The Greek Tradition in Republican Thought rewrites the standard history of republican political theory in Europe and America. It argues that an important republican tradition, derived from the central texts of Greek moral and political philosophy, emerged in sixteenth-century England and contributed significantly to the ideological framework of both the English Civil Wars and the American Founding. This tradition attached little importance to freedom as "non-dependence" and saw no intrinsic value in political participation. Its central preoccupations were not honor and glory, but happiness (*eudaimonia*) and justice – and it defined the latter, in Plato's terms, as the rule of the best men. This set of commitments yielded a startling readiness to advocate the corrective redistribution of wealth and even the outright abolition of private property. Dr Nelson offers significant reinterpretations of such central actors in the republican drama as Thomas More, James Harrington, Montesquieu, and Thomas Jefferson, as well as a radical reappraisal of ancient Roman historiography.

The Greek Tradition in Republican Thought is a powerful and imaginative piece of intellectual excavation, and will be of great interest to scholars and students of the history of ideas, political theory, early modern history, and American studies.

ERIC NELSON has been a Research Fellow of Trinity College, Cambridge and is currently a Junior Fellow in the Society of Fellows, Harvard University. This is his first book.

IDEAS IN CONTEXT

Edited by Quentin Skinner (*General Editor*), Lorraine Daston,
Dorothy Ross and James Tully

The books in this series will discuss the emergence of intellectual traditions and of related new disciplines. The procedures, aims and vocabularies that were generated will be set in the context of the alternatives available within the contemporary frameworks of ideas and institutions. Through detailed studies of the evolution of such traditions, and their modification by different audiences, it is hoped that a new picture will form of the development of ideas in their concrete contexts. By this means, artificial distinctions between the history of philosophy, of the various sciences, of society and politics, and of literature may be seen to dissolve.

The series is published with the support of the Exxon Foundation.

A list of books in the series will be found at the end of the volume.

THE GREEK TRADITION IN REPUBLICAN THOUGHT

ERIC NELSON

CAMBRIDGE
UNIVERSITY PRESS

PUBLISHED BY THE PRESS SYNDICATE OF THE UNIVERSITY OF CAMBRIDGE
The Pitt Building, Trumpington Street, Cambridge, United Kingdom

CAMBRIDGE UNIVERSITY PRESS
The Edinburgh Building, Cambridge, CB2 2RU, UK
40 West 20th Street, New York, NY 10011-4211, USA
477 Williamstown Road, Port Melbourne, VIC 3207, Australia
Ruiz de Alarcón 13, 28014 Madrid, Spain
Dock House, The Waterfront, Cape Town 8001, South Africa

http://www.cambridge.org

First published 2004

Printed in the United Kingdom at the University Press, Cambridge

Typeface Adobe Garamond 11/12.5 pt   *System* LATEX 2$_\varepsilon$ [TB]

A catalogue record for this book is available from the British Library

Library of Congress cataloguing in publication data

Nelson, Eric, 1977–
The Greek tradition in republican thought / Eric Nelson.
p.   cm. – (Ideas in Context; 69)
Includes bibliographical references and index.
ISBN 0 521 83545 3 (hardback)
1. Republicanism.   2. Republicanism – Greece.   I. Title.   II. Series.
JC421.N44 2004   321.8′6–dc22   2003055383

ISBN 0 521 83545 3 hardback

To my parents

Contents

Acknowledgments

The story of how I came to write this book is very much a tale of two Cambridges. It was in Cambridge, Massachusetts, as a Harvard undergraduate, that I was first introduced to the historical study of political thought, and it is, accordingly, a great pleasure to have the opportunity to acknowledge several important collegiate debts. For their friendship, encouragement, and generosity, I am deeply grateful to Rachel Barber, C. Thomas Brown, Jessamyn Conrad, Noah Dauber, Dov Glickman, Andrew Green, Mark Kishlansky, Barbara Lewalski, Harry Lewis, Bayley Mason, Gregory Nagy, Derek Pearsall, Daniel Schwartz, Noah Seton, Beth Stewart, Richard Thomas, and William Todd. I must also record a special debt of gratitude to Ernst Badian, who has been a constant source of guidance ever since the moment I first set foot in his classroom. Even in retirement, he has been kind enough to correspond with me about the vagaries of ancient Roman land law, and has read and commented on several sections of this study. It is, finally, a great honor to be able to thank James Hankins and Richard Tuck, the best of mentors and the most constant friends. They have invested more time and energy in my academic career than I can ever hope to repay or justify. Both have read the entirety of this study, and whatever merit it has is due largely to their extraordinary learning and abiding care.

The doctoral dissertation out of which this book emerged was written in Cambridge, England, and I am equally anxious to thank all of those on that side of the Atlantic whose kindness and support have made this project possible. I must begin by thanking the Marshall Aid Commemoration Commission for the award of a 1999 British Marshall Scholarship, which allowed me to pursue graduate studies in the United Kingdom. I am also deeply grateful to the Master and Fellows of Trinity College, Cambridge, who did me the honor of electing me to a Research Fellowship in October 2001, and whose financial assistance made possible my final year of doctoral work. During my time in Cambridge, I accumulated a remarkable number of professional and personal debts. For their generosity, advice, and erudition, I wish to thank Annabel Brett, James Carley, Paul Cartledge, Daniel Christ, Cathy Curtis, Anisha Dasgupta, Hannah Dawson, Paul de Bakker, Fillipo de Vivo, John Dunn, Peter Garnsey, Coulter George, Simon Goldhill, Tara Helfman, Alfred Hiatt, Istvan Hont, Melissa Lane, Sir Elihu Lauterpacht, Noel Malcolm, Sarah Michael, Leonidas Montes, Michael Pacold, Efraim Podoksik, Stefan Reif, Emma Rothschild, David Runciman, Malcolm Schofield, Jonathan Scott, Amartya Sen, Richard Serjeantson, Rabbi Julian Sinclair, Gareth Stedman Jones, Dagfinnur Sveinbjornsson, and Andrew Taylor. I am also immensely grateful to the examiners of my dissertation, David Armitage and Iain Hampsher-Monk, for much expert advice and encouragement.

During the revision process, I was privileged to receive the assistance of several eminent scholars. Bernard Bailyn reviewed the final three chapters of the manuscript with characteristic enthusiasm and insight, and Conal Condren was kind enough to do the same for the text as a whole. I must also reserve a special word of thanks for J. G. A. Pocock, who read and commented on the entire study with remarkable graciousness and good humor. The final product is unquestionably better for his suggestions.

My deepest debt of all is, however, to Quentin Skinner, who has self-lessly shepherded this project from inception to publication with consummate grace and astonishing learning. While his kindness is legendary across continents, up close it is simply staggering. I can only say that he embodies more completely than anyone I have ever met a great principle of the Talmud: "Let the honor of thy student be as dear to thee as thine own."

In preparing this study, I have made extensive use of several library collections. Thanks are due for much help and solicitude to the staff of the rare books room in the Cambridge University Library, and to the librarians of the various departmental libraries connected to the University. The Wren Library in Trinity College furnished me with a wonderful place in which to work, as well as unfettered access to the College's remarkable collection of early-modern books. I am also grateful to the staff of the Brooke Russell Astor Reading Room for Rare Books and Manuscripts at the New York Public Library, and to the librarians of the Houghton, Lamont, and Widener libraries at Harvard University.

An earlier and abridged version of chapter 1 appeared as "Greek Nonsense in More's *Utopia*" in *The Historical Journal* 44 (2001), and I am grateful to the *Journal* for permission to reproduce part of that essay here. Other material drawn from this study was presented to the Annual Conference of the Renaissance Society of America in Toronto, Canada (March 2003), the Cambridge Political Thought and Intellectual History Seminar (November

2002), the Fourth Annual Conference of the International Society for Intellectual History in Sydney, Australia (July 2002), and the Cambridge Graduate Seminar in Political Thought and Intellectual History (October 2000). A substantial portion of the argument was also incorporated into a series of lectures on "The Greek Tradition in Republican Thought," delivered to undergraduates in the University of Cambridge during Michaelmas Term, 2002. I am grateful to all of these audiences for many helpful comments.

Cambridge University Press has, from the first, been an ideal home for this project. My editor, Richard Fisher, has guided me with extraordinary skill and efficiency through the process of preparing a book for publication, ably assisted by Jackie Warren. I also wish to acknowledge the essential contribution of Jan Chapman, who has brought unparalleled rigor to the task of copy-editing the manuscript.

As this is my first book, I hope I may be forgiven for recording some older debts here as well. It is first of all a privilege to be able to acknowledge the kindness and inspiration of several early teachers. Warmest thanks to Thomas Golden, Alice Kjellgren, Ruth Levenson, Susan Martin, Marcia Picciotto, and William Younger of the Town School, and to Barry Bienstock, Gregory Donadio, Thomas LaFarge, David Schiller, Johannes Somary, and Susan Tiefenbrun of the Horace Mann School. I am also delighted to thank several of my oldest and dearest friends for many years of support and affection. I list them with the deepest gratitude: Leonie Baird, Sandra and Hector Bird, Judy Braun, Meryl and Phil Cedar, Raymond Dearie, Gil and Barbara Fishman, Neel Gandhi, Elisabeth Gitter, Mark and Ellen Harmon, Dennis and Judith Jacobs, Randy Komenski, Stuart Komenski, Adam Kreps, Susan Kronick, Suzanne Sacks, Ron Senio, Susan Shepard, Edward Shumsky, and Andrew Stern.

Lastly, I owe more than I can say to my brother, Adam Nelson, to my grandparents, Renee and Howard Nelson and Cela and Jack Sarna, to my aunt and uncle, Judy and Morris Sarna, and to the rest of my dear family.

This book is dedicated with love to Shirley Sarna and Steven Nelson, my first and greatest teachers.

Note on conventions

Bibliography. The bibliography lists only those primary and secondary sources on which I have relied in preparing this study. I have not attempted to provide a full, systematic accounting of the massive literature available on each of the subjects I discuss. Anonymous sources are listed by title. Apocryphal classical texts appear under the name of their putative author (e.g. Ps.-Cicero, *Rhetorica ad Herennium*).

Classical names and titles. I refer to ancient Greek and Roman authors using the most common English form of their names, even though standard practice is often inconsistent. For example, I speak of Sallust, but also of Valerius Maximus. Greek titles are given in English (e.g. Plato's *Republic*), but all other titles are reproduced in their original languages.

Dates. I employ the convention of referring to dates "BCE" (before the common era) and "CE" (of the common era).

References. I cite each source fully the first time it is referenced in a given chapter. Thereafter, I provide only the name of the author and an abridged title (e.g. Erasmus, *Adagia*, p. 10). Passages from classical authors are cited according to prevailing practice; for example, I refer to passages from Aristotle's *Politics* using both Bekker's division into pages, columns, and lines, and Schneider's division of the text into chapters and sections (e.g. *Pol.* 1281a22 [III.6]).

Transcriptions. When quoting from early-modern vernacular sources, I have tried, wherever possible, to preserve original capitalization, italicization, punctuation, and spelling. However, I normalize the long "s," expand contractions, and change "u" to "v" and "i" to "j" in accordance with contemporary orthography. I use "sic" only in cases where there are clear misprints. I do not, for example, correct Noah Webster's use of the form "hav." When quoting from early-modern Latin sources I change "u" to "v" and "j" to "i," expand contractions, and omit diacritical marks. On occasion I change a lower-case initial letter to an upper, or vice versa, in order to accommodate the demands of my own prose.

Translations. Wherever possible, I have quoted standard English translations of classical and foreign language sources, and have preferred to reproduce the original texts in the footnotes. On occasion, however, I have modified translations for the sake of accuracy or clarity; where this is done, it is duly noted. Translations of unpublished or untranslated works are my own.

Introduction

When Cicero observed in *De legibus* that Plato, "the most learned of men and the greatest of all philosophers," had written a book "on the republic" (*de republica*), he was bearing witness to a quiet revolution.[1] Aristotle had called his master's dialogue the "Politeia" (Πολιτεία),[2] employing a Greek term which could mean "citizenship," "constitution," "government," or, more generally, "way of life." Centuries later, Plato's editor Thrasyllus added the now customary subtitle, "On Justice" (περὶ δικαίου).[3] Cicero himself had called the dialogue "Politeia" earlier in his career, preferring simply to transliterate Plato's Greek into the Latin alphabet, rather than to search for a Latin analogue.[4] But in this passage from *De legibus* Cicero takes a fateful step; his rendering of "politeia" as "respublica" is not so much translation as authorization. Plato's dialogue is no longer a mere entertainment for the Roman erudite, a treatise written in Greek by a Greek author about a uniquely Greek political arrangement. It emerges instead as a text about the *respublica*, the constituent unit of Roman political life, and accordingly invites careful scrutiny by theorists interested in discovering the *optimus reipublicae status*, the best state of a republic.[5] With one innocuous gesture, Cicero brands Plato as a republican, ensuring that for the next two millennia important political theorists would derive their view of the "republic" from a Greek philosopher who had never even heard the term.

---

[1] *De leg.* II.14. Cicero, *De republica, De legibus*, ed. and trans. C. W. Keyes, Loeb Classical Library (Harvard University Press, 1928). "sed, ut vir doctissimus fecit Plato atque idem gravissimus philosophorum omnium, qui princeps de re publica conscripsit idemque separatim de legibus eius, id mihi credo esse faciundum . . ." This passage represents the first extant designation of Plato's dialogue as the "Republic."

[2] *Politics* 1261a6 (II.2). Aristotle, *Politics*, ed. and trans. H. Rackham, Loeb Classical Library (Harvard University Press, 1932). English translations are taken from this volume.

[3] Literally, "on the just thing." *Platonis opera*, ed. John Burnet, vol. IV, Oxford Classical Texts (Oxford: Clarendon Press, 1963), p. 327 (*app. crit.*).

[4] See *Ep. Att.* IV.16. Cicero, *Epistulae ad Atticum*, ed. and trans. E. O. Winstedt, vol. I, Loeb Classical Library (Harvard University Press, 1912).

[5] *De leg.* I.15.

Plato's assimilation to the republican tradition will, however, only be regarded as a watershed event if Greek and Roman political theory are seen to offer substantially different perspectives on the nature of the commonwealth. If Plato says much the same thing as Cicero, then his designation as an authority on "republics" should make little practical difference in the history of political thought. While it may seem on the face of it implausible that two men separated from each other by language, culture, and the span of three centuries should emerge with basically identical political theories (even if, as in this case, one has influenced the other), the argument for the fundamental unity of Greek and Roman political thought has recently acquired substantial scholarly support. Straussian scholars have long contended that the central pivot of Western intellectual history is that between the "ancients" and the "moderns," and that, accordingly, the classical authors were in substantial agreement on all essential points.[6] But scholars of "classical republicanism" too have increasingly found themselves committed to a similar conflation of Greece and Rome. After all, if republicanism is "classical" in any meaningful sense, then it must represent a coherent Graeco-Roman inheritance.

The argument that this is the case is chiefly associated with the work of Zera Fink and J. G. A. Pocock. Fink's study *The Classical Republicans*, first published in 1945, described the anti-monarchical authors of the English Civil War and Interregnum as heirs to a tradition of thought, stretching from Aristotle to Cicero, which advocated a "mixed constitution" as the only means of bringing permanence to otherwise transitory political arrangements.[7] Yet Fink's analysis, while path-breaking, neglected to ask whether, within this tradition of thought, there was any unanimity as to the moral and philosophical reasons one might have for preferring a mixed regime. Pocock attempted to address this objection in *The Machiavellian Moment* (1975), his magisterial survey of Florentine and Anglo-American republicanism. While he followed Fink in locating the source of the republican tradition in a defense of mixed constitutions, he explicitly argued that this advocacy of mixed regimes should be regarded as an expression of Aristotelian moral and political philosophy. In his crucial third chapter

---

[6] A recent statement of this view can be found in Paul A. Rahe, "Situating Machiavelli" in *Renaissance Civic Humanism: Reappraisals and Reflections*, ed. James Hankins (Cambridge University Press, 2000), pp. 270–308. See also Rahe, *Republics Ancient and Modern: Classical Republicanism and the American Revolution*, vol. 1 (Chapel Hill: University of North Carolina Press, 1992). Leo Strauss himself set out the best-known formulation of this view in his *Natural Right and History* (University of Chicago Press, 1953), esp. pp. 78, 134–36, 178–82.

[7] Zera S. Fink, *The Classical Republicans: an Essay in the Recovery of a Pattern of Thought in Seventeenth-Century England* (Evanston: Northwestern University Press, 1945). See esp. pp. 1–10.

Pocock defended this thesis by providing a reading of Aristotle's *Politics*: on this account, Aristotle's *polis* fulfills human nature by allowing the exercise of virtue, and is best ordered when each citizen is able to exercise his own particular virtue in its governance.[8] Accordingly, Pocock continues, within Aristotle's sixfold classification of constitutions, "polity" is identified as the best, since, as a "mixture" of the two predominant regimes (i.e. the rule of the few and the rule of the many), it allows all political classes to participate in governance in a fashion commensurate with their natures.

It is at this point that Pocock, like Fink before him, turns to Polybius. A Greek writing for a Roman audience in the second century BCE, Polybius devoted the sixth book of his *Histories* to an analysis of the different possible constitutions and the causes of revolution. He accepts the six-fold classification found in Aristotle, and argues that each pure constitution first degenerates into its corrupt counterpart and then yields another pure constitution in an endless cycle of change and disruption (ἀνακύκλωσις).[9] Although Polybius maintains that revolution is ultimately inevitable, he claims that it can be significantly delayed by the introduction of a mixed regime – one infused with "all the good and distinctive features of the best governments, so that none of the principles should grow unduly and be perverted into its allied evil."[10] In Pocock's analysis, Aristotle's ethical case for the mixed constitution, when wedded to the Polybian proposition that only mixed constitutions protect states from the ravages of continual revolution, yielded the philosophical framework of republican discourse from Cicero to Milton, and from Machiavelli to Harrington.[11]

Although brilliant and daring, this account faces a number of difficulties. An argument in favor of a mixed constitution, for example, need not be Aristotelian; and Pocock's suggestion that *cinquecento* authors such

---

[8] J. G. A. Pocock, *The Machiavellian Moment: Florentine Political Thought and the Atlantic Republican Tradition* (Princeton University Press, 1975), pp. 66–80.

[9] Polybius, *The Histories*, ed. and trans. W. R. Paton, vol. III, Loeb Classical Library (Harvard University Press, 1923), VI.9.

[10] Polybius, *Histories* VI.10.

[11] Jonathan Scott approximates this view when he writes that "English republican moral philosophy has rightly been called classical republicanism in that it owed a particular debt to the moral philosophy of Greek antiquity. Civic activity – the life of the polis – was the only means to achieve man's telos, or end: the life of virtue . . . It was Aristotle's most important innovation . . . to speak of the moral necessity of public citizenship, a theme subsequently amplified by Cicero" (p. 318). But, as we shall see, Cicero did not so much amplify this claim as replace it with an entirely different set of claims. Moreover, while the Aristotle of *Politics* I and III might seem to urge civic participation, the Aristotle of *Politics* VII and *Ethics* X can be read quite differently. See Jonathan Scott, *England's Troubles: Seventeenth-Century English Political Instability in European Context* (Cambridge University Press, 2000).

as Machiavelli and Guicciardini were committed to Aristotle's political teleology is difficult to sustain.[12] But perhaps *The Machiavellian Moment*'s most serious shortcoming is its assumption that Roman political philosophy was a straightforward off-shoot of the Aristotelian–Polybian synthesis, and that, as a result, early-modern theorists who consulted Aristotle would emerge with an account of political life identical in all important respects to the one they would have found in Cicero or Livy. In other words, Pocock and his followers err in assuming that there is a "republicanism" which is "classical." The present study, in contrast, assumes that Greek and Roman political theory were substantially different from one another, making it highly unlikely that the induction of Plato and Aristotle into the "republican" canon should have yielded a single, synthetic Graeco-Roman political theory. But what essentially separates Plato from Sallust, Aristotle from Justinian? The hint of an intriguing answer is to be found in an improbable source: Hegel's lectures on the philosophy of world history.

Although admired for their philosophical grandeur, Hegel's lectures have notoriously failed to win the respect of historians. Indeed, it is a commonplace that historiography developed in its recognizably "modern" form, through the writings of Niebuhr and Ranke, largely as a reaction against the kind of historical idealism championed by Hegel (through which, as Nietzsche put it, he arrived at the notion that "the apex and culmination of the world process coincided with his own existence in Berlin").[13] Much of this censure is justified, but nonetheless Hegel's analysis of the transition

---

[12] Plato had earlier generated a sixfold typology of constitutions in the *Statesman* (in addition to a somewhat different version in Books VIII and IX of the *Republic*), and praised a mixed constitution in Book III of the *Laws*. In this second text, he went so far as to claim that a mixed constitution was the only "real constitution," whereas the "pure" ones were only "settlements enslaved to the domination of some component section, each taking its designation from the dominant factor" – and therefore prone to revolution. It is, in fact, this Platonic account of constitutional change, not the Aristotelian one, that Polybius favors. Polybius refers to a "theory of the natural transformations" of states that has been "more elaborately set forth by Plato and certain other philosophers" (παρὰ Πλάτωνι καί τισιν ἐτέροις τῶν φιλοσόφων) (VI.5). For Polybius, the primary model is Plato, not Aristotle. This is because, although Aristotle provides his own sketch of constitutional change in *Politics* 1286b (III.10), in 1316a (V.10) he explicitly rejects Plato's argument that constitutions decay into their degenerate counterparts. He insists, rather, that "all constitutions more often change into the opposite form than into the one near them" (πλεονάκις γὰρ εἰς τὴν ἐναντίαν μεταβάλλουσι πᾶσαι αἱ πολιτεῖαι ἢ τὴν σύνεγγυς). As a result, he attacks the view championed by Plato (and later adopted by Polybius), according to which aristocracy changes "to oligarchy, and from this to democracy, and from democracy to tyranny." Aristotle does, however, offer an account more consistent with Plato's in *Ethics* 1160b (VIII.10). For the divergences between Aristotelian and Polybian ideas about the mixed constitution, see Wilfried Nippel, "Ancient and Modern Republicanism: 'Mixed Constitution' and 'Ephors'" in *The Invention of the Modern Republic*, ed. Biancamaria Fontana (Cambridge University Press, 1994), pp. 7–10.

[13] Friedrich Nietzsche, *Unfashionable Observations*, trans. R. T. Gray (Stanford University Press, 1995), p. 143.

from the "Greek" to the "Roman World" in *The Philosophy of History* contains a remarkable insight. Hegel sets himself the task of studying "universal history," the process through which Freedom (*Freiheit*) ultimately realizes itself in the union of universal and particular, the subjective and the objective. This union, for Hegel, occurs finally in the modern state, where each particular individual is conscious both of his subjectivity and the fact that he wills the universal (i.e. the universal is then no longer seen as something "external"). The journey begins in the "Oriental World" (*Die orientalische Welt*), where the subjective ("disposition, Conscience, formal Freedom") is not yet recognized, and government exists as the arbitrary will of a single man whose persona is assimilated to an all-powerful, external, prescriptive force.[14] In the "Greek World" (*Die griechische Welt*), however, subjectivity begins to make itself felt.

The Greeks are surrounded by a heterogeneous environment which gives them the consciousness of diversity and, as a result, "throws them back upon their inner spirit."[15] They find their *Geist* awakened by natural stimuli, and they express their subjectivity by acting upon those stimuli (hence Hegel argues that their "Spirit" is not yet truly free, since it requires external stimulation to call it into action).[16] The Greek spirit, then, is "artistic," in that, like the artist, it expresses its subjectivity in modifying the natural. The Greeks first exert their subjective agency on their bodies, producing what Hegel calls the "subjective work of art," and then create deities who are "objectively beautiful" (the "objective work of art"). The union of these is the "political work of art" (*Das politische Kunstwerk*), the state conceived of not as an abstract universal as opposed to concrete particulars, but rather as an objectively beautiful whole of which each individual is an organic part: it is "a living, universal Spirit, but which is at the same time the self-conscious Spirit of the individuals composing the community."[17] The Greeks, for Hegel, were not conscious of an external universal, and, as a result, did not discover particularity (they are "unconscious of particular interests").[18] It is, in short, in the Greek world "that the advancing Spirit makes *itself* the content of its volition and its knowledge; but in such a way that State, Family, Law, Religion, are at the same time objects aimed at by individuality, while the latter *is* individuality only in virtue of those aims."[19]

[14] G. W. F. Hegel, *Vorlesungen über die Philosophie der Weltgeschichte*, vol. XII, ed. Karl Heinz Ilting, Karl Brehmer, and Hoo Nam Seelmann; Vorlesungen: Ausgewählte Nachschriften und Manuskripte (Hamburg: Felix Meiner Verlag, 1996). G. W. F. Hegel, *The Philosophy of History*, trans. J. Sibree (New York: Prometheus Books, 1991), p. 111.
[15] Hegel, *Philosophy of History*, p. 233.   [16] Ibid., p. 238.   [17] Ibid., p. 250.   [18] Ibid., p. 252.
[19] Ibid., p. 223.

The transition from the Greek to the "Roman World" (*Die römische Welt*) results from the Greek discovery of reflection and particularity. Indeed, in *The Philosophy of Right*, Hegel interprets Plato's *Republic* as a response to this advent of individual interest. Plato, he writes, "could only cope with the principle of self-subsistent particularity, which in his day had forced its way into Greek ethical life, by setting up in opposition to it his purely substantial state."[20] Indeed, Plato "absolutely excluded it [i.e. particularity] from his state, even in its very beginnings in private property and the family, as well as in its more mature form as the subjective will, the choice of a social position, and so forth." But Plato could not withstand the force of the advancing Spirit, and Greece duly gave way to Rome. In Rome, Hegel argues, the state was at last conceived of as an abstract universal to which individuals owed obedience: "In Rome, then, we find that free universality, that abstract Freedom, which on the one hand sets an abstract state, a political constitution and power, over concrete individuality; on the other side creates a personality in opposition to that universality."[21] Once the universal is discovered, "personality" (its antithesis) comes along with it, "which gives itself reality in the existence of private property." *Proprietas* thus becomes the central Roman preoccupation. "The administration of government, and political privileges, receive the character of hallowed private property,"[22] and marriage itself "bore quite the aspect of a mere contract" which made the wife "part of the husband's property."[23]

It is a matter of the utmost importance that one of Hegel's chief examples of the clash between the Greek and Roman spirits is the question of agrarian laws.[24] He writes that in Rome "the plebeians were practically excluded from almost all the landed property, and the object of the Agrarian Laws was to provide lands for them."[25] These measures "excited during every period very great commotions in Rome," which Hegel explains in a fascinating passage:

We must here call special attention to the distinction which exists between the Roman, the Greek, and our own circumstances. Our civil society rests on other principles, and in it such measures are not necessary. Spartans and Athenians, who had not arrived at such an abstract idea of the State as was so tenaciously held by the Romans, did not trouble themselves with abstract rights, but simply desired

---

[20] G. W. F. Hegel, *The Philosophy of Right (Grundlinien der Philosophie des Rechts)*, ed. and trans. T. M. Knox (Oxford: Clarendon Press, 1942), p. 124.
[21] Hegel, *Philosophy of History*, p. 279.   [22] Ibid., p. 295.   [23] Ibid., p. 286.
[24] Indeed, it is striking that F. R. Christi neglects to discuss the agrarian laws in his analysis of the turn from Greece to Rome in the *Philosophy of History*. See F. R. Christi, "Hegel and Roman Liberalism" in *History of Political Thought* 5 (1984), 281–94.
[25] Hegel, *Philosophy of History*, p. 302.

that the citizens should have the means of subsistence; and they required of the state that it should take care that such should be the case.[26]

For Hegel, in short, the issue of agrarian legislation highlights a basic incommensurability between Greek and Roman values: the Greeks tended to see the *polis* as an organic whole, not an abstract universal against which individual rights could be asserted (and they conceived of principles such as "justice" first and foremost as properties of the whole). The Romans, on the other hand, developed the idea of legal personality, and invested the concept of *proprietas* with immense ideological significance.[27] As a result, on Hegel's account, opposition to agrarian laws must be regarded as a distinctively Roman phenomenon. In Greece, the charge of "injustice" brought against these laws simply would not arise.

As an attempt at social and economic history, this analysis is not terribly compelling. To state only its most obvious shortcoming, the Greeks were by no means generically incapable of articulating a case against redistributionism; such opposition was widespread throughout the Greek world in the classical period (Lycurgus, after all, had his eye put out by *somebody*).[28] Nor are we likely to be consoled by Hegel's argument that "if we wish to know what Greece really was, we find the answer in Sophocles and Aristophanes, Thucydides and Plato" because it is in the philosophical counter-culture, rather than the culture itself that "we find the historical expression of what Greek life actually was."[29] Yet, as a conceptual reflection on the character of the surviving ancient sources, Hegel's analysis is remarkably astute: the extant Roman historians do indeed bitterly attack the agrarian laws and their sponsors, while the ancient Greek historians of Rome almost uniformly praise them. And, as we shall see, this quarrel over *proprietas* emerges equally strongly from a comparison of the principal Greek and Roman texts of moral and political philosophy.

---

[26] Ibid., p. 303.

[27] Hegel is arguing here against the view of Niebuhr. See Alfred Heuss, *Barthold Georg Niebuhrs wissenschaftliche Anfänge: Untersuchungen und Mitteilungen über die Kopenhagener Manuscripte und zur europäische Tradition der lex agraria (loi agraire)* (Göttingen: Vandenhoeck & Ruprecht, 1981).

[28] See, for example, Doyne Dawson, *Cities of the Gods: Communist Utopias in Greek Thought* (Oxford University Press, 1992), pp. 99–102; J. W. Jones, *The Law and Legal Theory of the Greeks: an Introduction* (Oxford: Clarendon Press, 1956), pp. 84–87, 198–200; and Fritz M. Heichelheim, *An Ancient Economic History*, vol. II, trans. Joyce Stevens (Leyden: A. W. Sythoff, 1964), pp. 121–26, 134–53. Heichelheim does, however, argue that, while "levelling" programs in the Greek city-states often met with sharp resistance, the overall culture of the classical Greek *poleis* stressed the subordination of property arrangements to the public good.

[29] G. W. F. Hegel, *Lectures on the Philosophy of World History*, trans. H. B. Nisbet, with an introduction by Duncan Forbes (Cambridge University Press, 1975), p. 146. This passage is from the 1830 version of the lectures.

One of the benefits of taking Hegel's insight seriously is that it sheds a great deal of light on an interpretation of early-modern republicanism that has been gaining momentum in recent years. In 1955, Hans Baron published his controversial study *The Crisis of the Early Italian Renaissance*, introducing the English-speaking world to the concept of "civic humanism" (*Bürgerhumanismus*). Although Baron's claim that "civic humanism" burst suddenly on to the scene around the year 1400 as a result of Florentine anxiety about the growing hegemony of the Visconti has been largely discredited, his argument that Italian republicanism rested on a particular interpretation of Roman history has aged more gracefully. Baron noticed that his "civic humanists" uniformly explained the death of Roman virtue as a consequence of the collapse of the Republic. He points out that, while Dante had consigned Brutus and Cassius "into the maws of Lucifer, side by side with Judas Iscariot"[30] in the *Inferno*, the Florentine republicans of the *quattrocento* styled Caesar as a tyrant and drew strength from the recently rediscovered first book of Tacitus' *Historiae*, in which we read that, after Actium, virtue was replaced with fawning subservience.[31] Accordingly, Florentine republicans were committed to arguing that Florence was founded by the Romans when Rome was still a republic. They could then interpret Florentine history as the direct outgrowth of Ciceronian virtue and civic spirit.[32]

Quentin Skinner took Baron's insight as the starting-point for a comprehensive critique of Pocock. The Italian republicans, he argued, did not look to Aristotle for their political principles, but rather to a series of Roman sources which had significantly un-Aristotelian things to say about the principles of political organization. Skinner proceeded to identify a neo-Roman ethical system synthesized out of the *Codex* of Justinian and the works of Cicero, Sallust, Livy, and Tacitus, which provided the framework for the republicanism of the Italian city-states.[33] This neo-Roman account defines

[30] Hans Baron, *The Crisis of the Early Italian Renaissance: Civic Humanism and Republican Liberty in an Age of Classicism and Tyranny* (Princeton University Press, 1955), p. 39. See Dante, *Inferno* XXXIV.64–67. "Delli altri due c'hanno il capo di sotto, / quel che pende dal nero ceffo è Bruto / – vedi come si torce! e non fa motto!–; / a l'altro è Cassio che par sì membruto."

[31] *Historiae* I.I. See Tacitus, *The Histories*, ed. C. H. Moore, Loeb Classical Library (Harvard University Press, 1925), p. 3.

[32] Baron, *Early Italian Renaissance*, pp. 49, 103.

[33] See Quentin Skinner, *The Foundations of Modern Political Thought*, vol. I *The Renaissance* (Cambridge University Press, 1978); "Political Philosophy" in *The Cambridge History of Renaissance Philosophy*, ed. Charles B. Schmitt, Quentin Skinner, Eckhard Kessler, and Jill Kraye (Cambridge University Press, 1988); "Machiavelli's *Discorsi* and the Pre-Humanist Origins of Republican Ideas" in *Machiavelli and Republicanism*, ed. Gisela Bock, Quentin Skinner, and Maurizio Viroli (Cambridge University Press, 1990); *Liberty before Liberalism* (Cambridge University Press, 1998); "Classical Liberty and the Coming of the English Civil War" in *Republicanism: a Shared European Heritage*, vol. II, ed. Quentin

liberty as a status of non-domination (to be contrasted with slavery), and exalts it as the source of virtue. It insists that virtue encourages justice (*iustitia*), a quality defined in the Roman *Digest* as the "constant and perpetual aim of giving each person *ius suum*"[34] and interpreted as an imperative to respect private property.[35] For neo-Roman theorists, dedication to justice thus understood allows the cultivation of the common good (*commune bonum*), which produces concord (*concordia*) and peace (*pax*), and enables the state to seek *gloria*.[36] Implicit in all of this is that individuals should reject the contemplative life and embrace the life of civic engagement (*vita activa*), performing their *officia* to their friends and family, promoting the glory of their *civitas* or *patria*, and securing honor for themselves.[37]

Skinner and Martin van Gelderen (Cambridge University Press, 2002), pp. 9–28; *Visions of Politics*, vol. II *Renaissance Virtues* (Cambridge University Press, 2002), esp. chaps. 2–7, 11, 12.

[34] "Iustitia est constans et perpetua voluntas ius suum cuique tribuendi." *Digest* 1.1.10. See also *Institutes* 1.1.1. For Ciceronian and Stoic views on property, see Julia Annas, "Cicero on Stoic Moral Philosophy and Private Property" in *Philosophia Togata*, vol. I: *Essays on Philosophy and Roman Society*, ed. Miriam Griffith and Jonathan Barnes (Oxford University Press, 1989), pp. 151–73. For the neo-Roman exaltation of wealth and money-making, see Eugenio Garin, *Italian Humanism [Der italienische Humanismus]: Philosophy and Civic Life in the Renaissance*, trans. Peter Munz (Oxford: Basil Blackwell, 1965), esp. pp. 43–46. Garin famously placed the *quattrocento* notion that (in Davanzati's image) "money is to the city what blood is to an individual" at the center of the Renaissance remaking of European culture. See also James Hankins, "Humanism and Modern Political Thought" in *The Cambridge Companion to Renaissance Humanism*, ed. Jill Kraye (Cambridge University Press, 1996), pp. 126–27; and Mark Jurdjevic, "Virtue, Commerce, and the Enduring Florentine Moment: Reintegrating Italy into the Atlantic Republican Debate" in *Journal of the History of Ideas* 62 (2001), 721–43. This aspect of neo-Roman ideology also explains Steven Pincus's observation that many seventeenth-century English republicans were quite comfortable with commercial society. See Steven Pincus, "Neither Machiavellian Moment nor Possessive Individualism: Commercial Society and the Defenders of the English Commonwealth" in *American Historical Review* 103 (1998), 705–36.

[35] Cicero argues in the *De officiis* (1.20) that *iustitia* consists in doing no harm and respecting private property.

[36] Jacob Burckhardt long ago commented on the fundamentally Roman character of the Renaissance preoccupation with glory. In the chapter on "Glory" in his great study of Renaissance culture, he writes: "the Roman authors, who were now zealously studied, are filled and saturated with the concept of fame, and . . . their subject itself – the universal empire of Rome – stood as a permanent ideal before the minds of Italians." See Jacob Burckhardt, *The Civilization of the Renaissance in Italy*, ed. Peter Murray, trans. S. G. C. Middlemore, with an introduction by Peter Burke (London: Penguin, 1990), p. 104. See also Andrew Fitzmaurice, *Humanism and America: an Intellectual History of English Colonisation*, Ideas in Context (Cambridge University Press, 2003), esp. pp. 1–19, 32–35; Markku Peltonen, *Classical Humanism and Republicanism in English Political Thought: 1570–1640*, Ideas in Context (Cambridge University Press, 1995), pp. 34ff.; and Skinner, "Political Philosophy," pp. 413ff.

[37] For a helpful analysis of Roman ideology, see A. A. Long, "Cicero's Politics in *De Officiis*" in *Justice and Generosity: Studies in Social and Political Philosophy: Proceedings of the Sixth Symposium Hellenisticum*, ed. André Laks and Malcolm Schofield (Cambridge University Press, 1995), pp. 213–40. Long writes, "What do I mean by Roman ideology? I refer to the system of values expressed by such terms as *virtus, dignitas, honestas, splendor, decus* and, above all, *laus* and *gloria*. All of these words signify honour, rank, worth, status. They indicate at the limit what a noble Roman would give his life for. This Roman honour code . . . was a value system demanding both achievement in public life and public recognition of that achievement" (p. 216).

Hegel's chief insight seems to have been that, at the center of the ideological apparatus Skinner describes, is the Roman concept of *proprietas*. A republican ideology without this notion would, he realized, look remarkably different. The present study identifies just such an ideology: a view of republican government, accessible from the principal sources of Greek moral philosophy (and quite distinct from Pocock's participatory brand of Aristotelianism), which provided a viable alternative to neo-Roman ideology throughout the early-modern period. Indeed, now that the ideological underpinnings of the neo-Roman account have been identified, we can see how deeply antagonistic they are to Greek ethics. Although Plato and Aristotle produced widely different accounts of political life, they agreed on several propositions which run directly counter to the neo-Roman view just set out. To begin with, neither Plato nor Aristotle particularly values freedom (ἐλευθερία) as "non-dependence."[38] The freedom they value is the condition of living according to nature, and one of their cardinal assumptions is that most individuals cannot be said to be "free" in this sense unless they depend upon their intellectual and moral superiors (if a man ruled by his passions is left to rule himself, then he is enslaved).[39] Both also take it as axiomatic that the purpose of civic life is not glory – the irrelevant approval of non-experts – but happiness (εὐδαιμονία).[40] In Book v of the *Republic*, Plato states emphatically that "the object on which

---

[38] The farthest Aristotle goes in praising freedom as "non-dependence" is his claim in *Politics* 1283a15 (III.7) that while wealthy men [πλούσιοι] and free men [ἐλεύθεροι] "are indispensable for a state's existence" (because, as he explains, a state cannot consist entirely of poor men or of slaves), "justice [δικαιοσύνη] and civic virtue [πολιτικὴ ἀρετή] are indispensable for its good administration [οἰκεῖσθαι καλῶς]" and are, thus, more important (since the state aims at the good life). This tepid endorsement, however, does not approach the Roman and neo-Roman glorification of *libertas*. Aristotle defines "freedom" in this sense as the absence of "slavery" – the condition of being owned by another person, and living as a means rather than an end. But he does not, like the Roman authors, transform this claim into a broader argument against political dependence (i.e. being governed according to somebody else's will). On Aristotle's account, men can be said to be "free" in both monarchies and democracies, so long as they are not actually owned by others; this sort of freedom is therefore totally compatible with political dependence. Indeed, such dependence is often prescribed by nature – we read in *Politics* 1254b5 (1.2) that monarchs rule their subjects in the same way that the intellect rules the appetitive part of the soul. Moreover, Aristotle is clear that even "unfreedom" is to be preferred to living a life that is not according to nature; this conviction accounts in large part for his theory of natural slavery. For an interesting discussion of this issue, see Richard Mulgan, "Liberty in Ancient Greece" in *Conceptions of Liberty in Political Philosophy*, ed. Zbigniev Pelczynski and John Gray (London: The Athlone Press, 1984), pp. 7–26. Skinner also discusses this question in "The Republican Ideal of Political Liberty" in *Machiavelli and Republicanism*, ed. Bock, Skinner, and Viroli, p. 296.

[39] See, for example, Plato, *Republic* 431a (IV), 515c (VII), and *Laws* 860d (IX); see also Aristotle *Ethics* 1110b (III.1.14), and 1178a (X.7.9).

[40] See Richard Tuck's discussion in *Philosophy and Government: 1572–1651*, Ideas in Context (Cambridge University Press, 1993), pp. 6–9.

we fixed our eyes in the establishment of our state was . . . the greatest possible happiness [εὐδαιμονία] of the city as a whole,"[41] and in Book IX of the *Laws* he reiterates that the goal of the state is to teach its citizens how to lead a "happy life."[42] Aristotle agrees, establishing in Book I of the *Nicomachean Ethics* that "happiness . . . is the End at which all actions aim,"[43] and adding in *Politics* VII that it is "the best state [ἀρίστην], the one that does well, that is happy [εὐδαίμονα]."[44]

For both Plato and Aristotle, this preference has serious consequences for their evaluation of civic participation. In the *Republic*, Plato argues that, in order to achieve happiness, men must live according to their nature. In order to live this natural life, however, they must be led out of ignorance and brought to the awareness that the sensible world is only a flawed, misleading projection of the true, sublime reality. Plato dramatizes this transition from darkness to light in the Allegory of the Cave from *Republic* VII. After escaping from the world of shadows, the former prisoners turn to "the contemplation of things above" and their souls ascend to the level of intelligible reason, and the idea of the Good.[45] In the *Timaeus*, we learn further that this state of contemplation is actually the human soul's essential "motion" (κίνησις), and the source of human happiness.[46]

Needless to say, this emphasis on contemplation required Plato to take a very different position on civic participation from the one encountered in the neo-Roman authors. In the case of *Kallipolis*, Plato insists that those who have escaped from the cave and contemplated the world of Forms must become involved in the governance of the city, because a happy city (that is, one governed by the wisdom obtained through contemplation of ultimate reality) must not be ruled "by men who fight one another for shadows and wrangle for office as if that were a great good."[47] Socrates concedes that this will temporarily undermine the happiness of the illuminated souls, but reminds Glaucon that their goal is the happiness of the whole community – not just that of the guardians. In cities not ruled according to Platonic principles, however, the philosophers should opt instead for contemplation. In Book VI of the *Republic* Plato amplifies this point by having Socrates articulate an eerie prophecy of his own demise: he observes that a philosopher attempting politics in an actual city "would . . . before

---

[41] *Republic* 420b (IV). English translations from Plato are taken from *The Collected Dialogues, including the Letters*, ed. Edith Hamilton, Huntington Cairns, Bollingen Series 71 (Princeton University Press, 1989).

[42] *Laws* 858d (IX).

[43] *Ethics* 1097a (1.7.8). All translations from Aristotle's *Ethics* are found in Aristotle, *Nicomachean Ethics*, ed. and trans. H. Rackham, rev. edn., Loeb Classical Library (Harvard University Press, 1934).

[44] *Politics* 1323b30 (VII.1).   [45] *Republic* 517b (VII).   [46] *Timaeus* 90a.   [47] *Republic* 520d (VII).

he could in any way benefit his friends or the state, come to an untimely end without doing any good to himself or others."[48] Socrates concludes, "I say the philosopher remains quiet, minds his own affair," keeping out of the storm of ignorance that afflicts his countrymen. For Plato, the contemplative life is the truly happy life, and those able to pursue it relinquish that opportunity only under extremely rare circumstances – and never because they confuse public honor with the Good.[49]

Although he emerges with a less despairing analysis than Plato's, Aristotle's basic view of these issues is largely consistent with that of his teacher. In Book I of the *Nicomachean Ethics* Aristotle maintains that happiness is achieved when men exercise the virtues particular to their nature. As man's essential characteristic is his reason, the virtues that lead him to happiness are all to do with reason, and are divided into "intellectual" (διανοητικαί) and "moral" (ἠθικαί) virtues. The moral virtues, we learn, can all be explained as a mean between extremes, and Aristotle argues in Book VI that men rely on "practical wisdom" (φρόνησις), one of the intellectual virtues, to locate the mean in any given situation. The moral virtues are social, and, as a result, Aristotle can make his famous claim in *Politics* I that man is by nature suited for the *polis*. The *polis* allows him to realize his nature.

Thus far, Aristotle's political theory would seem to be straightforwardly oriented toward civic participation. But the story becomes more complicated when we introduce a second component of intellectual virtue. Aristotle explains that, whereas moral virtue relies on practical wisdom, intellectual virtue also comprehends "theoretical wisdom" (σοφία, with its particular activity θεωρία). In Book X of the *Ethics*, and again in Book VII of the *Politics*, he argues that it is the exercise of this intellectual virtue that is most intrinsic to man's nature, and that man achieves true happiness (εὐδαιμονία) only when he is left to contemplate the universe and assimilate himself momentarily to the divine. Aristotle makes clear that this life of contemplation (ὁ κατὰ τὸν νοῦν βίος) trumps the civic life (it is, in fact,

---

[48] *Republic* 496d (VI).

[49] This argument raises an important question: if the contemplative life is the happy life, and the city aims at happiness, how can the city itself lead a contemplative life? The most obvious answer – namely that a happy state is one in which everyone leads a contemplative life – is unavailable to Plato, since he insists that only a select group of citizens is capable of leading this kind of life. Instead, Plato relies on the analogy between man and city: when a man's soul is in a state of contemplation, it is not the case that every part of his soul contemplates. Rather, the rational element keeps the appetitive and spirited elements under control so that it can pattern the soul on the cosmos. Likewise, a "contemplative" *polis* is one ruled by philosophers (i.e. the rational part of the soul). It continually reorients itself through contemplation of ultimate reality.

the only activity which is a good in itself),[50] thus producing a tension in his overall account. And, although he goes to some lengths in *Politics* VII to explain how a *polis*, like a man, might live a contemplative life,[51] suffice it to say that his view of civic participation remains a deeply anti-Roman one.[52]

But if Greek and neo-Roman ethics diverge on the ends of civic life and the value of civic participation, perhaps their most important point of contention is on the nature of justice. Justice for Plato is not simply giving each person *ius suum* in the Roman sense.[53] As expressed in the *Republic*, Platonic justice (δικαιοσύνη) consists in an arrangement of elements according to nature. The *polis*, like the human soul, is made up of component elements (the rational, the spirited, and the appetitive), and, since it is natural for reason to rule, both the *polis* and the soul achieve justice when their elements are governed by reason. This view of justice as "balance among elements" leads Plato to endorse policies that would straightforwardly violate the Roman principle of justice. He concludes, for example, that because the unrestricted flow of property corrupts citizens and topples the rule of reason, the *polis* must – on grounds of justice – either abolish private property (as in the *Republic*) or sharply restrict its accumulation (as in the *Laws*).[54] Platonic justice is holistic, and is inextricably linked to an overall conception of nature and order.

Aristotle's theory of justice is more complex, and, conceptually speaking, represents something of a midpoint between the Platonic and Roman notions. In Book V of the *Ethics* Aristotle distinguishes between "universal" and "particular" justice. Universal justice concerns what is lawful, and "is applied to anything that produces and preserves the happiness . . . of the political community."[55] In this sense, he writes, justice includes all of virtue when oriented toward other human beings. Particular justice, on the other

---

[50] *Ethics* 1177a (X.7).   [51] *Politics* 1325b15–30 (VII.3).

[52] Peltonen describes how Francis Bacon, for example, defended the *vita activa* "against Aristotle," whom he took to have argued that "the contemplative way of living was the most valuable." See Peltonen, *Classical Humanism*, p. 141.

[53] In *Republic* I, Plato begins from Simonides' view that "it is just to give each person those things which are owed to him" (τὸ τὰ ὀφειλόμενα ἑκάστῳ ἀποδιδόναι δίκαιόν ἐστι) (331e) (the translation is my own), but he interprets this imperative in a revolutionary, holistic sense. For Plato, a person's "due" is his natural place within a rationally balanced, organic whole. As a result, Plato prefers to speak of justice as the natural ordering of elements – not, as in the Roman tradition, the protection of private property and the prevention of bodily harm.

[54] It would be more precise to say that the *Republic* bans private property among the guardians, and forbids extreme wealth and poverty throughout the city (*Republic* 421c [IV]). On this, see Malcolm Schofield, *Saving the City: Philosopher-Kings and Other Classical Paradigms* (London and New York: Routledge, 1999), p. 79.

[55] *Ethics* 1129b (V.1).

hand, concerns what is "fair" (τὸ ἴσον), and mandates that each person not take more than his proper share of goods or honor; its opposite is the particular vice of "rapacity" (πλεονεξία). One critic sums up the distinction by noting that "universal justice includes any ethical virtue in so far as it promotes and protects the good of the community, whereas particular justice involves specific sorts of actions affecting the common advantage."[56] In the subset of particular justice which Aristotle calls "distributive" (ἐν ταῖς διανομαῖς) (as opposed to "corrective" or "commutative"), the apportioning of property and political office according to desert (κατ᾽ ἀξίαν), we have the forerunner of the Roman standard of giving each person *ius suum*.[57]

But Aristotle makes clear that his theory of justice, like Plato's, is intimately connected to a claim about nature. For Aristotle, distributive justice in the political sense requires giving each person the role for which his nature suits him. In situations where all citizens have sufficient virtue to participate in governance, and where no single citizen or small group of citizens is supereminently virtuous, justice requires that political authority should be broadly shared (although, even in this case, high political offices should be assigned exclusively to the most excellent men).[58] However, when the virtue of one citizen, or that of a small group of citizens, towers above the rest, justice demands that the city should be governed as a monarchy or an aristocracy.[59] The principle here is that if the *polis* is to achieve its purpose (i.e. to allow human beings to fulfill their natures), then it must be ordered and governed by those most skilled at "living well" – those most expert at seeking and achieving the Good. People of inferior virtue should be ruled by their moral superiors for their own sakes. Accordingly, in Book I of the *Politics* we learn that there are natural slaves, and that it is just to go to war in order to put these unfortunates in their proper, natural place.[60]

Thus, Aristotle's idea of distributive justice is not the Roman notion that we should simply respect private property and do no bodily harm (as Cicero puts it in *De officiis* 1.20). It is revealing that, although Aristotle rejects the communism of Plato's guardians in Book II of the *Politics*, he nonetheless maintains in II.6 that levels of property must be kept proportionate in order to prevent the development of an unjust system in which wealthy,

---

[56] Fred D. Miller, Jr., *Nature, Justice, and Rights in Aristotle's Politics* (Oxford: Clarendon Press, 1995), p. 70.

[57] See also Aristotle, *Rhetoric* 1366b7 (1.9). "ἔστι δὲ δικαιοσύνη μὲν ἀρετὴ δι᾽ ἣν τὰ αὐτῶν ἕκαστοι ἔχουσι. καὶ ὡς ὁ νόμος." But compare 1373b (1.13). The Greek text is taken from Aristotle, *Rhetoric*, ed. and trans. John Henry Freese, Loeb Classical Library (Harvard University Press, 1926).

[58] *Politics* 1281b–1282a (III.6).   [59] *Politics* 1283b–1284a (III.7–8).

[60] For Aristotle's theory of natural slavery, see Peter Garnsey, *Ideas of Slavery from Aristotle to Augustine* (Cambridge University Press, 1996), esp. pp. 107–27.

but unvirtuous men are left to rule (1270a).[61] This passage introduces a theme which recurs throughout the *Politics*: political authority should rest with those who most contribute to the good life (i.e. the virtuous), rather than the wealthy, and only a temperate distribution of property secures this end.[62]

By way of summary, then, the Greek view does not particularly concern itself with freedom as "non-dependence," and it assumes that the purpose of civic life is not glory, but happiness (εὐδαιμονία), defined as the fulfillment that human beings achieve through contemplation. Most important for present purposes, it also exhibits a sharply contrasting theory of justice. Justice (δικαιοσύνη), on this Greek view, is not a matter of giving each person *ius suum* in the Roman sense, but is rather an arrangement of elements that accords with nature. In the case of the state, justice is instantiated by the rule of reason in the persons of the most excellent men; it results in a social existence which teaches citizens virtue. This view of justice as a natural balance among elements in turn leads to a completely anti-Roman endorsement of property regulations. If property is allowed to flow freely among citizens, both Plato and Aristotle reason, extremes of wealth and poverty will inevitably develop. The resulting rich and poor will both be corrupted by their condition: the rich will become effeminate, luxurious, and slothful, while the poor will lose their public spirit.[63] These corrupt souls will no longer defer to the rule of the best men, an "unjust" regime will develop, and virtue will be undermined.[64]

This "Greek view," as I have set it out, is clearly a minimal and composite summary, designed to highlight a certain orientation shared by Plato and Aristotle. In presenting it, I do not intend to minimize the extent to which medieval, Renaissance, and early-modern thinkers posited deep divisions

---

[61] See Miller's excellent summary of Aristotle's views on property, *Nature*, pp. 327–31.

[62] See esp. 1267b5 (II.4), 1281a5 (III.5), and the analysis of agricultural democracy at 1318b7–1319a19 (VI.4). See also *Rhetoric* 1391a (II.16).

[63] See, for example, Plato, *Republic* 421d–422a (IV), *Laws* 729a (V), 742e–743c (V), 744d–745b (V), and Aristotle, *Politics* 1295b4–1296a22 (IV.9). It should be noted, however, that, despite Plato's comments on the effects of wealth in *Republic* IV, his "oligarchic man" becomes avaricious, rather than opulent (*Republic* 554a–555a [VIII]). The corrupting effects of wealth were, needless to say, also a deep concern of Roman authors. Yet the surviving Roman authors found themselves constrained by their theory of justice, and could not bring themselves to endorse severe property regulations or redistribution programs.

[64] Aristotle argues that a state exhibiting extreme disparities in wealth may have one of two degenerate destinies: either it will become an "unmixed oligarchy" (ὀλιγαρχία ἄκρατος), or the poor might revolt and establish "extreme democracy" (δῆμος ἔσχατος) (*Politics* 1296a2 [IV.9]). Both resulting situations will soon develop into tyranny. Indeed, in cases where one citizen or a very small number of citizens possesses inordinate wealth, Aristotle goes so far as to recommend ostracism as a preemptive measure (1284b15–43 [III.13]). See also Plato, *Republic* 550c–553a (VIII).

between Plato and Aristotle, nor, indeed, to suggest that the works of Plato and Aristotle alone constitute "Greek thought" (any more than the works of Cicero, Sallust, Livy, and Tacitus constitute "Roman thought").[65] The intention is, rather, to emphasize that authors who took Plato or Aristotle for their model could (and often did) emerge with a substantially different kind of republican theory. In particular, they might, for the reasons set out above, come to base their republican frameworks either on the abolition of private property or on some mechanism designed to secure its egalitarian distribution – two proposals wholly incompatible with the Roman and neo-Roman view, which rejects any political interference in property distribution as a violation of the principle of justice.[66] Indeed, it is precisely on this issue of property distribution that several significant Renaissance and early-modern thinkers *did* insist on the compatibility of Plato and Aristotle. Erasmus, for example, observed that, while Plato advocated a society without private property, Aristotle had simply "tempered" this view by arguing that "ownership and title should be in the hands of certain individuals, but that, in every other respect, all things should be held in common, in accordance with the proverb [i.e. that 'among friends all things are common property'] for the sake of utility, virtue, and civil society."[67] Likewise, James Harrington, who listed More among his favorite philosophers and whose

---

[65] Plato and Aristotle are singled out in this study because they constituted by far the most important sources for Greek ethical and political theory in Renaissance and early-modern Europe – not because these two authors reflected the mainstream of Greek political philosophy. Indeed, Josiah Ober does well to remind us that Plato and Aristotle were critics, rather than purveyors of mainstream Greek political ideas and values. See Josiah Ober, *Political Dissent in Democratic Athens: Intellectual Critics of Popular Rule* (Princeton University Press, 1998). For a discussion of a different kind of "Greek republicanism," see my "'True Liberty': Isocrates and Milton's *Areopagitica*" in *Milton Studies* 40 (2001), 201–21.

[66] In Robert Nozick's vocabulary, we have here a quarrel between a "historical" theory of justice and a "patterned," or "end-result" theory. See Robert Nozick, *Anarchy, State, and Utopia* (New York: Basic Books, 1974), pp. 153–55. It is worth noting that even Seneca (himself an extremely rich man), whose *De otio* endorses significant aspects of the Platonist case and several of whose essays take a negative view of excessive property, emerges in *De vita beata* (XXIII.1–5) with an impassioned defense of private property and limitless money-making based on Roman *ius*. Seneca, *Moral essays*, vol. II, ed. and trans. John W. Basore, Loeb Classical Library (Harvard University Press, 1932). For an excellent discussion of Seneca's views of property see Miriam T. Griffin, "Seneca *Praedives*" in *Seneca: a Philosopher in Politics* (Oxford University Press, 1976), pp. 286–314.

[67] *Opera omnia Desiderii Erasmi Roterodami*, vol. XX, ed. M. L. van Poll-van de Lisdonk, M. Mann Phillips, and Chr. Robinson (Amsterdam: Elzevier, 1993), p. 84. "Aristoteles libro Politicorum ii. temperat Platonis sententiam volens possessionem ac proprietatem esse penes certos, caeterum ob usum, virtutem et societatem civilem omnia communia iuxta proverbium." Elsewhere, however, Erasmus was quick to criticize Aristotle for departing from the Platonic (and Apostolic) standard even to that extent. He writes in the *Dulce bellum inexpertis* (1515) that from Aristotle "didicimus non esse perfectam hominis felicitatem, nisi corporis & fortunae bonae accesserint. Ab hoc didicimus non posse florere rempublicam in qua sint omnia communia. Huius omnia decreta cum Christi doctrina conamur adglutinare, hoc est, aquam flammis miscere."

Oceana bears the mark of *Utopia*,[68] would later insist that Plato's *Laws* and Aristotle's *Politics* were of one mind in endorsing agrarian laws.[69]

In the confrontation between Greek and Roman republican values we can, therefore, detect the prehistory of two basic positions on the nature of property which continue to organize our political discourse. One sees the community as the ultimate owner of all goods, and empowers it to arrange the distribution of those goods in such a way as to advance some normative vision of human nature. The other views property as a trump against the power of the community, and insists that the *respublica* was originally constituted in order to protect private property. The Greek tradition is the foundational expression of the first position in Western political thought, while neo-Roman ideology is the archetype of the second.

In what follows I examine the winding road taken by the Greek tradition through the intellectual landscape of the early-modern period. It should be clear that, in speaking of a "Greek tradition," I do not mean a reified philosophical system, but rather an orientation on questions relating to justice, the good life, and property which early-modern thinkers drew out of the central texts of Greek moral and political philosophy, and which yielded a different set of referents for such key evaluative terms as "justice," "republic," "virtue," "freedom," and "happiness."[70] I argue that this tradition was revived in England during the early sixteenth century, and was then broadly influential throughout the seventeenth and eighteenth centuries, both in the Old World and the New. Careful attention to the *fortuna* of this style of political reasoning yields significant new interpretations of many of the leading characters in the republican drama, among them Thomas More, Niccolò Machiavelli, James Harrington, Montesquieu, and the theorists of the American Revolution and Constitution.

But this study makes no totalizing claims about the nature of "republicanism." The aim here is not to replace Pocock's "classical republicanism" and Skinner's "neo-Romanism" with the "Greek tradition," or to identify the feature (or features) that all these ideologies have in common. Indeed, I begin from the premise that the question "what is the essence of republicanism?" is badly posed. If by "republicanism" we mean a tradition

---

[68] *The Political Works of James Harrington*, ed. J. G. A. Pocock (Cambridge University Press, 1977), p. 395.

[69] Ibid., pp. 166, 234–35, 382, 412, 460.

[70] On the danger of heuristic devices taking on a life of their own, see Conal Condren, "*Natura naturans*: Natural Law and the Sovereign in the Writings of Thomas Hobbes" in *Natural Law and Civil Sovereignty: Moral Rights and State Authority in Early Modern Political Thought*, ed. Ian Hunter and David Saunders (Houndmills: Palgrave Macmillan, 2002), esp. pp. 61–62.

of taking the "republic" as the constituent unit of political life, then there will be as many "republicanisms" as there are uses of the word "republic." Rather than searching in vain for the "essence" that underlies all these uses, we should treat the word "republic" in the same way that Wittgenstein treats the word "game" in the *Philosophical Investigations*. He asks, what is common to all the things we call "games"? What is their essential, unifying characteristic? The answer is "nothing." "For if you look at them you will not see something that is common to all, but similarities, relationships, and a whole series of them at that."[71] I have no doubt that the word "republic" exhibits a patchwork of uses that is even less uniform. I claim only to have studied an important "family resemblance."

---

[71] Ludwig Wittgenstein, *Philosophical Investigations (Philosophische Untersuchungen)*, ed. G. E. M. Anscombe and R. Rhees, trans. G. E. M. Anscombe (Oxford: Basil Blackwell, 1958), p. 31.

CHAPTER I

Greek nonsense in More's Utopia

I

At the end of Sir Thomas More's *Utopia* the character "More" rejects Raphael Hythloday's suggestion that the Utopians have achieved the *optimus reipublicae status* ("the best state of a commonwealth"):

> When Raphael had finished his story, I was left thinking that not a few of the laws and customs he had described as existing among the Utopians were really absurd. These included their methods of waging war, their religious practices, as well as other customs of theirs; but my chief objection was to the basis of their whole system, that is, their communal living and their moneyless economy.[1]

This passage represents a pivotal moment in More's text. At issue is whether "More" the character should be identified in this instance with More the author, and whether in consequence we are meant to take the Utopian example as the true "best state of a commonwealth"[2] or as part of a rhetorical exercise. There is much to be said for both positions, but we should at least begin by noticing that, within the economy of the text, "More's"

---

[1] Thomas More, *Utopia*, ed. George M. Logan, Robert M. Adams, and Clarence H. Miller (Cambridge University Press, 1995), p. 247. All quotations from *Utopia* in Latin and English are taken from this edition. On occasion I have modified the translation for the sake of clarity; where this is done, it is duly noted. "Haec ubi Raphael recensuit, quamquam haud pauca mihi succurrebant quae in eius populi moribus legibusque perquam absurde videbantur instituta, non solum de belli gerendi ratione et rebus divinis ac religione, aliisque insuper eorum institutis, sed in eo quoque ipso maxime quod maximum totius institutionis fundamentum est, vita scilicet victuque communi sine ullo pecuniae commercio..." I am grateful to Abbé Germain Marc'hadour for calling to my attention several corrigenda in this chapter.

[2] The phrase "de optimo reipublicae statu" is found in Cicero, *De legibus* 1.15. In this passage, the character Atticus explicitly compares Cicero's enterprise to what "was done by your beloved Plato" (*Platonem illum tuum*). See Cicero, *De republica, De legibus*, ed. and trans. C. W. Keyes, Loeb Classical Library (Harvard University Press, 1928). The classic Greek discussion of the distinction between the "best possible political community" (ἡ κοινωνία πολιτικὴ ἡ κρατίστη πασῶν) and those communities which actually exist is found in Book II of Aristotle's *Politics* (1260b27 [II.1]). See Aristotle, *Politics*, ed. and trans. H. Rackham, Loeb Classical Library (Harvard University Press, 1932).

rejection of the Utopian system as "absurd" is precisely the result the reader is led to expect. Every time Raphael outlines the sort of Utopian advice he would give if he were a councillor, his interlocutor dismisses it as absurd or out of place, and adds that such advice would be greeted with derision by his fellow Europeans. In Book 1, Hythloday observes that, if he gave his sort of advice in court, he would be "either kicked out forthwith, or made into a laughing stock," and More readily agrees.[3] Later, when Raphael asks "More" whether men would greet his proposals with deaf ears, "More" replies "with completely deaf ears, doubtless" because Hythloday's stance is "outlandish."[4] A frustrated Hythloday is forced to insist that his advice should not be rejected as "outlandish to the point of folly" and his ideas as "outlandish and absurd" simply because they run counter to "corrupt custom."[5] Nonetheless, he knows full well that they will be, and the reader is not surprised when "More" ends up rejecting Hythloday's advice as nonsensical and contrary to *publica opinio*.

But "nonsense" is not an innocent idea in *Utopia*, and, while many scholars have stressed More's indebtedness to the Lucianic tradition of *serio ludere* ("playing seriously"), the fact that "nonsense" constitutes a structuring force in the text has gone largely undiscussed. More's network of Greek puns do not simply entertain; they organize. Hythloday is a distributor (δαίων) of nonsense (ὕθλος),[6] and almost everything he describes from his travels has a name coined from Greek words connoting "nonsense" or "non-existence" (a quality which renders things nonsensical). The Polylerites are people of much (πολύ) nonsense (λῆρος); the Achorians are people without a country (ἀχώριοι); Utopia is "no place" (οὔτοπος) – a pun on "happy place" (εὔτοπος) – and the title of its governor is Ademus, an official "without people" (ἄδημος); the river Anyder is without water (ἀνύδωρ), and runs through Amaurot, the unknown city (ἀμαυρός).[7] As we have seen, however, the content of Hythloday's account is "nonsense" *from a particular point of*

---

[3] More, *Utopia*, p. 83. "aut eiciendum aut habendum ludibrio."

[4] Ibid., p. 95. I have altered Adams's translation here. "surdissimis, inquam, haud dubie: neque hercule miror . . . Quid enim prodesse possit aut quomodo in illorum pectus influere sermo tam insolens . . ."

[5] Ibid., p. 99. "ita non video cur videri debeat usque ad ineptias insolens . . . Equidem si omittenda sunt omnia tamquam insolentia atque absurda quaecumque perversi mores hominum fecerunt ut videri possint aliena, dissimulemus oportet apud Christianos pleraque omnia quae CHRISTUS docuit . . ."

[6] See Nigel Wilson, "The Name Hythlodaeus" in *Moreana* 29 (1992), 33. Some scholars have wanted to derive "daeus" from δαίος, meaning "hostile" or "wretched," but also (very occasionally) "knowing" or "cunning." This interpretation draws strength from the fact that νέμω, not δαίω, is the regular Greek verb meaning "to distribute"; however, I tend to prefer the first alternative.

[7] For an account of More's toponymy, see James Romm, "More's Strategy of Naming in the *Utopia*" in *The Sixteenth Century Journal* 22 (1991), 173–83. Romm despairs of identifying any organizing rubric for More's nomenclature, largely because certain names seem to allow for an ethical, as well as "nonsensical" reading. But Romm interprets the organizing principle of "nonsense" too narrowly:

view, namely that of "More" and those whom he represents. But the name "More" is the most significant pun of all: *Utopia*'s readers would remember Erasmus' dedication to More in *The Praise of Folly* (*Moriae encomium*), in which he attributes the inspiration for his panegyric to "your family name of More [*Mori cognomen tibi*], which is as similar to the word for Folly [*Moriae vocabulum*], as you yourself are far from that quality,"[8] and concludes by exclaiming "farewell, most learned More, and zealously defend your Folly [*Moria*]."[9] More subsequently made frequent use of this pun,[10] and his readers would certainly have recorded that Hythloday's advice is dismissed as nonsense by a *moros*.[11]

So More's wordplay leaves us as witnesses to a dialogue between a speaker of nonsense and a fool, and it is our task to determine who the true *stultus* is. A possible way out of the impasse is to recall that Hythloday is not the first speaker of ὕθλος in the Western tradition: Socrates receives this epithet in a famous passage in the *Republic*,[12] and the conceit that Socratic and Platonic advice will always be laughed at by those still in "the cave" (i.e. Europe) is, as we shall see, one of the structuring elements in *Utopia*, as it was in *The Praise of Folly*. In the confrontation between "More" and Hythloday we have a clash between a man trapped in the cave and one who has seen the sun. But for More, a founding member of the group of "baby Greeks" (*Graeculi*), whom Erasmus so jovially satirizes, this confrontation is dramatized as a battle between Greece and Rome – between the values of the Roman

---

once we allow for the importance of point of view, we can see how More's meaning can be conveyed both by "no place" terms and by terms which seem to be nonsense, but actually contain moral significance. Ultimately, however, we should be wary of agonizing over these names to the point where we miss the joke.

[8] *Opera omnia Desiderii Erasmi Roterodami*, vol. IX, ed. Clarence H. Miller (Amsterdam: Elzevier, 1979), p. 68. All translations from Erasmus' Latin are my own. "Mori cognomen tibi gentile, quod tam ad Moriae vocabulum accedit, quam es ipse a re alienus."

[9] Ibid., p. 70. "Vale, disertissime More, et Moriam tuam gnaviter defende."

[10] See Richard Marius, *Thomas More* (London: Phoenix, 1999), p. 88. One prominent example is More's 1515 *Letter to Dorp* (*The Complete Works of St. Thomas More*, vol. XV, ed. Daniel Kinney [Yale University Press, 1986]), where he comments that Erasmus dedicated *The Praise of Folly* to "my patronage." See also letter 1087 from More to Erasmus (1520) in which More responds to the *Antimorus*, a diatribe against him written by Germain de Brie. *Opus epistolarum Des. Erasmi Roterodami*, ed. P. S. Allen and H. M. Allen, vol. IV, no. 1087 (Oxford University Press, 1922).

[11] Dominic Baker-Smith notes parenthetically that the name Morus "implies a family relationship to Folly," but neglects to identify the implications of this fact for interpreting More's text. See Dominic Baker-Smith, *More's Utopia* (London: HarperCollins, 1991), p. 52.

[12] In Book I, Thrasymachus characterizes Socrates' thoughts on justice as ridiculous, and exclaims "I won't accept it if you speak such nonsense as that" (ὡς ἐγὼ οὐκ ἀποδέξομαι ἐὰν ὕθλους τοιούτους λέγῃς) (336d). English translations from Plato are taken from *Plato: the Collected Dialogues, including the Letters*, ed. Edith Hamilton, Huntington Cairns (Princeton University Press, 1989). In this case, however, I have substituted my own translation for Shorey's less literal one. The Greek texts are taken from *Platonis opera*, ed. John Burnet, 5 vols., 2nd edn. (Oxford: Clarendon Press, 1963).

republican tradition and those of a rival commonwealth theory based on Greek ethics. *Utopia* suggests that, when seen from a Roman perspective, Greek advice looks like "nonsense." But, for More, that "nonsense" yields the *optimus reipublicae status*.

II

The political structure of the island of Utopia, with its governors,[13] senates, and assemblies, would surely have reminded More's readers of the standard "mixed constitution" recommended by Polybius, and authorized in Renaissance Europe by the stability of the Venetian regime. But republicanism in the Renaissance was far more than a set of claims about political structures: it was an ethical position.[14] Accordingly, in order to locate *Utopia* as precisely as possible within the intellectual landscape of the period, it becomes essential to identify the ethical framework of Utopian republicanism. In this respect, the most striking fact about More's text is its comprehensive rejection of the civic ideology that Quentin Skinner has dubbed "neo-Roman." Recall that, on this Roman view, liberty is conceptualized in opposition to slavery, and is deemed essential for the constitution of virtue. Virtue, in turn, is said to yield *iustitia*, defined in the classic formulation as an imperative to respect the *ius* of each individual. With virtue and justice in place, the state can achieve *concordia*, and ultimately *gloria*, its highest goal. Integral to this theory, as noted above, is a marked preference for *negotium* over *otium*, and a conviction that, in order for the state to maintain its liberty, each person must seek honor through the observance of public *officia*. In short, neo-Roman authors embrace republican government because they regard living in a free state as the only means of achieving virtue, and identify active civic participation as the only defense against enslavement.

In his important study of *Utopia* George Logan argues that More's dialogue should be seen as an attempt to muster Greek "city-state theory" to defend the "traditional humanist" or neo-Stoic program.[15] Now that Skinner and others have excavated that traditional, neo-Roman story more effectively, however, we can recognize that this is not the case. More was

---

[13] There is no "governor" (*princeps*) of Utopia as a whole; rather, each city's *phylarchs* (who represent thirty households each) elect that city's governor. See More, *Utopia*, pp. 122–23.

[14] This claim has been most recently disputed (unsuccessfully I think) in the case of English republicanism by Arihiro Fukuda in his otherwise excellent *Sovereignty and the Sword: Harrington, Hobbes, and Mixed Government in the English Civil Wars* (Oxford University Press, 1997). See Jonathan Scott's incisive review in *English Historical Review*, 115 (2000), 660–62.

[15] George M. Logan, *The Meaning of More's Utopia* (Princeton University Press, 1983), p. 111.

not criticizing the practices of contemporary republican theory from within the neo-Roman framework, but rather using the description of Utopia to reject that framework altogether. Machiavelli, who was writing the *Discorsi* as More was writing *Utopia*, furnishes an instructive comparison. Although Machiavelli's republican theory is utterly subversive across the spectrum, it nonetheless continues to inhabit the basic categories set out above. Machiavelli may turn the conventional content of *virtus* upside down, but his *virtù* still remains an instrument for the acquisition of *gloria* and *grandezza*. He still praises the *vivere libero* (1.2),[16] and insists that the central mission of a republic and all free people is actively *mantenere lo stato* – to avoid *servitù* (1.29).[17] He notoriously suggests that Christianity is antagonistic to a civic life dedicated to *gloria*, but leaves no doubt that glory wins the day and remains intact as the goal of civil association (11.2).[18] In short, the subversiveness of Machiavelli lies in his radical reappraisal of the traditional neo-Roman categories.

More's text, as we shall see, mounts an attack on these categories and asserts a different, fundamentally Greek ethical framework for political life. As Montesquieu observed acutely in *De l'esprit des lois*, More "wanted to govern all states with the simplicity of a Greek city."[19] This is not to repeat the familiar and obvious claim that Plato plays a significant role in *Utopia* and furnishes the source for Utopian communism. It is rather to stress that, for More, the abolition of private property was not the means to Roman *iustitia* and, thence, to Roman *gloria*, but rather part of an entirely separate schema – one that is essentially Greek and sharply divergent from *Romanitas*. This Greek view, as I have set it out, does not particularly value freedom (ἐλευθερία) as "non-dependence"; indeed one of its cardinal

---

[16] Niccolò Machiavelli, *Discorsi sopra la prima deca di Tito Livio*, ed. Giorgio Inglese, introduzione di Gennaro Sasso (Milan: Rizzoli, 1984), p. 68.

[17] Ibid., p. 126. "Perché avendo una città che vive libera duoi fini, l'uno lo acquistare, l'altro il mantenersi libera, conviene che nell'una cosa e nell'altra per troppo amore erri."

[18] Ibid., pp. 298–99. "Pensando dunque donde possa nascere che in quegli tempi antichi i popoli fossero più amatori della libertà che in questi, credo nasca da quella medesima cagione che fa ora gli uomini manco forti, la quale credo sia la diversità della educazione nostra dall'antica, fondata dalla diversità della religione nostra dalla antica. Perché, avendoci la nostra religione mostro la verità e la vera via, ci fa stimare meno l'onore del mondo; onde i Gentili, stimandolo assai e avendo posto in quello il sommo bene, erano nelle azioni loro più feroci."

[19] xxix.19. See Montesquieu, *De l'esprit des lois*, ed. Victor Goldschmidt, vol. 11 (Paris: Garnie-Flammarion, 1979), p. 308. "Thomas More ... voulait gouverner tous les Etats avec la simplicité d'une ville grecque." The translation is my own. Montesquieu followed in a long line of European thinkers who believed that Utopia did indeed represent More's *optimus reipublicae status*. To name another example, John Locke wrote in 1659 that More had made *Utopia* "the Subject of those Excellent formes of Government his brain had contriv'd, thereby teaching the World not what really was, but what ought to be "(Letter to William Godolphin, July 7, 1659). See *John Locke: Selected Correspondence*, ed. Mark Goldie (Oxford University Press, 2002), p. 8.

assumptions is that individuals cannot be "free" unless they depend upon their intellectual and moral superiors. Absent such an arrangement, they would be enslaved by their ignorance of the dictates of their own rational nature. Moreover, as we have seen, the Greek view expresses undisguised disdain for the pursuit of "glory," and takes as its ultimate *desideratum* "happiness" (εὐδαιμονία; *felicitas* or *beatitudo* in Latin), defined as the fulfillment that human beings achieve through contemplation. Most importantly, Greek "justice" (δικαιοσύνη) is an arrangement of elements according to nature, and consists in the rule of the wisest and most virtuous men. This theory of justice diverges sharply from Roman *iustitia*, and, as we have seen, can authorize the coercive regulation and redistribution of property in order to secure the rule of reason.

More's attraction to this Greek value system, and his antipathy to its neo-Roman counterpart, were as much cultural as theoretical, and, in order to understand them, we have to reconstruct a particular aspect of his intellectual context: his association with the Erasmian circle. These Oxford–London humanists, whom Erasmus befriended during his periods of residence in England (the longest of which lasted from 1509 to 1514), became the first Englishmen to dedicate themselves to the study of Greek, and to make a polemical point of preferring Greece to Rome.[20] Members of this Graecophile coterie (whom More dubbed *Graecistes*)[21] included William Grocyn (More's tutor and the first lecturer in Greek at Oxford),[22] John Colet (founder of St. Paul's school, and author of the Platonizing Oxford lectures on Paul's Epistle to the Romans), Thomas Linacre (the doctor-turned-priest who helped to introduce Erasmus to Greek studies), William Lily (author of a pioneering Latin grammar, and More's partner in translating Greek epigrams into Latin elegiacs), Richard Pace (a scholar of Greek who later opted for a diplomatic career), and, of course, More himself.[23] From 1514 to 1520, the general period of *Utopia*'s preparation and publication, this circle's advocacy of Greek culture took on a new intensity, as several of its members were called upon to defend Erasmus' controversial project of using the Greek New Testament to correct the Vulgate. As an irate 1518 letter from More to the University of Oxford makes clear, opposition

---

[20] Marius, *Thomas More*, p. 72; More, *Complete Works*, vol. xv, p. lxxxi.

[21] See, for example, More's *Letter to Dorp* (1515) in *Complete Works*, vol. xv, p. 96.

[22] Grocyn, however, preferred Aristotle to Plato, and Linacre contributed to the Aldine Aristotle. See *Contemporaries of Erasmus: a Biographical Register of the Renaissance and Reformation*, ed. Peter C. Bietenholz and Thomas B. Deutscher, vol. 11 (Toronto, 1986), pp. 135–36.

[23] Other associates included Richard Croke, Richard Foxe, William Latimer, Thomas Lupset, Cuthbert Tunstall, and Christopher Urswick. Ibid., vol. 1, p. 327.

to this form of Biblical criticism, and to the Greek learning which had engendered it, had indeed reached a fever pitch:

I have recently heard it reported by a number of people in London that certain scholars at your university, prompted either by hatred of Greek learning, by a misguided devotion to some other sort, or (as I think more likely) by a shameless addiction to joking and trifling, have formed a deliberate conspiracy to call themselves Trojans. One of them, who is said to be riper in years than in wisdom, has assumed the name "Priam," another the name "Hector," another the name "Paris" or else that of some other Trojan, and the rest have been doing the same, for the sole purpose of jokingly setting themselves up as a faction opposed to the Greeks to make fun of the students of Greek learning ... [One of these "Trojans"] openly called everyone a heretic who wished to pursue Greek learning, and he went on to brand lecturers in Greek as "archdevils," and students of Greek (in a more modest and wittier vain, as he thought) as "underdevils."[24]

The Erasmian circle responded energetically to this sort of abuse, and to the more scholarly criticism of the new Greek learning emerging from the universities (in particular, the University of Louvain). Erasmus himself led the way forward. In a 1515 reply to Maarten van Dorp, his famous antagonist, Erasmus announces that "without Greek, the study of the liberal arts is lame and blind."[25] He echoes these comments in the 1516 epistle dedicatory to his translation of Theodore Gaza's *Grammatica institutio*. In that context, he bemoans the University of Cologne's hostility to Greek studies and invites the dedicatee, Johannes Caesarius, to reflect on the burgeoning Greek revival:

I rejoice in our age, my dear Caesarius, in which we see Greek literature coming to life again everywhere! For as the neglect of Greek brought with it the "total

---

[24] More, *Complete Works*, vol. xv, pp. 132, 142. I have taken Kinney's translation here. "Ego quum Londini essem, audivi iam nuper saepius, quosdam scholasticos Academiae vestrae, sive graecarum odio literarum, seu pravo quopiam aliarum studio, seu quod opinor verius, improba ludendi nugandique libidine, de composito conspirasse inter sese, ut se Troianos appellent. Eorum quidam (senior quam sapientior ut ferunt) Priami sibi nomen adoptavit, Hectoris alius, alius item Paridis, aut aliorum cuiuspiam veterum Troianorum, caeterique ad eundem modum, non alio consilio, quam uti per ludum iocumque velut factio Graecis adversa graecarum studiosis literarum illuderent ... quicunque graecas appeterent literas, aperte vocavit haereticos: ad haec lectores earum diabolos maximos denotavit, auditores vero, diabolos etiam illos, sed modestius, et ut ipsi videbatur, facete, minutulos." For this episode's place in the rise of Erasmianism in Oxford and Cambridge, see James McConica, *English Humanists and Reformation Politics under Henry VIII and Edward VI* (Oxford University Press, 1965), pp. 88–93; see also Alistair Fox, "Facts and Fallacies: Interpreting English Humanism" in *Reassessing the Henrican Age: Humanism, Politics and Reform 1500–1550*, ed. Alistair Fox and John Guy (Oxford University Press, 1986), esp. pp. 12–14. For the broader European context of the debate over Greek, see Jean-Christophe Saladin, *La bataille du grec à la Renaissance* (Paris: Belles lettres, 2000). See also Simon Goldhill, *Who Needs Greek?: Contests in the Cultural History of Hellenism* (Cambridge University Press, 2002), chap. 1.

[25] *Opus epistolarum*, vol. ii, no. 337. "sine his mancum ac caecum esse litterarum studium."

destruction" of all good disciplines and all elegant authors, we may have hope also that, with Greek studies being revived, those disciplines and authors will once again flourish.[26]

That same year he writes playfully that he hopes to transform his patron, John Fisher, "from a Latin into a Greek; this is the 'metamorphosis' I myself have undertaken."[27]

But Erasmus' English defenders adopted a posture that was more overtly polemical. In the 1517 treatise *De fructu qui ex doctrina percipitur* (*On the Benefit of a Liberal Education*), Richard Pace provides a representative statement of what emerged as the Erasmian party line:

Whatever seems to have originated with the Romans, for example, in rhetoric and history, was all taken from the Greeks as if it were a loan. For Demosthenes and Isocrates produced Cicero, as great as he was in the art of oratory (Quintilian acknowledges this). In philosophy, indeed, Cicero called Plato and Aristotle the most learned of the Greeks, and he calls one of them "divine" and the other "most wise." But philosophy among the Romans was so feeble that nothing could seem more stupid to learned ears than to compare Roman philosophers to the Greeks. And I include Cicero in this group, if he'll forgive me for saying so.[28]

More evidently shared Pace's sentiments and polemical style. In his 1519 letter to the monk John Batmanson, he declares that the superiority of Greek culture is clear from "those arts they call liberal, along with philosophy, in which subjects the Romans wrote next to nothing," and offers similar observations in his *Letter to Oxford* and in his own reply to Dorp (1515).[29] In short, for More and his circle, an impassioned defense of the Erasmian

---

[26] Ibid., no. 428. "Gratulor, mi Caesari, nostro saeculo quo videmus passim repullescere Graecas litteras. Nam ut harum neglectus omnium bonarum disciplinarum, omnium elegantiorum autorum πανολεθρίαν invexit, ita spes est futurum ut his renatis et illa reflorescant."

[27] Ibid., no. 452 [to Andrew Ammonius]. "Interim e Latino Graecum reddam; hanc μεταμόρφωσιν in me recepi."

[28] Richard Pace, *De fructu qui ex doctrina percipitur*, ed. and trans. Frank Manley and Richard S. Sylvester (New York: Renaissance Society of America, 1967), p. 128. The translation is my own. "Apud Latinos vero, quicquid apparet proprium, ut in arte dicendi, & in historia, hoc totum quasi mutuo sumptum est ex Graecis. Nam Ciceronem, quantus est in arte Oratoria (Quintiliano id confitente) fecit Demosthenes & Isocrates. In Philosophia vero, Plato & Aristoteles, quorum alterum divinum, alterum sapientissimum, ut doctissimos Graecos saepe appellat. Sed Philosophia adeo apud Latinos manca est, ut nihil possit esse eruditis auribus stultius, quam Latinos Philosophos cum Graecis comparare. Quo in genere, nec Ciceronem ipsum (quod eius venia dictum sit) excipio." For an excellent discussion of Pace's *œuvre*, see Catherine M. Curtis's unpublished doctoral thesis, "Richard Pace on Pedagogy, Counsel, and Satire" (University of Cambridge, 1996).

[29] More, *Complete Works*, vol. xv, p. 220. "vel denique propter artes, quas liberales vocant, ac philosophiam, quibus de rebus Latini scripsere propemodum nihil." See also p. 99 and p. 143. Richard Croke offered a similar statement of the Erasmian case in his July, 1519 lecture at Cambridge, "De graecorum disciplinarium laudibus oratio." See Richard Croke, *Orationes Richardi Croci duae* (Paris, 1520).

project and the new Greek learning carried with it a corresponding attack on Rome in general, and on Roman philosophy in particular.[30]

But More was not undiscriminating in his affection for Greek philosophy. He evinced the same marked preference for Plato over Aristotle shared by almost all of the Oxford–London humanists.[31] This circle was deeply influenced by the writings of Giovanni Pico della Mirandola, the notorious syncretist,[32] whom the Erasmians admired for his thoroughly Platonic renunciation of the *vita activa*. In More's *Life of John Picus* (1510), for example, the protagonist appears as a man whose mind was "evermore on high cleued fast in contemplation & in thenserching of natures cownceill," unable to "let down hit selfe to the consideration and ouerseing of these base abiecte and vile erthly trifles."[33] Likewise, in a 1492 letter which More admired enough to translate, Pico insists to an interlocutor that he prefers "the rest and peace of my mynde" to "all your kingis palacis, all your commune besines, all your glory" (the phrase "all your glory" is, incidentally, More's own addition).[34]

---

[30] Needless to say, the attacks on Rome that we find in the writings of the Erasmian circle are polemical and, as a result, hyperbolic in character. An appreciation of the central role these comments play in the presentation of the Erasmian case does not entail taking them at face value. Indeed, to do so would be deeply mistaken. Erasmus himself annotated Cicero's *De officiis* and prepared an edition of Seneca, whom he admired.

[31] More did not, however, reject Aristotle along with scholasticism. He tried all his life to rescue Aristotle from the schoolmen, and to arrive at a temperate assessment of the philosopher's merit. As he puts it in his *Letter to Dorp*, "Ad Aristotelem ipsum venio quem et ego et supra multos, ita cum multis amo, quem tu [Dorp] in memorata oratione tua videris non supra multos modo, sed pro multis quoque atque adeo pro omnibus amplecti." See *Complete Works*, vol. xv, pp. 100ff.

[32] Pico quarreled with Ficino over the latter's attack on Averroës in the *Theologia platonica*, sought wisdom from occult, Arabic, and kabbalistic sources (a fact which More notably glosses over in his translation of the *Life*), and argued for the compatibility of Plato and Aristotle (for example, in *De ente et uno*). Kristeller suggested the term "syncretist," rather than "eclectic," to designate Pico's approach in order to differentiate it from that of the ancient eclectics (i.e. Pico never suggested that all great philosophers were in fundamental agreement). See Paul Oskar Kristeller, and "Introduction" to Pico's *Oration on the Dignity of Man* in *The Renaissance Philosophy of Man*, ed. Ernst Cassirer, Paul Oskar Kristeller, and John Herman Randall, Jr. (University of Chicago Press, 1948), p. 220. See also Kristeller, *Eight Philosophers of the Italian Renaissance* (Stanford University Press, 1964).

[33] *The Complete Works of St. Thomas More*, vol. 11, ed. Anthony S. G. Edwards, Katherine Gardiner Rodgers, and Clarence H. Miller (Yale University Press, 1997), p. 68. More's text is a free translation of the biography written by Pico's nephew, Giafrancesco.

[34] Ibid., p. 86. This passage appears in the letter to Andrea Corneo which More translates and appends to his *Life*. Pico's Latin reads: "meam animi pacem, regiis aulis, publicis negotiis . . . antepono" (p. 350). In his introduction, Edwards argues that More "softened" Pico's letter by adding the thought that one could lead both an active and a contemplative life. However, this thought is present in the Latin, and More's brief addition appears to be a mere explanatory gloss. The text reads: "Sed inquies, ita volo Martham amplectaris ut Mariam interim non deseras! Hac tibi parte non repugno, nec qui id faciunt damno vel accuso, sed multum abest ut a contemplandi vita ad civilem transisse error non sit, non transisse pro flagitio aut omnino sub culpae nota vel criminis censeatur."

But perhaps even more important than Pico to the Erasmian circle was Marsilio Ficino, author of the first complete Latin translation of Plato's dialogues.[35] Colet corresponded with Ficino during a visit to Italy (1493–96),[36] and Erasmus drew heavily on the Florentine's work (especially the 1469 *Commentarium in Convivium, De amore*) in his *Enchiridion militis christiani*.[37] Indeed, although More was accomplished in Greek, it is probable that he too consulted Ficino's translations. To take only one example, Ficino's *argumentum* for the *Republic* summarizes Plato's theory that cities made up of rich and poor are not one city, but two, and describes the philosopher's novel approach to this problem:

Whence he arrived step by step at his mystery, namely that everything should be held in common. Some would not have less, nor others more. And it is from the former circumstance that jealousies [*invidiae*], lies [*mendacia*], thefts [*furta*] are born, while extravagance [*luxuria*], pride [*superbia*], and sloth [*pigritia*] are born from the latter circumstance.[38]

This is not at all far from Hythloday's insistence that Platonic communism would eliminate theft (*furta*), frauds (*fraudes*), and a host of other crimes and seditions,[39] along with pride (*superbia*), and jealousy (*invidia*).[40] And, as we shall see, Ficino's characterization of Platonic "justice" as "the order

---

[35] Marsilio Ficino, *Platonis opera omnia* (Venice, 1517). For Ficino's translations of Plato and their influence, see James Hankins, *Plato in the Italian Renaissance* (Leiden: E. J. Brill, 1990), pp. 267ff.

[36] A. H. T. Levi, "Introduction" to Erasmus, *The Praise of Folly*, ed. A. H. T. Levi, trans. Betty Radice (Harmondsworth: Penguin Books, 1971), p. 23.

[37] See Maria Cytowska, "Erasme de Rotterdam et Marsile Ficin son maître" in *Eos*, 63 (1975), 165–79. In *Enchiridion*, Erasmus writes, "of the philosophers I should recommend the Platonists because in much of their thinking as well as in their mode of expression they are the closest to the spirit of the prophets and of the gospel" (*The Collected Works of Erasmus*, vol. LXVI, ed. John W. O'Malley [University of Toronto Press, 1988], p. 33). It is important to recall that both More and Erasmus were anxious to exploit the similarities between Christian and Platonic terminology: for example, when they use the word *felicitas* – a marked term in this chapter – they are happy to have their readers take that term as part of two different, yet intrinsically similar discourses (although *beatitudo* was the more pious term for "happiness"). Indeed, the case of *felicitas* represents a surprising omission in Hexter's otherwise excellent discussion of Christian terminology in *Utopia. The Complete Works of St. Thomas More*, vol. IV, ed. Edward Surtz and J. H. Hexter (Yale University Press, 1965), pp. lxxvff.

[38] Ficino, *Platonis opera*, p. 232. "Unde sensim descendit ad mysterium suum ut omnia videlicet sint communia, ne alii minus, alii vero plus habeant, & inde invidiae, mendacia, furta, & hinc luxuria, superbia, pigritiaque nascuntur." A similar passage from Lucian's *Cynicus* (which More translated into Latin in 1506) also seems to anticipate this aspect of More's argument in *Utopia*. In More's Latin, the Cynic declares: "Aurum vero, argentumque ne desideram unquam, neque ego, neque meorum amicorum quisquam. Omnia nanque mala inter homines ex horum cupiditate nascuntur, & seditiones, & bella, & insidiae, & caedes. Haec omnia fontem habent plus habendi cupiditatem." Gold and silver are particular targets of *Utopia* for precisely these reasons (More, *Utopia*, pp. 149ff.). See *The Complete Works of St. Thomas More*, vol. III (part I), ed. Craig R. Thompson (Yale University Press, 1974), p. 21.

[39] More, *Utopia*, p. 245.   [40] Ibid., p. 247.

and health of the society" (*civitatis ordo atque salus*) is very much the view of justice we encounter in *Utopia*.

But the text which most nearly anticipates More's Platonic reassessment of *Romanitas* is certainly Erasmus' *The Praise of Folly*. In Logan's phrase, Erasmus' encomium represents a sort of hall of mirrors in which the personification of Folly hails herself as the determining force in human affairs, and as the source of all blessings – leaving it to the reader to recall that some of what Folly praises *is* folly to praise. Many of the issues raised by Folly are picked up again in *Utopia* (often in precisely the same terms, as in the case of the "problem of counsel" and the Utopian rejection of hunting), but the correspondence between the approaches to Greek theory in the two texts is perhaps the most striking. Throughout Erasmus' mock panegyric, Folly insists that her gift of *stultitia* is what allows human beings to lead happy lives: in a foolish world, only fools are happy. Accordingly, she argues that the Greek philosophers led unpleasant, impractical lives because they did not accept her gift; they chose wisdom instead. Folly first addresses the subject in chapter twenty-four, attacking both Greeks and Romans, but reserving her worst venom for Socrates (on whom she unleashes every Aristophanic weapon in her arsenal):

As evidence of how useless philosophers are when it comes to the practices of real life take Socrates himself, dubbed the one wise man by Apollo's oracle, but chosen with little wisdom, since when he tried to do something in public life, he had to give up amidst the hearty laughter of all men . . . For while he philosophized about clouds and ideal forms, measured the feet of a flea, and wondered at the voice of a midge, he learned nothing at all relevant to civic life.[41]

Folly expands on this theme considerably, lamenting that philosophers are not foolish enough to be able to perform the essential *officia* of Roman ethics:

He [a philosopher] is not at all able to be of any use to himself, to his country, or to his own family, because he is ignorant of public business, and entirely out of touch with popular opinion and the practices of the masses. From which cause he unavoidably incurs hatred, without question due to the great gulf between normal life and minds like his. For what happens among mortals that is not full of folly, done by fools, among fools?[42]

---

[41] Erasmus, *Opera omnia*, vol. IX, p. 98. "Qui quidem quam sint ad omnem vitae usum inutiles, vel Socrates ipse, unus Apollinis oraculo sapiens, sed minime sapienter iudicatus, documento esse potest, qui nescio quid publice conatus agere summo cum omnium risu discessit . . . Nam dum nubes et ideas philosophatur, dum pulicis pedes metitur, dum culicum vocem miratur, quae ad vitam communem attinet non didicit."

[42] Ibid., p. 100. "Usqueadeo neque sibi neque patriae neque suis usquam usui esse potest, propterea quod communium rerum sit imperitus et a populari opinione vulgaribusque institutis longe lateque

Erasmus' implication is devastating. In a bitterly ironic paraphrase of Callicles' argument in the *Gorgias*,[43] Folly argues that philosophers live unhappy lives and are laughed at and scorned because their wisdom prevents them from being viable in a world of fools (Erasmus' μῶροι). Philosophy is incompatible with *popularis opinio* (recall that "More" condemns Hythloday's advice because it is contrary to *publica opinio*). And although Folly mentions Cicero briefly in her list of useless philosophers,[44] the passages quoted above along with Folly's suggestion that these philosophers lack *decorum*[45] reveal that Folly is engaged in a Ciceronian critique of Greek philosophy – precisely the sort of critique that "More" offers in *Utopia*.

Folly, we should recall, does not claim credit for the content of Greek philosophy, but, rather, for what occurs when Greek philosophers attempt to act in the "real world" of fools. And what happens in *The Praise of Folly* when someone tries to give Platonic advice in that real world? An important passage from chapter sixty-six provides the answer:

And so what is likely to come to pass for those men is, I believe, what happens in Plato's myth to those who are chained in a cave and wonder at the shadows of things, and also to that escapee who returns to the cave and announces that he has seen the true things and that those men are much mistaken who believe that nothing else exists besides the wretched shadows. And indeed this wise man commiserates and deplores the insanity of those men who are gripped by such a great error. But those men laugh at him as if he were deranged, and throw him out.[46]

The *miserae umbrae* which beguile the captives, it turns out, are nothing other than the ethics of Roman republican theory.

In chapter twenty-seven Folly asks "what state ever adopted the laws of Plato or Aristotle, or the teachings of Socrates?"[47] None, she replies, because they are all too busy chasing Roman *gloria*. She proceeds to identify two sets of martyrs to the Roman *patria* as her acolytes, and launches into a brutal satire of the Roman *vita activa*, claiming it as an instance of folly.

---

discrepet. Qua quidem ex re odium quoque consequatur necesse est, nimirum ob tantam vitae atque animorum dissimilitudinem. Quid enim omnino geritur inter mortales non stultitiae plenum idque a stultis et apud stultos?"

[43] See *Gorgias* 484d.   [44] Erasmus, *Opera omnia*, vol. IX, p. 98.   [45] Ibid., p. 100.

[46] Ibid., p. 190. "Itaque solet iis usuvenire, quod iuxta Platonicum figmentum opinor accidere iis, qui in specu vincti rerum umbras mirantur, et fugitivo illi, qui reversus in antrum veras res vidisse se praedicat, illos longe falli, qui praeter miseras umbras nihil aliud esse credant. Etenim sapiens hic commiseratur, ac deplorat illorum insaniam, qui tanto errore teneantur. Illi vicissim illum veluti delirantem rident, atque eiiciunt." Recall that Hythloday predicted he would be "thrown out" (*eiiciendum*) for the same reason (More, *Utopia*, p. 83).

[47] Erasmus, *Opera omnia*, vol. IX, p. 102. "quae civitas unquam Platonis aut Aristotelis leges aut Socratis dogmata recepit?"

Cicero's famous dictum in Book II of the *De officiis* that *summa et perfecta gloria* depends on "the affection, the confidence, and the mingled esteem of the people"[48] is surely Erasmus' target:

> Besides, what was it that prevailed upon the Decii, so that they offered themselves of their own free will to the gods of the underworld? What dragged Q. Curtius into the chasm, if not vain glory, the sweetest Siren, but one denounced passionately by those wise men of yours? What could be more foolish, they ask, than for a man seeking office to flatter the mob, to purchase support with gifts, to pursue the applause of all the fools, to be pleased with their acclamations, to be carried about in triumph as if he were some image to be gazed at by the people, and to stand in the forum cast in bronze. Add to these things adopted names and family-names. Add divine honors bestowed on little men, and even the most wicked tyrants being transformed into gods in public ceremonies . . . This is the folly which spawns states; dominions are established by it, as are magistracies, civil religion, councils, and law courts. Nor is human life anything other than some game of folly.[49]

Folly could hardly be more clear: in case we were unsure which kind of *inanis gloria* we were talking about, Folly makes sure we know it is the sort of *gloria* for which men organize *civitates* and *imperia*, *consilia* and *magistratus* – that is, the institutions of *Romanitas*.

In the Erasmian framework, Platonic philosophy is thought ridiculous by those living amidst the ethical categories of Roman theory – what Folly later calls the "middle, quasi-natural affections" such as love of country and family, when valued for themselves and not as manifestations of the *summum bonum*.[50] The Platonism that Erasmus opposes to *Romanitas* is deeply metaphysical, drawn, as we have seen, from Ficino and from the broader context of the Greek revival in England. Erasmus uses Folly to demonstrate that the Roman *vita activa* is incompatible with an interior life

---

[48] Cicero, *De officiis*, ed. and trans. Walter Miller, Loeb Classical Library (Harvard University Press, 1913), p. 198.

[49] Erasmus, *Opera omnia*, vol. IX, p. 102. "Tum autem quae res Deciis persuasit, ut ultro sese diis manibus devoverent? Quid Q. Curtium in specum traxit nisi inanis gloria, dulcissima quaedam Siren, sed mirum quam a sapientibus istis damnata? Quid enim stultius, inquiunt, quam supplicem candidatum blandiri populo, congiariis favorem emere, venari tot stultorum applausus, acclamationibus sibi placere, in triumpho veluti signum aliquod populo spectandum circumferri, aeneum in foro stare? Adde his nominum et cognominum adoptiones, adde divinos honores homuncioni exhibitos, adde publicis ceremoniis in deos relatos etiam sceleratissimos tyrannos . . . Haec stulticia parit civitates, hac constat imperia, magistratus, religio, consilia, iudicia, nec aliud omnino est vita humana quam stulticiae lusus quidam." A similar passage appears in *Enchiridion* (*The Collected Works of Erasmus*, vol. LXVI, p. 27); the Decii and Curtius are discussed in identical terms in the *Ciceronianus* (*The Collected Works of Erasmus*, vol. XXVIII, ed. and trans. Betty I. Knott [University of Toronto Press, 1986], p. 385).

[50] Erasmus, *Opera omnia*, vol. IX, p. 191. "Deinde sunt quidam affectus medii quasique naturales, ut amor patriae, charitas in liberos, in parentes, in amicos."

lived on correct, Platonic terms. Nonetheless, Erasmus does not hesitate to identify the social and political implications of his Platonism. In the 1508 Aldine edition of the *Adagia*, he explains Plato's use of the proverb "friends have everything in common" (τὰ τῶν φιλῶν κοινά) by stating that "through this passage [Plato] tries to demonstrate that the happiest state of a commonwealth consists in the common ownership of all things."[51] "If it were only possible for mortals to be persuaded of this," Erasmus muses, "in that very instant war, envy and fraud would depart from their midst."[52] However, Erasmus was under no illusions. In the 1515 edition of the text he writes: "But it is exceedingly strange that this community of possessions advocated by Plato should so displease Christians that they attack it with stones, since nothing ever said by a pagan philosopher is more similar to the judgment of Christ."[53]

In the *Dulce bellum inexpertis* of 1515 Erasmus blames several phenomena for the slow degeneration of Christian Platonism. One is, quite predictably, the reintroduction of Aristotle, who taught "that there cannot be perfect human happiness unless there are goods of the body and of fortune."[54]

---

[51] Erasmus, *Opera omnia Desiderii Erasmi Roterodami*, vol. xx, ed. M. L. van Poll-van de Lisdonk, M. Mann Phillips, and Chr. Robinson (Amsterdam: Elzevier, 1993), p. 84. "Quo loco conatur demonstrare felicissimum reipublicae statum rerum omnium communitate constare." David Wootton adduces this passage in his excellent discussion of Erasmus' "proto-Utopianism." See Wootton, "Friendship Portrayed: a New Account of *Utopia*" in *History Workshop Journal* 45 (1998), 25–47; and Wootton, "Introduction" to Thomas More, *Utopia, with Erasmus's The Sileni of Alcibiades*, ed. and trans. David Wootton (Indianapolis: Hackett Publishing 1999), p. 8. See also John C. Olin, "Erasmus's *Adagia* and More's *Utopia*" in *Miscellanea Moreana: Essays for Germain Marc'hadour*, ed. Clare M. Murphy, Henri Gibaud, and Mario A. Di Cesare (Binghamton, New York: Medieval & Renaissance Texts & Studies, 1989), pp. 127–36; and Kathy Eden, *Friends Hold All Things in Common: Tradition, Intellectual Property, and the* Adages *of Erasmus* (Yale University Press, 2001). While Eden includes much interesting information, she does not, it seems to me, sufficiently recognize the fundamental differences between the attitudes of Greek and Roman authors on the subject of property.

[52] Erasmus, *Opera omnia*, vol. xx, p. 61. "Quae si mortalibus persuaderi queat, ilico facessant e medio bellum; invidia, fraus, breviter universum malorum agmen semel e vita demigret." This discussion bears a striking resemblance to a passage from Pace's *De fructu* (indeed, Pace mentions the *Adagia* several times in his work): "Apud homines vero, ubi abest aequalitas, ibi adest magna confusio, innumeras ingenerans pestes, ut avaritiam, dolum, fraudem, & id genus alias, quas longum esset recensere . . . Porro communitas illa quam Pythagoras in amicitia postulavit, non nisi aequabilitas intelligenda est, astipulante ipso Platone, sic scribente in sexto de legibus, ἰσότης φιλίαν ἀπεργάζεται, id est, aequalitas amicitiam facit" (Pace, *De fructu*, p. 58).

[53] Erasmus, *Opera omnia*, vol. xx, p. 84. "Sed dictu mirum quam non placeat, imo quam lapidetur a Christianis Platonis illa communitas, cum nihil umquam ab ethnico philosopho dictum sit magis ex Christi sententia." Recall Hythloday's observation that Jesus' doctrines would seem strange (*aliena*) among contemporary Christians (More, *Utopia*, p. 98), and his comment that "neque mihi quidem dubitare subit quin vel sui cuiusque commodi ratio vel CHRISTI servatoris auctoritas . . . totum orbem facile in huius reipublicae leges iamdudum traxisset . . ." (p. 245).

[54] Erasmus, *Dulce bellum inexpertis* (Louvain, 1517). "Ab hoc didicimus non esse perfectam hominis felicitatem, nisi corporis & fortunae bonae accesserint."

But Erasmus seems to assign the preponderance of blame to his second culprit: the Roman law. Christians, he explains, came to embrace the "leges Caesaris" because of their reputation for "equity," and then, in order to reconcile these precepts with Christian civilization, distorted the message of the Gospel (*Evangelium doctrinam*). Erasmus goes on to list the several sins of Justinian's *Codex*: "The Roman law permits men to repel force with force; it permits each person to pursue what is his [*ius suum*]; it approves of commerce; it allows usury, so long as it is in moderation, just as it extols war as a glorious thing, so long as it is undertaken for the sake of *ius*."[55] As a result, Erasmus explains, Europe has inherited two Roman pathologies: the love of glory and the love of wealth. The first issues straightforwardly in wars, while the second ensures that, in Europe, "he is thought to be the best who is the richest."[56] In short, because of Roman *gloria* we have lost *eudaimonia*, and because of Roman *ius* we have lost *dikaiosune*. If we are to recover what has been lost, we must return to Platonic and Apostolic principles.

In 1519, three years after the initial publication of *Utopia*, More would offer an extended discussion of precisely this theme:

God showed great foresight when he instituted that all things should be held in common; Christ showed as much when he tried to recall mortals again to what is common from what is private. For he perceived that the corrupt nature of mortals cannot cherish what is private without injury to the community, as experience shows in all aspects of life. For not only does everyone love his own plot of land or his own money, not only does everyone cherish his own family or his own set of colleagues, but to the extent that we call anything our own it absorbs our affections and diverts them from the service of the common good.[57]

More's solution to this problem, like Plato's, was Utopia, the land without private property where the entire community was one large family.[58] In

---

[55] Ibid. "Recepimus nonnihil & a Caesaris legibus, propter aequitatem, quam prae se ferunt, & quo magis convenirent, Evangelium doctrinam ad eas quo ad licuit destorsimus. At hae permittunt vim vi repellere, suum quemque ius persequi, probant negociationem, recipiunt usuram modo moderatam, bellum ceu rem praeclaram efferunt modo iustum."

[56] Ibid. "His gradibus paulatim eo ventum est, ut is optimus habeatur, qui sit locupletissimus."

[57] *Complete Works*, vol. xv, p. 279. I have modified Kinney's translation here. "Multum providit deus cum omnia institueret communia, multum Christus cum in commune conatus est rursus a privato revocare mortales. Sensit nimirum corruptam mortalibus naturam non sine communitatis damno deamare privatum, id quod res, omnibus in rebus docet. Nec enim tantum suum praedium amat, aut suam quisque pecuniam, nec suo duntaxat generi studet, aut suo quisque collegio, sed ut quicque est quod aliquo modo vocemus nostrum ita in se illud affectus nostros a communium cultu rerum sevocat." This passage would seem to contradict Neal Wood's claim that, outside *Utopia*, More never showed any sympathy for communism. See Neal Wood, *Foundations of Political Economy: Some Early Tudor Views on State and Society* (Berkeley, CA: University of California Press, 1994), pp. 95–96.

[58] More, *Utopia*, p. 147.

composing a Platonic account of the *felicissimus reipublicae status* which could stand up to the neo-Roman tradition, More was taking up the task that Erasmus had begun. The Utopians, we should recall, also put up statues of their great men in the marketplace.[59] But their great men are of a very different sort, and their statues are put up for very different reasons.

III

The dichotomy between Greece and Rome is made explicit from the very outset of More's text. Hythloday is first introduced as a "stranger," much like the "strangers" (ξένοι) who serve as Platonic alter-egos in the *Sophist*, the *Statesman*, and the *Laws*. Giles then explains to "More" that Hythloday has not sailed around (*navigavit*) like Palinurus, the unfortunate watchman of Roman epic, but rather like the Greek Ulysses, or "even more" like Plato.[60] The allusion is most likely to the account of Plato's travels found in Cicero's *De finibus* and Diogenes' *Lives*,[61] and later presented as the *Navigatio Platonis* in Ficino's text.[62] Both Ulysses and Plato surveyed the manners of different societies (Homer introduces Odysseus as the man who "saw the cities of many men, and knew their minds"),[63] but Hythloday, like Plato, has studied them as a philosopher. Giles then tells "More" that, while Hythloday is not ignorant of Latin, he is extremely learned in Greek.[64] In fact, Giles reports, Hythloday has studied Greek instead of Latin because his main interest is philosophy, and "he recognized that, on that subject, nothing very valuable exists in Latin except certain works of Seneca and Cicero."[65] More himself makes a similar statement in his *Letter to Oxford*: "For in philosophy, apart from those works which Cicero and Seneca left behind, the schools of the Latins have nothing to offer that is not either Greek

---

[59] Ibid., p. 195.   [60] Ibid., p. 44.

[61] Cicero, *De finibus* v.87 (see Cicero, *De finibus bonorum et malorum*, ed. and trans. H. Rackham, Loeb Classical Library [Harvard University Press, 1967], p. 490); Diogenes, *Lives* III.6 (see Diogenes Laertius, *Lives of Eminent Philosophers*, ed. and trans. R. D. Hicks, vol. 1, Loeb Classical Library (Harvard University Press, 1966), p. 281). The first extant, authentic description of Plato's travels is found in Cicero, *De republica*. 1.16 (which, however, remained lost during the Renaissance).

[62] Ficino, "Militia et Navigatio Platonis Trina."

[63] Homer, *The Odyssey*, ed. W. B. Stanford, vol. 1 (London: Bristol Classics Press, 1958). 1.3. "πολλῶν δ' ἀνθρώπων ἴδεν ἄστεα καὶ νόον ἔγνω." A further indication that we are to connect Hythloday and Odysseus in this manner comes in Peter Giles's prefatory letter. Speaking of Hythloday, he writes "homo mea quidem sententia regionum, hominum, et rerum experientia vel ipso Ulysse superior" (p. 25).

[64] More, *Utopia*, p. 45.

[65] I have altered the translation here. "qua in re [philosophia] nihil quod alicuius momenti sit, praeter Senecae quaedam ac Ciceronis, exstare Latine cognovit."

or translated from Greek."[66] But when Hythloday recommends books to the Utopians, he goes even further. He states clearly that "we thought that, except for the historians and poets, there was nothing in Latin that they would value."[67] This more extreme iteration, as we have seen, anticipates a passage from More's *Letter to a Monk*. On that occasion, More argues that "speakers of Latin write practically nothing" in "those arts they call liberal, along with philosophy."[68] Accordingly, Hythloday gives the Utopians most of Plato's works, and some of Aristotle's – none of Cicero's or Seneca's – and continues by noting that the Utopian language is related to Greek.[69] This opposition between Greece and Rome works itself out through the same sort of clash between ethical systems that I located in *The Praise of Folly*.

Thomas White's study of More's use of Plato in *Utopia* identifies a wide range of Platonic references in the text, and this present analysis will not attempt to reinvent that particular wheel.[70] Rather, it will hope to assess how More structures the Utopian story around the essentially Greek value

[66] "Nam in philosophia, exceptis duntaxat his, quae Cicero reliquit et Seneca, nihil habent latinorum scholae, nisi vel graecum, vel quod e greca lingua traductum est." See *Complete Works*, vol. xv, p. 143. I have modified Kinney's translation here.

[67] More, *Utopia*, p. 181, "nam in Latinis praeter historias ac poetas nihil erat quod videbantur magnopere probaturi.'"

[68] "quibus de rebus Latini scripsere propemodum nihil." More, *Complete Works*, vol. xv, p. 220. Neither Kinney nor the editors of the Cambridge *Utopia* text adduce this passage when discussing Hythloday's second comment.

[69] More, *Utopia*, p. 181. This is my primary reason for doubting John Parrish's daring claim that the name "Utopia" should be read as a nod to the penultimate sentence of Seneca's *De otio*, in which the ideal republic is said to be "nusquam" (nowhere) (John Michael Parrish, "A New Source for More's 'Utopia'" in *The Historical Journal* 40 [1997], 493–98). Parrish is correct that More referred to his treatise as "Nusquama" in his correspondence throughout the early fall of 1516 (see, for example, letters 461 and 467 in Erasmus, *Opus epistolarum*, vol. 11). But, unlike "Utopia" (an original coinage), "nusquam" is a ubiquitous adverb, making any specific source for More's initial title difficult to establish. Indeed, Baker-Smith points out that, in Ficino's version of *Republic* ix, Glaucon tells Socrates that his republic "in terris vero nusquam, ut arbitror, exstat" (Baker-Smith, *More's Utopia*, p. 97). Moreover, several of the Utopian positions that Parrish derives from the Stoics to support his case are not exclusively Stoic. For example, to account for Utopian communism he cites Diogenes' comment from the "Life of Zeno" that "by friendship they [the Stoics] mean a common use of all that has to do with life." But this is a common Greek saying. In the *Adagia*, Erasmus points out that the proverb τὰ τῶν φιλῶν κοινά is found in Plato's *Laws*, and makes other appearances in the works of Aristotle, Cicero, and Pythagoras (Erasmus, *Opera omnia*, vol. xx, p. 86). Also, while Zeno's *Republic* embraced communal property (and communal wives), later Stoics such as Chrysippus, Panaetius, and Posidonius rejected this aspect of Zeno's system (as did Seneca himself). My own thought about the title is that More may have had in mind the most famous gag in Greek literature: Odysseus' declaration to Polyphemus that his name is Οὖτις, "Nobody" (*Od.* ix.366). This (along with the pun on 'eutopia') would help to explain the otherwise perplexing fact that More employs the negating adverb 'ou'. The implication of the Homeric allusion would be clear enough: "Outis" is not nobody, and "Outopia" is not simply nowhere.

[70] Thomas White, "Pride and the Public Good: Thomas More's Use of Plato in *Utopia*" in *Journal of the History of Philosophy* 20 (1982), 329–54. See also Surtz's discussion of Plato in More, *Complete Works*, vol. iv, pp. clviff., and Baker-Smith, "Uses of Plato by Erasmus and More" in *Platonism and*

system that I have identified, and opposes it to *Romanitas*. In this respect, it is best to begin at the beginning. Book I occupies itself with the "problem of counsel," a standard humanist topic which inevitably relates to the quarrel between *otium* and *negotium* to which I have already alluded. This theme is announced unmistakably by all the prefatory letters which various humanists appended to the 1517 and 1518 editions of the text. Erasmus' letter (first included in 1518) raises the issue in the guise of a standard *captatio benevolentiae*, an attempt to earn the goodwill of the reader by pointing out what a busy man the author is, and under what harried conditions the work was produced. But, as a preface to *Utopia*, this is more than a *topos*. "Apart from the cares of a married man and the responsibilities of his household, apart from his official post and floods of legal cases, he [More] is distracted by so many and such important matters of state business [*tantisque regni negotiis*] that you would marvel he finds any free time [*otium*] at all for books."[71] Guillaume Budé follows suit, and observes that reading about the *mores* and *instituta* of the Utopians made him disdainful of his *negotium* and his obsession with *industria oeconomica*.[72] It is, however, More's own letter which frames the issue most explicitly:

Well, little as it was, that task [of writing *Utopia*] was rendered almost impossible by my many other obligations [*negotia mea*]. Most of my day is given to the law – pleading some cases, hearing others, arbitrating others and deciding still others; this man is visited for the sake of duty [*officii causa*], that man for the sake of business [*negotii*]; and so almost all day I'm out dealing with other people, and the rest of the day I give over to my household; and then for myself – that is, my studies – there's nothing left.[73]

The reader is being prepared for a humanist showdown between the Roman values of *officia* and *negotium* and the Greek *vita contemplativa*.

In Book 1, as Skinner has shown conclusively, the figure of "More" becomes the *porte-parole* for the Ciceronian *vita activa*, and counters Hythloday's defense of *otium* with what are in effect quotations from the

the *English Imagination*, ed. Anna Baldwin and Sarah Hutton (Cambridge University Press, 1994), pp. 86–99.
[71] More, *Utopia*, p. 5. "Praeter rem uxoriam, praeter curas domesticas, praeter publici muneris functionem et causarum undas, tot tantisque regni negotiis distrahitur, ut mireris esse otium vel cogitandi de libris."
[72] Ibid., p. 9.
[73] Ibid., p. 33. I have modified the translation of this passage. "Sed huic tamen tam nihilo negotii peragendo, cetera negotia mea minus fere quam nihil temporis reliquerunt. Dum causas forenses assidue alias ago, alias audio, alias arbiter finio, alias iudex dirimo, dum hic officii causa visitur, ille negotii, dum foris totum ferme diem aliis impertior, reliquum meis; relinquo mihi, hoc est literis, nihil."

De officiis.[74] What is remarkable about *Utopia*, however, is not simply that Hythloday defends *otium*, but *why* he does. In response to "More's" insistence that he should become a councillor, Hythloday argues (clearly echoing Erasmus' Folly) that Latinized Europeans will not accept Greek advice. Hythloday understands that "More" and his ilk will find Utopian advice absurd (just as, he notes, Dionysius of Syracuse found Plato's absurd)[75] because they have been imbued with Roman views on justice and the ends of civic life – two positions that Hythloday spends the whole of *Utopia* attacking from a Greek perspective. He asks, "what if I told them the kind of thing that Plato imagines in his republic, or that the Utopians actually practise in theirs," and answers that, no matter how superior, "here they [the practices] would seem alien [*aliena*]."[76] His views are only confirmed when "More" champions a "*philosophia civilior*" (one more suited to the *vivere civile*) over what he dismisses as Hythloday's "*philosophia scholastica*" (where *scholastica* is clearly another "nonsense" word).[77] Hythloday is forced to conclude that, in attempting to advise Europeans "deeply immersed as they are and infected with false values from boyhood on"[78] and languishing in the grasp of *stultitia* (another nod to Erasmus),[79] he would simply end up acquiring the disease he was trying to cure.[80]

"More" begins with the Ciceronian claim that, in becoming a councillor, Hythloday would advance his own interests as well as those of his family and friends[81] (see *De officiis* 1.17), and proceeds to offer the standard humanist

---

[74] Quentin Skinner, "Sir Thomas More's *Utopia* and the Language of Renaissance Humanism" in *The Languages of Political Theory in Early-Modern Europe*, ed. Anthony Pagden (Cambridge University Press, 1987), esp. pp. 132–35. Baker-Smith largely follows Skinner in his analysis of Book 1 (Baker-Smith, *More's Utopia*, pp. 98–102). He rightly emphasizes the self-conscious Platonism of those who defended the *vita contemplativa* against the Ciceronian *vita activa*, but neglects to locate that Platonist commitment within the context of a wider ethical and political theory, or to acknowledge the explicit critique of *Romanitas*.

[75] More, *Utopia*, p. 83.

[76] Ibid., p. 99. "Quod si aut ea dicerem quae fingit Plato in sua republica aut ea quae faciunt Utopienses in sua, haec quamquam essent (ut certe sunt) meliora, tamen aliena videri possent . . ."

[77] Ibid., p. 95. The contrast between this Ciceronian *philosophia civilior* and Platonic political theory is picked up in precisely these terms by Thomas Starkey in his *A Dialogue between Pole and Lupset* (ca. 1530). Starkey has Pole explain to Lupset that "we loke not for such hedys as plato descrybeth in his pollycy for that ys out of hope wyth us to be found . . . but aftur a more cyvyle & commyn sort . . ." See Thomas Starkey, *A Dialogue between Pole and Lupset*, ed. T. F. Mayer (London: Royal Historical Society, 1989), p. 108.

[78] More, *Utopia*, p. 83. "perversis opinionibus a pueris imbuti atque infecti penitus." Compare Hythloday's prediction that his advice will be assailed for contravening "perversi mores" (p. 99).

[79] Ibid., p. 101.   [80] Ibid., p. 97.

[81] Ibid., p. 51. This argument is also advanced by Callicles during his exchange with Socrates in *Gorgias* 483b–486d – a discussion which largely mirrors the debate between "More" and Hythloday in Book 1.

observation that a "philosophic nature" is suited to advising princes[82] (a view, "More" tells Hythloday, that is shared by "your Plato")[83] – and, later, that it is every good man's *officium* to do so.[84] Hythloday replies that he would not part with his precious *otium* (his ability "to live as he likes," a privilege Cicero rejects as un-civic)[85] on that account, since courtiers are incredulous and defensive when "a man should suggest something he has read of in other ages or seen in practice elsewhere" (part of his constant insistence that his advice would be ill-received by Europeans).[86] When "More" retorts that he should not be so impatient to "pluck up bad ideas by the root," but should rather aim to make the regime as good as possible, Hythloday replies that such conduct would simply force him to imitate the degeneracy of the multitude. He illustrates his point by taking an image out of the *Republic*:

This is why Plato in a very fine comparison declares that wise men are right in keeping away from public business [*a capessenda republica*]. They see the people swarming through the streets and getting soaked with rain; they cannot persuade them to go indoors and get out of the wet. If they go out themselves, they know they will do no good, but only get drenched with the others. So they stay indoors and are content to keep at least themselves dry, since they cannot remedy the folly of others [*alienae stultitiae*].[87]

The analogy to which Hythloday refers is found at the end of a passage in Book VI – one which surely must have been in More's thoughts when he composed this debate. Earlier in the passage, Plato writes as follows:

[The enlightened few realize] that no one can do anything sound, so to speak, concerning the business of cities, nor is there an ally with whose aid the champion

---

[82] More, *Utopia*, p. 53.

[83] Ibid., p. 81. This is a particularly significant detail, since Hythloday has not yet referred to Plato directly. Here, without being told, "More" reveals his awareness that Hythloday is ventriloquizing Plato.

[84] Ibid.

[85] Ibid., p. 51. See Cicero, *De officiis* 1.70. Interestingly, this is an aspect of the debate that More stresses repeatedly in his *Life of John Picus*. In the biography itself, More writes of Pico that "liberte a boue all thing he loued to which both his owne naturall affection & the study of philosophy enclined him" (*Complete Works*, vol. 11, p. 68), and in the letter to Corneo we read that philosophers "love liberte; they can not bere the prowde maners of estates: they can not serve" (p. 85). The first clause of this second passage is More's own interpolation (the Latin is simply "mores pati & servire nesciunt"). Baker-Smith provides an illuminating account of the similarities between the letter and Book 1 of *Utopia*, although he does not stress the theme of "liberte" in the earlier work. See Baker-Smith, *More's Utopia*, esp. pp. 18–20, 99.

[86] More, *Utopia*, p. 53.

[87] Ibid., p. 101. "Quamobrem pulcherrima similitudine declarat Plato cur merito sapientes abstineant a capessenda republica. Quippe quum populum videant in plateas effusum assiduis imbribus perfundi, nec persuadere queant illis ut se subducant pluviae tectaque subeant: gnari nihil profuturos sese si exeant quam ut una compluantur, semet intra tecta continent, habentes satis quando alienae stultitiae non possunt mederi si ipsi saltem sint in tuto."

of justice could escape destruction, but, rather, that he would be as a man who has fallen among wild beasts, unwilling to share their misdeeds and unable to hold out against the savagery of all, and that he would thus, before he could in any way benefit his friends or the state, come to an untimely end, useless to himself and others – for all these reasons I say the philosopher remains quiet, minds his own affair...[88]

In its emphasis on the inability of a philosopher to help his friends, himself, or the state by entering public service in a commonwealth not ruled by philosophers (and its rejection of "More's" sort of collusion as "sharing the misdeeds" of the rulers), this passage encapsulates the debate between "More" and Hythloday – and reveals it to be a debate between Cicero and Plato, between Rome and Greece.[89]

Moreover, Plato's portrayal of the philosopher as a "champion of justice" in the midst of those who argue over the "shadows of justice"[90] frames the extensive discussion of *iustitia* in Book I and its distinctive treatment in Book II. In the midst of the debate on *negotium*, Hythloday recounts how he participated in a discussion on the punishment for theft at the court of Cardinal Morton, More's patron and the only European in *Utopia* who appreciates Greek advice. Hythloday repeats his argument that the practice of hanging thieves is unjust and ineffective, and offers two principal reasons. First, the punishment is disproportionate; second, "it would be much better to enable every man to earn his own living, instead of being driven to the awful necessity of stealing and then dying for it."[91]

This second objection is fleshed out extensively and develops into an attack on Roman "iustitia" (giving each person *ius suum*) and a defense of

---

[88] *Republic* 496c (VI). I have altered Shorey's translation here. "καὶ ὅτι οὐδεὶς οὐδὲν ὑγιὲς ὡς ἔπος εἰπεῖν περὶ τὰ τῶν πόλεων πράττει οὐδ᾽ ἔστι σύμμαχος μεθ᾽ ὅτου τις ἰὼν ἐπὶ τὴν τῷ δικαίῳ βοήθειαν σώζοιτ᾽ ἄν, ἀλλ᾽ ὥσπερ εἰς θηρία ἄνθρωπος ἐμπεσών, οὔτε συναδικεῖν ἐθέλων οὔτε ἱκανὸς ὢν εἷς πᾶσιν ἀγρίοις ἀντέχειν, πρίν τι τὴν πόλιν ἢ φίλους ὀνῆσαι προαπολόμενος ἀνωφελὴς αὑτῷ τε καὶ τοῖς ἄλλοις ἂν γένοιτο – ταῦτα πάντα λογισμῷ λαβών, ἡσυχίαν ἔχων καὶ τὰ αὑτοῦ πράττων..." Consider also Hythloday's claim that "there is no way for you to do any good when you are thrown among colleagues who would more readily corrupt the best of men than be reformed themselves. Either they will seduce you by their evil ways, or, if you remain honest and innocent, you will be made a screen for the knavery and folly of others" (More, *Utopia*, p. 101).

[89] Brendan Bradshaw provides an excellent account of the relationship between the "More"–Hythloday debate and *Republic* VI, although he neglects to comment on "More's" Ciceronianism, or to emphasize that More imports an extremely specific thought from his source (i.e. that the advice of philosophers will seem like nonsense to those in the cave) which has implications for our overall view of *Utopia*. Bradshaw also concludes that "More" is the victor in the debate. See Brendan Bradshaw, "More on Utopia" in *The Historical Journal* 24 (1981), 1–27.

[90] *Republic* 517d (VII). "περὶ τῶν τοῦ δικαίου σκιῶν."

[91] More, *Utopia*, p. 57. "potius multo fuerit providendum uti aliquis esset proventus vitae, ne cuiquam tam dira sit furandi primum dehinc pereundi necessitas."

Greek δικαιοσύνη.[92] In the Platonic framework, as we have seen, "justice" indicates an arrangement of elements that accords with nature; it relies on σωφροσύνη, or "balance," which produces "harmony" and prevents the corruption of the established order; the arrangement of the whole, when just and balanced, reflects itself on to the souls of the citizens and molds their characters. Justice is, indeed, in Ficino's phrase, the *civitatis ordo atque salus*, and just institutions are essential for the cultivation of virtue. Logan notices More's focus on "institutions" or "root-causes," but attributes it mistakenly to a "scholastic" strain in his thought.[93] There is no trace of the scholastic idiom in *Utopia*; we find no references to *ius naturale, lex naturalis, iurisdictio, dominium, imperium, universitas*, or any of the other standard scholastic vocabulary (which, lest we forget, both Erasmus and More ridicule mercilessly).[94] On the contrary, More has Hythloday articulate a fundamentally Greek, holistic concept of justice which he proceeds to oppose to the more narrow, *ad hoc* Roman notion. Nor should we be surprised that it is Cardinal Morton's fool who comes to Hythloday's aid when he has finished speaking – and that More chooses the uncommon word *morio* to designate the fool so that he can pun on μόριον, "councillor."[95]

It quickly becomes apparent that Hythloday's "justice" does not consist in giving each person what belongs to him (and punishing those who take what is another's by *ius*), but in producing a natural and harmonious institutional arrangement:

Restrict the right of the rich to buy up anything and everything, and then to exercise a kind of monopoly. Let fewer people be brought up in idleness. Let agriculture be restored, and the wool-manufacture revived as an honest trade, so there will be useful work for the idle throng... Certainly unless you cure these evils it is futile to boast of your justice [*iustitia*] in punishing theft. Your policy may look

[92] Thomas White tries to connect More's "justice" to Aristotelian distributive justice and, more broadly, to ideas about the "common good." While helpful, however, his analysis ignores the most basic, holistic sense in which More intends the term – and, thus, the explicit critique of Roman *ius*. See Thomas White, "Aristotle and *Utopia*" in *Renaissance Quarterly* 29 (1976), 657.

[93] Logan, *More's Utopia*, p. 79.

[94] There is, however, one notorious allusion to the *naturae praescriptum* in Hythloday's account of Utopian colonialism (More, *Utopia*, p. 136). For an analysis of the scholastic idiom during the sixteenth century, see Annabel Brett, *Liberty, Right and Nature: Individual Rights in Later Scholastic Thought* (Cambridge University Press, 1997), and Richard Tuck, *Natural Rights Theories: Their Origin and Development* (Cambridge University Press, 1979), esp. chap. 2.

[95] More, *Utopia*, p. 77. For an instance of the word being used in this way, see Aristotle, *Politics* 1282a37 (III.6): "τῶν δὲ ῥηθέντων ἕκαστος μόριόν ἐστι τούτων (λέγω δὲ μόριον τὸν βουλευτὴν καὶ τὸν ἐκκλησιαστὴν καὶ τὸν δικαστήν)". Wootton is correct to point out that the word is "unusual" in Latin, and I believe this is a plausible solution to the conundrum. See Wootton, *Utopia*, p. 29.

superficially like justice, but in reality it is neither just nor expedient [*speciosam quam aut iustam aut utilem*]. If you allow young folk to be abominably brought up and their characters corrupted little by little, from childhood; and if then you punish them as grown-ups for committing the crimes to which their training has consistently inclined them, what else is this, I ask, but first making them thieves and then punishing them for it?[96]

Hythloday endorses the Platonic notion that justice as an arrangement of the soul is produced and reinforced by justice in the arrangement of the state. The justice "they" boast of in punishing theft is Roman *iustitia* – applying a punishment for a crime that has been committed. But Hythloday argues that this *iustitia* is hollow; he later says that he finds "no trace" of justice in the "justice of the nations."[97] When souls are unjust (that is, not balanced according to nature) education (which we should recall is *part* of the institutional arrangement, as well as, more broadly, a result of it) is to blame. Accordingly, Hythloday praises the practice of the Polylerites (those people of "much nonsense"), who force thieves to make restitution (a practice reminiscent of the one that Plato endorses in the *Laws*)[98] and insist that the purpose of punishment is educative. Plato had written that "the purpose of the penalty [δίκη] is not to cancel the crime – what is once done can never be made undone – but to bring the criminal . . . to complete renunciation of such criminality [ἀδικίαν], or at least to recovery in great part from the dreadful state,"[99] and Hythloday extols the Polylerite custom in similar terms: "It is clear how mild and practical they are, for the aim of the punishment is to destroy vices and save men. The men are treated so that they necessarily become good, and they have the rest of their lives to make up for the damage done."[100]

This notion of justice as δικαιοσύνη, in turn, becomes the essential justification for Utopian communism as praised by Hythloday in Book I, and then described in Book II. The Utopians agree with Plato that, in a just society, "no one can ever be reduced to poverty or forced to beg,"[101]

---

[96] More, *Utopia*, p. 67. "Refrenate coemptiones istas divitum ac velut monopolii exercendi licentiam. Pauciores alantur otio, reddatur agricolatio, lanificium instauretur ut sit honestum negotium quo se utiliter exerceat otiosa ista turba . . . Certe nisi his malis medemini, frustra iactetis exercitam in vindicanda furta iustitiam, nempe speciosam magis quam aut iustam aut utilem. Siquidem quum pessime sinitis educari et mores paulatim ab teneris annis corrumpi, puniendos videlicet tum demum quum eta flagitia viri designent quorum spem de se perpetuam a pueritia usque praebuerant, quid aliud, quaeso, quam facetis fures et iidem plectitis?"

[97] Ibid., p. 243.   [98] *Laws* 857a (IX).   [99] *Laws* 934a–b (XI).

[100] More, *Utopia*, p. 75. "Qui quantum habeat humanitatis et commodi facile patet, quando sic irascitur ut vitia perimat, servatis hominibus atque ita tractatis ut bonos esse necesse sit, et quantum ante damni dederunt tantum reliqua vita resartiant."

[101] Ibid., p. 145. See *Laws* 936c (XI).

and, therefore, they have abolished private property.[102] Hythloday shares their view, and argues that a society based on private property cannot be just:

> But as a matter of fact, my dear More [*mi More* – note the pun], to tell you what I really think, wherever you have private property, and money is the measure of all things, it is hardly ever possible for a commonwealth to be just or prosperous – unless you think justice can exist where all the best things [*optima*] are held by the worst citizens [*pessimi*], or suppose happiness can be found where the good things of life are divided among the very few, where even those few are always uneasy.[103]

This passage introduces three interconnected claims about why private property produces injustice, all dependent on the Greek tradition. The first has to do with rulership. Hythloday and the Utopians – like Plato – take it as axiomatic that justice requires the rule of the better over the baser: in a Platonic universe, there are those naturally suited to rule (Hythloday uses the image of shepherds who rule for the good of their flock, recalling Plato's treatment of rulership in the *Republic* and the *Statesman*),[104] just as there are those who are suited by nature to soldiering, or weaving, or any other τέχνη (art). This Platonic claim about just rulership represents the point of contact between *Utopia* and the humanist tradition of equating *virtus* with *vera nobilitas*.[105] Articulated in a series of important fifteenth-century treatises (such as Buonaccorso's *Controversia de nobilitate*, and Poggio Bracciolini's *De nobilitate*), this trope developed in opposition to the scholastic tradition of equating *nobilitas* with *longae divitiae* (that is, long-established wealth), and its attendant *splendor* and *magnificentia*.[106] Taking aim at the schoolmen, humanists declared (citing a variety of classical authorities) that true worth was not determined by pomp and pedigree, but by personal virtue.

Because the contrary position is rooted in scholastic sources (and because the phrase itself derives from Juvenal, Horace, and Cicero), the temptation

---

[102] Hexter and others have stressed, however, that while Plato's communism in the *Republic* may be restricted to the class of guardians, More's is generalized. See *Complete Works*, vol. IV, pp. lxxxvii, cixff. Nonetheless, More leaves no doubt that he views the abolition of private property as a Platonic measure.

[103] More, *Utopia*, p. 101. "Quamquam profecto, mi More (ut eta vere dicam quae meus animus fert), mihi videtur ubicumque privatae sunt possessiones, ubi omnes omnia pecuniis metiuntur, ibi vix umquam posse fieri ut cum republica aut iuste agatur aut prospere, nisi vel ibi sentias agi iuste ubi optima quaeque perveniunt ad pessimos, vel ibi feliciter ubi omnia dividuntur in paucissimos, nec illos habitos undecumque commode, ceteris vero plane miseris."

[104] Ibid., p. 93. See, for example, *Republic* 345c (1), and *Statesman* 261d.

[105] Skinner discusses this issue from a different point of view ("Sir Thomas More's *Utopia*," pp. 135–47).

[106] Ibid., p. 137.

is to see the ideology behind *virtus vera nobilitas* as essentially Roman. But we should recall that the notion is as Platonic as it is Ciceronian (Cicero, after all, took the concept from Plato),[107] and that the scholastic defense of *longae divitiae* was itself a bowdlerization of Aristotle's claim in *Politics* IV that "nobility [εὐγένια] means ancient wealth [ἀρχαῖος πλοῦτος] and virtue [ἀρετή]."[108] It is important to place this statement in its precise context. Aristotle argues that there are generally three qualities which carry with them claims to political authority: freedom, wealth, and virtue ("nobility" as conventionally understood does not constitute an additional quality because it is simply an amalgam of the final two). A regime which satisfies the claims of wealth and freedom alone is a kind of "polity," while a regime which satisfies the claims of wealth, freedom, and virtue to varying degrees is a kind of approximate aristocracy. However, Aristotle makes clear that a true aristocracy, which is much to be preferred, assigns rulership only on the basis of virtue. Some wealth is, to be sure, a prerequisite of virtue on the Aristotelian account: in *Politics* III Aristotle argues that manual laborers "cannot practise the pursuits in which goodness is exercised,"[109] and in *Ethics* 1122a (IV.2) he offers a qualified defense of *magnificentia* (μεγαλοπρέπεια) not unlike Cicero's.[110] That said, he also argues explicitly in *Politics* IV that rule by the "middle class" is best, because both extreme wealth and extreme poverty corrupt,[111] and he heaps scorn on the claims of the conventional "nobility" in Book II of the *Rhetoric* (1390b [II.15]). Thus, as Jacob Burckhardt observed almost 150 years ago,[112] it was entirely possible to defend the equation of *virtus* with *vera nobilitas* from an Aristotelian perspective. Indeed, when Thomas Starkey addresses the issue in his *Dialogue between Pole and Lupset*, he does precisely that. Starkey has Pole endorse Aristotle's position that external, worldly goods are required for the cultivation of virtue, but has him add that "vertues of the mynd... passe and excelle al vertues & powarys of ther body, & al other ryches & wordly tresore, as thos thyngys wych be chefely & above al other to be extymyd & regardyd" (this is a simple paraphrase of *Politics* 1280a26–1281a8

---

[107] See *De officiis* II.69–71. Skinner points out that Poggio made this connection. See Skinner, "Political Philosophy," p. 423.

[108] *Politics* 1294a21 (IV.6).   [109] Ibid. 1278a21 (III.3).

[110] Cicero, *De officiis* II.55–60. It is worth noting that Cicero cites Aristotle as his source for a temperate assessment of *magnificentia*.

[111] *Politics* 1295a39–1296a22 (IV.9).

[112] "From a theoretical point of view, when the appeal was made to antiquity, the conception of nobility could be both justified and condemned from Aristotle alone." See Burckhardt, *The Civilization of the Renaissance in Italy*, ed. Peter Murray, trans. S. G. C. Middlemore, with an introduction by Peter Burke (Harmondsworth: Penguin Books, 1990), p. 231.

[III.7–15]).[113] Ultimately, both Aristotle and Plato agree that the just polity is one in which the most virtuous men rule.

More, in turn, uses the *virtus vera nobilitas* trope to assert the connection between rulership and δικαιοσύνη, and to insist that the abolition of private property is necessary for that connection to be realized. In Utopia, Hythloday tells us, "virtuti pretium sit" – virtue has its reward.[114] The Utopians, indeed, find it downright bizarre that "a dunderhead who has no more brains than a post, and who is as vicious as he is foolish, should command a great many wise and good men, simply because he happens to have a big pile of gold coins."[115] In a society of private property, however, where "money is the measure of all things" and the wealth goes to the *pessimi*, the worst citizens will tend to rule, thus producing an unjust arrangement by definition (that is, rule by the appetitive over the rational – which Hythloday, following Plato, calls contrary to "nature").[116] Hythloday rejects the claim that simple legislation will prevent public offices "which ought to go to the wise"[117] from going to the wealthy, and identifies such usurpations as the inevitable result of private property. But because all their property is held in common, the Utopians are able to favor the most

---

[113] Starkey, *Dialogue*, p. 25. Starkey plays an important role in the English reception of Greek ethics. In his *Dialogue* he has Pole argue very much like Hythloday, even using Plato's "rain simile" (*Republic* 496d [VI]) to defend *otium* – although he attributes it to Plutarch (p. 16). Lupset clearly speaks for the author in this first section, and he rejects Pole's argument; he urges Pole to "folow not the exampul of plato, whose ordur of commyn wele no pepul apon erth to thys days coud ever yet attayn, wherfor hyt ys reputyd of many men but as a dreme, & vayne imygynatyon wych never can be brought to effect" (p. 18). Nonetheless, Starkey has Pole carry out an exercise very reminiscent of the one Socrates performs in the *Republic* (although in reverse, since Pole moves from man to *polis*, rather than from *polis* to man). He agrees with More (and the Greeks) that "felycyte" is the end of civic life (p. 38), and that the "just pollycy" and the "veray & true commyn wele" consist "not in the helth of one partycular parte thereof, but in the gud and natural affecte & dysposyton of every parte couplyd to other," where every part does its own "offyce & duty, to them appoyntyd & determyd" (p. 39) – and where, as in any Platonic state, reason rules over the appetitive and the spirited (pp. 33–34). Justice for Starkey lies in "the dew proportyon of the . . . partys togyddur, so that one parte ever be agreabul to a nother, in forme & fastyon quantyte & nombur" (p. 33). In short, we have justice as δικαιοσύνη. He also agrees with More that poverty amidst luxury "ys the mother of envy & malyce dyssensyon & debate, & many other myschefys ensuyng" (p. 34).

[114] More, *Utopia*, p. 101.

[115] Ibid., p. 155. "usqueadeo ut plumbeus quispiam et cui non plus ingenii sit quam stipiti nec minus etiam improbus quam stultus, multos tamen et sapientes et bonos viros in servitute habeat, ob id dumtaxat quod ei magnus contigit aureorum numismatum cumulus." This passage underscores why Wood is incorrect to suggest that More was mounting a critique of the Greek theory of distributive justice (N. Wood, *Foundations*, pp. 100–101). More's argument is that an unequal distribution of wealth makes the just distribution of political power impossible. Distributive justice, for Plato and Aristotle, is above all the assigning of rulership to the most virtuous. This would, perhaps, explain the various "undemocratic" aspects of Utopian life with which Wood is so concerned.

[116] More, *Utopia*, p. 163.   [117] Ibid., p. 103.

excellent members of society: those who should rule by nature.[118] In domestic matters (in conformity with both Platonic and Aristotelian doctrine),[119] "wives act as servants to their husbands, children to their parents, and generally the younger to their elders,"[120] while government is reserved for those who "from childhood have given evidence of excellent character, unusual intelligence, and a mind inclined to the liberal arts."[121] This small Platonic elite is excused from labor, and left to cultivate itself for future service to the *respublica*.[122] Because the Utopian republic is reconciled with nature and justice in this manner, Hythloday tells us that it will "last forever" – a claim not even made by Plato on behalf of *Kallipolis*.[123]

Hythloday later adds to this first argument by claiming that the unnatural rulership brought about by private property topples the institutional arrangement of the state by causing it to lose sight of its own nature. In Greek thought, the state aims at αὐτάρκεια (self-sufficiency), and, for Plato, justice is, above all, the natural ordering of the elements which are necessary to produce this quality. In the *Republic*, when Socrates builds *Kallipolis* from scratch, self-sufficiency dictates that the very first, most essential members of the society are the farmers, the builders, the weavers, and other craftsmen.[124] However, in a society of private property, Hythloday argues, this natural priority is subverted:

Now isn't this an unjust and ungrateful commonwealth? It lavishes rich rewards on so-called gentry, goldsmiths and the rest of that crew, who don't work at all or are mere parasites, purveyors of empty pleasures. And yet it makes no proper provision for the welfare of farmers and colliers, labourers, carters, and carpenters, without whom the commonwealth would simply cease to exist . . . Before, it appeared to be unjust that people who deserve most from the commonwealth should receive least. But now, by promulgating law, they have transmuted this perversion into justice.[125]

---

[118] More emphasizes this aspect of Utopian political thought in a letter to Erasmus dated October 31, 1516. Professing himself to be gratified that men such as Giles and Busleyden approve of his treatise, he writes "in illa republica nostra illi tales viri, litteris ac virtute tanti, principes plane essent futuri; quum in suis quanticumque sint (sunt sane magni) magnos tamen habeant nebulones authoritate ac potentia pares, ut ne dicam superiores" (*Erasmus, Opus epistolarum*, vol. 11).

[119] See ploto, *Republic* 412c (111), *Aristotis, Politics* 1254b (1).

[120] More, Utopia, p. 137.

[121] Ibid., p. 155. I have altered the translation here; Adams's "devotion to learning" fails to capture the particular kind of learning implied by "bonas artes." "hi videlicet in quibus a pueritia egregiam indolem, eximium ingenium, atque animum ad bonas artes propensum deprehendere."

[122] Ibid., p. 131.

[123] Ibid., p. 147. Plato inists in *Republic* 546a (v111) that even *Kallipolis* would eventually decay.

[124] See *Republic* 370d (11).

[125] More, *Utopia*, p. 243. "An non haec iniqua est et ingrata respublica, quae generosis, ut vocant, et aurificibus et id genus reliquis aut otiosis aut tantum adulatoribus et inanium voluptatum artificibus,

Private property and the warped rulership that accompanies it under-mine the connection between justice and self-sufficiency – they subvert the natural ordering of the essential elements which compose the state.

But above all, as we have come to expect, Hythloday argues that com-munism is essential for justice because private property and its accompany-ing institutions corrupt the souls of citizens. In Platonic thought, no one emerges unscathed from this process: in the *Republic*, Socrates argues that wealth brings "luxury" and "idleness,"[126] while poverty makes the poor un-able to discharge their natural functions, denying them happiness. Likewise, Hythloday observes that wealth makes the rich "rapacious, wicked, and use-less,"[127] and, as for the poor, "bitter necessity, then, forces them to think that they must look out for themselves, rather than for the people"[128] – and, as we have seen, turns them into criminals. Utopian communism prevents all of this, Hythloday argues, and ensures that the citizens are brought up with "sound principles" which "their education and the good institutions of their republic both reinforce"[129] – that is, the Utopians preserve justice in its true, Greek sense.[130]

It only remains to point out that, for Hythloday and the Utopians, the purpose of justice is to produce happiness (Greek εὐδαιμονία) – the quality which they agree with the Greeks in identifying as the end of human and civic life. *Felicitas* is among the most ubiquitous words in More's text, and is often explicitly opposed to forms of *gloria*.[131] The Polylerites, for example, have a system of justice which has allowed them to "live in a useful rather

---

tanta munera prodigit? agricolis contra, carbonariis, mediastinis, aurigis et fabris, sine quibus nulla omnino respublica esset . . . Ita quod ante videbatur iniustum, optime de republica meritis pessimam referre gratiam, hoc isti depravatum etiam fecerunt, tum provulgata lege, iustitiam."

[126] *Republic* 422a (iv).

[127] More, *Utopia*, p. 103. "rapaces, improbi, atque inutiles."

[128] Ibid., p. 241. "eoque necessitas urget ut sui potius quam populi, id est aliorum, habendam sibi rationem censeat."

[129] Ibid., p. 213. I have replaced Adams's "society" with "republic" in this instance, in order to reflect More's concern with constitutional structures. "Postremo rectae opiniones (quibus et doctrina et bonis reipublicae institutis imbuti a pueris sunt) virtutem addunt."

[130] I am now in a position to dispute Hexter's claim that, for More, "equality is justice" (*Complete Works*, vol. iv, p. cxxiii). I should say rather that the abolition of private property (and the level social order it creates) is a *necessary condition* for the emergence of justice. Justice itself is the rational ordering of all elements which contribute to self-sufficiency. Athanasios Moulakis endorses Hexter's position. See Moulakis, "Pride and the Meaning of *Utopia*" in *History of Political Thought* 11 (1990), 247.

[131] Thomas White, among others, observes that happiness is the aim of Utopian life in his study of More's Aristotelianism. The hope here is to build on that common observation by noticing that, in this respect, More is challenging the traditional values of *Romanitas*, and, thus, of the republican tradition as understood in his lifetime. See White, "Aristotle and *Utopia*", 640. See also similar comments in Logan, *More's Utopia*, p. 185.

than splendid manner, more happy than renowned or famous...they are hardly known by name to anyone but their immediate neighbors."[132] Anonymity is not, to say the least, a pillar of the Roman value system; but the Polylerites aim for happiness, not glory, so it does not disturb them.

This is even more true of the Utopians, who have understood that happiness (*felicitas*) cannot be achieved without justice – and that justice requires the abolition of private property.[133] Only if goods are held in common can mortals live happily (*feliciter*),[134] which explains, for Hythloday, why the Utopians live more happily than Europeans – indeed more happily than any other commonwealth.[135] Again, at the end of Book II, Hythloday claims that, as a result of their "structures of life," the Utopians live "the most happily" (*felicissime*), and he contrasts this "happiness of the Utopian republic" to the wretchedness of all societies built around private property. As for glory, the Utopians (again echoing Erasmus' Folly) despise the *gloria* won in battle,[136] and, when they are forced to fight, they have no thought of *laus* (praise) or *fama* (fame).[137] Rather, in direct opposition to Cicero's injunction in the *De officiis* (1.41), they make unrepentant use of *fraus* (fraud) and overwhelming *vis* (force) in order to end their wars as quickly as possible: they traffic in assassinations, bribes, seditions, mercenaries, and various other instruments of *ars et dolus* (skill and cunning) in order to carry the day.[138] They endorse these practices, not (as Machiavelli does in *Il Principe*) because they believe that *vis* and *fraus* will ultimately secure them *gloria*, but because glory is not the point of their actions. In their ethical system, the "first concern" is to identify the nature of "human happiness," and then pursue "true happiness" (*vera felicitas*) as the primary goal of human life.[139] It is in this context that the Utopians intervene in

---

[132] More, *Utopia*, p. 71. I have modified the translation here: "haud perinde splendide atque commode, felicesque magis quam nobiles aut clari degunt. Quippe ne nomine quidem opinor praeterquam conterminis admodum satis noti."

[133] Ibid., p. 101.   [134] Ibid., p. 103.   [135] Ibid., p. 179.

[136] Ibid., p. 202. See, for example, Erasmus, *Opera omnia*, vol. IX, p. 96.

[137] More, *Utopia*, p. 205.

[138] Ibid., pp. 205–17. Thus, More takes Plato's case for "happiness" to its logical conclusion in a way that Plato never did. See Surtz on the un-Platonic military practices of the Utopians (More, *Complete Works*, vol. IV, p. clix). The classic work on the Erasmian and Utopian rejection of military glory remains Robert P. Adams, *The Better Part of Valor: More, Erasmus, Colet, and Vives, on Humanism, War and Peace, 1496–1535* (Seattle: University of Washington Press, 1962). Adams's analysis, however, is colored by his argument that the Erasmian political programme was almost exclusively "neo-Stoic."

[139] More, *Utopia*, p. 161.

the debate between *otium* and *negotium* (a debate which, we should recall, is waged in terms of *felicitas* in Book 1):[140]

The structure of their republic is dedicated above all to this objective: that, as far as public needs permit, all citizens should be free to withdraw as much time as possible from the service of the body and devote themselves to the freedom and culture of the mind. For in that, they think, lies the happiness of life [*vitae felicitas*].[141]

With this connection between justice, happiness, and the *vita contemplativa* established, the story comes full circle.

IV

More's formulation of the Greek tradition is uncompromising and profoundly deterministic. If private property is not abolished outright, he argues, then it will inevitably produce wealth and poverty. The resulting rich and poor will both be corrupted by their condition, and the rule of reason and virtue (i.e. justice) will be toppled. Once private property has been consigned to the "ash-heap of history," however, the republic can embrace true justice, achieve happiness through contemplation, and shun the absurd quest for worldly glory. It can then achieve immortality, a precious reprieve from the Polybian cycle unheard of in the Roman tradition. Every subsequent text in the Greek tradition would bear the mark of *Utopia*, but few would embrace More's belief that private property could not be sufficiently regulated to preserve and protect the rule of the best men. If it is not property *per se* that corrupts, but broad differentials in property, then the central challenge confronting political theory becomes the task of keeping fortunes temperate. Classical history furnished a notorious example of just such a project in the agrarian laws. Lycurgus had equalized property in founding the Spartan commonwealth, and Agis and Cleomenes had attempted to revive the Lycurgan program in the midst of Sparta's precipitous decline. But it was first and foremost the Roman agrarian laws that captured the early-modern imagination, and, accordingly, it is to them that I now turn.

---

[140] See, for example, Giles's claim that being a counselor would make More "happier" (*felicior*). Ibid., p. 51.

[141] Ibid., p. 135. I have replaced Adams's translation of the first sentence. "quandoquidem eius reipublicae institutio hunc unum scopum in primis respicit: ut quoad per publicas necessitates licet, quam plurimum temporis ab servitio corporis ad animi libertatem cultumque civibus universis asseratur. In eo enim sitam vitae felicitatem putant."

CHAPTER 2

The Roman agrarian laws and Machiavelli's modi privati

I

Alone among Shakespeare's plays, *Coriolanus* opens with a scene of mob violence. A throng of Roman plebeians comes on stage brandishing "staves, clubs, and other weapons," and resolves to carry out a murder:

FIRST CIT. First, you know Caius Martius is chief enemy to the people.
ALL. We know't, we know't.
FIRST CIT. Let us kill him, and we'll have corn at our own price. Is't a verdict?
FIRST CIT. No more talking on't; let it be done. Away, away! (1.1.6–11)[1]

When a second citizen attempts to intervene, calling out "One word, good citizens," the mob's leader turns on him:

FIRST CIT. We are accounted poor citizens, the patricians good. What authority surfeits on would relieve us. If they would yield us but the superfluity while it were wholesome, we might guess they relieved us humanely; but they think we are too dear: the leanness that afflicts us, the object of our misery, is as an inventory to particularise their abundance; our sufferance is a gain to them. Let us revenge this with our pikes, ere we become rakes. For the gods know, I speak this in hunger for bread, not in thirst for revenge. (1.1.14–24)

At issue is the corn shortage of 492 BCE, a state of affairs precipitated by the secession of the plebs in the previous year (during which fields could not be cultivated). In response to the crisis, the senate imported massive quantities of corn from Sicily, and the plebs demanded that the distribution of the corn effectively be subsidized by the state.

This episode produced the first instance of what would later become the agrarian and frumentarian laws: laws which transferred wealth from the patricians to the plebs, in the form of land, subsidies, or the abolition of debts. Indeed, Shakespeare's demagogue groups these measures together.

---

[1] All quotations from *Coriolanus* are taken from Shakespeare, *Coriolanus*, ed. Philip Brockbank, The Arden Shakespeare (London: Methuen, 1976).

When the reasonable second citizen admonishes the first not to attack "the helms o'th'state, who care for you like fathers," the demagogue replies as follows:

Care for us? True indeed! They ne'er cared for us yet. Suffer us to famish, and their store-houses crammed with grain; make edicts for usury, to support usurers; repeal daily any wholesome act established against the rich, and provide more piercing statutes daily, to chain up and restrain the poor. If the wars eat us not up, they will; and there's all the love they bear us. (1.1.78–85)

Menenius Agrippa, a cool-headed and respected senator, is chosen to respond to the plebeian sedition. He proceeds to offer an allegory, reported identically by Livy, Plutarch, and Dionysius,[2] which must represent the first appearance of "trickle-down economics" in Western literature. He tells how, long ago, the limbs and organs of the human body rebelled against the belly: they asked why the belly should get all the food, while they did much of the work. Menenius gives the belly's reply:

> "True is it, my incorporate friends," quoth he,
> "That I receive the general food at first
> Which you do live upon; and fit it is,
> Because I am the store-house and the shop
> Of the whole body. But, if you do remember,
> I send it through the rivers of your blood
> Even to the court, the heart, to th'seat o'th'brain;
> And through the cranks and offices of man,
> The strongest nerves and small inferior veins
> From me receive that natural competency
> Whereby they live . . . "
>
> (1.1.129–39)

Menenius explains that "[t]he senators of Rome are this good belly, / And you the mutinous members," and insists that "[n]o public benefit which you receive" has its origin outside the senate. He concludes by denigrating the seditious first citizen as "the great toe of this assembly," and labels him the "lowest, basest, poorest" and a "rascal."

The ferment continues, however, and the man who emerges as the great enemy of the plebs is the hero of Shakespeare's play: Gnaeus Marcius, dubbed "Coriolanus" following his conquest of the city of Corioli. Coriolanus, of whom Menenius says "[h]is nature is too noble for the world" (III.1.253), is brought to ruin because he refuses to court public opinion and

---

[2] Livy II.32; Plutarch, *Coriolanus* 6; Dionysius, *Roman Antiquities* VI.86. See also Ps.-Sextus (Aurelius Victor), *De viris illustribus urbis Romae* 18. Menenius was in fact responding to the previous year's insurrection, but Shakespeare conflates the two episodes.

win the support of the masses by supporting the corn subsidy. In the first act, he bitterly mocks the protestations of the plebs:

> They said they were an-hungry, sigh'd forth proverbs –
> That hunger broke stone walls; that dogs must eat;
> That meat was made for mouths; that the gods sent not
> Corn for the rich men only. With these shreds
> They vented their complaining, which being answer'd
> And a petition granted them, a strange one,
> To break the heart of generosity
> And make bold power look pale, they threw their caps
> As they would hang them on the horns o'th'moon,
> Shouting their emulation.
>
> (I.I.204–13)

He concludes that "[w]hoever gave that counsel, to give forth / The corn o'th'storehouse gratis, as 'twas us'd / Sometime in Greece ... Though there the people had more absolute power– / I say they nourish'd disobedience, fed / The ruin of the state" (III.I.113–17). Coriolanus rejects the Greek practice. The plebs, he argues, do not deserve the corn because "[t]hey ne'er did service for't," and he prophesies that the corn rebellion will yield a situation where "gentry, title, wisdom, / Cannot conclude but by the yea and no / Of general ignorance."

The positions in *Coriolanus* are quite clear. The plebs insist on the transfer of wealth from the rich to the poor on grounds of fairness and balance (explicitly taking Greek practice as their model), and the patricians such as Coriolanus and Menenius argue that the plebs are not entitled to what they have not earned, and that redistributionary schemes constitute a dangerous capitulation to demagoguery. Shakespeare's representation is apt. These two positions collided throughout the long and troubled saga of the Roman agrarian and frumentarian laws. The struggle culminated in the reforms of the Gracchi in the second century BCE, a moment in the Roman past to which Renaissance and early-modern thinkers would return incessantly for guidance. Did the agrarian laws promote injustice and sedition, bringing about the collapse of the republic (as Shakespeare suggests), or were they an appropriate, if inadequate response to the great public evil of material inequality? For theorists attempting to discover whether extremes of wealth and poverty doomed a republic – or whether the cure was worse than the disease – this was no obscure, antiquarian question: it was of central importance. These thinkers scoured the ancient sources for answers, and found, as Hegel observed, a great quarrel between the home-grown Roman historians and the Greek historians who wrote Roman history. This quarrel would give agrarian laws a central, although heretofore unremarked place in the confrontation between Greek and Roman republican theories.

II

Irrespective of their later symbolic import, it is essential to understand that Roman agrarian laws did not, strictly speaking, affect private property. From the proposal of the very first agrarian law in 486 BCE until the fall of the republic, these measures dealt exclusively with the *ager publicus*, state lands either captured in war or bequeathed to Rome by foreign princes (as in the case of Pergamum). Cultivated portions of *ager publicus* could be bought from the *quaestors* by individuals who then received full property rights (although the state nominally retained ultimate ownership), or were assigned by lot to citizens in blocks of two *iugera*. The uncultivated tracts of *ager publicus*, however, proved to be a source of great and prolonged turmoil. Initially, citizens were allowed to "occupy" these lands and farm them for their own profit, although they did not receive *dominium* (property rights) over the land. While the state could in principle remove such tenants for compelling state reasons, it could not displace one tenant in favor of another. *Possessores* of uncultivated sections of *ager publicus* were obligated to pay a certain portion of their profits from corn, vineyards, fruit-trees, or grazing land to the state, and, as a result, these lands were theoretically a source of substantial state revenue. In effect, however, the uncultivated lands came to yield almost no revenue, and vast tracts were soon consolidated in the hands of the wealthiest patricians. These patricians acquired hegemony over the uncultivated *ager publicus* by means of fraud and violence, and then assiduously neglected to pay the required tithe to the republic – forcing the state to levy taxes in order to compensate for lost income. Even some of the most rabidly anti-Gracchan Roman authors were forced to speak disapprovingly of this aspect of patrician practice. However, by the time of the Gracchan laws (133 and 122 BCE) these tracts of land had been in private hands for generations, and had acquired the aura of private property.[3]

---

[3] Passages from classical sources relevant to the Gracchan agrarian laws are catalogued in A. H. J. Greenidge and A. M. Clay (eds.), *Sources for Roman History: 133–70 BC* (Oxford: Clarendon Press, 1960). Important studies of the agrarian laws in general and the Gracchan episode in particular include Ernst Badian, *Foreign Clientelae* (Oxford: Clarendon Press, 1958), esp. pp. 168–91; Badian, "From the Gracchi to Sulla: 1940–59" in *Historia* 11 (1962), 197–245; A. H. Bernstein, *Tiberius Gracchus: Tradition and Apostasy* (Ithaca: Cornell University Press, 1978); Jérome Carcopino, *Autour des Gracques: études critiques* (Paris: Belles Letters, 1967); Giuseppe Cardinali, *Studi Graccani* (Rome: "L'Erma" di Bretschneider, 1965); D. Kontchalkovsky, "Recherches sur l'histoire du mouvement agraire des Gracques" in *Revue Historique* 153 (1926), 161–86; and David Stockton, *The Gracchi*

The first agrarian law, like each of its many successors, proposed to re-divide the uncultivated *ager publicus* and distribute it to the plebs in an egalitarian fashion. The fullest Roman account of this first venture appears in Book II of Livy's *Ab urbe condita*. Livy, although by no means wholly uncritical of the patricians, emerges as a solid opponent of the agrarian laws and, as Ogilvie points out, deliberately presents the first agrarian law's sponsor as a proto-Gracchus in order to ground an infamous, more con-temporary evil in the remote past.[4] Spurius Cassius Vicellinus submitted his agrarian law during his third term as consul in 486 BCE. The immediate occasion for the measure was the defeat of the Henrici, and the subsequent appropriation of two-thirds of their land as Roman *ager publicus*. Livy tells us that Spurius Cassius proposed to divide the land between the Latins and the plebs, and that "to this gift he wished to add some part of that land which, he charged, was held by individuals, although it belonged to the state" (II.41).[5] In response, Livy continues, "many of the Fathers, be-ing themselves in possession of the land, took fright at the danger which threatened their interests. But the senators were also concerned on public grounds, namely, that the consul by his largesses should be building up an influence perilous to liberty" (II.41).[6] Livy then deftly uses the relatively recent storms of the Triumviral period against Spurius Cassius: "this was the first proposal for agrarian legislation, and from that day to within living memory it has never been brought up without occasioning the most serious disturbances" (II.41).[7]

The plebs, Livy continues, ultimately turned on Spurius Cassius because they suspected that he was using the agrarian law to amass monarchical power, and because they were offended that he had included the Latins in the redistribution proposal. Accordingly, the first proponent of the agrarian law was executed. But, as Livy recounts, only a year later "the desires of the

(Oxford: Clarendon Press, 1979), esp. chaps. 1–4. See also the summary account of the agrarian movement in John Henry Freese's 'Introduction' to Cicero's *De lege agraria* in Cicero, *Pro Publio Quinctio, Pro Sexto Roscio Amerino, Pro Quinto Roscio Comoedo, De lege agraria* I, II, III, ed. and trans. John Henry Freese, Loeb Classical Library (Harvard University Press, 1930), pp. 330–40. I am deeply grateful to Professor Badian for reviewing my analysis of the ancient sources.

[4] R. M. Ogilvie, *A Commentary on Livy Books 1–5* (Oxford: Clarendon Press, 1965), p. 339. Livy himself lived through the Triumviral period, from which he probably derived his horror of land reform.

[5] All quotations from Livy are taken from Livy, *History of Rome*, ed. and trans. B. O. Foster et al., 14 vols., Loeb Classical Library (Harvard University Press, 1919–59). I have generally reproduced the Loeb translations, while making minor adjustments. "Adiciebat huic muneri agri aliquantum, quem publicum possideri a privatis criminabatur."

[6] "Id multos quidem patrum, ipsos possessores, periculo rerum suarum terrebat; sed et publica patribus sollicitudo inerat, largitione consulem periculosas libertati opes struere."

[7] "Tum primum lex agraria promulgata est, numquam deinde usque ad hanc memoriam sine maximis motibus rerum agitata."

people were . . . again excited by the charms of the agrarian law" (II.42).[8] Livy notes bitterly that the tribunes, thirsty for supremacy, "tried to keep their popular power in the foreground with a popular law, while the senators, who thought there was frenzy enough and to spare in the populace shuddered at the thought of land-grants and encouragements to rashness" (II.42).[9] The patricians, on Livy's account, had every reason to complain that the tribunes were attempting to amass political power "by a generosity exhibited at other men's expense" (III.I).[10]

Livy's account of the Gracchan land reforms themselves is lost, but if the epitome that survives as the *Periochae* is any guide, his assessment of this episode was characteristically negative. In the summary of Book LVIII we read as follows:

Tiberius Sempronius Gracchus, a tribune of the plebs, carried a land law against the desires of the senate and the order of knights, to the effect that no one should occupy more than a thousand *iugera* of public land; Gracchus then went so insane as to remove from office by special enactment his colleague Marcus Octavius, who was supporting the other side of the controversy . . . He also proposed a second land law, in order to put more land at his disposal, that the same commissioners [i.e. those administering the first law] should judge which land was public and which private. Then when there was less land than could be divided up without incurring the hostility of the commons too, because Gracchus had stirred them up to be greedy enough to hope for a large amount, he declared that he would propose a law that the fortune which had belonged to King Attalus [of Pergamum] should be divided among those who ought to receive land under the Sempronian Law.[11]

If anything, Livy's view of Caius Gracchus seems to have been even more unrelentingly critical. Caius is introduced in the summary of Book LX as "Caius Gracchus, the brother of Tiberius and a better speaker than his brother" who

carried as tribune of the plebs several pernicious laws, among which were: a law on the grain supply, that grain should be sold for six and one-third *asses* to the

---

[8] "Sollicitati et eo anno sunt dulcedine agrariae legis animi plebis."

[9] "Tribuni plebi popularem potestatem lege populari celebrabant: patres satis superque gratuiti furoris in multitudine credentes esse, largitiones temeritatisque invitamenta horrebant."

[10] "largiendo de alieno." For another attack on agrarian legislation, see Livy VI.II. Here he writes of Manlius: "Et non contentus agrariis legibus, quae materia semper tribunis plebi seditionum fuisset, fidem moliri coepit."

[11] "Tib. Sempronius Gracchus tribunus plebis cum legem agrariam ferret adversus voluntatem senatus et equestris ordinis, ne quis ex publico agro plus quam mille iugera possideret, in eum furorem exarsit, ut [M.] Octavio collegae causam diversae partis defendenti . . . Promulgavit et aliam legem agrariam, qua sibi latius agrum patefaceret, ut idem triumviri iudicarent, qua publicus ager, qua privatus esset. Deinde cum minus agri esset quam quod dividi posset sine offensa etiam plebis, quoniam eos ad cupiditatem amplum modum sperandi incitaverat, legem se promulgaturum ostendit, ut his, qui Sempronia lege agrum accipere deberent, pecunia, quae regis Attali fuisset, divideretur."

plebs; a second agrarian law, such as his brother also had carried; and a third law, as a means of seducing the order of knights, which was at that time in harmony with the senate [i.e. a law which gave the knights a two-to-one majority in the senate].[12]

For Livy, the Gracchi were dangerous demagogues whose reckless proposals had thrust Rome into prolonged chaos.

This intensely polemical portrayal of agrarian laws and their propo-nents was significantly amplified by Livy's Roman successors.[13] In Lucan's *Pharsalia*, the Gracchi, "who dared to bring about immoderate things" (*ausosque ingentia Gracchos*), appear in the underworld alongside Catiline and Drusus in the *turba nocens* which rejoices at Rome's civil war, while the blessed dead weep.[14] Velleius Paterculus takes up the Gracchan movement in Book II of his *Res gestae divi Augusti* (II.2–4), and emerges with a scathing indictment of Tiberius Gracchus and the agrarian law. Gracchus, he writes, "by proposing agrarian laws which all immediately desired to see in opera-tion, turned the state upside down, and brought it into a position of critical and extreme danger."[15] Velleius then praises Publius Scipio Nasica for op-posing Gracchus by gathering together "the optimates, the senate, the larger and better part of the equestrian order, and those of the plebs who were not yet infected by pernicious theories."[16] Florus writes even more boldly in his *Epitome* that the Gracchan laws may have had the "appearance of equity" (*species aequitatis*), in that they claimed to give the plebs their *ius*, but in fact the agrarian laws brought the state to ruin (*perniciem*). Florus asks, "how could the plebs be restored to the land without dispossessing those who possessed it, who were themselves part of the people and held estates left to them by their forefathers by a kind of right [*ius*]?"[17]

---

[12] "... tribunus plebis... perniciosas aliquot leges tulit, inter quas frumentariam, ut senis et triente frumentum plebi daretur; alteram legem agrariam, quam et frater eius tulerat; tertiam, qua equestrem ordinem, tunc cum senatu consentientem, corrumperet ..."

[13] Following Cardinali (*Studi Graccani*, p. 14), I include Dio Cassius, a Roman senator and administrator under Commodus, in this category, even though he wrote in Greek. That said, the surviving fragments of Book XXIV of Dio's history, which contain his account of the Gracchan reforms, were not printed until the eighteenth century. As a result, they do not figure in the present story.

[14] *Ph.* VI.794. See Lucan, *The Civil War*, ed. and trans. J. D. Duff, Loeb Classical Library (London: William Heinemann, 1928).

[15] Quotations from Velleius are taken from Velleius Paterculus, *Res gestae divi Augusti*, ed. and trans. Frederick W. Shipley, Loeb Classical Library (New York: G. P. Putnam's Sons, 1924). "simul etiam promulgatis agrariis legibus, omnibus statim concupiscentibus, summa imis miscuit et in praeruptum atque anceps periculum adduxit rem publicam."

[16] "Tum optimates, senatus atque equestris ordinis pars melior et maior, et intacta perniciosis consiliis plebs ..."

[17] II.i.13. See L. Annaeus Florus, *Epitome*, ed. and trans. Edward Seymour Forster, Loeb Classical Library (Harvard University Press, 1929). "et reduci plebs in agros unde poterat sine possidentium eversione, qui ipsi pars populi erant, et iam relictas sibi a maioribus sedes aetate quasi iure possidebant?" I have

The only hole in this united front of Roman authors – the exception that proves the rule – is Sallust, who hailed from a plebeian family, and whose sympathies toward the popular party are well known. Indeed, his *Bellum Iugurthinum* tells a rather different story.[18] Before the destruction of Carthage, Sallust observes, Rome was governed harmoniously, and public morals were maintained (XLI.2).[19] After the Punic Wars, however, peace brought corruption, and "the nobles began to abuse their position and the people their liberty, and every man for himself robbed, pillaged, and plundered" (XLI.5).[20] Thus, "the community was split into two parties, and between these the state was torn to pieces [*dilacerata*]." So far, Sallust appears to distribute blame fairly evenly between the factions. But he soon makes clear that, since the party of the patricians had greater power, it ended up making greater mischief. "Generals divided the spoils of war with a few friends. Meanwhile the parents or little children of the soldiers, if they had a powerful neighbour, were driven from their homes" (XLI.7–8).[21] The power of *avaritia* waxed so great that "as soon as nobles were found who preferred true glory [*vera gloria*] to unjust power [*iniusta potentia*], the state began to be disturbed and civil dissension to arise like an upheaval of the earth" (XLI.10).[22] Among these noble souls Sallust numbers the Gracchi, who "began to assert the freedom of the commons [*vindicare plebem in*

---

departed somewhat from Forster's translation here. See also *De vir. ill.* 64–65. This account is less explicitly partisan, although Ps.-Sextus does have Scipio Nasica order "all to follow him who wished the republic to be healthy" (*sequi se iussit, qui salvam republicam vellent*).

18 We also find a somewhat less comprehensively hostile view of the Gracchi in Valerius Maximus. He does dismiss Caius Gracchus as "a young man happier in his eloquence than in his aims, for with his shining talent he could have been a splendid defender of the commonwealth, but preferred to be an impious revolutionary" (VIII.10.1). But his verdict on Tiberius is more complex: "[Rome] punished with death the Tribune of the Plebs T. Gracchus, who dared to promulgate an agrarian law. The same senate commendably voted that land be divided equally among the people by a board of three according to Gracchus' law, removing at the same time both the cause of a very serious internal conflict and its instigator (VII.2.6)." (Translations are taken from Valerius Maximus, *Memorable Doings and Sayings*, ed. and trans. D. R. Shackleton Bailey, Loeb Classical Library [Harvard University Press, 2000]). Thus, from Valerius Maximus we get a split decision. Tiberius was a dangerous and audacious figure who was justly dispatched; but the agrarian law itself was salutary and addressed a serious problem. For a pathos-filled account of Ti. Gracchus' death (although not a favorable treatment of the agrarian laws) see Ps.-Cicero, *Rhetorica ad Herennium* IV.55.68.

19 See Sallust, *Bellum Iugurthinum*, ed. and trans. J. C. Rolfe. Loeb Classical Library (Harvard University Press, 1921).

20 "Namque coepere nobilitas dignitatem, populus libertatem in libidinem vortere, sibi quisque ducere, trahere, rapere. Ita omnia in duas partes abstracta sunt, res publica, quae media fuerat, dilacerata."

21 "praedas bellicas imperatores cum paucis diripiebant. Interea parentes aut parvi liberi militum, uti quisque potentiori confinis erat, sedibus pellebantur."

22 "Nam ubi primum ex nobilitate reperti sunt qui veram gloriam iniustae potentiae anteponerent, moveri civitas et dissensio civilis quasi permixtio terrae oriri coepit."

libertatem] and expose the crimes of the oligarchs" (XLII.I).[23] Sallust does grudgingly concede that "it must be admitted that the Gracchi were so eager for victory that they had not shown a sufficiently moderate spirit [*haud satis moderatus animus*]" (XLII.2),[24] but his overall vision of the Gracchan episode is decidedly outside the Roman mainstream.[25] That said, even the mighty voice of Sallust would be more than drowned out by the expansive rhetoric of the agrarian law's greatest ancient opponent: Marcus Tullius Cicero.

As a practicing politician, Cicero was quite capable of taming his anti-agrarian leanings to suit the needs of the moment. In 64 BCE, for example, P. Servilius Rullus proposed an agrarian law which placed exclusive control over the sale and regulation of lands in a commission of ten whose numbers were to be drawn entirely from the democratic party. Cicero opposed the law in several speeches before the senate and popular assembly, tailoring his rhetoric to the demands of his audience. When addressing the plebs, he insisted that he opposed Rullus' law on the grounds that it created a tyrannical power, not because it was an agrarian law. Indeed, in making his case he had very conciliatory things to say about the agrarian movement and even the Gracchi:

> For, to speak frankly, Romans, I do not disapprove of every kind of agrarian law in itself. For I remember that two of the most illustrious citizens, the most able and the most devoted friends of the Roman people, Tiberius and Gaius Gracchus, settled plebeians in public lands, formerly occupied by private persons. I am not one of those consuls who, like the majority, think it a crime to praise the Gracchi, by whose advice, wisdom, and laws I see that many departments of the administration were set in order. (*De lege agraria* II.10)[26]

When unconstrained by political necessity, however, Cicero let loose with overt polemics against the agrarian laws, reserving his harshest invective for the Gracchi. In Book III of *De legibus* Cicero attacks the office of tribune ("a mischievous thing, born in civil strife and tending to civil strife" [III.19][27]),

---

[23] "vindicare plebem in libertatem et paucorum scelera patefacere coepere . . ."

[24] "Et sane Gracchis cupidine victoriae haud satis moderatus animus fuit."

[25] Although it must be said that even in the case of Sallust, we do not find a defense of the Gracchi based on the intrinsic desirability of an equal distribution of wealth. For such a view, early-modern writers would have to turn to the Greeks.

[26] Quoted from the Loeb edition, ed. and trans. J. H. Freese; see n. 3 above. "Nam, vere dicam, Quirites, genus ipsum legis agrariae vituperare non possum. Venit enim mihi in mentem duos clarissimos, ingeniosissimos, amantissimos plebei Romanae viros, Tiberium et Gaium Gracchos, plebem in agris publicis constituisse, qui agri a privatis antea possidebantur. Non sum autem ego is consul, qui, ut plerique, nefas esse arbitrer Gracchos laudare, quorum consiliis, sapientia, legibus multas esse video rei publicae partes constitutas."

[27] Quotations from *De legibus* are taken from Cicero, *De republica, De legibus*, ed. and trans. C. W. Keyes, Loeb Classical Library (Harvard University Press, 1928). "nam mihi quidem pestifera videtur, quippe quae in seditione et ad seditionem nata sit."

insisting that from its inception "its first acts – deeds worthy of its impious nature – were to deprive the senators of all their privileges, to make the lowest equal to the highest everywhere, and to produce utter confusion and disorder" (III.19).[28] His chief complaint is posed as a rhetorical question: "what rights did the tribunate of Tiberius Gracchus leave to the best citizens?"[29] Furthermore, Cicero places the blame for Rome's extended civil wars squarely on Caius Gracchus' shoulders: "was it not the overthrow of Caius Gracchus and the casting of daggers into the forum (this is Gracchus' own description of what he did) that brought about, through the tribunate, a complete revolution in the State?" (III.20)[30]

But Cicero's most extended and bitter diatribe against the agrarian laws and their notorious sponsors appears in Book II of *De officiis*, perhaps the central text of the neo-Roman tradition. In discussing the duties of statesmen, Cicero declares that "the man in administrative office . . . must make it his first care that everyone shall have what belongs to him [*suum quisque teneat*] and that private citizens suffer no invasion [*deminutio*] of their property rights by act of the state" (II.73).[31] As his example of this kind of *deminutio*, he submits that "ruinous policy" (*perniciose*) of the consul Philippus called the *lex agraria*. This policy, he continues, favored an "equal distribution of property" (*ad aequationem bonorum pertinens*). "What plague could be worse?" (*qua peste quae potest esse maior*), he asks, especially since it negates the basic purpose for which people enter civil association – namely the preservation of their private property (*custodia rerum suarum*). Later, Cicero expands on this argument:

But they who pose as friends of the people, and who for that reason either attempt to have agrarian laws passed, in order that the occupants may be driven out of their homes, or propose that money loaned should be remitted to borrowers, are undermining the foundations of the commonwealth; first of all they are destroying harmony, which cannot exist when money is taken away from one party and

---

[28] "qui primum, ut impio dignum fuit, patribus omnem honorem eripuit, omnia infima summis paria fecit, turbavit, miscuit."

[29] "quid iuris bonis viris Ti. Gracchi tribunatus reliquit?" See *De republica* III.41: "Asia Ti. Gracchus, perseveravit in civibus, sociorum nominisque Latini iura neglexit ac foedera. quae si consuetudo ac licentia manare coeperit latius imperiumque nostrum ad vim a iure traduxerit, ut, qui adhuc voluntate nobis oboediunt, terrore teneantur, etsi nobis, qui id aetatis sumus, evigilatum fere est, tamen de posteris nostris et de illa immortalitate rei publicae sollicitor, quae poterat esse perpetua, si patriis viveretur institutis et moribus." See also *In Catilinam* 1.3, and *Tusculanae disputationes* IV.51.

[30] "C. vero Gracchi ruinis et iis sicis, quas ipse se proiecisse in forum dixit, quibus digladiarentur inter se cives, nonne omnem rei publicae statum permutavit?"

[31] Quotations from *De officiis* are taken from Cicero, *De officiis*, ed. and trans. Walter Miller, Loeb Classical Library (Harvard University Press, 1913). "In primis autem videndum erit ei, qui rem publicam administrabit, ut suum quisque teneat neque de bonis privatorum publice deminutio fiat."

bestowed on another; and second, they do away with equity, which is utterly subverted, if the rights of property are not respected. For, as I said above, it is the peculiar function of the state and the city to guarantee every man the free and undisturbed control of his own particular property. (*De officiis* II.78)[32]

Cicero continues by noting that these agrarian laws brought about the downfall of Lysander and Agis in Sparta, plunging Greece into chaos, and adds "what shall we say of our own Gracchi, the sons of that famous Tiberius Gracchus and the grandsons of Africanus? Was it not strife over the agrarian issue that caused their downfall and death?"[33] In short, Cicero characterizes the agrarian movement as seditious, dangerous, and violently unjust. For what is an agrarian law, he asks, but an initiative "to rob one man of what belongs to him and to give to another what does not belong to him?" (II.84).[34] This was the most powerful and lasting Roman assessment of the agrarian movement and the Gracchan reforms.

The Greeks, however, tended to take a very different view,[35] and, because the two most substantial surviving accounts of the Gracchan episode

---

[32] "Qui vero se populares volunt ob eamque causam aut agrariam rem temptant, ut possessores pellantur suis sedibus, aut pecunias creditas debitoribus condonandas putant, labefactant fundamenta rei publicae, concordiam primum, quae esse non potest, cum aliis adimuntur, aliis condonantur pecuniae, deinde aequitatem, quae tollitur omnis, si habere suum cuique non licet. Id enim est proprium, ut supra dixi, civitatis atque urbis, ut sit libera et non sollicita suae rei cuiusque custodia."

[33] "Quid? nostros Gracchos, Ti. Gracchi summi viri filios, Africani nepotes, nonne agrariae contentiones perdiderunt?"

[34] "Quid est aliud aliis sua eripere, aliis dare aliena?"

[35] As far as I have been able to make out, this broad ideological division between Greek and Roman historians on the agrarian laws has hardly been discussed in the scholarly literature. Stockton wonders whether we should "look to the possible influence of Greek political experience and theory for his [i.e. Ti. Gracchus'] inspiration" (Stockton, *Gracchi*, p. 84), a point made explicitly in A. H. J. Greenidge, *A History of Rome*, vol. I (London: Methuen, 1904), pp. 104–6, and also in several other sources – although Badian is dubious (see Badian, "From the Gracchi to Sulla," 201). Greenidge points out that the Gracchi were taught by two Greeks, Diophanes of Mitylene and Blossius of Cumae, and that contemporaries "held the belief that Tiberius was spurred to his political enterprise by the direct exhortation of these teachers" (p. 104). For his part, Greenidge concludes that "there can be little doubt that the teaching of the two Greeks exercised a powerful influence on the political cast of his mind." But these scholars do not connect the alleged "Greekness" of the Gracchan program to the stunningly favorable treatment the Gracchi receive in Greek, as opposed to Roman sources. One scholar who does notice the contrast in tone between Livy's account and Plutarch's is R. B. Rose in his "The 'Red Scare' of the 1790s: the French Revolution and the 'Agrarian Law'" in *Past and Present* 103 (1984), 114–15. Rose does not, to be sure, consider whether there might be an ideological Graeco-Roman divide on the *lex agraria* (he adduces no other sources). But he does observe that Plutarch's account, unlike that of Livy, is "sympathetic" and dramatizes a conflict between "the high-minded Gracchus brothers" and "the corrupt and selfish Patricians." Likewise, Mouza Raskolnikoff remarks that Plutarch is "favorable" to the Gracchi, by which, presumably, she means to contrast him with Livy or Cicero (see Mouza Raskolnikoff, *Histoire romaine et critique historique dans l'Europe des Lumières: la naissance de l'hypercritique dans l'historiographie de la Rome antique* [Strasbourg: AECR, 1992]). Raskolnikoff also argues that Greek historians like Plutarch and Appian share a common focus on the economic basis of revolution, a subcategory she takes from Jean Marie Goulemot, *Le règne de l'histoire: discours historiques et révolutions (XVIIeme–XVIIIeme siècle)* (Paris: Albin Michel,

come down to us from Plutarch and Appian, this Greek view is of more than middling historical importance and influence.³⁶ Indeed, it is hardly surprising, given what I have said about the contrast between Greek and Roman sensibilities, that Plutarch in particular would reject Cicero's verdict on the Gracchi. A Greek of the first century CE who held Roman citizenship but made his home in Chaeronea, Plutarch studied in Athens and maintained close ties to the Platonic Academy throughout his life. His biographies of the two Gracchi are companion pieces to his lives of Agis and Cleomenes, and his enthusiasm for the Lycurgan project and its latter-day revival indisputably colored his view of the infamous Roman tribunes. Plutarch introduces the Gracchi as "men of most generous natures" who "had a most generous rearing, and adopted generous political principles" (*Agis* 11.4).³⁷ He compares them to Agis and Cleomenes, the Spartan kings who restored the Lycurgan regimen in Sparta, on the grounds that "these also tried to exalt the people, just as the Gracchi did, and tried to restore an honourable and just civil polity [πολιτείαν καλὴν καὶ δικαίαν] which had lapsed for a long time; and like the Gracchi they incurred the hatred of the powerful men, who were unwilling to relax their usual rapacity [πλεονεξίαν]" (11.6).³⁸ Plutarch continues by blaming a change in land laws for the toppling of the Lycurgan system, the introduction of material inequality, and the state's attendant moral collapse (v.1). The Gracchi, he claims,

1996 [orig. 1975]), pp. 148–56. If this is meant to suggest that Cicero, Livy, Lucan, and Florus were somehow unaware that the Roman seditions arose from conflicts between the rich and poor, then it is surely mistaken. Rather, both the Greek and Roman historians understood the economic roots of civic conflict; they simply applied radically different value judgments to the canonical episodes of Roman history.

³⁶ Dionysius of Halicarnassus does not discuss the Gracchan episode (but for a brief, negative reference at 11.11.3, which does not, however, offer an evaluation of the agrarian law). That said, he does include an account of Spurius Cassius' agrarian law which conforms very much to the program to be encountered in Plutarch and Appian. This is particularly noteworthy, considering his patrician sympathies. See Dionysius VIII.68–80 in *Roman Antiquities*, ed. and trans. Earnest Cary, vol. V, Loeb Classical Library (London: William Heinemann, 1945). The dissenting voice among Greek historians is that of Diodorus Siculus. Like Valerius Maximus among the Romans, however, he splits his verdict. He joins Plutarch and Appian in praising Tiberius Gracchus, but he launches a scathing attack on Caius (although, interestingly enough, not because of the agrarian law, but because of Caius' reengineering of the senate). See Diodorus XXXIV/V.5–29 in *Diodorus of Sicily*, ed. and trans. Francis R. Walton, vol.XII, Loeb Classical Library (London: William Heinemann; and New York: G. P. Putnam's Sons, 1933). The only relevant passage from Polybius is at 11.21.8, where he records the decision of Gaius Flaminius to divide conquered territory among Roman citizens, and criticizes this measure for its tendency to stir up anti-Roman sentiment in Gaul and elsewhere.

³⁷ Quotations from Plutarch are taken from Plutarch, *Lives*, vol. X, ed. and trans. Bernadotte Perrin, Loeb Classical Library (New York: G. P. Putnam's Sons, 1921). "οὓς κάλλιστα μὲν φύντας, κάλλιστα δὲ τραφέντας, καλλίστην δὲ τῆς πολιτείας ὑπόθεσιν λαβόντας . . ."

³⁸ "καὶ γὰρ οὗτοι τὸν δῆμον αὔξοντες, ὥσπερ ἐκεῖνοι, καὶ πολιτείαν καλὴν καὶ δικαίαν ἐκλελοιπυῖαν πολὺν χρόνον ἀναλαμβάνοντες, ὁμοίως ἀπηχθάνοντο τοῖς δυνατοῖς μὴ βουλομένοις ἀφεῖναι τὴν συνήθη πλεονεξίαν."

were attempting to alleviate just such a problem in Rome – one inextricably connected to land laws.

At the outset of his *Life of Tiberius and Caius Gracchus*, Plutarch narrates how Rome arrived at her desperate state:

Of the territory which the Romans won in war from their neighbours, a part they sold, and a part they made common land, and assigned it for occupation to the poor and indigent among the citizens, on payment of a small rent into the public treasury. And when the rich began to offer larger rents and drove out the poor, a law was enacted forbidding the holding by one person of more than five hundred *iugera* of land. For a short time this enactment gave a check to the rapacity of the rich, and was of assistance to the poor, who remained in their places on the land which they had rented and occupied the allotment which each had held from the outset. (*T. Gracchus* VIII.1)[39]

The solution did not hold for long, however. Soon thereafter "the neighbouring rich men, by means of fictitious personages, transferred these rentals to themselves, and finally held most of the land openly in their own names."[40] This land policy yielded a sharp population decline, and led to the replacement of yeoman farmers by slaves. It was this evil, records Plutarch, which Tiberius Gracchus set out to address.

Plutarch's inclusion of this narrative in his account of the Gracchan reforms is itself very telling: Plutarch wants to make the story of the agrarian laws a tale of the rapacity (πλεονεξία) of the rich, not the unreasoning envy of the poor. Indeed, when Gracchus finally draws up the agrarian law, Plutarch casts it as an example of good and responsible government:

[Gracchus] did not, however, draw up his law by himself, but took counsel with the citizens who were foremost in virtue and reputation, among whom were Crassus the pontifex maximus, Mucius Scaevola the jurist, who was then consul, and Appius Claudius, his father-in-law. And it seems that a law dealing with injustice [ἀδικίαν] and rapacity [πλεονεξίαν] so great was never drawn up in milder and gentler terms. For men who ought to have been punished for their disobedience and to have surrendered with payment of a fine the land which they were illegally enjoying, these men it merely ordered to abandon their unjust acquisitions upon

[39] "Ῥωμαῖοι τῆς τῶν ἀστυγειτόνων χώρας ὅσην ἀπετέμοντο πολέμῳ, τὴν μὲν ἐπίπρασκον, τὴν δὲ ποιούμενοι δημοσίαν ἐδίδοσαν νέμεσθαι τοῖς ἀκτήμοσι καὶ ἀπόροις τῶν πολιτῶν, ἀποφορὰν οὐ πολλὴν εἰς τὸ δημόσιον τελοῦσιν, ἀρξαμένων δὲ τῶν πλουσίων ὑπερβάλλειν τὰς ἀποφορὰς καὶ τοὺς πένητας ἐξελαυνόντων, ἐγράφη νόμος οὐκ ἐῶν πλέθρα γῆς ἔχειν πλείονα τῶν πεντακοσίων. καὶ βραχὺν μὲν χρόνον ἐπέσχε τὴν πλεονεξίαν τὸ γράμμα τοῦτο, καὶ τοῖς πένησιν ἐβοήθησε κατὰ χώραν μένουσιν ἐπὶ τῶν μεμισθωμένων καὶ νεμομένοις ἣν ἕκαστος ἐξ ἀρχῆς εἶχε μοῖραν."

[40] "τῶν γειτνιώντων πλουσίων ὑποβλήτοις προσώποις μεταφερόντων τὰς μισθώσεις εἰς ἑαυτούς, τέλος δὲ φανερῶς ἤδη δι' ἑαυτῶν τὰ πλεῖστα κατεχόντων …"

being paid their value, and to admit into ownership of them such citizens as needed assistance. (*T. Gracch.* IX.I)[41]

For Plutarch, the Gracchan laws were too mild! Indeed, he goes out of his way to praise the mercy and benignity of the plebs, who "although the rectification of the wrong was so considerate" were "willing to let bygones be bygones if they could be secure from such wrong in the future."[42] But the rich responded differently:

The men of wealth and property, however, were led by their rapacity [πλεονεξία] to hate the law, and by their wrath and contentiousness to hate the law-giver, and tried to dissuade the people by alleging that Tiberius was introducing a redistribution of land for the confusion of the body politic, and was stirring up a general revolution. (*T. Gracch.* IX.3)[43]

The great Roman charge against the Gracchi – that their laws disordered the state and positioned it for civil war – appears here as a trumped up canard popularized by the rapacious opposition.

For Plutarch, then, the Gracchi were virtuous social reformers attempting to subdue the destructive passion for wealth. Indeed, if the Gracchi suffer in the comparison to Agis and Cleomenes, Plutarch insists that is because Tiberius and Caius did not go far enough. He observes that "the chief proof that the Gracchi scorned wealth and were superior to money lies in the fact that they kept themselves clear from unrighteous gains during their official and public life" (*Comparative Lives* I.4).[44] Agis, however, had gone far beyond this level of scrupulousness; he donated all of his wealth to the state. "How great a baseness, then," writes Plutarch in a clever play on words, "would unlawful gain have been held to be by one in whose eyes even the lawful having [ἔχειν] of more [πλέον] than another was rapacity [πλεονεξία]?"[45] Likewise, for Plutarch, the agrarian laws of the Gracchi

---

[41] "Οὐ μὴν ἐφ᾽ αὑτοῦ γε συνέθηκε τὸν νόμον, τοῖς δὲ πρωτεύουσιν ἀρετῇ καὶ δόξῃ τῶν πολιτῶν συμβούλοις χρησάμενος, ὧν καὶ Κράσσος ἦν ὁ ἀρχιερεὺς καὶ Μούκιος Σκαιβόλας ὁ νομοδείκτης ὑπατεύων τότε καὶ Κλαύδιος Ἄππιος ὁ κηδεστὴς τοῦ Τιβερίου. καὶ δοκεῖ νόμος εἰς ἀδικίαν καὶ πλεονεξίαν τοσαύτην μηδέποτε πρᾳότερος γραφῆναι καὶ μαλακώτερος. οὓς γὰρ ἔδει δίκην τῆς ἀπειθείας δοῦναι καὶ μετὰ ζημίας ἣν παρὰ τοὺς νόμους ἐκαρποῦντο χώραν ἀφεῖναι, τούτους ἐκέλευσε τιμὴν προσλαμβάνοντας ἐκβαίνειν ὧν ἀδίκως ἐκέκτηντο, καὶ παραδέχεσθαι τοὺς βοηθείας δεομένους τῶν πολιτῶν."

[42] "ἀλλὰ καίπερ οὕτω τῆς ἐπανορθώσεως οὔσης εὐγνώμονος, ὁ μὲν δῆμος ἠγάπα, παρεὶς τὰ γεγενημένα, παύσασθαι τὸ λοιπὸν ἀδικούμενος . . ."

[43] "οἱ δὲ πλούσιοι καὶ κτηματικοὶ πλεονεξίᾳ μὲν τὸν νόμον, ὀργῇ δὲ καὶ φιλονεικίᾳ τὸν νομοθέτην δι᾽ ἔχθους ἔχοντες, ἐπεχείρουν ἀποτρέπειν τὸν δῆμον, ὡς γῆς ἀναδασμὸν ἐπὶ συγχύσει τῆς πολιτείας εἰσάγοντος τοῦ Τιβερίου καὶ πάντα πράγματα κινοῦντος."

[44] "καὶ μὴν τῆς γε Γράγχων ἀφιλοχρηματίας καὶ πρὸς ἀργύριον ἐγκρατείας μέγιστόν ἐστιν ὅτι λημμάτων ἀδίκων καθαροὺς ἐν ἀρχαῖς καὶ πολιτείαις διεφύλαξαν ἑαυτούς."

[45] "πηλίκον οὖν ἐνόμιζε κακὸν εἶναι τὸ κερδαίνειν ἀδίκως ὁ καὶ δικαίως πλέον ἔχειν ἑτέρου πλεονεξίαν ἡγούμενος;"

were too mild and isolated a corrective. In true Greek style, Plutarch prefers the holistic approach of Agis and Cleomenes:

Agis and Cleomenes in their reforms, considering that the application of trifling and partial remedies and excisions to the disorders of the state was nothing more than cutting off a Hydra's head (as Plato says), tried to introduce into the constitution a change which was able to transform and get rid of all evils at once; though perhaps it is more in accordance with the truth to say that they banished the change which had wrought all sorts of evils, by bringing back the state to its proper form and establishing it therein. (*Comp.* 11.2)[46]

In short, Agis and Cleomenes, like good Platonists, restored "the unwritten laws concerning balance and the equality of property [περὶ σωφροσύνης καὶ ἰσότητος]" which Sparta had received from Lycurgus, and which Lycurgus had received from Pythian Apollo. Nonetheless the Gracchi receive Plutarch's praise. He insists that they were not "fond of power and strife" (τυραννικὸν καὶ πολεμοποιόν) as their enemies suggest, and closes by asking "what could have been more just [δικαιότερον] and honorable than their original design?" (*Comp.* v.5).[47]

Plutarch, then, goes considerably farther even than Sallust, by far the most philo-Gracchan Roman author. Sallust had attacked the patricians for their unjust acquisitions (although, to be sure, in far less extensive a manner than Plutarch) and had supported the Gracchan program as a remedy against the wrongful appropriation of individual property. In all of this, the Roman standard of justice went unchallenged. Plutarch, however, makes the broader Platonist case that the agrarian laws were praiseworthy because virtue and justice require the equal distribution of wealth. His narrative amounts to a powerful *a fortiori* argument in favor of the Gracchan laws: if the actions of the patricians count as crimes even under the morally dubious Roman standard of justice (*cuique tribuere ius suum*), how much more so do they violate the principle of justice rightly understood? This judgment unambiguously sets Plutarch apart; it is difficult to imagine a Roman ever writing such a thing.

Appian, a second-century Greek from Alexandria, follows Plutarch's lead.[48] Indeed, he places his account of the Gracchan reforms at the

---

[46] "ὁ δὲ Ἄγιδος καὶ Κλεομένους νεωτερισμός, τὸ μικρὰ καὶ κατὰ μέρος τῶν ἡμαρτημένων ἰᾶσθαι καὶ ἀποκόπτειν ὕδραν τινὰ τέμνοντος, ὥς φησιν ὁ Πλάτων, ἡγησάμενος εἶναι, τὴν ἅμα πάντα ἀπαλλάξαι κακὰ καὶ μετασκευάσαι δυναμένην μεταβολὴν ἐπῆγε τοῖς πράγμασιν. ἀληθέστερον δ' ἴσως εἰπεῖν ἐστιν ὅτι τὴν πάντα ἀπεργασαμένην κακὰ μεταβολὴν ἐξήλαυνεν, ἀπάγων καὶ καθιστὰς εἰς τὸ οἰκεῖον σχῆμα τὴν πόλιν."

[47] "ἐπεὶ τῆς γε πρώτης ὑποθέσεως τί κάλλιον ἢ δικαιότερον ἦν ..."

[48] The classic work on Appian's sources is Emilio Gabba, *Appiano e la storia delle guerre civili* (Florence: La Nuova Italia, 1956); on Plutarch, see esp. pp. 39, 227–28. Gabba discusses Appian's account

beginning of his history of the Roman civil wars, suggesting that he considered the agrarian question to be at the center of Rome's internal crisis. The very first sentence of the work announces that "the plebeians and the Senate of Rome were often at strife with each other concerning the enactment of laws, the canceling of debts, the division of lands, or the election of magistrates."[49] Appian then formally begins his history by telling much the same story as Plutarch about the development and abuse of the *ager publicus*, albeit with a more marked emphasis on the condition of Rome's Italian *socii*:

The Romans, as they subdued the Italian peoples successively in war, used to seize a part of their lands and build towns there, or enrol colonists of their own to occupy those already existing, and their idea was to use these as outposts; but of the land acquired by war they assigned the cultivated part to the colonists, or sold or leased it. Since they had no leisure as yet to allot the part which then lay desolated by war (this was generally the greater part), they made proclamation that in the meantime those who were willing to work it might do so for a toll of the yearly crops, a tenth of the grain and a fifth of the fruit . . . They did these things in order to multiply the Italian race, which they considered the most laborious of peoples, so that they might have plenty of allies at home. (1.7)[50]

---

of the Gracchan reforms on pp. 34–73. He rightly stresses the monarchism of Appian's account: for Appian, the civil wars were indicative of the instability of republican rule, and were finally transcended by the ὁμόνοια and ἐυταξία of the principate. Gabba is also right to point out that, unlike Plutarch's narrative, Appian's is more concerned with "le finalità politico-militari della legge agraria, rispetto a quella della giustizia sociale" (p. 42). See also Gregory Bucher, "The Origins, Program, and Composition of Appian's *Roman History*" in *Transactions of the American Philological Association* 130 (2000), 411–58. Bucher canvasses the two possible explanations for the obvious similarities between passages in Plutarch and Appian: (1) Appian read and used Plutarch; or (2) both had a common source, now lost (pp. 452–53). In either case, the scholarly consensus is that, in addition to Plutarch, Appian drew freely from a wide range of Roman sources, including the lost civil-war history of Asinius Pollio.

49　Quotations from Appian are taken from Appian, *The Civil Wars*, Book 1 in *Roman History*, ed. and trans. Horace White, vol. III, Loeb Classical Library (London: William Heinemann, 1913). "Ῥωμαίοις ὁ δῆμος καὶ ἡ βουλὴ πολλάκις ἐς ἀλλήλους περί τε νόμων θέσεως καὶ χρεῶν ἀποκοπῆς ἢ γῆς διαδατουμένης ἢ ἐν ἀρχαιρεσίαις ἐστασίασαν." The third volume of J. G. A. Pocock's ongoing study of Gibbon discusses Appian from a rather different point of view. Unfortunately, it was released too late to be considered in any detail in the present study. I have, however, benefited from extensive conversations with Professor Pocock on this subject. See J. G. A. Pocock, *Barbarism and Religion*, vol. III: *The First Decline and Fall* (Cambridge University Press, 2003), esp. pp. 32–60.

50　"Ῥωμαῖοι τὴν Ἰταλίαν πολέμῳ κατὰ μέρη χειρούμενοι γῆς μέρος ἐλάμβανον καὶ πόλεις ἐνῴκιζον ἢ ἐς τὰς πρότερον οὔσας κληρούχους ἀπὸ σφῶν κατέλεγον. καὶ τάδε μὲν ἀντὶ φρουρίων ἐπενόουν, τῆς δὲ γῆς τῆς δορικτήτου σφίσιν ἑκάστοτε γιγνομένης τὴν μὲν ἐξειργασμένην αὐτίκα τοῖς οἰκιζομένοις ἐπιδιήρουν ἢ ἐπίπρασκον ἢ ἐξεμίσθουν, τὴν δ' ἀργὸν ἐκ τοῦ πολέμου τότε οὖσαν ἢ δὴ καὶ μάλιστα ἐπλήθυεν, οὐκ ἄγοντές πω σχολὴν διαλαχεῖν ἐπεκήρυττον ἐν τοσῷδε τοῖς ἐθέλουσιν ἐκπονεῖν ἐπὶ τέλει τῶν ἐτησίων καρπῶν, δεκάτῃ μὲν τῶν σπειρομένων, πέμπτῃ δὲ τῶν φυτευομένων . . . καὶ τάδε ἔπραττον ἐς πολυανδρίαν τοῦ Ἰταλικοῦ γένους, φερεπονωτάτου σφίσιν ὀφθέντος, ἵνα συμμάχους οἰκείους ἔχοιεν."

But, as Appian goes on to explain, the result of the policy was quite different from the one intended:

But the very opposite thing happened; for the rich, getting possession of the greater part of the undistributed lands, and being emboldened by the lapse of time to believe that they would never be dispossessed, absorbing any adjacent strips and their poor neighbours' allotments, partly by purchase under persuasion and partly by force, came to cultivate vast tracts instead of single estates, using slaves as labourers and herdsmen, lest free labourers should be drawn from agriculture into the army. At the same time the ownership of slaves brought them great gain from the multitude of their progeny, who increased because they were exempt from military service. Thus certain powerful men became extremely rich and the race of slaves multiplied throughout the country, while the Italian people dwindled in numbers and strength, being oppressed by penury, taxes, and military service.[51]

Fearing that they would run out of Italian allies and find themselves overrun by slaves, the Romans sought to address this problem. Nonetheless, writes Appian in a nod to Roman sensibilities, they recognized that it would be "not at all just" (οὐδὲ πάντη δίκαιον) to deprive individuals of their fields after so much had been invested in the form of capital improvements. They settled instead on the Licinian law, which limited personal holdings to 500 *iugera* of *ager publicus*, and appointed monitors to make certain that the law was enforced.

But, Appian continues, the people never received their land, and the rich circumvented the new law with abandon: "But there was not the smallest consideration shown for the law or the oaths. The few who seemed to pay some respect to them conveyed their land to relations fraudulently, but the greater part disregarded it altogether . . ." (1.8.).[52] In response, Tiberius Gracchus proposed an agrarian law which Appian, like Plutarch, praises for its mildness. Gracchus, writes Appian, "brought forward the law, providing that nobody should hold more than 500 *iugera* of public domain. But he added a provision to the former law, that the sons of the occupiers might

---

[51] "ἐς δὲ τοὐναντίον αὐτοῖς περιῄει. οἱ γὰρ πλούσιοι τῆσδε τῆς ἀνεμήτου γῆς τὴν πολλὴν καταλαβόντες καὶ χρόνῳ θαρροῦντες οὔ τινα σφᾶς ἔτι ἀφαιρήσεσθαι τά τε ἀγχοῦ σφίσιν ὅσα τε ἦν ἄλλα βραχέα πενήτων, τὰ μὲν ὠνούμενοι πειθοῖ, τὰ δὲ βίᾳ λαμβάνοντες, πεδία μακρὰ ἀντὶ χωρίων ἐγεώργουν, ὠνητοῖς ἐς αὐτὰ γεωργοῖς καὶ ποιμέσι χρώμενοι τοῦ μὴ τοὺς ἐλευθέρους ἐς τὰς στρατείας ἀπὸ τῆς γεωργίας περισπᾶν, φερούσης ἅμα καὶ τῆσδε τῆς κτήσεως αὐτοῖς πολὺ κέρδος ἐκ πολυπαιδίας θεραπόντων ἀκινδύνως αὐξομένων διὰ τὰς ἀστρατείας. ἀπὸ δὲ τούτων οἱ μὲν δυνατοὶ πάμπαν ἐπλούτουν, καὶ τὸ τῶν θεραπόντων γένος ἀνὰ τὴν χώραν ἐπλήθυε, τοὺς δ' Ἰταλιώτας ὀλιγότης καὶ δυσανδρία κατελάμβανε, τρυχομένους πενίᾳ τε καὶ ἐσφοραῖς καὶ στρατείαις."

[52] "φροντὶς δ' οὐδεμία ἦν οὔτε τῶν νόμων οὔτε τῶν ὅρκων, ἀλλ' οἵτινες καὶ ἐδόκουν φροντίσαι, τὴν γῆν ἐς τοὺς οἰκείους ἐπὶ ὑποκρίσει διένεμον, οἱ δὲ πολλοὶ τέλεον κατεφρόνουν . . ."

each hold one-half of that amount . . . " (1.9).[53] The remainder of the land was to be divided among the plebs by a commission of three men. The rich, who were "no longer able to disregard the law" or to get around it by consolidating several allotments (a practice which Gracchus explicitly forbade), inveighed against the new law in the expected manner. At this point, Appian rather evenhandedly summarizes the primary arguments employed by the plebs and the patricians: the patricians cry out against the injustice of being deprived of lands they have tilled and cultivated, while the plebs insist that public lands should be divided among the public, and that the patricians have driven those responsible for Roman glory into penury (1.10). Gracchus himself then comes before the people, and Appian portrays him as the soul of reason and honor. He asks the plebs

whether it was not just [δίκαιον] to let the commons divide the common property; whether a citizen was not worthy of more consideration at all times than a slave; whether a man who served in the army was not more useful than one who did not; and whether one who had a share in the country was not more likely to be devoted to the public interests. (1.11)[54]

Gracchus concludes by exhorting the patricians to embrace this mild law, and to address Italy's population crisis. The agrarian law is then enacted.

So far Appian himself has not characterized the Gracchan law, although the manner of his narration is suggestive. The reader must wait until the story's *dénouement* in order to hear the author's own opinion. After Gracchus' death, his younger brother Caius attempted to carry out the provisions of the land law. However, it proved impossible to settle exactly which land belonged to which occupants, and whether any given plot was public or private. As Appian puts it, "the injustice [ἀδίκημα] done by the rich, although great, was not easy to ascertain" (1.18).[55] The failure of the first Gracchan law led to more unrest, and ultimately, to the "sedition of the younger Gracchus." After the fall of Caius, Appian explains, a new law was passed allowing landholders to sell their land to whomever they chose – a practice forbidden by Tiberius' law. Appian's account of what happened next contains his overarching assessment of the Gracchan laws:

At once the rich began to buy the allotments of the poor, or found pretexts for seizing them by force. So the condition of the poor became even worse than it was

---

[53] "ἀνεκαίνιζε τὸν νόμον μηδένα τῶν πεντακοσίων πλέθρων πλέον ἔχειν. παισὶ δ᾽ αὐτῶν ὑπὲρ τὸν παλαιὸν νόμον προσετίθει τὰ ἡμίσεα τούτων."

[54] "εἰ δίκαιον τὰ κοινὰ κοινῇ διανέμεσθαι καὶ εἰ γνησιώτερος αἰεὶ θεράποντος ὁ πολίτης καὶ χρησιμώτερος ὁ στρατιώτης ἀπολέμου καὶ τοῖς δημοσίοις εὐνούστερος ὁ κοινωνός."

[55] "καὶ τὸ τῶν πλουσίων ἀδίκημα καίπερ ὂν μέγα δυσεπίγνωστον ἦν."

before, until Spurius Thorius, a tribune of the people, brought in a law providing that the work of distributing the public domain should no longer be continued, but that the land should belong to those in possession of it, who should pay rent for it to the people, and that the money so received should be distributed; and this distribution was a kind of solace to the poor, but it did not help to increase the population. By these devices the law of Gracchus – a most excellent and useful one, if it could have been carried out – was once and for all frustrated . . . (1.27)[56]

Appian continues, "the rent itself was abolished at the instance of another tribune. So the plebeians lost everything . . ."[57] For this Greek historian, the Gracchan law was "excellent and useful" (ἄριστος καὶ ὠφελιμωτάτος); and, while he does not share Plutarch's more explicitly Platonizing stance, he agrees that it was the greedy intransigence of the rich that decimated the Roman state.[58]

We can see, then, that the historiography of the Gracchan reforms and the agrarian movement became the locus for a great confrontation between Greek and Roman political principles. Roman historians who embraced the standard, Roman theory of justice (*cuique tribuere ius suum*) excoriated the agrarian laws as dangerous and unjust, while Greek historians tended to praise the Gracchi for attempting to create a just society, and blamed the rich for precipitating the Roman civil wars. To be sure, it is not the case that approval of the Roman agrarian laws logically requires an attachment to the Greek principle of justice. One could, like Sallust, defend the Gracchan reforms on Roman grounds (i.e. on the grounds that returning conquered lands to the plebs was a matter of *ius*). Nor is it the case that opposition to the agrarian laws necessarily suggests antagonism to the Greek principle of justice. One might, for example, oppose redistribution on purely prudential grounds, all the while approving of it in principle. Yet, as we shall see, it is almost invariably the case that early-modern thinkers who praised the Roman agrarian movement understood it (like Plutarch in particular) as a comprehensive attempt to equalize holdings in the state, in accordance

---

[56] "καὶ εὐθὺς οἱ πλούσιοι παρὰ τῶν πενήτων ἐωνοῦντο, ἢ ταῖσδε ταῖς προφάσεσιν ἐβιάζοντο. καὶ περιῆν ἐς χεῖρον ἔτι τοῖς πένησι, μέχρι Σπούριος Θόριος δημαρχῶν εἰσηγήσατο νόμον, τὴν μὲν γῆν μηκέτι διανέμειν, ἀλλ' εἶναι τῶν ἐχόντων, καὶ φόρους ὑπὲρ αὐτῆς τῷ δήμῳ κατατίθεσθαι καὶ τάδε τὰ χρήματα χωρεῖν ἐς διανομάς. ὅπερ ἦν μέν τις τοῖς πένησι παρηγορία διὰ τὰς διανομάς, ὄφελος δ' οὐδὲν ἐς πολυπληθίαν. ἅπαξ δὲ τοῖς σοφίσμασι τοῖσδε τοῦ Γρακχείου νόμου παραλυθέντος, ἀρίστου καὶ ὠφελιμωτάτου, εἰ ἐδύνατο πραχθῆναι, γενομένου . . ."

[57] ". . . καὶ τοὺς φόρους οὐ πολὺ ὕστερον διέλυσε δήμαρχος ἕτερος, καὶ ὁ δῆμος ἀθρόως ἁπάντων ἐξεπεπτώκει."

[58] An overtly Platonist stance would be extremely uncharacteristic of Appian, given his celebrated attack on Athenian philosophers in *Mithridatic Wars* 28 (*Roman History* XII.5).

with Greek principles.[59] Likewise, early-modern thinkers who attacked the agrarian laws almost always agreed with Cicero that, irrespective of the vagaries of Roman land law, the impulse behind agrarian legislation was the establishment of an equal distribution of property and the abandonment of *ius*. As a result, attitudes toward the agrarian movement prove to be a valuable indicator of broader ideological allegiances.

III

It is, accordingly, unsurprising that among the neo-Roman authors of the *quattrocento* in Italy, the Ciceronian attitude toward the Gracchi and their laws went more or less unchallenged.[60] These thinkers fully embraced the Roman theory of justice and its attendant reverence for private property; indeed all of the major figures whom Hans Baron dubbed "civic humanists" listed public and private wealth among the chief *desiderata* of a flourishing republic.[61] The prevailing Ciceronian view of the Roman agrarian laws was so deeply ingrained in Italian Renaissance culture that relatively few references to Spurius Cassius or the Gracchi find their way into the political literature of the time – there was simply nothing to discuss.[62] When the

---

[59] Alfred Heuss notes that humanists tended to understand the Roman agrarian movement as "a classical model of equality" (*einem klassischen Gleichheitsmodell*) along the lines of those recommended by Greek *Staatsphilosophie*, in particular the writings of Plato and Aristotle. He might have added that Plutarch provided the classic statement of this position – his works encouraged readers to see Rome through Greek eyes. See Alfred Heuss, *Barthold Georg Niebuhrs wissenschaftliche Anfänge: Untersuchungen und Mitteilungen über die Kopenhagener Manuscripte und zur europäische Tradition der lex agraria (loi agraire)* (Göttingen: Vandenhoeck & Ruprecht, 1981), p. 216.

[60] This is presumably the point that Heuss is trying to make when he writes as follows: "Für den Humanisten besteht da das gewichtige Präjudiz, daß die römische Tradition im allgemeinen negativ urteilt und sie als ein Element der inneren Auflösung betrachet" (ibid., p. 245). But Heuss neglects to distinguish this "Roman tradition" from its counterpart (the account of the Gracchan reforms found in the Greek historians), or to distinguish the Italian humanists of the *quattrocento* from subsequent generations of "humanists" who endorsed that second narrative. Nor does he examine the ideologies behind these respective positions.

[61] On this, see Mark Jurdjevic, "Virtue, Commerce, and the Enduring Florentine Moment: Reintegrating Italy into the Atlantic Republican Debate" in *Journal of the History of Ideas* 62 (2001), 721–43. This is not, of course, to say that elements of the Greek account were wholly absent from *quattrocento* political theory. To take one example, Giovanni Pontano's *De obedientia* (*c.* 1470) contains a strong repudiation of the *opinio vulgi*, and of the pursuit of *honores*, *magistratus*, and *imperia* (in short, the *vita activa* as understood by Roman sources). But this text also includes a comprehensive defense of the Roman theory of justice: "Restat nunc dicendum de iustitia hac, quae pars est eius. Cuius cum proprium sit, cuique quod suum reddere, declaratur nobis, eius officia ad alios potissimum pertinere, ipsamque in commune niti, ac late ad plurimorum res conferre" (Pontano, *Opera omnia soluta oratione composita*, vol. 1 [Venice, 1518], p. 13).

[62] This was due in large part to the comparative scarcity of editions of Greek historians in the first century of printing. As Peter Burke has shown in an important article, even the least popular Roman historian of the period 1450–99 (Florus) was more ubiquitous than the most popular Greek

Gracchi were mentioned at all, it was generally in the spirit of Boccaccio's characterization in the preface to *De mulieribus claris* (1362). Alerting the reader that he intends to discuss several women who were famous but wicked, Boccaccio defends this decision by remarking that he has often read accounts of famous men which included even "the treacherous Iugurtha" and "the most seditious Gracchi" (*seditiosissimos Graccos*).[63] Accordingly, in the *De optimo cive* (composed between 1457 and 1461), Bartolomeo Sacchi (better known as Platina) classes the Gracchi with Saturninus, Drusus, and Spurius Melius, all rabble-rousers "whose entire lives were based on vain display."[64] Writing later in the *Dialogus de falso et vero bono*, Platina compares the schemes of the Gracchi to the "savageness, wantonness, and avarice" of Rome's other famous traitors, even going so far as to liken the agrarian laws to the rape of Virginia by Appius Claudius.[65] Likewise, Francesco Patrizi of Siena, writing in the 1460s in his *De institutione, statu, ac regimine reipublicae*, observes that, while the Gracchi were sons of a venerable father, they themselves "turned out to be the most factious and seditious men" (*turbulentissimi, & seditiosissimi*).[66] "One of them," he continues, "was overcome by Scipio Nasica in the Capitol for the health of the republic, and the other was forced to take his own life."[67] Poggio Bracciolini follows suit in

historian (Plutarch). While Sallust's *Catiline* appeared in forty-six editions, Valerius in twenty-nine, and Livy in twenty-three, Plutarch appeared in only eight. The period 1550–99, however, saw the rise of interest in Plutarch, with the number of editions rising to twenty-seven (Livy appeared in forty-five editions during the same period). See Peter Burke, "A Survey of the Popularity of Ancient Historians, 1450–1700" in *History and Theory* 5 (1966), 135–52. One might add that, while Pier Candido Decembrio prepared a Latin translation of Appian in the late 1450s, the *editio princeps* did not appear until 1551 (on Decembrio's Appian, see Massimo Zaggia, "La traduzione latina da Appiano di Pier Candido Decembrio: per la storia della tradizione" in *Studi Medievali* 34 [1993], 193–243). Likewise, the *editio princeps* of Dionysius appeared in 1546, although one Latin translation was published by Lapus Biragus at Treviso in 1480 (See John Edwin Sandys, *A History of Classical Scholarship*, vol. II [Cambridge University Press, 1908], pp. 103–5).

[63] Giovanni Boccaccio, *De mulieribus claris*. ed. and trans. Virginia Brown. I Tatti Renaissance Library (Harvard University Press, 2001), p. 10.

[64] Platina, *De optimo cive*, Book I, in *B. Platinae cremonensis de vita & moribus summarum pontificum historia . . . eiusdem de optimo cive* (Cologne, 1529). "Testes sunt autem Saturninus tribunus plebis, Sp. Melius, Gracchi duo, M. Drusus, quorum vita tota in ostentatione fundata erat."

[65] Ibid. *De falso et vero bono*, Book II. "Nam ut malo contagione quadam malos fieri dicimus, sic bono meliores effici necesse est. Verum tantum abest ut bonos magistratus faciant, ut etiam plerosque ad supremam saevitiam, libidinem & avaritiam perduxerint, ut de Appio illo decemviro, qui Virginiam Virginii filiam ob magistratum & potentiam stuprare est ausus. Quid vero egerint duo Gracchi, quid Saturninus, quid Spurius Melius, quid Clodius, quid plerique alii apud Romanos in magistratibus constutiti, ex rebus eorum gestis facillime deprehendimus."

[66] Francesco Patrizi [of Siena], *Francisci Patricii Senensis, pontificis Caietani, de institutione reipublicae libri IX. Ad senatum populumque Senesem scripti* (Strasbourg, 1594), p. 36. "Titus Grachus pater, summae probitatis vir extitit . . . hic tamen filios habuit Tiberium & Caium Grachos, qui turbulentisimi, & seditiosissimi extiterunt."

[67] Ibid. "Et alter in Capitolio ob Reip. salutem a Scipione Nasica oppressus est, alter ad voluntariam mortem compulsus."

the *In laudem reipublicae Venetorum* (1459), where he includes the agrarian laws in the long catalogue of *tumulti* with which he reproaches the Roman plebs. He derides "the quarrels and feuds, the uprisings of a fickle populace, the great and frequent struggles between the fatherland and the mob" which characterized life in the Roman republic.[68] He mentions the "theft and plunder, proscription of citizens and fine men driven into exile" and particularly attacks "the Secession of the Plebs, the willfulness of the decemvirs, the exiles of Coriolanus and Camillus" – all instances of popular folly to which the great serenity of the Venetian *governo stretto* is favorably compared.[69] For Poggio, in short, the agrarian laws were simply part of a general pattern of Roman popular "plunder."

In the early sixteenth century, however, the Florentine circle connected to the *Orti Oricellari* developed a significantly different attitude toward property, and ultimately initiated a reappraisal of the agrarian laws. In August 1512, Francesco Guicciardini penned a short, unpublished treatise generally known as the *Discorso di Logrogno* (or sometimes *Del modo di ordinare il governo popolare*), in which he outlined how he would reform the Florentine republic. In that text, he argues passionately for the creation of a Florentine senate – reminiscent of the Venetian *Consiglio di Pregati* – in order to secure an end to the popular *tumulti* which had plagued Florence, and to institute the rule of the wise. At the end of his essay he includes a remarkable coda. He insists that all the constitutional alterations he has endorsed would greatly strengthen Florentine civic life, but concludes that "in order for it to be raised to a higher level, we should need to remedy the fundamental causes of our over-refined sensibilities and weak spirits . . .":[70] "It would be necessary to eliminate the excessive regard and esteem for wealth, because

[68] Poggio Bracciolini, *Opera omnia*, ed. Riccardo Fubini, vol. II (Turin: Bottega D'Erasmo, 1966), p. 928. "quantae dissensiones, discidia, seditiones in mobili populo viguerunt, quot quantaque patriae et plebis certamina sunt excitata . . ." The English text is taken from Martin Davies's translation in *Cambridge Translations of Renaissance Philosophical Texts*, ed. Jill Kraye, vol. II (Cambridge University Press, 1997), p. 138.

[69] Ibid. "furta, rapinae, proscriptiones civium, optimorum virorum exilia . . . plebis secessio, decemvirum libido, Coriolani Camillique exilia . . ."

[70] *Opere inedite di Francesco Guicciardini*, ed. Piero and Luigi Guicciardini, vol. II (Florence, 1858), p. 311. "Perché a volerla condurre in maggiore grado, bisognerebbe venire alla radice delle delicatezze e mollizie delli animi nostri, che fanno li uomini effemminati e danno causa a infiniti mali; bisognerebbe tagliare il tanto pregio, la tanta riputazione in che sono le ricchezze, lo appetito immoderato delle quali leva il desiderio della vera gloria, aliena li animi dal cercare le virtù, e li introduce in mille usurpazioni e in mille disonestà." English text is taken from Russell Price's translation in *Cambridge Translations of Renaissance Philosophical Texts*, ed. Jill Kraye, vol. II (Cambridge University Press, 1997), p. 230.

the craving for riches erodes the desire for true glory, prevents the cultivation of the virtues and results in countless seizures of what belongs to others, as well as many other dishonourable actions." The reference to "seizures of what belongs to others" (*usurpazioni*) reveals that we are still firmly within the Roman tradition, as does the basic argument that the desire for wealth stifles the quest for "true glory" (*vera gloria*), the proper goal of any state. But what Guicciardini goes on to say would have been unimaginable coming from Bruni or Poggio.[71] He notes that "there are, perhaps, some remedies that could alleviate these evils somewhat," but argues that the *malattia* is so deeply rooted in the common culture that "Lycurgus' knife would be needed" in order to solve the problem (*bisognerebbe a tagliarla il coltello di Licurgo*): "In one day he [Lycurgus] eradicated from Sparta all wealth and sumptuousness; he put together all the property of all the inhabitants, then divided it equally among them; he prohibited the use of money and all the activities for which wealth is sought: sumptuous display, banquets, many servants, luxurious clothes and fine houses."[72] This was "certainly a most remarkable achievement, bringing about in one day in his city such moderation in living and such zeal for virtue and such low esteem for wealth, as well as the many fine and glorious activities he made to flourish in it."[73]

Guicciardini's deep internalization of key aspects of the Greek story is striking here, especially his insistence that equality of property is necessary to make virtue the coin of the realm (J. G. A. Pocock is quite correct to notice the Platonism of this claim).[74] Nonetheless, writes Guicciardini, although "we can marvel at and praise such a remarkable achievement . . . we are not

---

[71] Quentin Skinner makes this observation in *The Foundations of Modern Political Thought*, vol. 1: *The Renaissance* (Cambridge University Press, 1978), p. 170.

[72] Kraye, *Cambridge Translations*, p. 231. "il quale estirpò in uno di da Lacedemone tutte le ricchezze e suntuosità accumulando insieme le facultà di tutti, dividendole di poi per equali parti, vietando i danari, levando tutti li usi perché le ricchezze si desiderano, di suntuosità di conviti, di copia di servi, di bellezze di veste e masserizie" (*Opere inedite*, p. 312).

[73] *Opere inedite*, p. 312 "cosa certo mirabile, in quanta continenza, e in quanto ardore di virtù e poca estimazione della roba conducessi in uno giorno la città sua, e di quanti belli e gloriosi esercizi la empiessi."

[74] J. G. A. Pocock, *The Machiavellian Moment: Florentine Political Thought and the Atlantic Republican Tradition* (Princeton University Press, 1975), p. 123. It is, thus, particularly surprising that Athanasios Moulakis takes the *Discorso* as an expression of a new, post-classical preference for a "realist constitution" which simply seeks "to assure the security of persons and property" and gives up on classical virtue. Indeed, Moulakis does not refer to the final section of the treatise. See Athanasios Moulakis, "Civic Humanism, Realist Constitutionalism, and Francesco Guicciardini's *Discorso di Logrogno*" in *Renaissance Civic Humanism: Reappraisals and Reflections*, ed. James Hankins (Cambridge University Press, 2000), pp. 200–22.

allowed to hope for it, or even to desire it."[75] Accordingly, he proposes
several more moderate measures:

> I certainly believe that making our city well-armed, and thus creating the chance
> for Florence to achieve glorious victories, giving public office to men of good
> reputation and conduct, making it easy to punish the crimes of anyone who
> follows evil paths: all these measures together would result in the rich being less
> esteemed than they are today.[76]

This passage represents a striking modification of the Greek view. Recall
that the Greek account of property is profoundly deterministic: if there are
extremely wealthy citizens in a given state, those citizens will necessarily
become corrupted by their wealth and will no longer defer to the rule of
the best men. In other words, disproportionate wealth and poverty lead to
a societal preference for wealth over virtue. For Guicciardini the terms of
the argument are reversed. He suggests that the societal practice of reward-
ing wealth over virtue (and placing the wealthy above the law) secures an
undue esteem for the rich and, in consequence, creates a cultural obsession
with money-making. Accordingly, Guicciardini believes that if virtue, not
wealth, is rewarded by the state, then public enthusiasm for the acquisition
of large fortunes will be abated (i.e. it is the glorification of wealth which
produces large fortunes, not the other way around). His view, therefore,
provides a non-coercive means of rectifying inequalities – one that does not
conflict with his principle of justice.

None of this is to say that Guicciardini recommends no measures which
problematize his relationship with the neo-Roman tradition. For example,
in order to topple wealth from its place at the apex of social goods, he
proposes restricting the right of citizens to wear "sumptuous clothes and
jewelry, which make the differences between rich and poor people so obvious and spur men on to seek wealth."[77] He also proposes reducing dowries
to "moderate proportions" so as to encourage "the maintenance of equality between relatives and noble families" and "because this would greatly

---

[75] "A noi è rimasto il poterci maravigliare ed esclamare di cosa tanto notabile, ma di ridurla in atto
non ci è lecito non che sperarlo, appena desiderarlo" (*Opere inedite*, p. 313). I have altered Price's
translation here; he renders "lecito" as "possible," which fails to capture the normative thrust of the
word.

[76] Ibid. "Credo che dandosi la città alle arme, ed essendo aperta la via di diventare glorioso con quelle,
distribuendosi i magistrati con riguardo della buona fama e portamenti delli uomini, sendo facile il
punire i delitti di chi errassi, tutte queste cose insieme farieno i ricchi essere in meno estimazione
che non sono oggi."

[77] Ibid. "di limitare e moderare quanto fossi possibile li ornamenti e suntuosità del vestine, le quali
fanno apparire la differenza dal povero al ricco i sono causa di infiammare li uomini al desiderio
delle ricchezze."

benefit men who are worthy but poor, who find it much harder to marry off their daughters than men who are rich and unscrupulous."[78] But ultimately, while he goes considerably further than his Florentine predecessors, he is still committed to a Roman theory of justice (a commitment which he amplifies in the 1524 *Dialogo del reggimento di Firenze*[79]), and concludes that the "knife of Lycurgus" is neither possible nor desirable for contemporary republics. As a result, nothing in his account calls for a reconsideration of the agrarian laws. It would be a second Florentine, writing a discourse on the first ten books of Livy's *Ab urbe condita*, who would carry out that reevaluation.

IV

Recent scholarship on Niccolò Machiavelli has stressed his continuing allegiance to a broadly Roman set of moral and political principles. Quentin Skinner in particular has shown that, despite Machiavelli's revolutionary attack on the cherished Roman ideal of *concordia*, the author of *Il Principe* and the *Discorsi* remained in many ways a firmly neo-Roman writer, convinced that the chief aim of the state was the pursuit of glory, and that *virtù* was the quality which allowed the state to reach this goal.[80] As Machiavelli puts it in Book v of the *Istorie Fiorentine*, "from order comes *virtù*, and from this comes glory and good fortune."[81] That for him remains the central formula. Yet, for present purposes, an essential element of Machiavelli's thought emerges from his response to a tension, if not an incoherence, within the Roman view itself. Although thus far I have focused primarily on the Greek anxiety about wealth, ancient Roman writers were almost equally concerned about this phenomenon and its social consequences. Beginning with Sallust's *Bellum Catilinae*, and continuing through the writings of Livy, Horace, and the later satirists, Roman authors expressed their fear that the influx of wealth and luxury into the Roman state would spawn idleness, sloth, femininity, and the outright abandonment of the civic enterprise (although, unlike their Greek counterparts, they did not

[78] Ibid. "e in ultimo perché si farebbe uno grande beneficio alli uomini virtuosi e poveri, i quali non hanno più difficultà di maritare le loro figliuole, che non hanno i ricchi viziosi."

[79] Guicciardini, *Dialogue on the Government of Florence*, ed. Alison Brown (Cambridge University Press, 1994), pp. 49, 52, 85.

[80] Quentin Skinner, "Machiavelli's *Discorsi* and the Pre-Humanist Origins of Republican Ideas" in *Machiavelli and Republicanism*, ed. Gisela Bock, Quentin Skinner, and Maurizio Viroli. Ideas in Context (Cambridge University Press, 1990), pp. 121–41.

[81] Machiavelli, *Opere*, ed. Mario Bonfantini (Milan: Riccardo Ricciardi, 1963), p. 773. "dall'ordine virtù, da questa gloria e bona fortuna."

focus their attention on the effects of *differentials* in wealth).[82] Roman political theory had at its heart a conviction that only a disciplined, rugged, moderate people were capable of republican government. But, as we have seen, this same Roman view was characterized by a particular theory of justice which made any coercive attempt to restrict or redistribute wealth unacceptable. Society itself, Cicero argues in the *De officiis*, was primarily constituted to protect private property, and measures such as the agrarian laws make a mockery of that trust. They are simply "unjust."

Thus, Florentine writers of the *cinquecento*, distressed over the civic implications of Medici ascendance, received a decidedly muddled message from their Roman sources: the effects of disproportionate wealth would doom the republic, but there was nothing the republic could legitimately do about it. For Guicciardini and the other writers who remained solidly within the Roman tradition, the "knife of Lycurgus" was simply not an option. Machiavelli directs his attentions to precisely this impasse. His solution is to jettison the Roman theory of justice. If civic glory is truly the highest goal of the state, and *virtù* is simply what allows the state to reach that goal, then, for Machiavelli, justice drops out of the equation. Untethered from the principle of *cuique tribuere ius suum*, he is able to embrace the knife of Lycurgus to solve the problem of wealth – and he begins with the agrarian laws.

Machiavelli first broaches the subject in the thirty-seventh chapter of his first discourse. Initially, his comments appear to represent a ringing endorsement of the Ciceronian view. The chapter is entitled "What scandals the agrarian law gave birth to in Rome" (*Quali scandoli partorì in Roma la legge agraria*), offering a none-too-subtle hint as to Machiavelli's overall attitude. He begins by stating two central psychological assumptions of his theory: first, people are restless, no matter how well off they may be, and, relatedly, nature dictates that human beings want everything, and so are never satisfied. These facts of life combine to subject men to the wiles of fortune, causing them to agitate against their neighbors and risk war. From this sort of wrangling between the senate and the people of Rome, Machiavelli claims, "arose the disease [*il morbo*] that gave birth to the contention over the Agrarian law, which in the end was the cause of the destruction of the republic" (*che infine fu causa della distruzione della Republica*).[83] Machiavelli's choice of words here is extremely significant. He

---

[82] See, for example, Sallust, *Bel. Cat.* XI.4–7, XII.1–2; Horace, *Satirae* I.1, II.3; Juvenal, *Satirae* VI.293.

[83] Quotations from the *Discorsi* are taken from Machiavelli, *Discorsi sopra la prima deca di Tito Livio*, ed. Giorgio Inglese (Milan: Rizzoli, 1984). English translations are based substantially on the text

identifies the agrarian laws as the result of a *morbo* just as Cicero had called them a *pestis*. He also reiterates the standard Ciceronian argument that these laws led directly to the fall of the republic, an opinion which he forcefully reiterates in chapter twenty-four of the third discourse. The agrarian law, he explains, had two provisions: it "set forth that no citizen could possess more than so many *jugera* of land" and "that fields taken from enemies should be divided among the Roman people."[84] Machiavelli maintains that these two statutes so inflamed the hatred between senate and people that Rome was led to civil war and, finally, to Caesar's tyranny – ensuring that "never again was that city free" (*mai fu poi libera quella città*).[85]

It would seem at first glance, therefore, that Machiavelli unhesitatingly accepts the Roman verdict on the agrarian laws. Yet a brief look at a central passage in this chapter reveals that this is not the case. The agrarian laws did indeed provoke unprecedented turmoil, but for a particular reason:

Because well-ordered republics have to keep the public rich and their citizens poor, it must be that in the city of Rome there was a defect in this law. Either it was not made at the beginning so that it did not have to be treated again every day; or they delayed so much in making it because looking back might be scandalous; or if it was well ordered at first, it had been corrupted later by use. So whatever the case may have been, one never spoke of this law in Rome without turning the city upside down. (1.37)[86]

Machiavelli is clear, as he puts it later in the chapter, that the agrarian laws were propounded to address a real "disorder": the fact that Rome had failed to keep itself rich and its citizens poor. In Machiavelli's view, the overall intention of the Gracchan laws was salutary. He notes that "the motors of this disorder were the Gracchi, whose intention one should praise more than their prudence."[87] The difficulty was that the "disorder" in question

---

found in Machiavelli, *Discourses on Livy*, ed. and trans. Harvey C. Mansfield and Nathan Tarcov (University of Chicago Press, 1996). I have, however, modified the translations for the sake of clarity on occasion. *Discorsi*, p. 140. "Da questo nacque il morbo che partorì la contenzione della legge agraria, che infine fu causa della distruzione della Republica."

[84] Ibid. "Aveva questa legge due capi principali. Per l'uno si disponeva che non si potesse possedere per alcuno cittadino più che tanti iugeri di terra; per l'altro che i campi di che si privavano i nimici si dividessono intra il popolo romano."

[85] Ibid., p. 142.

[86] *Discorsi*, p. 140. "E perché le republiche bene ordinate hanno a tenere ricco il publico e gli loro cittadini poveri, convenne che fusse nella città di Roma difetto in questa legge; la quale o non fusse fatta nel principio in modo che la non si avesse ogni dì a ritrattare, o che si differisse tanto in farla che fosse scandaloso il riguardarsi indietro, o, sendo ordinata bene da prima, era stata poi dall'uso corrotta: talché, in qualunque modo si fusse, mai non si parlò di questa legge in Roma che quella città non andasse sottosopra."

[87] *Discorsi*, p. 142. "Del quale disordine furono motori i Gracchi, de' quali si debbe laudare più la intenzione che la prudenza."

had (for whatever reason) become so great and was of such long duration that any attempt to eliminate it would violate a central Machiavellian principle. As Machiavelli puts it in chapter thirty-three of the first discourse, "when an inconvenience that arises either in a republic or against a republic, caused by an intrinsic or extrinsic force, has become so great that it begins to bring fear to everyone, it is a much more secure policy to temporize [*temporeggiarsi*] with it than to attempt to extinguish it."[88] Machiavelli's great example of this principle is the case of Cosimo de' Medici. By the time the *grandi* of Florence became aware of the supereminent status that Cosimo had acquired in the city, any attempt to extinguish his power and influence had the paradoxical effect of augmenting them. Indeed, when the *grandi* expelled Cosimo from Florence, his party became so resentful that it promptly engineered his return and made him *principe della republica* (1.33). Rome faced the same sort of problem when it came to the distribution of *ager publicus*. Machiavelli writes of the agrarian laws that "to try to take away a disorder that has grown in a republic, and because of this to make a law that looks very far back, is an ill-considered policy."[89]

The dangerous flaw in the agrarian laws was that they were "backward-looking": they attempted to ameliorate a real evil, but one which had already passed beyond effective redress. Thus, Machiavelli's insistence that the agrarian laws caused the fall of the republic should by no means be taken as an uncomplicated endorsement of the Ciceronian verdict. Indeed, his view that republics should keep themselves rich and their citizens poor, repeated throughout the *Discorsi*, alerts us to a profoundly anti-Roman strain in his thought. Machiavelli was convinced that the accumulation of wealth produced "corruption" (*corruzione*) – the utter abandonment of the public good – and should actively be prevented by the state. He argues that wealth can produce this "corrupt" condition in several ways. First, as he suggests in the second discourse, a failure to keep citizens poor has the familiar effect of introducing luxuriousness into the state, a circumstance which distracts citizens from the quest for civic glory. Accordingly, Machiavelli worries in particular about the consequences for a non-corrupt state of conquering rich and exotic countries. He quotes Livy's remark that when the Romans conquered luxuriant Capua "with

---

[88] Ibid., p. 132. "quando uno inconveniente che surga o in una republica o contro una republica, causato da cagione intrinseca o estrinseca, è diventato tanto grande che e'cominci a fare paura a ciascuno, è molto più sicuro partito temporeggiarsi con quello che tentare di estinguerlo."

[89] Ibid., p. 142. "Perché a volere levar via uno disordine cresciuto in una republica, e per questo fare una legge che riguardi assai indietro, è partito male considerato."

its means for every pleasure," the experience "diverted the charmed spirits of the soldiers from the memory of their fatherland" (11.19).[90] Machiavelli also agrees with Juvenal that gratuitous spoils of war have the effect of granting the defeated nation a strange sort of victory: he records the satirist's observation that, as a result of its conquests, "thrift and other excellent virtues" abandoned the Roman republic, and that "gluttony and luxury have made their home and avenge a conquered world."[91] For Machiavelli, wealth and its attendant luxury were deeply hostile to the demands of the civic enterprise.

But there is a second and more significant sense in which wealth produces *corruzione* in Machiavelli's thought. This emerges out of his notion of "inequality" (*inequalità*) – an aspect of the Machiavellian system which has received a great deal of scholarly attention, but which has not, it seems to me, been properly related to the philosopher's view of wealth.[92] Indeed, scholars have been very hesitant to identify any substantial connection between Machiavellian "inequality" and inequalities in property. Pocock, for example, recognizes the central role of *inequalità* in Machiavelli's thought, but insists that his concept of inequality "connotes neither inequality of wealth nor inequality of political authority – there is no reason to suppose that Machiavelli objected to either."[93] Gisela Bock takes issue with Pocock, but ultimately concludes that "Machiavelli's 'equality' is not economic or social, but legal and political, meaning equality before the law and equal access to office; in the terms of the *Discorsi*, it is not 'equalità di sustanze'

---

[90] Ibid., p. 347 (quoted in Latin). "Iam tunc minime salubris militari disciplinae Capua, instrumento omnium voluptatum, delinitos militum animos avertit a memoria patriae." This passage provides a helpful reminder that Roman authors too identified wealth as a source of social decay; the key difference between the Greek and Roman traditions is that the Greeks possessed an understanding of "justice" which allowed them to take aggressive action to regulate and redistribute wealth.

[91] Ibid. "e in cambio di parsimonia e d'altre eccellentissime virtù, 'gula et luxuria incubuit, victumque ulciscitur orbem.' "

[92] This observation applies also to Felix Gilbert's analysis. Gilbert notices Machiavelli's hostility to wealth, and his antagonism to the Florentine aristocracy, but does not, I feel, identify Machiavelli's primary concern: that wealth will produce *inequalità* and raise the specter of *modi privati* (his closest approximation to this claim appears on p. 189). See Felix Gilbert, *Machiavelli and Guicciardini: Politics and History in Sixteenth-Century Florence* (Princeton University Press, 1965), esp. pp. 174–77. After writing the above, I was pleased to read Benedetto Fontana's most recent article, which makes several of the same points that I go on to make in the following pages (see Benedetto Fontana, "Sallust and the Politics of Machiavelli" in *History of Political Thought* 24 [2003], 86–108). I disagree, however, with his claim that Machiavelli's "critique of great wealth is not so much moral as political and social" (p. 105n); to the extent that disproportionate wealth prevents the republic from preserving *libertà* and acquiring *gloria*, Machiavelli's quarrel with it is intensely moral. Fontana also tries to trace Machiavelli's account of the agrarian laws to Sallust, while I feel that Cicero and Livy were much more important sources.

[93] Pocock, *Machiavellian Moment*, p. 209.

or 'della roba,' but 'equalità di grado' or 'de onori.'"[94] These explanations fail to acknowledge the central role Machiavelli assigns to wealth in the development of *inequalità*. Both authors are certainly correct in claiming that "inequality" for Machiavelli refers to the presence in the state of supereminent individuals (e.g. Cosimo de' Medici), but how on Machiavelli's account do such individuals become supereminent, and what is it about their supereminence that dooms the republic? The answers to these questions make sense of Machiavelli's passionate insistence on "keeping the citizens poor," and must be sought by investigating the place of *inequalità* in his broader republican theory.

In the second chapter of the first discourse Machiavelli offers a powerful defense of republican government, drawing heavily upon the theory of the "cycle of regimes" (ἀνακύκλωσις) popularized by Polybius. The three good regimes – monarchy, aristocracy, polity – tend to decay into their corrupt analogues (tyranny, oligarchy, democracy), yielding an endless cycle of constitutional transformation. Indeed, Machiavelli argues that only the brief lifespan of a given state prevents it from experiencing the cycle in full:

> It is while revolving in this cycle that all republics are governed and govern themselves. But rarely do they return to the same governments, for almost no republic can have so long a life as to be able to pass many times through these changes and remain upon its feet. But indeed it happens that in its travails, a republic always lacking in counsel and forces becomes subject to a neighboring state that is ordered better than it; assuming this were not so, however, a republic would be capable of revolving for an infinite time in these governments. (1.2)[95]

These pure forms of government, then, are inherently unstable and lead ultimately to the subjugation of the state by a foreign power. Machiavelli's solution, like that of his predecessors, is the mixed constitution. He praises those lawgivers who "having recognized this defect [i.e. the flimsiness of pure regimes], avoiding each of these modes by itself, chose one that shared in all, judging it firmer and more stable; for the one guards the other, since in one and the same city are the principality, the aristocrats, and

---

[94] Gisela Bock, "Civil Discord in Machiavelli's *Istorie Fiorentine*" in *Machiavelli and Republicanism*, ed. Bock, Skinner, and Viroli, p. 189.

[95] *Discorsi*, p. 67. "E questo è il cerchio nel quale girando tutte le repubbliche si sono governate e si governano: ma rade volte ritornano ne' governi medesimi, perché quasi nessuna repubblica può essere di tanta vita che possa passare molte volte per queste mutazioni e rimanere in piede. Ma bene interviene che nel travagliare una repubblica, mancandole sempre consiglio e forze, diventa suddita d'uno stato propinquo che sia meglio ordinato di lei; ma posto che questo non fusse, sarebbe atta una repubblica a rigirarsi infinito tempo in questi governi."

the popular government."⁹⁶ This mixed arrangement removes the state (at least temporarily) from the fluctuations of the Polybian cycle, maintaining a dynamic balance among elements. Moreover, as Machiavelli would argue at length in the second discourse, mixed republics surpass all other regimes in their ability to acquire glory and greatness (*grandezza*) (II.2), which he, like Guicciardini, identifies as the true goal of civic association.

The signal example of this republican achievement, according to Machiavelli, is the Roman constitution. After the expulsion of the Tarquins, Rome was governed by consuls and the senate, representing the monarchical and aristocratic elements of the mixed constitution. The *tumulti* between the patricians and the plebs secured the creation of the tribunal power, thus adding the final, democratic ingredient. Machiavelli ends chapter two predictably enough by observing that, once constituted on these lines, Rome "made a perfect republic" (*una republica perfetta*). But he then adds the unexpected claim that Rome achieved this state of perfection "through the disunion of the plebs and the senate."⁹⁷ Machiavelli justifies this novel hypothesis in chapter four by introducing his theory of the *umori*. Those who revile the Roman *tumulti*, he argues, "do not consider that in every republic are two diverse humors, that of the people and that of the great, and that all laws in favor of freedom arise from their disunion" (I.4).⁹⁸ Machiavelli foreshadows this passage in the ninth chapter of *Il Principe*: "For in every city are found two diverse humors, and this arises from the fact that the people desire not to be commanded or oppressed by the great, while the great desire to command and oppress the people."⁹⁹ In each city, according to Machiavelli, we find those who wish to rule and those who simply wish not to be ruled; these wishes correspond to indelible temperaments which the state must accommodate and balance against each other.

---

⁹⁶ Ibid. "Talché avendo quelli che prudentemente ordinano leggi conosciuto questo difetto, fuggendo ciascuno di questi modi per se stesso, ne elessero uno che participasse di tutti, giudicandolo più fermo e più stabile, perché l'uno guarda l'altro, sendo in una medesima città il Principato, gli Ottimati e il Governo Popolare."

⁹⁷ *Discorsi*, p. 69. "per la disunione della Plebe e del Senato."

⁹⁸ Ibid., p. 71. "Io dico che coloro che dannano i tumulti intra i Nobili e la Plebe mi pare . . . che e' non considerino come e' sono in ogni republica due umori diversi, quello del popolo e quello de' grandi; e come tutte le leggi che si fanno in favore della libertà, nascano dalla disunione loro."

⁹⁹ Italian texts from the *Istorie Fiorentine* and *Il Principe* are taken from Machiavelli, *Opere*, ed. Mario Bonfantini (Milan: Riccardo Ricciardi, 1963). English translations from the *Istorie Fiorentine* are based on the text found in Machiavelli, *Florentine Histories*, ed. and trans. Laura F. Banfield and Harvey C. Mansfield, Jr. (Princeton University Press, 1988). This passage is found in *Opere*, p. 32. "Perché in ogni città si truovano questi dua umori diversi; e nasce da questo, che il populo desidera non essere comandato né oppresso da' grandi, e li grandi desiderano comandare e opprimere il populo." See also *Istorie Fiorentine* III.1 (*Opere*, p. 680). Translations from *Il Principe* and the *Discursus* are my own.

On the one hand, Machiavelli makes clear in his *Discursus florentinarum rerum post mortem iunioris Laurentii Medices* (*c.* 1520) that those men of great dynamism who wish to rule must be satisfied in order for the state to survive:

And although in Florence there is equality . . . nonetheless there are in the state some men who are of elevated souls, and it seems that they merit being given precedence over others, and it is necessary to order the republic to satisfy these men; nor for any other reason did the previous state come to ruin than because it did not satisfy this humor.[100]

Nonetheless, these *grandi* must be counterbalanced by the *popolo* – those who simply wish to ward off *servitù* – if the state is to avoid tumbling back into the Polybian cycle. Accordingly, Machiavelli praises the hectic confrontations between the patricians and plebs in Rome as the source of Roman greatness. Men have different temperaments, and their disunion preserves the equilibrium of the mixed state.

Machiavelli sharply contrasts this "productive disunion" between *umori* to another sort of division which is substantially less salutary – one intimately connected to what Machiavelli calls *inequalità*. He encapsulates the difference between the two sorts of disunion in a passage from Book VII of the *Istorie Fiorentine*. He begins this discussion by restating his belief that "those who hope that a republic can be unified are very much deceived in this hope,"[101] and continues by making a central distinction:

It is true that some divisions are harmful to republics and some are helpful. Those are harmful that are accompanied by sects and partisans; those are helpful that are maintained without sects and partisans. Thus, since a founder of a republic cannot provide that there be no enmities in it, he has to provide at least that there be no sects. (VII.1)[102]

On Machiavelli's view, the formation of parties or sects signals *corruzione*, an abandonment of the public good brought about by the preparedness

---

[100] Machiavelli, *Il Principe e altri scritti minori*, ed. Michele Scherillo (Milan: Ulrico Hoepli, 1916), p. 263. "E benchè in Firenze sia quella egualità . . . nondimeno sono in quella alcuni che sono di animo elevato, e pare loro meritare di precedere agli altri, a' quali è necessario nell'ordinare la repubblica satisfare; nè per altra cagione rovinò lo Stato passato, che per non si essere a tale umore satisfatto."

[101] *Opere*, p. 875 [p. 276]. "coloro che sperano che una republica possa essere unita, assai di questa speranza s'ignannono."

[102] Ibid. "Vera cosa è che alcune divisioni nuocono alle republiche e alcune giovono. Quelle nuocono che sono dalle sètte e da partigiani accompagnate, quelle giovono che sanza sètte e sanza partigiani si mantengono. Non potendo adunque provedere uno fondatore di una republica che non sieno inimicizie in quella, ha a provedere almeno che non vi sieno sètte."

of a people to seek private, rather than public means of advancement and protection. Sects can arise for several different reasons in Machiavellian politics; very early in the first discourse (1.7) we are told, for example, that the two *umori* require regular, structured opportunities to "vent" (*sfogarsi*) their frustration and anger over particular issues (his chief example of such a structured opportunity is the power of one Roman citizen to accuse another). If these institutionalized means of conveying discontent are absent from the state, then passions will build to the point where "extraordinary means" are required to express them. These extraordinary means – most often extreme violence and private vendetta – cause such fear that citizens band together in sects and put their trust in powerful leaders (this is precisely what transpired in the case of the agrarian laws [1.37]). The result is that citizens no longer seek public solutions to their problems; they rely entirely on their party.

But, for Machiavelli, by far the most prominent inducement to faction is the presence in the state of men who have acquired "reputation" (*riputazione*) through "private means" (*modi privati*). Machiavelli explains what he means by this phrase in an important passage in the third discourse:

So one ought to examine the means by which citizens get reputation, which are in effect two: either public or private. The public means are when one individual by counseling well, by working better in the common benefit, acquires reputation. One ought to open to citizens the way to this honor and to put up rewards both for counsel and for works so that they have to be honored and satisfied with them. If these reputations, gained by these ways, are clear and simple, they will never be dangerous; but when they are gained by private means, which is the other way cited before, they are very dangerous and altogether hurtful. The private ways are doing benefit to this and to that other private individual – by lending him money, marrying his daughters for him, defending him from the magistrates, and doing for him similar private favors that make men partisans to oneself and give spirit to whoever is favored to be able to corrupt the public and to breach the laws. (III.28)[103]

---

[103] *Discorsi*, p. 536. "E però si debbe esaminare i modi con i quali e'pigliano riputazione, che sono in effeto due: o publici o privati. I modi publici sono quando uno, consigliando bene, operando meglio in beneficio comune, acquista riputazione. A questo onore si debba aprire la via ai cittadini, e preporre premii e ai consigli e alle opere, talché se ne abbiano a onorare e sodisfare. E quando queste riputazioni prese per queste vie siano stiette e semplici, non saranno mai pericolose; ma quando le sono prese per vie private, che è l'altro modo preallegato, sono pericolosissime e in tutto nocive. Le vie private sono faccendo beneficio a questo e a quello altro privato, col prestargli danari, maritargli le figliuole, difenderlo dai magistrati e faccendogli simili privati favori, i quali si fanno gli uomini partigiani e danno animo, a chi è così favorito, di potere corrompere il publico e sforzare le leggi."

Machiavelli took this question of *modi privati* so seriously that he offered a yet more expansive, powerful statement of his position in the *Istorie Fiorentine*:

> And therefore it is to be known that citizens in cities acquire reputation in two ways: either by public means or by private means. One acquires it publicly by winning a battle, acquiring a town, carrying out a mission with care and prudence, advising the republic wisely and prosperously. One acquires it by private means by benefiting this or that citizen, defending him from the magistrates, helping him with money, getting him unmerited honors, and ingratiating oneself with the plebs with games and public gifts. From this latter way of proceeding, sects and partisans arise, and the reputation thus earned offends as much as reputation helps when it is not mixed with sects, because that reputation is founded on a common good, not a private good. (VII.I)[104]

For Machiavelli, the presence in the state of men who have acquired reputation through private means constitutes "inequality" – a situation in which some men are dependent on other men, rather than on the state. In an uncorrupt republic (one free from inequality), the state is the sole patron and the undisputed source of benefits; in corrupt republics, individuals rely instead on the patronage of particular *grandi*, and no longer see their own good as bound up with the common good. The essential enabler in this corrupt system of individual patronage is wealth, which explains why keeping the state rich and the citizens poor is such a priority for Machiavelli.

This danger of private *riputazione* is encapsulated in Machiavelli's writings in the person of Cosimo de' Medici. In Book IV of the *Istorie Fiorentine* Machiavelli explains through the figure of Niccolò da Uzzano how Cosimo had acquired his supereminent stature in Florence through *modi privati*, and how difficult it became to attack these *modi* in public:

> The deeds of Cosimo that make us suspect him [of seeking princely power] are these: because he helps everyone with his money, and not only private individuals but the public, and not only Florentines but the condottieri; because he favors this or that citizen who has need of the magistrates; because by the good will that he has in the generality of people he pulls this or that friend to higher ranks of honor. Thus one would have to allege as the causes for driving him out that he is merciful,

---

[104] *Opere*, p. 875. "E però è da sapere come in due modi acquistono riputazione i cittadini nelle città: o per vie publiche o per modi privati. Publicamente si acquista vincendo una giornata, acquistando una terra, faccendo una legazione con sollecitudine e con prudenza, consigliando la republica saviamente e felicemente: per modi privati si acquista beneficando questo o quell'altro cittadino, defendendolo da' magistrati, suvvenendolo di danari, tirandolo immeritamente agli onori, e con giuochi e doni publici gratificandosi la plebe. Da questo modo di procedere nascono le sètte e i partigiani, e quanto questa reputazione così guadagnata offende, tanto quella giova quando ella non è con le sètte mescolata, perché la è fondata sopra un bene commune, non sopra un bene privato."

helpful, liberal, and loved by everyone. So tell me: what law is it that forbids or that blames and condemns in men mercy, liberality, and love? And although these are all means that send men flying to a princedom, nonetheless they are not believed to be so, nor are we adequate to the task of making them be so understood, because our ways have destroyed their faith in us, and the city, which is naturally partisan and, since it has always lived with parties, is corrupt, cannot give a hearing to such accusations. (IV.27)[105]

Cosimo has used his private wealth to acquire a partisan following. Moreover, his *modi privati* were difficult to stigmatize due to their overwhelmingly beneficent effects. The *grandi*, faced with no institutionalized way of "venting" against him, were shortly to embrace "extraordinary" – and futile – means to secure his exile. To be sure, Cosimo's "unequal" status was more than a matter of wealth: his overall *stato* must be understood as a function of raw power, widespread patronage, and popular sympathy. But Machiavelli makes clear that money is the great engine of private *riputazione*. As he puts it later in the *Istorie Fiorentine*, Cosimo "surpassed every other man of his times not only in authority and riches but also in liberality ... for there was no citizen who had any quality in that city to whom Cosimo had not lent a large sum of money" (VII.5).[106]

Throughout the *Discorsi* Machiavelli insists that an uncorrupt republic will simply not have citizens who are capable of such "liberality." The state will actively and coercively prevent this from happening. In the thirty-fourth chapter of the first discourse he writes that one who wishes to develop princely stature "must have many qualities that in a non-corrupt republic he can never have. For he needs to be very rich and to have very many adherents and partisans, which he cannot have where the laws are observed."[107] Machiavelli turns again to this issue in chapter fifty-five, where

---

[105] See also *Discorsi* 1.33 for the same episode. *Opere*, p. 761. "L'opere di Cosimo che ce lo fanno sospetto sono: perché gli serve de' suoi danari ciascuno e non solamente i privati ma il publico, e non solo i Fiorentini ma i condottieri; perché favorisce quello e quell'altro cittadino che ha bisogno de' magistrati; perché e' tira con la benivolenzia che gli ha nello universale questo e quell'altro suo amico a maggiori gradi di onori. Adunque converrebbe addurre le cagioni di cacciarlo, perché gli è piatoso, officioso, liberale e amato da ciascuno. Dimmi un poco: quale legge è quella che proibisca o che biasimi o danni negli uomini la pietà, la liberalità, lo amore? E benché sieno modi tutti che tirono gli uomini volando al principato, nondimeno e' non sono creduti così, né noi siamo sufficienti a dargli ad intendere, perché i modi nostri ci hanno tolta la fede, e la città che naturalmente è partigiana e, per essere sempre vivuta in parte, corrotta, non può prestare gli orecchi a simili accuse."

[106] Ibid., p. 880. "non solamente superò ogni altro de' tempi suoi di autorità e di ricchezze ma ancora di liberalità ... perché non era cittadino alcuno che avesse nella città alcuna qualità, a chi Cosimo grossa somma di danari non avesse prestata."

[107] *Discorsi*, p. 135. "conviene ch'egli abbia molte qualità le quali in una republica non corrotta non può mai avere: perché gli bisogna essere richissimo e avere assai aderenti e partigiani, i quali non può avere dove le leggi si osservano."

he observes that "those republics in which a political and uncorrupt way of life is maintained do not endure that any citizen of theirs either be or live in the usage of a gentleman; indeed, they maintain among themselves an even equality . . ." (1.55).[108] These *gentiluomini* occupy a special place in Machiavellian thought:

> I say that those are called gentlemen who live idly in abundance from the returns of their possessions without having any care either for cultivation or for other necessary trouble in living. Such are pernicious in every republic and in every province, but more pernicious are those who, beyond the aforesaid fortunes, command from a castle and have subjects to obey them. (11.55)[109]

Thus, Machiavelli lists two sorts of *gentiluomini*: those who are extremely rich and idle, and those who are extremely rich, idle, and in possession of castles and private armies. While the second category is yet more "pernicious" than the first, either breed will suffice to lead a republic straight into corruption, and thence back into the Polybian cycle.

Indeed, Machiavelli insists that anyone who wishes to establish princely power in a republic will meet with failure "unless he draws from that equality many of ambitious and unquiet spirit and makes them gentlemen in fact, and not in name, granting them castles and wealth and giving them favor in belongings and men" (1.55).[110] He explains this admonition in some detail in the 1520 *Discursus*. Observing once again that "in order to create a principality in Florence, where there is extremely great equality, it would be necessary to first institute inequality, and to make for yourself many nobles with castles and villas,"[111] Machiavelli argues that "a prince alone, stripped of nobles, cannot sustain the weight of the principality; because it is necessary that between him and the masses there should be a middle level which helps him to sustain that weight."[112] These *gentiluomini* who facilitate the state's return to the Polybian cycle are not simply rich men;

---

[108] Ibid., p. 175. "quelle republiche, dove si è mantenuto il vivere politico e incorrotto, non sopportono che alcuno loro cittadino né sia né viva a uso di gentiluomo: anzi mantengono intra loro una pari equalità."

[109] Ibid. "dico che gentiluomini sono chiamati quelli che oziosi vivono delle rendite delle loro possessioni abbondantemente, sanza avere cura alcuna o di coltivazione o di altra necessaria fatica a vivere. Questi tali sono perniziosi in ogni republica e in ogni provincia; ma più perniziosi sono quelli che oltre alle predette fortune comandano a castella, e hanno sudditi che ubbidiscono a loro."

[110] Ibid., p. 176. "se non trae di quella equalità molti d'animo ambizioso e inquieto, e quelli fa gentiluomini in fatto, e non in nome, donando loro castella e possessioni e dando loro favore di sustanze e di uomini."

[111] *Scritti minori*, p. 261. "a volere un principato in Firenze, dove è una grandissima egualità, sarebbe necessario ordinarvi prima la inegualità, e farvi assai nobili di castella e ville."

[112] Ibid., p. 262. "un principe solo, spogliato di nobiltà, non può sostenere il pondo del principato; però è necessario che infra lui e l'universale sia un mezzo che l'aiuti sostenerlo."

but enormous wealth is a necessary cause of their ascendance. It is their widespread private patronage which produces corruption and the end of civic greatness.

v

We see, then, that Machiavelli's approach to the agrarian laws derives from a comprehensive reassessment of the social and political effects of wealth and represents a substantial shift away from the standard Roman and neo-Roman approach. Although he agrees with the Romans that the agrarian laws precipitated the fall of the republic, Machiavelli's reasons for making that argument are idiosyncratic and are accompanied by a powerful conviction that the agrarian laws aimed at addressing a very real disorder in the Roman state: the rise of very rich men whose private patronage produced *inequalità, corruzione*, and, ultimately, a return to the Polybian cycle. All that having been said, Machiavelli's theory is clearly not an instance of the "Greek view" as I have described it. To begin with, as has been noted repeatedly, Machiavelli is not at all interested in "justice," so feels no compulsion to offer arguments for why the agrarian laws, though imprudent, may have been "just." Indeed, in this respect Machiavelli's account lacks the moral apparatus that would make real dialogue with the Roman or Greek traditions possible. His willingness to empty *virtù* of its conventional content and to endorse reprehensible actions for the sake of *grandezza* places him outside the debate. Take, for example, the question of the relationship between wealth and virtue. The Greeks had insisted that men who possessed disproportionate wealth would become corrupted, and that, as a result, the rule of the rich implied the rule of the unvirtuous. If, however, one man or a few men were supereminent in virtue, then the Greeks would insist that those individuals should rule on grounds of justice. Machiavelli, on the other hand, fully allows that great wealth and *virtù* might go together in the persons of the *grandi* (Cosimo is a perfect example),[113] and argues that even rule by a single man of unparalleled *virtù* (whom he calls, in terms which would have struck his predecessors as oxymoronic, "uno tiranno virtuoso")[114] is bad for the state – such an arrangement would send the republic back into the Polybian cycle and deprive it of *grandezza*. On Machiavelli's account, as we have seen, both *umori* (those who wish to rule and those

---

[113] See, for example, *Istorie* vi.6 (*Opere*, p. 831), where Cosimo is said to have earned the respect of the Florentine armies "con la virtù e con i meriti"; see also vii.5 (*Opere*, p. 882), where Machiavelli writes "E così la virtù e fortuna sua spense tutti i suoi nimici e gli amici esaltò."

[114] *Discorsi* ii.2 (p. 297).

who simply wish not to be ruled) must be incorporated into government and left to tame each other. The *virtuosi* (who are very different indeed from Cicero's *viri virtutis*) must not be left unchecked.[115]

Machiavelli's view is, thus, substantially different from the Greek account we have been following. Yet his theory offered a new and complex analysis of how wealth might undermine republican government, and also rejected the standard of justice which made "keeping the state rich and the citizens poor" morally impossible. This new attitude toward property necessitated a reassessment of the Roman agrarian laws, and guaranteed that those laws would become an issue of central importance for early-modern political theory. But Machiavelli's disciples in the seventeenth century would face a fairly predictable problem. Terrified as they were by Machiavelli's account of the corrosive effects of wealth, they were nonetheless simply unable to countenance a political theory unmoored from justice. The "knife of Lycurgus" could not be embraced simply because it would bring the state glory; it had to be rendered "just." The Roman view could not perform this alchemy. Only the Greek view could legitimize the knife. It is, therefore, unsurprising that Machiavelli's greatest English disciple, James Harrington, would make the marriage of Machiavelli and the Greek tradition his life's work.

---

[115] Machiavelli also embraces the same inverted view of the relationship between large fortunes and the esteem for wealth that we found in Guicciardini's *Discorso di Logrogno*. In the third discourse, he repeats his assertion that "the most useful thing that may be ordered in a free way of life is that the citizens be kept poor" (III.25.1), and adds that the poverty of Roman citizens in the first four centuries of the republic had a definite cause: "Nor can one believe that any greater order produced this effect other than seeing that the way to any rank whatever and to any honor whatever was not prevented for you because of property, and that one went to find virtue in whatever house it inhabited. That mode of life made riches less desirable" (III.25.1). For Machiavelli, as for Guicciardini, it was the undue regard for wealth which produced the drive for money-making and the acquisition of large fortunes, not (as the Greeks would have it) the other way around.

CHAPTER 3

James Harrington and the "balance of justice"

I

Ever since J. G. A. Pocock tried to place James Harrington's *The Commonwealth of Oceana* at the center of an "Atlantic republican tradition," controversy has swirled around this text to an unprecedented degree.[1] Recent scholars have wanted to see Harrington as a "republican," a "civic humanist," a Hobbesian, a "natural philosopher," an Aristotelian, and, most influentially, as a Machiavellian. Accordingly, *Oceana*'s argument has been said to turn on a defense of the citizen soldier, a search for effective civic religion, an application of Hobbesian "mechanism," an endorsement of widespread political participation, an embrace of Venetian serenity, or an enthusiasm for Roman liberty.[2] But Harrington himself announces the basic theme of *Oceana* in the epigraph on the title page – a passage which has gone almost completely unnoticed:

> Tantalus a labris sitiens fugientia captat
> Flumina: quid rides? mutato nomine, de te
> Fabula narratur.[3]

---

[1] J. G. A. Pocock, *The Machiavellian Moment: Florentine Political Thought and the Atlantic Republican Tradition* (Princeton University Press, 1975).

[2] For Harrington as a theorist of the citizen soldier, see J. G. A. Pocock, "Introduction" to *The Political Works of James Harrington* (Cambridge University Press, 1977). For Harrington and civil religion, see Mark Goldie, "The Civil Religion of James Harrington" in *The Languages of Political Theory in Early-Modern Europe*, ed. Anthony Pagden (Cambridge University Press, 1987). For Harrington as a Hobbesian, see Arihiro Fukuda, *Sovereignty and the Sword: Harrington, Hobbes, and Mixed Government in the English Civil Wars* (Oxford University Press, 1997); see also Jonathan Scott, "The Rapture of Motion: James Harrington's Republicanism" in *Political Discourse in Early Modern Britain*, ed. Nicholas Phillipson and Quentin Skinner (Cambridge University Press, 1993). For Harrington and Machiavelli (together with an ingenious account of Hobbes's role in Harrington's thought) see Felix Raab's classic *The English Face of Machiavelli: a Changing Interpretation 1500–1700* (London: Routledge, 1964), esp. chap. 6. For Harrington and the philo-Venetian tradition, see Pocock, *Machiavellian Moment*, esp. chap. 11. For Harrington and the neo-Romans, see Quentin Skinner, *Liberty Before Liberalism* (Cambridge University Press, 1998).

[3] Harrington, *Political Works*, p. 155.

Harrington introduces and encapsulates his treatise with the lines: "Thirsty Tantalus grasps at streams escaping from his lips. What are you laughing at? With the name changed, the story is told about you."

Scholars have rarely commented on this passage, except to point out that, for Harrington, the story of *Oceana* is actually told about England "with the name changed." This is certainly the case, but what exactly *is* the story we are being told? A brief look at the source of this passage makes clear that there is much more to be said. These lines are taken from the first poem in Book I of Horace's *Satires*,[4] a meditation on the theme that "for all men, and especially for the avaricious, their own lot in life is hard to bear" (*omnibus, maxime vero avaris, sortem suam gravem esse*). In this satire, which serves as the dedication of Book I to Maecenas, Horace argues mischievously that a man "misled by blind desire" (*decepta cupidine falso*) who hoards wealth believing that *quantum habeas sis* – however much you have is what you are – makes his own life miserable. Such a man comes to value the possession of wealth, not its uses, and so finds himself in the position of Tantalus, the mythical king of Lydia condemned to stand chin-high in a pool of water in Hades for all eternity. To quench his thirst, he tries to drink the water, only to have it recede at his every attempt. The man who hoards wealth sleeps "with open mouth on money-bags piled up from all sides" but is forced "to lie awake half-dead with fear, to be in terror night and day of wicked thieves, of fire, of slaves . . ." (1.71–77).[5] "Is this so pleasant?" (*hoc iuvat?*), the poet asks. When it comes to such goods, he would choose rather to be "the poorest of the poor" (*pauperrimus*).

Horace's injunction is simple and powerful: "set bounds to the quest of wealth, and as you increase your means let your fear of poverty lessen, and when you have won your heart's desire, begin to bring your toil to an end" (1.92–94).[6] In selecting this satire as the source of his epigraph, Harrington makes clear from the very outset that *Oceana* is a book about greed. He foregrounds his conviction that the miserly pursuit of disproportionate wealth represents the central threat to English civic life, and that such wealth renders even its owners wretched and uneasy. If England is to avoid becoming Tantalus, it must adopt the Harringtonian program, the primary, foundational feature of which Harrington calls the "equal agrarian." In

---

[4] Horace, *Satires, Epistles, Ars Poetica*, ed. and trans. H. R. Fairclough, Loeb Classical Library, rev. edn. (Harvard University Press, 1929). My translations are based on Fairclough's, although I have made several adjustments.

[5] ". . . congestis undique saccis / indormis inhians . . . an vigilare metu exanimem, noctesque diesque / formidare malos fures, incendia, servos."

[6] "Denique sit finis quaerendi, cumque habeas plus, / pauperiem metuas minus et finire laborem / incipias, parto quod avebas . . ."

order to defend this signature proposal, he summons the combined strength of the Greek and Machiavellian inheritances, fusing them into a new and powerful whole.

II

Harrington was acutely aware, as he put it, that "agrarian laws of all others have ever been the greatest bugbears."[7] Early in the seventeenth century Sir Walter Raleigh had declared in his *Discourse of the Original and Fundamental Causes of . . . War* that the "state-phrensy of sedition" which had gripped ancient Rome "was occasioned by the reviving of the Agrarian Law, by which the Lands taken from their enemies, and formerly divided among the nobility, should be shared among the people of Rome."[8] "The contention about this law," Raleigh insisted, following Machiavelli, "kindled such a hatred between the people and the senate, that it never ended but with the loss of the liberty of Rome, and the dissolution of that republic."[9] Likewise, in the 1633 poem *The Reigne of King Henry the Second,* Thomas May attributed the Roman agrarian laws to the personified figure of Sedition, about whose "denn" we read: "storyes carued there / Of his atchieuements numberlesse were seene, / Such as the Gracchis factious stirres had beene / In ancient Rome . . ." (1.532–35).[10] Nor were such laws considered any less abhorrent by Harrington's immediate contemporaries. In the 1640s Edmund Waller worried that a comprehensive assault on episcopal prerogatives might mean that the "next demand might be *Lex Agraria,* the like equality of things Temporall" – a terrifying prospect.[11] For his part, Milton vilified the agrarian movement even up to the eve of the Restoration. In *The readie and easie way to establish a free Commonwealth* (1660), his last defense of his nation's "expiring libertie," he argues in plainly Ciceronian tones that (*pace* Harrington) the construction

---

[7] *Political Works*, p. 231.

[8] Sir Walter Raleigh, *A Discourse of the Original and Fundamental Cause of Natural, Arbitrary, Necessary, and Unnatural War* in *The Works of Sir Walter Raleigh, Kt.*, ed. T. Birch and W. Oldys, vol. VIII (Oxford University Press, 1829), p. 292.

[9] Raleigh is willing to consider that the law may have been "just and reasonable," but argues, like Machiavelli, that not all reasonable laws are "at all times fit to be promoted." He continues his discussion with a direct paraphrase of *Discorsi* 1.37.3: "it is plain by this also, how much more men esteem wealth rather than honours; for the nobility of Rome ever gave way to the people, where it touched matter of honour without any extraordinary distaste; but when their wealth was concerned, how obstinately did they defend it, even to madness" (*Works*, p. 293).

[10] Thomas May, *The Reigne of King Henry the Second Written in Seauen Bookes*, ed. Götz Schmitz (Tempe, AZ: Arizona Center for Medieval and Renaissance Studies, 1999), p. 17.

[11] *A Speech Made by Master Waller Esquire . . . Concerning Episcopacie* (London, 1641), p. 5.

of a free state "requires no perilous, no injurious alteration or circumscription of mens lands and properties."[12] Once "temporal and spiritual lords" have been removed, "no man or number of men can attain to such wealth or vast possession, as will need the hedge of an Agrarian law (never succesful, but the cause rather of sedition, save only where it began seasonable with first possession) to confine them from endangering our public libertie."

In the same vein, Marchamont Nedham, writing in *The Case of the Commonwealth of England, Stated* (1650), attacks the agrarian laws as the root of the infamous Leveller movement.[13] To make his case, he sketches a progression of popular plunder. First, he suggests, the masses of the people tend to insult and punish the well-to-do "for the most part without any cause but merely to exercise their own spleen, which takes the same course of enmity likewise against all that are wealthy, be they high or low." But the sins of the plebs do not end there: "Nor is that alone sufficient, but they fly out ever and anon into violence; and from plundering to those Licinian and agrarian laws made by the populacy of Rome whereby it was provided that no man should grow too rich nor be master of above fifty acres of land."[14] Nedham specifically cites that "insolent passage recorded by Livy" in which the plebs demanded of the senate "how they durst possess more than fifty acres a piece yet find fault with a division made of two acres apiece to the people!" From here, Nedham writes, the next expression of plebeian degeneracy is "to introduce an absolute community," although he adds that "neither the Athenian nor Roman levelers ever arrived to this

---

[12] John Milton, *The readie and easie way to establish a free Commonwealth* in *The Riverside Milton*, ed. Roy Flannagan (New York: Houghton Mifflin, 1998), p. 1143. On Milton's critique of Harrington in *The readie and easie way*, see Barbara K. Lewalski, *The Life of John Milton: a Critical Biography* (Oxford: Blackwell, 2000), pp. 394–95.

[13] For the Leveller preoccupation with the example of the Roman plebs, see Samuel Dennis Glover, "The Putney Debates: Popular Versus Elitist Republicanism" in *Past and Present* 164 (1999), 47–80. Glover does not notice the ideological divide between Greek and Roman sources on the Roman *tumulti* (he also somewhat puzzlingly lists Florus as an anti-patrician writer), but he does make the important point that the Levellers generated a "plebeian" narrative of the fall of the republic. As a result, Leveller pamphlets furnished an important part of the background to Harrington's reconceptualization of the agrarian laws. See in particular John Lilburne, *The Upright Mans Vindication* (London, 1653), p. 22. Glover is correct that Lilburne compares one of his plans to the Roman "*Lex Agraria*," but it is important to note that this pamphlet does not propose a division of existing lands, or a cap on future accumulations. See also Glover, "The Classical Plebeians: Radical Republicanism and the Origins of Leveller Thought," Ph.D. dissertation, University of Cambridge, 1994. For Leveller political theory, see Iain Hampsher-Monk, "The Political Theory of the Levellers: Putney, Property and Professor Macpherson" in *Political Studies* 24 (1976), 397–422.

[14] Marchamont Nedham, *The Case of the Commonwealth of England, Stated*, ed. Philip A. Knachel (Charlottesville: University Press of Virginia, 1969), p. 109.

high pitch of madness." In short, Nedham offers an uncritical restatement of the standard Ciceronian verdict on agrarian laws.[15]

By the time he came to publish his 1656 treatise, *The Excellencie of a Free State*, however, Nedham had moved significantly beyond this view.[16] Given his peculiar propensity for vacillation, that is perhaps not much of a surprise. But Nedham's project in the 1650s required him to come to grips with the agrarian laws in a new and important way. *The Excellencie of a Free State*, published anonymously, reproduces a series of editorials that Nedham wrote for the Parliamentary broadsheet, *Mercurius Politicus*, during the tumultuous year 1651–52.[17] Cromwell had by then already floated the idea of reintroducing a monarchical element into the English constitution, and had even gestured at assuming the crown himself. Nedham resisted these developments by writing furiously in his newspaper of the need to give the democratic, popular element a dominant role in public decision-making. These sentiments were hardly less timely in 1656 (the year of *Oceana*), with the Protectorate at its height, and, accordingly, Nedham reissued and reordered these editorials in order to produce a bold, comprehensive case for genuinely popular government in lieu of kingly or senatorial rule.

In the midst of this sweeping polemical agenda the agrarian laws have a most uneasy place. Nedham spends a great deal of his time defending popular regimes against the charge that they foster sedition, tumults, and "levelling." Indeed, the very first hypothetical "objection" he addresses is "that the erecting of such a [popular] government would be to set on levelling and confusion."[18] "For an answer," he replies, "if we take levelling in the common usage and application of the term in these days, it is of an odious signification, as if it levelled all men in point of estates, made all things common to all, destroyed propriety." But popular regimes, he

---

[15] A further illustration of the prevalence of this Ciceronian approach to property in the 1640s and early 1650s is found in Samuel Hartlib's *Macaria*. It is deeply significant that Hartlib's utopia, which self-consciously models itself on More's in so many other respects, noticeably lacks an agrarian law and heaps praise on private wealth (only threatening state intervention in cases of conspicuous waste). See Samuel Hartlib, *A Description of the Famous Kingdome of Macaria* (London, 1641).

[16] The situation becomes even more complex if we accept Blair Worden's suggestion that Nedham had a hand in the 1646 pamphlet *Vox Plebis* (which ostentatiously takes the side of the Roman plebs). See Blair Worden, "'Wit in a Roundhead': the Dilemma of Marchamont Nedham" in *Political Culture and Cultural Politics in Early Modern England*, ed. Susan Amussen and Mark Kishlansky (Manchester University Press, 1995).

[17] For the background to *The Excellencie of a Free State*, see Blair Worden, "Marchamont Nedham and English Republicanism" in *Republicanism, Liberty, and Commercial Society: 1649–1776*, ed. David Wootton (Stanford University Press, 1994), esp. pp. 66–81.

[18] Marchamont Nedham, *The Excellencie of a Free State* (London, 1767), p. 47.

flatly suggests, have never been responsible for instituting "levelling." In defense of this position he proceeds to give a truly contorted, nearly comical rendition of Spartan and Roman history purporting to demonstrate that the infamous leveling practices of antiquity were instituted uniquely by kingly and senatorial regimes, and were promptly suspended once the people acquired rulership.[19] In all of this, the agrarian laws represent a very palpable absence. Whenever ancient "levelling" practices were mentioned, all of Nedham's readers would have thought immediately of Spurius Cassius, the Gracchi, Agis and Cleomenes, and their ilk, but Nedham never once alludes to any of them. He includes a passing reference now and then to "the usury and exactions of the great ones"[20] (a striking repudiation of his more conventional account of the Roman tumults in *The Case of the Commonwealth of England, Stated*), by way of vindicating the plebs, but shies away from the "bugbear" of agrarian levelling.

Finally, at the very end of the book, he turns to address the agrarian laws. What is remarkable about this attempt is Nedham's evident, acute awareness of the delicate tightrope he must walk. He must acquit the plebs of the charge of greed and envy (in order to justify his broader claims about the desirability of popular rule), and yet he must also reject the agrarian movement as seditious. At long last mentioning "that famous contention which lasted for three hundred years in Rome betwixt the senate and the people, about the dividing of such lands as were conquered and taken from the enemy," Nedham proceeds to give an extremely careful account of the quarrel:

The senators, they sharing the lands amongst themselves, allowed little, or none, unto the people; which gave such discontents, that the people made a law to curb them; enacting, that no senator should possess above 500 acres of land. The senators cried it was against their liberty, thus to be abridged by the people; and the people cried, it was inconsistent with liberty, that the senators should thus greaten themselves by an ingrossment of wealth and power into their own hands. Livy saith, "The people in this said right, and the senators did wrong: but that they both did ill, in making it a ground of civil dissension," for in process of time, when the Gracchi, who were supposed great patrons of liberty, took upon them to side with the people, they did, instead of finding out some moderate ways and expedients to reduce the senators to reason, proceed with such heat and violence [that they brought on the civil war].[21]

---

[19] Ibid., pp. 52–54. Nedham tries to square the circle by arguing that kingly and oligarchical regimes are the true "levellers," in that they reduce all subjects to a common state of servitude (in which property rights are not respected). On Nedham's inverted account, Lycurgus actually puts an end to "levelling" in Sparta.

[20] Ibid., p. 9.   [21] Ibid., p. 126.

Livy said no such thing about the Licinian law.[22] But Nedham (perhaps thinking of Machiavelli's account) endorses pseudo-Livy's verdict. "The occasion" of the civil war, he writes, "was given by the senators, (for, there was no reason they should grandize themselves in so gross a manner as they did) but yet the occasion ought not to have been taken, and prosecuted with such violence as it was by the people."[23] Despite his desperate desire to justify the plebs, Nedham still feels bound to condemn the agrarian movement itself. Indeed, even the notoriously vacillating Nedham could only vacillate so far when it came to the Gracchi. But the Nedham of 1656 had moved a long way. While he still maintained that the agrarian laws ultimately caused the collapse of the Roman republic, and did not endorse Machiavelli's conviction that the presence of wealthy men in the state represents a "disorder" *per se*, his political program forced him to rewrite the agrarian story in a strongly un-Ciceronian manner.

Harrington, however, went much farther than Nedham. Indeed, even when seen against the backdrop of Nedham's "second" view of the agrarian laws, Harrington's account is truly shocking in its iconoclasm. He first expresses his view of the Roman experiment in the "Preliminaries" to *Oceana*:

> Their [the Romans'] agrarian laws were such whereby their lands ought to have been divided among the people, either without mention of a colony, in which case they were not obliged to change their abode; or with the mention and upon condition of a colony . . . The lands assigned, or that ought to have been assigned, in either of these ways were of three kinds. Such as were taken from the enemy and distributed unto the people; or such as were taken from the enemy and, under colour of being reserved unto the public use, were by stealth possessed by the nobility; or such as as were bought with the public money to be distributed. Of the laws offered in these cases . . . such as drove at dispossessing the nobility of their usurpations, and dividing the common purchase of the sword among the people, were never touched but they caused earthquakes, nor could ever be obtained by the people or, being obtained, be observed by the nobility, who not only preserved their prey but, growing vastly rich upon it, bought the people by degrees quite out of those shares that had been conferred upon them. This the Gracchi coming too late to perceive, found the balance of the commonwealth to be lost.[24]

The efforts of the Gracchi to restore the essential republican "balance" proved fruitless: "putting the people (when they had least force) by forcible

---

[22] See Livy VI.35–42. Nedham may have been thinking of IV.51, but this passage does not pronounce a verdict on the Licinian law (nor, of course, does it discuss the case of the Gracchi). More likely, he was thinking of Sallust, *Bellum Iugurthinum* XXII.
[23] Nedham, *Excellencie*, p. 127.   [24] *Political Works*, p. 189.

means unto the recovery of it [the balance], did ill, seeing it neither could tend unto any more than to show them, by worse effects, that what the wisdom of their leaders had discovered was true." As Harrington puts it elsewhere, "by the time of Tiberius Gracchus the nobility had almost eaten the people quite out of their lands . . . whereupon the remedy being too late and too vehemently applied, that commonwealth was ruined."[25] But even the "vehemence" of the Gracchi is excused, since "if a cure be necessary, it excuseth not the patient, his disease being otherwise desperate, that it is dangerous; which was the case of Rome."[26] Harrington's verdict is simple: "the nobility of Rome, under the conduct of Sulla, overthrew the people and the commonwealth."[27]

Harrington certainly did not derive this account from Roman sources – not even from Sallust, who, for all his sympathy toward the *popularis* party, blamed both plebs and patricians for the advent of corruption, and condemned the Gracchi for their lack of "moderation." In the first edition of *Oceana*, a marginal gloss on Harrington's discussion refers the reader to "Sigonius, de Ant. Rom.," shorthand for the *De antiquo iure civium Romanorum* of the great Italian antiquarian Carlo Sigonio.[28] Sigonio, in turn, attributes the inspiration for his own analysis of the Roman *ager publicus* to Appian, and credits Plutarch with prompting his reflections on the Gracchi.[29] Indeed, Harrington's account, with its meticulous reconstruction of authentic Roman land law, its emphasis on the "usurpations" of the nobles (their πλεονεξία), its characterization of the Gracchi as men who tried to address a real disorder in the state, and its insistence that

---

[25] Ibid., p. 184.   [26] Ibid., p. 235.   [27] Ibid., p. 189.

[28] James Harrington, *The Commonwealth of Oceana* (London, 1656), p. 31.

[29] *Caroli Sigonii De antiquo iure civium Romanorum* (Paris, 1576), pp. 61, 65, and esp. p. 72. Caius Gracchus is here dubbed "iuris plebis retinentissimus" (p. 31). It is of considerable importance that Sigonio also wrote the *Respublica Hebraeorum* of 1582, with which Harrington was also familiar (see *Political Works*, p. 383). Antiquarian Hebraists of the late sixteenth and early seventeenth centuries began to see Biblical property regulations as instances of agrarian laws, and, accordingly, were increasingly prepared to question the polemical anti-Gracchism of their Roman sources (if God had framed such laws in his own commonwealth, surely they could not have been the instruments of sedition and injustice described by Cicero). A central example in this respect is Petrus Cunaeus' *De republica Hebraeorum libri III* of 1617. In 1.2 Cunaeus identifies the Biblical division of lands and the institution of the jubilee as *leges agrariae*, and praises them unreservedly (his key source is the section on *Halacha Shemita ve-Iovel* – the laws regarding the sabbatical year and the jubilee – in Maimonides' *Mishneh Torah*). In the following chapter, he compares the Hebrew agrarian scheme to the Roman Licinian law, and the story he tells of patrician plunder is drawn straight out of Plutarch (pp. 12–13). While the Greek account of the Roman agrarian laws undoubtedly held pride of place in Harrington's thinking on this subject, he was certainly influenced by the antiquarian tradition, and followed Cunaeus in praising the "equal agrarian" of ancient Israel (see *Political Works*, pp. 174–75, 634–35). For a recent discussion of this aspect of Harrington's thought, see Adam Sutcliffe, *Judaism and Enlightenment*, Ideas in Context (Cambridge University Press, 2003), pp. 49–57.

greedy patricians were to blame for the overthrow of the republic, is unmistakably Greek. However, if textual similarities and scattered marginalia are not enough to establish the provenance of Harrington's perspective on the agrarian laws, he himself removes any doubt on that score. In Book I of *The Art of Lawgiving* (1659), as a support for his agrarian proposal, he exclaims, "Let a man read Plutarch in the lives of Agis and of the Gracchi; there can be no plainer demonstration of the Lacedaemonian or Roman balance" (he regrets only that, in the *Moralia*, Plutarch "maketh no use, no mention at all of any such thing.").[30] Again in Book III, he writes, "for he who, considering the whole story or only that of the Gracchi in Plutarch, shall judge aright, must confess that, had Rome preserved a good agrarian but in Italy, the riches of her provinces could not have torn up the roots of her liberty."[31] Harrington sees the Roman agrarian laws through the eyes of a Greek.

Indeed, Harrington takes far more than a simple assessment of the Roman agrarian laws from Plutarch; he takes a view of wealth and its social and political consequences. In *The Stumbling-Block of Disobedience and Rebellion* (1658) Harrington writes of his principle of "balance" that "the truth is thus recorded by Plutarch in the *Life of Agis*":

So soon as the Lacedaemonians, having ruined Athens, became full of gold and silver, the commonwealth began to break; nevertheless, the lots or division of lands made by Lycurgus yet remaining, the equality of the foundation held good till Epitadeus, an ill-natured fellow, became Ephor, and having a mind to disinherit his son, got a law to pass whereby any man might dispose of his lot as he pleased, This, by him pursued of mere malice to his son, was hurried on by the avarice of others, whose riches came thus to eat the people so clearly out of their lands, that in a short time there remained not above an hundred freeholders in all Sparta.[32]

Harrington continues by tracing the birth of Spartan oligarchy to this moment, and insists that "Agis and Cleomenes, by the restitution of the lots of Lycurgus, were assertors of popular power." In short, he uses Plutarch's account to arrive at a general principle about the relationship between the distribution of wealth and the assignment of political dominance. Behind this assertion lurks a claim drawn from Harrington's Greek source about avarice and its destructive effects: the hoarding of large fortunes topples commonwealths.

Harrington later amplifies his endorsement of the Greek account of the agrarian laws by adding a scathing attack on the Roman sources. In the

---

[30] *Political Works*, p. 607. [31] Ibid., p. 689. [32] Ibid., p. 571.

body of *Oceana*, he returns to a familiar passage from Livy to defend his equal agrarian. Recall that, in Book II of Livy's *Ab urbe condita* (dramatized by Shakespeare in *Coriolanus*), during the secession of the plebs the senate dispatches Menenius Agrippa to attempt a reconciliation. He offers the plebs the allegory of the "belly" (which I characterized earlier as an instance of "trickle-down economics") in which the disproportionate wealth of the patricians is explained as a source of benefits for the people at large. Harrington takes aim at this classic Roman riposte to the agrarian movement:

notwithstanding the fable out of Aesop whereby Menenius Agrippa, the orator that was sent from the senate unto the people at Mount Aventine, showed the fathers to be the belly and the people to be the arms and legs, which except that, how slothful soever it might seem, were nourished, not these but the whole body must languish and be dissolved; it is plain that the fathers were a distinct belly, such an one as took the meat indeed out of the people's mouths but, abhorring the agrarian, returning it not in the due and necessary nutrition of the commonwealth.[33]

He concludes that "as the people that live about the cataracts of Nilus are said not to hear the noise, so neither the Roman writers, nor Machiavel the most conversant with them, seem among so many tribunician storms to hear their natural voice." In fact, he writes, in attributing the cause of these storms to strife "about the agrarian," the Roman writers were mistaking the "remedy for the disease." Harrington thus explicitly sides with the Greeks against the Romans in analyzing the "natural voice" of Roman upheaval. This self-conscious turn from Rome to Greece was his true innovation.[34]

III

Given his evident sympathy for this Greek perspective on agrarian laws, it should come as no surprise that Harrington's *Oceana* also relies deeply on the thought and approach of the Greek tradition's most prominent early-modern disciple, Sir Thomas More.[35] During the century between the publication of *Utopia* and *Oceana*, More's particular vision of the Greek

---

[33] Ibid., p. 276.
[34] A reckoning with this extremely loaded ideological position would, I believe, have improved Fergus Millar's analysis of Harrington's use of the Roman model. See Fergus Millar, *The Roman Republic in Political Thought* (University Press of New England, 2002), pp. 86–96.
[35] This, in my view, points to the major shortcoming in the analysis of Alan Cromartie. While Cromartie helpfully challenges Pocock's characterization of Harrington as a straightforward Machiavellian, he ignores the overt Hellenism of Harrington's text and its fundamental reliance on More (and Plato). See Alan Cromartie, "Harringtonian Virtue: Harrington, Machiavelli, and the Method of the Moment" in *The Historical Journal*, 41 (1998), 987–1009.

tradition had remained fresh in the learned imagination. In 1576, Jean Bodin published his *Six Livres de la République*, in which he asserted the absolute and indivisible character of sovereignty at the height of the French Wars of Religion. In Book v of this work he turns to a discussion of sedition and revolution within states, and comes up against the specter of economic inequality. It cannot be denied, he writes, that "of all the causes of seditions and changes in the Republic, there is none greater than the excessive wealth of a few subjects, and the extreme poverty of the majority."[36] Indeed, he continues, history is full of episodes in which those "who have given many reasons for their discontent about their status, have always taken the first opportunity that presents itself to despoil the rich of their possessions."[37]

Bodin, in his patented *in utramque partem* style, proceeds to delineate two reputable positions on this redistribution of wealth, in a section entitled "Les deux pestes de toutes Republiques." On the one hand, he writes, Plato "called wealth and poverty the ancient plagues of Republics,"[38] and, in order to redeem the state from these diseases, "it has been suggested that we should seek an equality, such as many have greatly praised, calling it the nursing mother of peace and friendship between subjects."[39] Conversely, these same thinkers have considered "inequality to be the source of all enmities, factions, hatreds, and partialities,"[40] because "he who has more than another, and who realizes that he is richer in goods, wishes also to be higher in honor, in delights, in pleasures, in food, and clothing. He wishes to be revered by those same poor people whom he disdains and treads underfoot."[41] In the Latin version Bodin adds that the rich man, in seeking superiority over his fellows solely on the basis of wealth, "has no regard,

---

[36] Jean Bodin, *Les Six Livres de la République*, ed. Christiane Frémont, Marie-Dominique Couzinet, and Henri Rochais, vol. v (Paris: Fayard, 1986), p. 59. My translations from Bodin's French are based somewhat on M. J. Tooley's, although I depart from his text significantly. See Jean Bodin, *Six Books of the Commonwealth* (abridged), trans. M. J. Tooley (Oxford: Basil Blackwell, 1955). "De toutes les causes des seditions, et changemens de Republiques, il n'y en a point de plus, / grande que les richesses excessives de peu de sujects, et la pauvreté extreme de la pluspart."

[37] Bodin, *Six Livres*, p. 59. "qui ont pretendu plusieurs causes du mescontentement qu'ils avoyent de l'estat, ont tousjours empoigné le premiere occasion qui s'est presentée, pour despouiller les riches de leurs biens."

[38] Ibid., p. 60. ". . . Platon appelloit les richesses, et la pauvreté, les anciennes pestes des Republiques."

[39] Ibid. "on cerchoit une equalité, que plusieurs ont fort loüée, l'appellant mere nourrice de paix et amitié entre les sujects."

[40] Ibid. "l'inequalité source de toutes inimitiez, factions, haines, partialitez."

[41] Ibid. "celuy qui a plus qu'un autre, et qui se void plus riche en biens, il veut aussi estre plus haut en honneur, en delices, en plaisirs, en vivres, en habits: il veut estre reveré des povres qu'il mesprise et foule au pied."

or only very little, for virtue."[42] The poor, on the other hand, "develop an envy and an extreme jealousy, born of the realization that they are as worthy, or even more worthy than the wealthy, and are nonetheless afflicted with poverty, hunger, misery, and contempt."[43] Accordingly, many ancient legislators, such as Lycurgus, Agis, and Plato himself, "divided goods equally among all subjects," and "in our own memory Thomas More, Chancellor of England, in his *Republic*, said that the only path to public well-being is if men live in a community of goods, which can never be where there is private property."[44]

This first position on the redistribution of wealth is, in short, what I have been calling the "Greek" view. Bodin traces it to the legislators of Greek antiquity, and to their contemporary acolyte, Sir Thomas More (whose *Utopia* is revealingly rechristened).[45] This position justifies the confiscation and redistribution of private property (or, indeed, its outright abolition) on the grounds that disproportionate wealth gives its possessors a false and invidious claim on political authority and public goods, and convulses the state with envy and mutual recrimination. Bodin stresses the dominance of this view in the classical period, and notes that "although the Romans were more equitable and better understood the principle of Justice than the other peoples, even they often decreed a general rescinding of debts . . . and had no better method of appeasing tumults and seditions quickly."[46] But the Romans, who understood "la Justice," also furnish the source of Bodin's second, and favored position on the redistribution of wealth. Compelling as the Greek case may be, he observes, "on the other hand one could argue that the equality of goods is very pernicious for Republics, which have no support or foundation more sound than confidence, without which neither justice nor any kind of society can prove durable. And confidence abides

---

[42] *Io. Bodini Andegavensis, De republica libri sex, latine ab autore redditi, multo quam antea locupletiores* (Paris, 1586), p. 525. "Nam quo quisque alios opibus superat, honoribus etiam, voluptatibus ac deliciis superior esse, de virtute nihil aut parum admodum solicitus." The translation is my own. Richard Knolles included this phrase in his 1606 English translation. See *The Six Bookes of A Commonweale*, trans. Richard Knolles (London, 1606), p. 569. "for he that hath more than another, and sees himselfe to have greater wealth, he will also be higher in honor, in delights, in pleasures, in diet and in apparell, having no great regard of virtue."

[43] *Six Livres*, p. 60. "conçoyvent une envie et jalousie extreme, de se voir autant ou plus dignes que les riches, et neantmoins estre accablez de povreté, de faim, de misere, de contumelie."

[44] Ibid., p. 61. "divisoyent les biens egalement à chacun des sujects . . . de nostre memoire Thomas le More Chancelier d'Angleterre, en sa Republique, dit, que la seule voye de salut public est, si les hommes vivent en communauté de biens: ce qui ne peut estre faict où il y a proprieté."

[45] Bodin retains the title "Utopia" in the Latin version. See Bodin, *De republica*, p. 525.

[46] *Six Livres*, p. 61. "quoy que les Romains ayent esté plus equitables et mieux entendus au faict de la Justice que les autres peuples, si ont-ils souvent ottroyé la rescision generale des debtes . . . et n'avoyent moyen plues expedient d'appaiser soudain les troubles et seditions."

where promises are honored."[47] He continues that "if then obligations are cancelled, contracts annulled, debts abolished, what else should one expect other than the complete undermining of the state? For no one would have any faith in anyone else."[48] Bodin exclaims that, when it comes to redistributionary proposals, "one can say that such sharing out of the goods of others is theft under the banner of equality."[49] If the fact that Bodin is simply paraphrasing Cicero's *De officiis* is not yet clear enough, he ends on a rather unambiguous note: "Let us then leave behind the opinion of those who seek to bring about equality in pre-existing Republics by appropriating the goods of others, when they should be preserving for each man what belongs to him, in order to establish natural justice."[50]

Thus, in Bodin the Roman theory of justice stands vindicated. But the interesting fact is that Bodin meticulously and self-consciously reconstructs the opposing viewpoint, faithfully representing its organizing principles and fully conscious of its pedigree. Indeed, Bodin may well have been More's most insightful sixteenth-century reader. He recognized in *Utopia* an endorsement of a coherent Greek system of thought which was fundamentally at odds with the more conventional Roman approach. He could not, to be sure, bring himself to endorse More's position, but he had a vivid sense of it. Indeed, later in Book v, Bodin makes an interesting attempt to stake out the middle ground. The abolition of debts and the redistribution of land and wealth will simply not do, he concludes, but perhaps the risk of excessive wealth and poverty could be somewhat tamed by certain revisions in inheritance laws. Monarchies and aristocracies must retain primogeniture in order to guarantee the continued survival of the great families. But "when it comes to the popular state, which seeks equality in all things, how could it support such a great inequality within families that one inherits everything, and the rest die of hunger? We see that all the seditions which took place in Rome and Greece had their origins in this issue."[51]

---

[47] Ibid., p. 62. "d'autre part on peut dire, que l'eqalité de biens est tres-pernicieuse aux Republiques, lesquelles n'ont appuy ni fondement plus assuré que la foy, sans laquelle ni la justice, ni societé quelconque ne peut estre durable: or la foy gist aux promesses des conventions legitimes."

[48] Ibid. "si donc les obligations sont cassees, les contracts annullez, les debtes abolies, que doit-on attendre autre chose que l'entiere eversion d'un estat? car il n'y aura fiance quelconque de l'un à l'autre."

[49] Ibid. "on peut dire que tel partage du bien d'autruy est une volerie sous le voile d'equalité."

[50] Ibid., p. 64. "Laissant donc en arriere l'opinion de ceux qui cerchent l'equalité és Republiques ja formees, prenans le bien d'autruy, au lieu qu'ils devoyent conserver à chacun ce qui luy appartient, pour establir la justice naturelle."

[51] Ibid., p. 78. "quant a l'estat populaire, qui demande l'equalité en toutes choses, comment pourroit-il supporter l'inequalité si grande en les familles, que l'un emportast tout, et que les autres mourussent de faim? veu que toutes les seditions, qui sont advenuës en Rome et en Grece, n'estoyent fondees

Bodin's remarks were prescient indeed. As we shall see, for those thinkers committed to the Greek program in the seventeenth and eighteenth centuries, inheritance laws offered an opportunity for redistribution which was less ostentatiously inconsistent with the Roman theory of justice. Such laws would become a central battleground in the ideological wars of the Revolutionary period.

Before returning to the seventeenth century, however, it is worth glancing briefly at a second classic representation of the Morean position in the late sixteenth century: the magnificent epitome provided by Edmund Spenser in the *Fairie Queene*. In Book v, entitled "The Legend of Artegall, or Of Justice," the knight Artegall and his companion Talus come upon a giant speaking to a mob of people by the seaside. The Giant, "admired much of fooles, women, and boys" (v.ii.30)[52], holds aloft a "ballance" and shouts that "all the world he would weigh equallie," assigning to each element its just proportion:

> For why, he sayd they all vnequall were,
> And had encroched vppon others share. . .
> And so were realmes and nations run awry
> All which he vndertooke for to repaire,
> In sort as they were formed aunciently;
> And all things would reduce vnto equality.
> (v.ii.32).

He describes his program violently, but, beneath the violence, his argument should sound familiar:

> Were it not good that wrong were then surceast,
> And from the most, that some were given to the least?

> Therefore I will throw downe these mountaines hie,
> And make them levell with the lowly plaine:
> These towering rocks, which reach vnto the skie,
> I will thrust downe into the deepest maine,

---

que sur ce poinct là." It is also worth noting that Bodin gives a fairly sympathetic account of the agrarian laws and the Gracchi, which he explicitly takes from Appian and Plutarch (pp. 75–76). Bodin approves of the proposal to divide newly conquered land among the plebs on prudential grounds, although not on grounds of "justice." Bodin's reliance on the Greek historians of Rome is explained in the 1565 *Methodus*, where he praises the unbiased eye of foreign historians, and singles out Dionysius, Polybius, and Plutarch to make his case (Bodin, *Method for the Easy Comprehension of History*, ed. and trans. Beatrice Reynolds [Columbia University Press, 1945], pp. 44–48, 63). He also lists Plutarch, Dionysius, and Appian among the historians most valuable for "civil training" (*Method*, p. 54). That said, in this earlier text he takes a rather less favorable view of the Gracchi. See esp. *Method*, pp. 184, 237.

52 All references to Spenser designate book, canto, and stanza. Quotations are taken from Edmund Spenser, *The Faerie Queene*, ed. A. C. Hamilton, Longman Annotated English Poets (London: Longman, 1977).

And as they were, them equalize againe.
Tyrants that make men subiect to their law,
I will supresse, that they no more may raine;
And Lordings curbe, that commons ouer-aw;
And all the wealth of rich men to the poor will draw.

                                                                    (v.ii.38).

Spenser surely must have intended the Giant to appear as a More-like figure.[53] In order for the natural and political worlds to be balanced and, therefore, capable of upholding justice (this book of the poem is, after all, "On Justice"), he argues, there must be equality of property. Justice is δικαιοσύνη, the natural, balanced ordering of elements.

The masses, who hope to gain "great good, / And wondrous riches by his innouation" (v.ii.51), flock to the Giant, but Artegall will have none of it. He insists much like Cicero (*De officiis* II.81–84), that in equalizing property the Giant "In stead of right me seemes great wrong dost shew" (v.ii.34). The Almighty, he argues, "pulleth down, he setteth vp on hy; / He giues to this, from this he takes away" (v.ii.42). Those who have amassed property were meant to amass it, and are therefore entitled to it. This view reinforces Spenser's claim in the proem that "justice" is giving each man his "owne" (v.i.3) – that is, the Roman *ius suum*. Artegall then concludes that "All change is perillous, and all chaunce vnsound. / Therefore leaue off to weigh them all againe . . ." (v.ii.36). The episode ends with Talus pushing the Giant off the cliff, and watching him and his Utopian view of justice drown below.

But Talus did not succeed in finishing off Greek ethics. Seventy years later, we find these words spoken not by Spenser's Giant, but rather by the Lord Archon in Harrington's *Oceana*.

The balance of a commonwealth that is equal is of such nature that whatever falleth into her empire must fall equally, and if the whole earth fall into your scales, it must fall equally and so you may be a greater people and yet not swerve from your principles one hair. Nay, you will be so far from that, that you must bring the world in such a case unto your balance, even unto the balance of justice.[54]

---

[53] It is surprising that this fact has not been more extensively discussed by Spenser scholars. In the most important book-length study of Book v, Jane Aptekar notices that the Giant "is advocating universal cosmic and social equalization," but actually argues that Artegall is the More-like figure, in that he attempts to put down the rebellion through the use of eloquence (she is thinking, most probably, of the characterization of More in Ps.-Shakespeare, *Sir Thomas More*, ed. Revd. Alexander Dyce [London: The Shakespeare Society, 1844]). This seems to me a much less plausible reading. See Jane Aptekar, *Icons of Justice: Iconography and Thematic Imagery in Book v of* The Fairie Queene (Columbia University Press, 1969), pp. 35–36.

[54] *Political Works*, p. 322.

The Archon's insistence that the world itself must be weighed in a scale and divided according to an equal balance certainly recalls the rhetoric of the Giant, who held aloft his "ballance" and promised that "all the world he would equally weigh." From the point of view of contemporary Harrington scholarship, however, the similarity between the two passages must appear somewhat strange. Spenser's Giant is, after all, a very More-like figure, and the view of justice as "balance" that he articulates is deeply reminiscent of the particular view of δικαιοσύνη we encountered in *Utopia*. Yet most scholars seem singularly reluctant to group Harrington with More in any but the most superficial ways. Pocock, for example, takes great pains to argue that *Oceana* "is not a utopia" in More's sense because "it does not portray a no-place or *outopia*, an imaginary island in unknown seas, but a fictionalized yet instantly recognizable England."[55] He urges us to see it instead as "a civil history of the sword and a civil history of property."[56] Charles Blitzer argues similarly that *Oceana* is not "Utopian" because "the author makes no attempt to conceal the fact that Oceana is England, although it is an England transformed . . . If we mean a state of ideal perfection, Oceana is not a utopia . . . It can perhaps more profitably be compared to the 'best possible states' of Plato and Aristotle, among others, rather than to More's 'nowhere.'"[57]

These comments misrepresent the character of *Utopia*, and, as a result, obscure *Oceana*'s deep structural and theoretical reliance on More's text. More never claims that Utopia constitutes "a state of ideal perfection," but, rather, the *optimus reipublicae status* – precisely the sort of "best possible state" argument that Blitzer attributes to Plato and Aristotle. And, while Pocock is surely right to draw attention to Harrington's preoccupation with history, I must at least begin by acknowledging that *Oceana* also presents itself as the *optimus reipublicae status*, the "perfect and immortal commonwealth."[58] Furthermore, the claim that Utopia is a simple "nowhere" in

---

[55] See Pocock, "Introduction" to James Harrington, *The Commonwealth of Oceana and A System of Politics*, ed. J. G. A. Pocock (Cambridge University Press, 1992), p. xvii. See also *Harrington, Political Works*, ed. Pocock), p. 74.

[56] *Political Works*, p. 43.

[57] Charles Blitzer, *An Immortal Commonwealth: the Political Thought of James Harrington* (Yale University Press, 1960), p. 32.

[58] *Political Works*, p. 209. In 1914 H. F. Russell Smith noted that *Oceana* is "written in the form of a Utopia," but concluded that it was not really Utopian because "it was meant neither for the skies nor for some spot on earth that did not exist, but for England." See H. F. Russell Smith, *Harrington and His Oceana: a Study of a 17th Century Utopia and its Influence in America* (Cambridge University Press, 1914), p. 12. In his study of English "Utopianism" J. C. Davis notes that "it has been a persistent feature of Harrington scholarship to deny his Oceana . . . the character of a utopia" and rejects this habit. See J. C. Davis, *Utopia and the Ideal Society: a Study of English Utopian Writing:*

contrast to Harrington's fictionalized England ignores the fact that Utopia is also a "possible England" – an England transformed by Greek ethics. I have already discussed how the name "Utopia" fits into a network of "nonsense" puns which cannot be taken at face value, but More also tells us that the island of Utopia is much the same size as England, and that it comprises fifty-four cities (England comprised fifty-three counties, together with the city of London).[59] He adds that its capital city Amaurot lies "at the navel of the land" (*in umbilico terrae*), and that the river Anyder runs through it, clearly recalling London and the Thames.[60]

While it is certainly true that Harrington's fictionalization is less extensive (and less creative) than More's, he carries it out on precisely More's terms: all the places and most of the people in his commonwealth are given Greek names. In this respect, we should begin by pointing out that Harrington derives his names for England, Scotland, and Ireland from Greek mythology. Harrington makes clear that "Oceana" does not simply refer to the sea in general, but to Okeanos (Ὠκεανός), the Great Outward Sea (as opposed to the Mediterranean),[61] and the offspring of Ouranos (heaven) and

---

1516–1700 (Cambridge University Press, 1981), p. 206. However, he then proceeds to structure his analysis around the claim that, in *Oceana*, we find a conflict between "classical republicanism" and "utopianism," where the former refers to Pocock's participatory brand of Aristotelianism, and the latter to a disposition to harness "men's natural behavior into a harmonious social whole" (p. 238). Likewise, Jonathan Scott finds *Oceana*'s "utopian form" unusual "within the republican tradition," and, citing Harrington's ordinance that bells must be rung at a particular hour, writes "one can only imagine the bafflement of Machiavelli" at such an order; Scott, "The Rapture of Motion," p. 149. Fair enough – but such a requirement would come as no surprise whatever to either Plato or More. Davis and Scott accept an unnecessarily narrow definition of what constituted "classical republicanism" and, as a result, have to segregate "Utopian" writing from it. The ideology that Davis identifies as "Utopian" is best explained as an account of the commonwealth based on Greek, rather than Roman ethics.

59 Thomas More, *Utopia*, ed. George M. Logan, Robert M. Adams, and Clarence H. Miller (Cambridge University Press, 1995), pp. 109, 113. Logan, Adams, and Miller notice the geographical similarities between England and Utopia in their notes. See also Brian R. Goodey, "Mapping 'Utopia': A Comment on the Geography of Sir Thomas More," in *The Geographical Review* 60 (1970), 13–30. Goodey illustrates the extensive similarities between the geography of Utopia and that of England as described in the *St. Albans Chronicle* (1515).

60 More, *Utopia*, p. 113.

61 Liljegren supplies a revealing comment by Toland: Oceana, he says, is "a name by which he [Harrington] design'd *England*, as being the noblest Iland of the *Northern* Ocean": the name Okeanos specifies the "northern," rather than "southern ocean"; S. B. Liljegren, *James Harrington's Oceana* (Heidelberg, 1924), p. 229. It is also worth noting that Okeanos is introduced as the offspring of earth and heaven in the *Timaeus*, a dialogue with which Harrington was extremely familiar, and one to which I will turn later in this chapter. Most important, however, in *Oceana* Harrington distinguishes between the "goods of fortune" and the "goods of the mind" (which he also calls "empire" and "authority"), and writes the following: "I come unto the principles of authority, which are internal and founded upon the goods of the mind. These the legislator that can unite in his government with those of fortune, cometh nearest unto the work of God, whose government consisteth of heaven

Gaia (earth). Hence the opening invocation of Oceana as a nation built on "the bounties of heaven and earth."[62] Ireland, on the other hand, is christened "Panopea." S. B. Liljegren derives this name from Panopeus, a Phocian city, and suggests that Harrington was comparing the pastoral settings of the two places.[63] If Harrington meant to refer to Panopeus, however, he more likely had in mind its reputation for being barren and uncultivated. Pausanias (x.4.1), for example, records that "Panopeus [is] a city of the Phocians, if one give the name of a city to those who possess no government offices, no gymnasium, no theater, no market-place, and no water descending to a fountain, but live in bare shelters just like mountain cabins, right on a ravine."[64] That said, in keeping with his designation of England as "Oceana," Harrington may well have had in mind Panope (Πανόπη, actually referred to as Πανόπεια in Hesiod, *Theogony* 250), one of the Nereids (sea-nymphs) and a daughter of the sea-god.[65] Nymphs had the reputation of inducing sloth and femininity (e.g. Odysseus' Kalypso), which would seem to explain Harrington's characterization of Panopea as "the soft mother of a slothful and pusillanimous people"[66] (there is also a possible pun on πανωπήεις, "visible from all sides" – i.e. an island).

Scotland's name, "Marpesia," is more complex. Liljegren seems aware that Marpessa (Μάρπησσα) was the wife of the hero Idas, but he confuses *Idas* with *Ida* (Ἴδη), the mountain range at Troy (and he suggests, therefore, that the allusion is to "the forests of Ida," and their Scotland-like terrain).[67] My own explanation for the name goes as follows: in Greek myth, Idas was the "strongest of men" (Homer *Iliad* IX.558), a symbol of brute valor, whom Marpessa chose over her abductor Apollo, the god of order, refinement, and civilization. Harrington is probably suggesting that the Scots (those "hardy people" who are the most "difficult to be held" of any nation, but are, nonetheless "cattle"),[68] like Marpessa, chose valor over refinement. As with

---

and earth" (*Political Works*, p. 169). Oceana unites the bounties of heaven and earth – an idea that Harrington promptly connects to Plato's dictum that philosophers will rule in the best state.

[62] *Political Works*, p. 157.

[63] Liljegren, Harrington's, Oceana, p. 231. Although I take issue with several of Liljegren's etymologies, he deserves credit for being the only Harrington scholar this century to discuss Harrington's nomenclature.

[64] Pausanias, *Description of Greece*, ed. and trans. J. G. Frazer, Loeb Classical Library (London: Macmillan, 1898).

[65] See Henri II Estienne, Θησαυρὸς τῆς Ἑλληνικῆς Γλώσσης (*Thesaurus Graecae Linguae*), vol. v (Paris, 1842–46), pp. 157–58.

[66] *Political Works*, p. 159.   [67] Liljegren, *Harrington's Oceana*, p. 231.

[68] *Political Works*, pp. 159, 331, 240.

Panopea, however, there is also a probable pun here: μάρπτω, the verb "to conquer" or "to seize," provides an etymology for Marpessa's name (she was "seized" by Apollo), and Scotland too has been conquered.

This pattern of Greek nomenclature continues within Oceana itself. London becomes Emporium (ἐμπόριον), a "trading-place," and includes another city (standing in for Westminster) called Hiera (ἱερά), "holy" or "glorious" place. Hiera, we are told, comprises two tribes: the Agoraea (ἀγοραῖοι), "assembly men," and the Propola (πρόπολα), "clergy."[69] Emporium itself has three tribes: Scazon (σκάζων), the tribe that causes a "limp" because it is larger than the other two, Metoche (μετοχή), named for "participation," and Telicouta (τηλικοῦτος), "great" tribe.[70] Oceana's chief magistrate is an *archon*, its counselors are *prytans*, the president of its senate is a *strategos*, its tribes are governed by *phylarchs* ("tribunes as it is in the vulgar Latin")[71] just as in Utopia,[72] and in the past it was governed by a series of kings with Greek names (two uncharacteristically humorous ones are "Adoxus" (foolish) for King John, and "Panurgus" (knave) for Henry VII).[73] Just like *Utopia*, Harrington's *optimus reipublicae status* sounds very Greek.

But that is not a sufficient characterization of *Oceana*, and a passage from Harrington's *The Prerogative of Popular Government* indicates why we should be wary about oversimplifying his reliance on More and the Greek tradition. In defending himself against Matthew Wren's accusation that he is an armchair political theorist, Harrington names his role models:

It was in the time of Alexander, the greatest prince and commander of his age, that Aristotle, with scarce inferior applause and equal fame, being a private man, wrote that excellent piece of prudence in his cabinet which he called his *Politics*, going upon far other principles than those of Alexander's government, which it hath long out-lived. The like did Titus Livy in the time of Augustus, Sir Thomas More in the time of Henry the Eighth, and Machiavel when Italy was under princes that afforded him not the ear. These works nevertheless are all of the most esteemed and applauded in this kind; nor have I found any man whose like endeavours have been persecuted, since Plato by Dionysius.[74]

---

[69] Ibid., p. 298. Liljegren correctly identifies all of the Greek coinages listed in this paragraph.

[70] Ibid., p. 296.　[71] Ibid., p. 210.　[72] More, *Utopia*, p. 123.　[73] *Political Works*, p. 191 (note).

[74] Ibid., p. 395. This passage calls into question Davis's statement that "Harrington may have read and been influenced by the *Utopia*. We do not know" (*Utopia and the Ideal Society*, p. 3). More's name would probably not have appeared on this list if Harrington had neither read nor been influenced by him.

The unremarked fact that More's *Utopia* appears on this list of Harrington's most esteemed political texts should reinforce our sensitivity to similar views of justice and the nature of civic life in the Harringtonian corpus – especially since More appears here alongside Plato and Aristotle. But all three are joined on this list by Livy and Machiavelli, which should alert us to the presence of a rival element in Harrington's thought. Indeed, Machiavelli's influence was central to the development of the Harringtonian program in general and the equal agrarian in particular.

IV

Harrington's Machiavellism has received a prodigious amount of scholarly attention over the last fifty years. Most notably, Pocock's *The Machiavellian Moment* described Harrington as a Machiavellian historian of civil life who became a pillar of the English and North American republican traditions.[75] In casting Harrington in this light, Pocock was following and expanding on the work of Charles Blitzer, whose *An Immortal Commonwealth* (1960) constituted the most important study of Harrington's *Oceana* from the previous generation. These two works highlighted an unquestionable aspect of Harrington's thought. At the start of *Oceana*, Machiavelli is called "the only politician of later ages,"[76] and, at the end of *A System of Politics*, Harrington insists that "corruption in government is to be read and considered in Machiavel," just as human diseases are to be studied in the writings of Hippocrates.[77] Nor is this idle flattery. Harrington derived several of his most essential political ideas from Machiavelli, including (but not limited to) his reverence for the single, great legislator (and the accompanying quintet of Moses, Theseus, Lycurgus, Solon, and Romulus), his distinction between governments for "preservation" and governments for "increase," and, most importantly, his insistence on the value of an armed citizenry.[78]

---

[75] Pocock, *Machiavellian Moment*, esp. pp. 383–400. Pocock's chapter on Harrington in *The Ancient Constitution* is also extremely important, and includes an interesting discussion of the relationship between Harrington and the Levellers. See J. G. A. Pocock, *The Ancient Constitution and the Feudal Law: a Study of English Historical Thought in the Seventeenth Century* (Cambridge University Press, 1957), p. 124ff.

[76] *Political Works*, p. 162.   [77] Ibid., p. 854.

[78] See ibid., pp. 207, 180, 201, 203, for example. That said, Jeffrey Barnouw points out that Pocock very severely overemphasizes the centrality of the "citizen soldier" in Harrington's thought. While I disagree with the substance of Barnouw's analysis, I think this point is well taken. See Jeffrey Barnouw, "American Independence: Revolution of the Republican Ideal; a Response to Pocock's Construction of 'the Atlantic Republican Tradition'" in *The American Revolution and Eighteenth-Century Culture:*

But Harrington makes clear that, to the extent that he honors Machiavelli, he does so largely because the Florentine was the "learned disciple"[79] of the ancients, and the "only politician that hath gone about to retrieve" ancient prudence[80] (what he calls in *The Prerogative of Popular Government* "the policy of a commonwealth").[81] In other words, Harrington values Machiavellian ideas insofar as they accord with a premodern political science synthesized out of the authors and commonwealths of Greece and Rome. We should, therefore, expect Harrington's Machiavellism to hinge upon the powerful neo-Roman element in Machiavellian thought (especially since, as we have seen, Harrington considered Machiavelli to be "the most conversant" with the authors of ancient Rome) – and this is indeed the case. In particular, as Quentin Skinner has shown, Harrington's works reveal a characteristic, neo-Roman emphasis on "freedom."[82] Harrington routinely praises the "free state"[83] (*civitas libera*), and places the word LIBERTAS in capital letters over the Lord Archon's final proclamation in *Oceana*.[84] He also accepts the characteristic republican thesis that Caesar was a tyrant (rather than a martyr) dedicated to "extinguishing liberty."[85]

Even more importantly, Harrington often adopts the neo-Roman practice of describing *libertas* as a status to be contrasted with slavery.[86] In a climactic moment in *Oceana*, he has the Orator proclaim that "this free-born nation liveth not upon the dole or bounty of one man but, distributing her annual magistracies and honours with her own hand, is herself King People"[87] (a republican nod to the famous frontispiece of Hobbes's *Leviathan*, published five years earlier). The free state does not

---

Essays from the 1976 Bicentennial Conference of the American Society for Eighteenth-Century Studies, ed. Paul J. Korshin (New York: AMS Press, 1986), esp. pp. 54, 63.

[79] *Political Works*, p. 162.   [80] Ibid., p. 161.   [81] Ibid., p. 397.

[82] Quentin Skinner, *Liberty Before Liberalism*, p. 46.

[83] *Political Works*, p. 687.   [84] Ibid., p. 339.   [85] Ibid., p. 161.

[86] Nonetheless, it must be noted that Harrington at the same time deploys another view of freedom which is not, strictly speaking, neo-Roman: the Stoic topic of the "bondage of the passions." For example, in *Oceana* Harrington insists that "the liberty of a man" consists in "the empire of his reason," and claims that the absence of this freedom relegates a man to "the bondage of his passions" (*Political Works*, p. 170). On another occasion, he writes "whatever was passion in the contemplation of a man, being brought forth by his will into action is vice and the bondage of sin; so whatever was reason in the contemplation of a man, being brought forth by his will into action, is virtue and the freedom of the soul." This view of liberty as "freedom from passion" would probably fall under the rubric of the more conventional "negative liberty" (non-interference), even though Isaiah Berlin specifies external interference in his "Two concepts of liberty" in *Four Essays on Liberty* (Oxford University Press, 1969). As we shall see, this rival view of freedom fits in well with Harrington's Platonist worldview.

[87] *Political Works*, p. 229.

live under the power of any other entity; it is subject to no will but its own. When the people are "under a yoke," however, Harrington agrees with Sallust and Tacitus that they are "of a broken, slavish, a pusillanimous spirit . . ."[88] These ideas combine to yield the zenith of Harrington's neo-Romanism in Book II of *The Prerogative of Popular Government*: "The Romans of all nations under heaven were endowed, as with the highest virtues, so with the greatest human glory; which proceeded from this especially, that they were in love with such as were in love with their liberty."[89]

With Harrington, however, there is always a "but" – and when it comes to his neo-Roman sensibilities, the "but" is even more substantial than usual. The problem is that, in Harrington's view, the Roman commonwealth was deeply pathological and unsound. In fact, in *The Art of Lawgiving*, he goes so far as to call it "the most unequal commonwealth" in history,[90] and takes the highly unusual step of preferring even Athens to Rome (he uses the stigmatized term "democracy," rather than "republic," to designate his ideal "commonwealth").[91] Later, in *Oceana*, he explains his reasons: "Rome was crooked in her birth, or rather prodigious; her twins the patricians and plebeian orders came . . . into the world one body with two heads, or rather two bellies."[92] For Harrington, Rome's pathology derived from the fact that it comprised two classes with two sets of competing and antagonistic interests. The Roman system, he writes, required "conniving and temporising with the enmity between the senate and the people as a necessary step unto Roman greatness."[93]

In his *Brief Directions* (1658) he sums up his view of the Roman model more fully:

In this frame the senate, by the optimacy of the first and second *classes* (which seldom or never disagree), carrieth all, to the exclusion of the main body of the people; whence ariseth continual feud or enmity between the senate and the people, who . . . endeavour to curb their power by weakening their balance or diminishing of their estates. All these tumultuously and to the alternation of the government,

---

[88] Ibid., p. 737. The language here echoes Harrington's designation of the Irish as a "slothful and "pusillanimous people."

[89] Ibid., p. 506.   [90] Ibid., p. 694.

[91] Ibid., p. 785; see also pp. 839, 851. Harrington praises Athens enthusiastically for its rotation of offices, and suggests that only the want of an effective nobility doomed the city (see pp. 184, 480). Also on p. 184, Harrington observes that Athens had at least a "timid" agrarian, whereas Rome had none.

[92] Ibid., p. 276.

[93] Ibid., p. 278. Recall that "temporizing" (*temporeggiarsi*) is a central Machiavellian concept (see, for example, *Discorsi* 1.33).

with so frequent changes under so divers shapes as make a very Proteus of the commonwealth till, having been all her life-time afflicted with anarchy, she end her days in tyranny.[94]

The overall pattern here is straightforwardly Polybian: popular government degenerates into anarchy, which, in turn, yields tyranny. But Polybius had argued in Book IV of his *Histories* that this cycle (ἀνακύκλωσις) could be temporarily escaped through the introduction of a mixed constitution, and Machiavelli claimed in the *Discorsi* that Roman government had attained "perfection" (*perfezione*) precisely because it embodied this Polybian mixture. The *tumulti* between the one, the few, and the many (the consuls, senate, and tribunes) produced Roman longevity and dynamism (1.2).[95] Yet, while Machiavelli praised the *buoni ordini* of the Roman state for producing this civic energy, Harrington strongly criticizes this view. He states explicitly that he is arguing "against the judgment of Machiavel."[96] For Harrington, this matrix of competing interests was the hallmark of "modern prudence," most comprehensively expressed by England's combination of king, lords, and commons.[97] Harrington asserts that "this [English] government, being indeed the masterpiece of modern prudence, hath been cried up to the skies . . . whereas indeed it hath been no other than a wrestling match."[98] The alternative to the Roman and English "wrestling match" is a set of *ordini* which produce common, not competing interests. And for Harrington, such *ordini* depend on an egalitarian distribution of property.

Harrington believed that Machiavelli had glimpsed this principle, but that he had failed to elucidate and apply it successfully (he had not, as we have seen, heard the "natural voice" of civic strife). On the very first page of the "Preliminaries," Harrington observes that "Machiavel . . . harps much upon a string which he hath not perfectly tuned, and that is the balance of dominion or property."[99] In other words, Harrington attributes to Machiavelli an undeveloped, inner intuition that the balance of property yields the balance of power, and that, accordingly, a commonwealth can only be instituted and preserved if fortunes are kept relatively equal. In this respect, Harrington is particularly drawn to the Machiavellian argument about *gentiluomini* and *modi privati* that has been discussed above. "The

---

[94] *Political Works*, p. 588.

[95] Niccolò Machiavelli, *Discorsi sopra la prima deca di Tito Livio*, ed. Giorgio Inglese (Milan: Rizzoli, 1984), pp. 68–69. English text is taken from *Discourses on Livy*, ed. and trans. Harvey C. Mansfield and Nathan Tarcov (University of Chicago Press, 1996).

[96] *Political Works*, p. 273.   [97] Ibid., p. 397.   [98] Ibid., p. 196.   [99] Ibid., p. 157.

balance as I have laid it down," writes Harrington, "though unseen by Machiavel, is that which interpreteth him, and that which he confirmeth by his judgment."[100] He then approvingly reproduces the following passage from the *Discorsi* (1.55):

he who will go about to make a commonwealth where there be many gentlemen, unless he first destroy them, undertakes an impossibility: and he who goes about to introduce monarchy where the condition of the people is equal shall never bring it to pass, unless he cull out such of them as are the most turbulent and ambitious, and make them gentlemen or noblemen, not in name but in effect, that is by enriching them with lands, castles, and treasures, that may gain them power amongst the rest and bring in the rest unto dependence upon themselves, to the end that, they maintaining their ambition by the prince, the prince may maintain his power by them.[101]

Harrington adds the phrase "that they may gain power amongst the rest and bring in the rest unto dependence upon themselves" (which is not present in the Italian)[102] as an explanatory gloss: he wants to emphasize Machiavelli's notion that wealth creates dependence, which in turn destroys commonwealths. As he puts it in the second part of the "Preliminaries," "where there is inequality of estates, there must be inequality of power, and where there is inequality of power, there can be no commonwealth."[103] Harrington concludes, "I agree with Machiavel that a nobility or gentry, overbalancing a popular government, is the utter bane and destruction of popular government."[104]

---

[100] Ibid., p. 166.

[101] Ibid. Note that Harrington fails to translate "favore ... di uomini" and reverses the order of items in line 6 so that "lands" (his rendering of *possessioni*) appears first. The Italian reads as follows: "Che colui che vuole fare dove sono assai gentiluomini una republica, non la può fare se prima non gli spegne tutti; e che colui che dove è assai equalità vuole fare uno regno o uno principato, non lo potrà mai fare se non trae di quella equalità molti d'animo ambizioso e inquieto, e quelli fa gentiluomini in fatto, e non in nome, donando loro castella e possessioni e dando loro favore di sustanze e di uomini, acciocché, posto in mezzo di loro, mediante quegli mantenga la sua potenza ed essi mediante quello la loro ambizione" (*Discorsi*, p. 176).

[102] Harrington may have intended this phrase as a rendering of the line that appears immediately after the above passage in Machiavelli's Italian: "e gli altri siano constretti a sopportare quel giogo che la forza, e non altro mai, può fare sopportare loro." But, if so, Harrington has totally transformed this passage, translated it two lines early, and rearranged it in such a way as to stress that the riches themselves *brought* dependence.

[103] *Political Works*, p. 198.

[104] Ibid., p. 166. Sir Walter Raleigh had offered a similar discussion of "overbalancing" in his *Maxims of State*. In a section dealing with the "Mysteries, or sophisms of State," Raleigh argues that rulers must "provide by all means, that the same degree or part of the commonwealth do not exceed both in quantity and quality. In quantity, as that the number of the nobility, or of great persons, be not more than the state or commonwealth can bear. In quality, as that none grow in wealth, liberty, honours, &c. more than it is meet for that degree. For as in weights, one heavier weight bear down

This, incidentally, is the same position as that which Harrington attributes to Aristotle through the use of some creative translation. He praises "the good commonwealthsman" for "where he sayeth that democracies, when a lesser part of their citizens overtop the rest in wealth, degenerate into oligarchies and principalities."[105] He expands on this claim in a fascinating passage from *The Prerogative of Popular Government* (1658):

If a man shall translate the words ἀρετή, δύναμις πολιτική, *virtus et facultas civilis*, political virtue or faculty, where he finds them in Aristotle's *Politics* (as I make bold, and appeal unto the reader whether too bold, to do) by the words "political balance," understood as I have stated the thing, it will give such a light unto the author as will go nearer than anything alleged . . . to deprive me of the honour of that invention. For example, where Aristotle saith: "If one man or such a number of men, as to the capacity of government come within the compass of the few, excel all the rest κατ' ἀρετῆς, in balance, or in such manner that the δύναμις πολιτική, political faculties or estates, of all the rest be not able to hold weight with him or them, they will never condescend to share equally with the rest in power, whom they excel in balance; nor is it to any purpose to give them laws, who will be, as the gods, their own laws . . . For this cause (he adds), cities that live under popular power have instituted ostracism, for the preservation of equality; by which, if a man increase in riches, retinue, or popularity above what is safe, they can remove him."[106]

Harrington has indeed "made too bold" with Aristotle here. In this passage, which appears in Book III of the *Politics*, Aristotle distinguishes between two sorts of supereminence: that arising from virtue (κατ' ἀρετῆς), and that arising from "wealth, popularity, or some other political strength" (πλοῦτον ἢ πολυφιλίαν ἤ τινα ἄλλην πολιτικὴν ἰσχύν).[107] Degenerate regimes will ostracize both sorts of supereminent men, but the best regime will eject only the latter sort. The exceptionally rich and popular should be ostracized even from the best regime because they warp the proportionate order of the city. However, the best regime will not eject supereminently virtuous men; it will, on the contrary, make them rulers in accordance with the principle of justice. So Harrington muddies the waters considerably when he translates ἀρετή as "balance" in this context. Nonetheless, he is certainly right to highlight Aristotle's intense anxiety about disproportionate wealth.

the scale; so in commonwealths, that part or degree that excelleth the rest in quality and quantity overswayeth the rest after it, whereof follow alterations and conversions of state." See Raleigh, *Works*, vol. VIII, p. 8.

[105] *Political Works*, p. 235.   [106] Ibid., p. 461.

[107] *Politics* 1284a4–25 (III.8). Aristotle, *Politics*, ed. and trans. H. Rackham, Loeb Classical Library (Harvard University Press, 1932), pp. 241–47.

That anxiety finds expression in Aristotle's endorsement of ostracism as a means of neutralizing the supereminently rich, and in his further assertion that "it is better for the lawgiver to so constitute the state at the outset that it does not need this medicine."[108] It is, therefore, with some justification that Harrington appropriates Aristotle along with Machiavelli as a prophet who prepared the way for *Oceana*.

But Harrington goes further than his sources, and finds himself explicitly at odds with Machiavelli on a central point. He insists that "to make a commonwealth unequal is to divide it into parties, which setteth them at perpetual variance, the one party endeavouring to preserve their eminence and inequality, and the other to attain unto equality."[109] This, he asserts, was "whence the people of Rome derived their perpetual strife with the nobility or senate." In other words, Harrington wants to argue that Machiavelli did not sufficiently think through the implications of his own argument in the *Discorsi*: if the *inequalità* brought about by wealth and dependence creates parties and sects, then the absence of *inequalità* should remove them and, with them, the cause of all internal conflict. If the Romans had "attained in perfection" the equal agrarian, Harrington insists, "there could have been no more enmity between the senate and the people of Rome than there was between those orders in Lacedaemon or is in Venice."[110] The *tumulti* were, thus, the result of faulty *ordini*, not, as Machiavelli would have it, a necessary mechanism for balancing divergent *umori*.[111] An equal agrarian would remove any need for civil strife.

Yet, despite all his exhortations about "keeping the state rich and the citizens poor," at the end of the day Machiavelli had still attacked the Roman agrarian laws as a *morbo* – a characterization completely unacceptable to Harrington. Indeed, Harrington realized that, on Machiavelli's view, his attempt to introduce an equal agrarian into the English "Gothic" constitution would count as a dangerous, "backward-looking" measure. Machiavelli would instead counsel "temporizing" with England's property woes in order to forestall civic upheaval. Once a problem becomes evident, he would caution, it has already passed beyond effective redress. In order to refute this claim, Harrington takes the extraordinary step of creating a character, Philautus ("self-lover" in Greek), who ventriloquizes the Machiavellian position. Philautus does not mince words: "that an agrarian

---

[108] *Political Works*, p. 245 (Politics 1284b18). "βέλτιον μὲν οὖν τὸν νομοθέτην ἐξ ἀρχῆς οὕτω συστῆσαι τὴν πολιτείαν ὥστε μὴ δεῖσθαι τοιαύτης ἰατρείας."
[109] *Political Works*, p. 180.   [110] Ibid., p. 277.
[111] On this point see Vickie Sullivan, "The Civic Humanist Portrait of Machiavelli's English Successors" in *History of Political Thought* 15 (1994), esp. 80–81.

is dangerous unto a commonwealth is affirmed upon no slight authority, seeing Machiavel is positive that it was the dissension which happened about the agrarian that caused the destruction of Rome."[112] But Harrington has the Lord Archon reply (in a passage that I have already had occasion to discuss) that "I cannot see how an agrarian, as to the fixation or security of a government, can be less than necessary. And if a cure be necessary, it excuseth not the patient, his disease being otherwise desperate, that it is dangerous; which was the case of Rome, not so stated by Machiavel, where he saith that the strife about the agrarian caused the destruction of that commonwealth."[113] To argue in such a manner, the Lord Archon explains, is to take the absurd position that "when a senator was not rich (as Crassus held) except he could pay an army, that commonwealth could have done other than ruin; whether in strife about the agrarian, or without it." The "greatest danger" for a commonwealth, he concludes, "must be from the absence of an agrarian, which is the whole truth of the Roman example." In other words, Harrington ridicules Machiavelli for attacking the agrarian laws when the Roman republic, enmeshed in corrupt inequality, would have collapsed in any case. The agrarian cure may have been "dangerous," but its proponents at least sought to give the commonwealth a fighting chance.

Once Machiavelli's reticence about the Roman agrarian laws had been discounted in this manner, however, the Machiavellian analysis of *inequalità* and *modi privati* provided a perfectly satisfactory foundation for Harrington's central principle: the balance of property yields the balance of power, and, accordingly, a commonwealth must maintain relatively equal fortunes in order to survive. But a great difficulty remained. Irrespective of any descriptive account of how a particular property arrangement might be necessary for maintaining a commonwealth, there remained a powerful conviction that any coercive attempt to create such an arrangement would be fundamentally unjust. Harrington was fully aware of this objection. In *Oceana*, after the agrarian law is formally proposed, he has Philautus insist that the "commonwealth should have the innocence of the dove," and should never attack the established families which had secured Oceana her liberty: "Let us leave this purchase of her birth unto the serpent, which eateth herself out of the womb of her mother."[114] Philautus then assails (in Ciceronian style) "such assaults and sallies upon men's estates as may slacken the nerve of labour, and give others reason to believe that their sweat is vain" – that is, that their private property will not be respected.[115]

---

[112] *Political Works*, p. 232.　　[113] Ibid., p. 235.　　[114] Ibid., p. 232.　　[115] Ibid.

Harrington's critic Matthew Wren picked up precisely this Roman theme in comments quoted in *The Prerogative of Popular Government*: "How great a sin would it be against the first and purest notion of justice, to bring in a government not only different from, but directly destructive unto the settled property of Oceana . . ."[116]

In this way Harrington, like Machiavelli before him, was forced to confront a palpable tension. On the one hand, he arrived at an analysis of the social effects of wealth which stressed the need to preserve equal fortunes; on the other, his culture's most prominent theory of justice (*cuique tribuere ius suum*) precluded any coercive attempts to secure that goal. As we have seen, Machiavelli's response to this impasse was simple: he jettisoned justice as an important civic value. Harrington, however, could not follow suit. It was not enough for him that the agrarian law was salutary; it also had to be just. In his vocabulary, it was true enough that the "goods of fortune" (i.e. property) produced "empire" (political power). But he needed to show that only a "popular balance" of those goods could produce a "just" society. In order to make this claim, Harrington turned to the Greek tradition, and to Plato as its chief exponent. There are also "goods of the mind" (i.e. virtue and wisdom), he argued, and these goods yield "authority." Only when the goods of the mind and the goods of fortune (authority and empire) are united can the state be just.

> I come now unto the principles of authority, which are internal and founded upon the goods of the mind. These the legislator that can unite in his government with those of fortune cometh nearest unto the work of God, whose government consisteth of heaven and earth; which was said by Plato, though in different words, as "when princes should be philosophers, or philosophers princes, the world would be happy."[117]

The central claim of Harrington's theory is that such a union of empire and authority can only be achieved in a commonwealth. In what remains of this chapter, I will outline the content of the Harringtonian agrarian and analyze how Harrington justifies it by placing it at the center of an explicitly Greek account of political life.

v

In his *Aphorisms Political* Harrington calls the "establishment of an equal or apt division of territory" the only "equal foundation" upon which the "equal

---

[116] Ibid., p. 467.   [117] Ibid., p. 169.

superstructures" (i.e. "orders") of political life can be based.[118] He insists that the "balance" of property in a given state must be located in at least five thousand landholders in order for that state to qualify as a commonwealth, and that, accordingly, in the case of England, the largest lawful estate should yield no more than £2,000 in annual revenue (i.e. the revenue yielded by one five-thousandth of the total land).[119] Harrington also seems to be attached to this figure because it works out to four times the value of a middling English estate.[120] As set out in *Oceana*, the agrarian law secures the desired distribution of wealth by mandating that no citizen currently possessing less than the maximum estate may purchase any property which would raise his revenue above the £2,000 mark (in Marpesia, the maximum value is £500). Rather than confiscating property from the present generation, however, the Harringtonian agrarian seeks to break up large fortunes through a series of laws regulating inheritances and other gifts. Dowries are restricted to the value of £1,500, and further wedding gifts banned; primogeniture is eliminated in families whose fortunes exceed the maximum revenue, ensuring that large estates are divided relatively equally among children. According to this agrarian law, all those found to have acquired properties exceeding the legal limit will forfeit the excess to the state.[121]

Harrington leaves a clue as to the source of these proposals in Book I of *The Prerogative of Popular Government*. In the course of defending the equal agrarian, he reproduces Aristotle's defense of moderate property arrangements from Book II of the *Politics*. He begins by recording that "it hath seemed to some (says Aristotle) the main point of institution in government to order riches right; whence otherwise derives all civil discord?"[122] He then points out, following Aristotle's example, that "Plato in his *Laws* allows not increase unto a possession beyond certain bounds."[123] This reference,

---

[118] Ibid., p. 778.   [119] Ibid., pp. 236, 425, 610.

[120] Ibid., p. 604. This passage records a second computation that Harrington used in order to arrive at his maximum annual revenue; £500 is not a given minimum, but rather the annual revenue of a middling landholder. The plausibility of this figure is confirmed in R. H. Tawney, "The Rise of the Gentry, 1558–1640" in *Economic History Review* 11 (1941), 4 (note 4).

[121] *Political Works*, p. 231. Excess revenues are only to be permitted if they have been acquired through lawful inheritance under the agrarian law. On the mechanics of the agrarian, see Andrew Reeve, "Harrington's Elusive Balance" in *History of European Ideas* 4 (1984), 401–25.

[122] *Political Works*, p. 460.

[123] This reference refutes Blitzer's puzzling claim that "Harrington in all his writings never explicitly referred to the *Laws*" (Blitzer, *Immortal Commonwealth*, p. 291). Blitzer notices that Harrington's reliance on this dialogue was substantial, but concludes that, rather than taking specific proposals from Plato, Harrington simply tried to do "for his own age and country what the Athenian had done for his" (p. 292). This view neglects the substantial similarity between the agrarian proposals

I will suggest, holds the key to understanding the Platonic structure of Harrington's agrarian proposal.

The *Laws* represents Plato's "second-best society," one governed by inflexible laws, rather than by the creative rule of philosophers. The passage to which Aristotle refers appears in Book v, in the context of the "Athenian's" analysis of wealth. The Athenian admits that the best society (the type envisaged in the *Republic*) would be structured around common friendship, and would be characterized by "a community in womenfolk, in children, in all possessions whatsoever – if all means have been taken to eliminate everything we mean by the word 'ownership' from life."[124] He acknowledges, however, that such a society is beyond the "birth, breeding, and education" of the average Greek,[125] and Harrington agrees in *A System of Politics* that "to hold that government may be founded upon community is to hold that there may be a black swan or a castle in the air."[126] Nonetheless, the Athenian maintains that extremes of wealth and poverty undermine the state, and he advocates a system of private property which establishes "a certain equality of possessions."[127]

He proposes a virtuous community of 5,040 landholders "who can be armed to fight for their holdings," and among whom the land is sensibly divided.[128] The number 5,040 became very influential as a quantification of the perfectly self-sufficient society of landholders. It was seductively close to the five thousand members of the Athenian assembly described by Thucydides (a figure which Harrington referred to quite frequently), and

in Plato and Harrington – which this chapter will proceed to explore – and leads Blitzer to the incorrect conclusion that Harrington's agrarian is of a "highly original character" (p. 228). H. F. Russell Smith perhaps comes closest to my view when he states that *Oceana* resembles Plato's *Laws* in part because "by regulating property and establishing a system of checks and balances" it hopes to maintain equilibrium (*Harrington and His Oceana*, p. 73). He too, however, neglects to notice the deep structural similarities between the two texts. On this point, see also Judith Shklar, "Ideology Hunting: The Case of James Harrington" in *American Political Science Review* 53 (1959), p. 686; and Wilfried Nippel, "Ancient and Modern Republicanism: 'Mixed Constitution' and 'Ephors'" in *The Invention of the Modern Republic*, ed. Biancamaria Fontana (Cambridge University Press, 1994), p. 21.

[124] All quotations from Plato in English are taken from *Plato: the Collected Dialogues, including the Letters*, ed. Edith Hamilton, Huntington Cairns, Bollingen Series 71 (Princeton University Press, 1989). The Greek text is drawn from *Platonis opera*, ed. John Burnet, 5 vols., Oxford Classical Texts, 2nd edn. (Oxford: Clarendon Press, 1963). This quotation is from *Laws* 739c.

[125] *Laws* 740a.   [126] *Political Works*, p. 808.   [127] Plato, *Laws* 684d.

[128] *Laws* 737e. This fact might have cleared up Macpherson's confusion as to why Harrington attached such significance to the number 5,000. See C. B. Macpherson, *The Political Theory of Possessive Individualism: Hobbes to Locke* (Oxford University Press, 1962), p. 185. Macpherson's Marxist reading of Harrington follows in the tradition of R. H. Tawney, "Harrington's Interpretation of His Age" in *Proceedings of the British Academy* (1941), 199–223.

corresponds roughly to the six thousand households in each city of Utopia (another statute in this section inspired the Utopian practice of sending excess people off to found colonies).[129] Plato adds that a single individual should be entitled to amass up to four times the value of the standard land allotment, but that, if he accumulates more than that amount, he should be forced to "consign the surplus to the state and its gods."[130] The Athenian also bans the practice of dowries,[131] and attacks lavish inheritances. He declares "let no man covet wealth for his children's sake, that he may leave them in opulence; 'tis not for their own good nor for the state's."[132] If we recall Harrington's restriction of dowries, regulation of inheritance, strict minimum of five thousand substantial landholders, and insistence that fortunes above a fixed level (which is four times greater than a stipulated amount) must be surrendered to the state, we can see Plato's handwriting clearly.[133] Indeed, the fact that Harrington took the substance of his agrarian proposals from Plato is no trifling detail. It reveals that his fundamental notion of a "balance" which is undermined by extremes in wealth is embedded within a fundamentally Greek theoretical context very reminiscent of the one actualized in More's *Utopia*.

In the "Preliminaries" to *Oceana* Harrington states that "government is no other than the soul of a nation or city."[134] This comment calls to mind several Greek texts, not least Isocrates' *Areopagiticus*, an oration that Harrington quotes several times in his writings: "For the soul of a state is nothing other than its constitution" (ἔστι γὰρ ψυχὴ πόλεως οὐδὲν ἕτερον ἢ πολιτεία).[135] But the statement is part of a broader pattern in Harrington's writings that must be explained with reference to Plato's *Timaeus*.[136] In this

---

[129] Compare Plato, *Laws* 740e with More, *Utopia*, p. 135. James Cotton notices the relationship between the number 5,000 and the size of the Athenian assembly. See James Cotton, *James Harrington's Political Thought and Its Context* (New York and London: Garland Pubishing, 1991), p. 30.

[130] *Laws* 744e.   [131] *Laws* 742c.   [132] *Laws* 729a.

[133] The major difference between the two proposals is that, while Plato ordains that only eldest sons should inherit property, and that the rest should be given away to families without offspring, Harrington abolishes primogeniture (*Political Works*, p. 231 [*Laws* 740c]). Scott is right to note that Harrington resorts to Aristotle to defend his "concept of the balance" (Scott, "The Rapture of Motion," p. 147), a point also made by James Cotton (see Cotton, *Harrington's Political Thought*, pp. 44–47). But the structure of the agrarian is Platonic, as, I believe, is the overall argument into which it fits.

[134] *Political Works*, p. 170.

[135] Isocrates, *Orations*, ed. and trans. George Norlin, vol. II, Loeb Classical Library (Harvard University Press, 1929), p. 112.

[136] For the reception of this dialogue in the Renaissance, see James Hankins, "Galileo, Ficino, and Renaissance Platonism" in *Humanism and Early Modern Philosophy*, ed. Jill Kraye and M. W. F Stone (New York and London: Routledge, 2000); Hankins, "Pierleone da Spoleto on Plato's

dialogue Plato (in the person of Timaeus) provides an account of creation in which God infuses the universe with a soul, producing order (κόσμος) out of chaos.[137] The soul of the world is harmonized when its elements are balanced according to reason, and its "perfect balance" is what prevents it from decaying. This balanced arrangement is called "justice," and, when God turns to create man's soul on the model of the ordered cosmos, he imbues man with the same sublime proportions. However, in order to prevent undue perfection in his creature, God commands his underlings to warp the "circles" of man's soul, toppling reason from its throne.[138] In order to restore balance and justice, man must be drawn to perfection by the contemplation of the cosmos. He must imprint the cosmic pattern onto his soul, and, also, onto the soul of his polity: "by learning the harmonies and revolutions of the universe, [each man] should correct the courses of the head which were corrupted at our birth . . . so that having assimilated them he may attain to that best life which the gods have set before mankind."[139] Once this state is achieved, the soul will perform its intended "motion" (κίνησις), the exercise of reason and contemplation.[140] In short, in the *Timaeus* Plato connects his theory of justice from the *Republic* to a broader theory of the universe, in which the cosmos, man, and state are seen to partake of the same fundamental order in their souls.[141]

This is precisely the view we find in Harrington. Throughout *Oceana* and Harrington's other works, the soul of the state is envisioned as an image of the soul of man, and the soul of man is seen as patterned on the cosmos.[142] In the "Preliminaries" we are first told that the "life or motion" of "the soul of

Psychogony (Glosses on the *Timaeus* in Barb. lat. 21)" in *Roma, magistra mundi. Itineraria culturae medievalis. Mélanges offerts au Père L. E. Boyle à l'occasion de son 75e anniversaire*, ed. Jaqueline Hamesse, vol. 1 (Louvain-la-Neuve: F.I.D.E.M., 1998); and Hankins, "The Study of the *Timaeus* in Early Renaissance Italy" in *Natural Particulars: Nature and the Disciplines in Renaissance Europe*, ed. Anthony Grafton, and Nancy Siraisi (Cambridge, MA: MIT Press, 2000).

[137] Plato, *Timaeus* 30a.

[138] *Timaeus* 43d–e. I am simplifying what is an extremely complex discussion. Plato actually imagines that, after man is given a body, he develops an "inferior soul" which is appetitive and spirited; it then becomes the task of the original, divine soul (intellection, which is located in the head) to govern the inferior soul. For present purposes, however, it suffices to show that the soul of man has its image in the soul of the cosmos, and that the soul of the state has its image in the soul of man. See *Timaeus* 69c.

[139] *Timaeus* 90d.   [140] *Timaeus* 90c.

[141] In fact, the *Timaeus* can be read as an extended gloss on Socrates' comment at the end of *Republic* IX that the "pattern" of the ideal city is "laid up in heaven for him who wishes to contemplate it, and so beholding to constitute himself its citizen": " Ἀλλ', ἦν δ' ἐγώ, ἐν οὐρανῷ ἴσως παράδειγμα ἀνάκειται τῷ βουλομέν ὁρᾶν καὶ ὁρῶντι ἑαυτὸν κατοικίζειν" (592b).

[142] Harrington may well have encountered a similar reading of the *Timaeus* in Erasmus' *Enchiridion*. Erasmus compares the composition and order of the state to the description of the soul found in the *Timaeus*, and imagines reason as enthroned like a king when soul and state are ruled according to nature. While Harrington never refers to the *Enchiridion* itself, he quotes from Erasmus' edition

man" is "perpetual contemplation or thought."[143] In his essay on "Natural Philosophy in Harrington's Political Thought" W. C. Diamond connects this concept of "motion" to the broader question of *spiritus* in Harrington's thought.[144] The more particular reference, however, is surely to the passage in the *Timaeus* that I already identified.[145] And Harrington makes clear that thought is the basic motion of the soul because we "raise ourselves" through the "contemplation of virtue,"[146] and that virtue is expressed in the cosmos. As he puts it in *A System of Politics*, "the contemplation of form is astonishing to man, and . . . exalts his soul to God."[147] He later adds that "to be raised upon contemplation of natural things" is "natural to man as he is a philosophical creature" and that the "form of government" consists "in contemplation of, and in conformity to the soul of man."[148] Harrington's clearest statement of this view, however, makes the connection to the *Timaeus* explicit. In the "Corollary" to *Oceana*, Harrington describes the mood of Lycurgus after he had instituted the Spartan commonwealth:

For the rest . . . when he saw that his government had taken root and was in the very plantation strong enough to stand by itself, he conceived such a delight within him, as God is described by Plato to have done, when he had finished the creation of the world, and saw his own orbs move below him. For in the art of man, being the imitation of nature which is the art of God, there is nothing so like the first call of beautiful order out of chaos and confusion as the architecture of a well-ordered commonwealth.[149]

---

of Suetonius (*Works*, p. 455) and his *In acta apostolorum paraphrasis* (*Works*, p. 503), and praises Erasmus as "a man as for his learning not inferior to any, so for his freedom not addicted unto interests or parties" (*Works*, p. 502). See *The Collected Works of Erasmus*, ed. John W. O'Malley, vol. LXVI (University of Toronto Press, 1988), pp. 42–46.

[143] *Works*, p. 169.

[144] Wm. Craig Diamond, "Natural Philosophy in Harrington's Political Thought" in *Journal of the History of Philosophy* 16 (1978), 387–98. Diamond's essay constitutes the only available discussion of Harrington's neoplatonic metaphysics and their impact on his political thought, and I am indebted to it. Since he is more interested in the conflict between "natural" and "new mathematical" philosophy, however, Diamond does not explore the connection between the concepts of justice, reason, and balance in Harrington's thought and the anti-Roman character of the agrarian proposal – which is my intention in what remains of this chapter. Similarly, Jonathan Scott identifies a Platonist strain in seventeenth-century English republicanism, but his emphasis is on metaphysics, not politics, and Harrington does not figure prominently in his discussion. See Jonathan Scott, *Algernon Sidney and the English Republic, 1623–1677* (Cambridge University Press, 1988), pp. 21ff.

[145] *Timaeus* 90c. "τ δ᾽ ἐν ἡμῖν θεί συγγενεῖς εἰσιν κινήσεις αἱ τοῦ παντὸς διανοήσεις καὶ περιφοραί."

[146] *Political Works*, p. 169.   [147] Ibid., p. 837.   [148] Ibid., p. 838.

[149] Ibid., p. 341. Harrington uses the conclusion of Plutarch's *Lycurgus* as the basis for this quotation, but then alters it substantially (*Lycurgus* XXIX, 1–11). He adds the references to the "orbs," and the entire sentence beginning "For in the art of man." That passage may well refer to the opening sentence of Hobbes's *Leviathan*: "Nature (the *Art* whereby God hath made and governes the World) is by the

Immediately after this passage (a paraphrase of the conclusion to Plutarch's *Lycurgus*), the Lord Archon himself is described as revelling in the "joy and harmony" of his "spheres." In short, Harrington asserts the unity of cosmos, individual, and state, and insists that their balance is the same.

But what exactly is this balance? In the *Timaeus* we saw that it constituted an ordering of elements that accords with reason, and we should not be surprised to find this same view in Harrington. In a direct quotation of Socrates in the *Gorgias* (464b), Harrington makes clear that "policy" constitutes a "philosophy of the soul" and adds that "the main of this philosophy consisteth in deposing passion and advancing reason unto the throne of empire."[150] The rule of reason is the will of God, and, as a result, Harrington adds in the "Preliminaries" that "where, by the lusts or passions of men, a power is set above that of the law, deriving from reason which is the dictate of God, God is in that sense rejected or deposed..."[151] The next step in the argument comes when Harrington claims, like Plato, that the state is ruled according to reason when it is governed by the best men. In the "Preliminaries" Harrington claims that, even in a commonwealth of only twenty people, "there will be such difference in them that about a third will be wiser, or at least less foolish than all the rest."[152] This third, "as stags that have the largest heads," will "lead the herd," and the other citizens will "hang upon their lips as children upon their fathers" ("a commonwealth," Harrington agrees with More and Plato, "is but a great family").[153] Coining a phrase which would echo throughout the republican writings of the next century, Harrington argues that these men constitute a "natural aristocracy diffused by God throughout the whole body of mankind to this end and purpose," and that the people have "not only a natural but a positive obligation to make use of their guides."[154] In another passage Harrington states his point even more emphatically, and derives it explicitly from Plato: "where

---

Art of man, as in many other things, so in this also imitated, that it can make an Artificial Animal." See Thomas Hobbes, *Leviathan*, ed. Richard Tuck, rev. edn. (Cambridge University Press, 1996), p. 9; Plutarch, *Lives*, ed. and trans. B. Perrin, vol. 1, Loeb Classical Library (Harvard University Press, 1914). Here Harrington takes what is clearly a Platonic thought in Hobbes and places it in an even more explicitly Platonic context.

[150] *Political Works*, p. 415.   [151] Ibid., p. 178.   [152] Ibid., p. 172.

[153] Ibid., p. 414. This in itself is an indication of a deeply Greek orientation. Under Roman law, children, like slaves, are not *sui iuris*, and, as a result, a neo-Roman theorist would never use the image of a child to describe a citizen. For Plato, More, and Harrington, however, the state is a "family" where the better (the most virtuous) rule over the baser like parents over children. Compare, for example, More, *Utopia*, p. 147.

[154] *Political Works*, p. 173. This emphasis on the moral importance of the rule of the best men seems to me to be the missing element in David Norbrook's otherwise excellent analysis (his discussion of Harrington's interaction with Virgil is particularly fine). Norbrook argues instead that Harrington's

men excel in virtue, the commonwealth is stupid and unjust if accordingly they do not excel in authority: wherefore this is both the advantage of virtue, which hath her due encouragement, and the commonwealth, which hath her due services. These are the philosophers which Plato would have to be princes . . ."[155] As in More's *Utopia*, if *virtus* does not constitute *vera nobilitas*, the state is rendered "unjust" because the rational ordering of its elements is toppled.

Harrington does, however, add a crucial caveat. Although he believes sincerely that the rule of the best men constitutes justice, Harrington also insists that the best men must not both "debate" and "resolve," lest power corrupt them and "put out their light."[156] Harrington, in short, rejects the purely Platonic rule of philosopher kings on the grounds that, by giving the best men absolute rule, one would endanger the very virtue upon which their claim to rulership depends. Disproportionate power would corrupt the wise just as surely as disproportionate wealth. Accordingly, Harrington is committed to a genuinely popular regime, in which an assembly of ordinary citizens acts to balance the natural aristocrats. The rule of the best men, therefore, takes on a revised character in *Oceana*: it refers to the circumstance in which the counsel of the natural aristocrats is able to guide the commonwealth effectively. But, Harrington reaches the paradoxical

---

attachment to the aristocracy derived from his Hobbesian focus on "stability." See David Norbrook, *Writing the English Republic: Poetry, Rhetoric and Politics, 1627–1660* (Cambridge University Press, 1999), pp. 357–78. For Harrington's response to Virgil, see his *An Essay vpon Two of Virgil's Eclogues and Two Books of his Aeneis* ([London, 1658]; Ann Arbor, MI: University Microfilms International, 1984). In the concluding "Note upon the fore-going Eclogues," Harrington reaffirms his analysis of the Roman balance: "That the Roman Empire was never founded upon a sufficient ballance of absolute Monarchy, is very true; but not truer then that this was the cause of that impotency and misery in the same, which oppressed both Prince and People."

[155] *Political Works*, p. 182. So far as I have been able to tell, H. F. Russell Smith is alone in recognizing that Harrington's moderate nobility would "be to Oceana almost what the guardians were to Plato's Republic" (*Harrington and His Oceana*, p. 33) – although he neglects to adduce this passage in support of his view. Harrington's defense of a landed (rather than purely intellectual) nobility is, however, perhaps the most explicitly Aristotelian element of his thought – and it would be jettisoned by his eighteenth-century acolytes. In *Oceana*, Harrington insists that the nobility be retained, and asks "For how else can you have a commonwealth that is not altogether mechanic . . . Your mechanics, till they have first feathered their nests – like the fowls of the air, whose whole employment is to seek their food – are so busied in their private concernments that they have neither leisure to study the public, nor are safely to be trusted with it . . . " He adds that nobles are necessary "especially when their families come to be such as are noted for their service done unto the commonwealth, and so take into their ancient riches ancient virtue, which is the second definition of nobility, but such an one as is scarce possible in nature without the former" (*Political Works*, p. 259). The "mechanics" in this passage are clearly Aristotle's *banausoi*, and the discussion of the relationship between "ancient riches" (*longae divitiae* or ἀρχαῖος πλοῦτος) and virtue is taken directly from *Politics* IV (1294a23). Harrington's phrase "the second definition of nobility" reveals that he is working from Aristotle's definition.

[156] *Political Works*, p. 173.

conclusion that, in order to institute such a regime, he must assign to non-aristocrats the power to make final decisions.

All of this, in turn, requires an egalitarian distribution of property. Following More once again, Harrington proceeds to base his defense of an "equal balance" on the argument that it makes possible the rule of reason. More had maintained that the sort of agrarian Harrington proposes, in which laws are made such that "no one should own more than a certain amount of land or receive more than a certain income,"[157] would prove ultimately ineffective in eliminating "poverty and anxieties" because such statutes would keep private property in place. Harrington disagrees with More on this point, but he nonetheless defends the agrarian on More's terms. He argues that extremes in wealth warp character, banish virtue, and, as a result, render the state "unjust" in the Greek sense.

When the "form" of the commonwealth is secure, Harrington insists, "the government maketh evil men good."[158] On another occasion, he adds that "orders of a government" should "constrain this or that creature to shake off that inclination which is more peculiar unto it and take up that which regards the common good."[159] In particular, in language that should sound quite familiar, Harrington claims that "the nature of orders in a commonwealth rightly instituted" are "void of all jealousy."[160] Just as More had explained the absence of envy from Utopia by virtue of the fact that men are "free from anxieties, and without worries about making a living" and that "everyone can feel secure of his own livelihood and happiness, and that of his whole family,"[161] Harrington argues that the agrarian excludes "ambition and covetousness" because it "taketh away the greatest of worldly cares." It "gives us the sweat of our brows without diminution" (perhaps a nod to Cicero's attack on *deminutio*), it "prepares our table," it "makes our cup to overflow," and eases our worries by "providing for our children."[162] For Harrington, like More, the equal state was the only path to the world envisioned by "our religion," where "*justice shall run down like a river, and judgment like a mighty stream.*"[163]

When the state is unequal, however, "government maketh good men evil." When their balance is undermined, Harrington writes, states "let in the sink of luxury."[164] He later adds that, just as an equal balance "abateth the luxury of the nobility" and restores "justice and right reason," in an unequal state "luxury is introduced in the place of temperance" and a deep "corruption of manners" results.[165] Harrington follows More and Plato in

[157] More, *Utopia*, p. 103.   [158] *Political Works*, p. 763.   [159] Ibid., p. 172.   [160] Ibid., p. 203.
[161] More, *Utopia*, p. 241.   [162] *Political Works*, p. 239.   [163] Ibid., p. 333.   [164] Ibid., p. 188.
[165] Ibid., p. 202.

arguing that extremes of wealth and poverty corrupt both rich and poor, and explains this corruption using a simile from the *Timaeus*. Plato compares imbalance in the soul to "a body which has one leg too long, or which is unsymmetrical in some other respect" and, as a result, is unable to do its work and "stumbles through awkwardness."[166] Likewise, Harrington denies that "a political body is rendered any fitter for industry, by having one gouty and another withered leg, than a natural."[167] Again, like Plato in Book IV of the *Republic*,[168] he argues that a city characterized by extremes of wealth and poverty is really "two commonwealths"[169] – a city of the rich and a city of the poor – and that corruption follows when there are "some who have no need of their trading, and others that are not able to follow it."[170] Indeed, Harrington so connected the absence of equity to idleness among the rich that he argued that the Swiss and Dutch had achieved "an implicit agrarian" simply because they lived in places "not alluring inhabitants unto wantonness, but obliging them unto universal industry."[171]

The final step of the argument is that, for Harrington (like More), rulership is determined by property.[172] It is simply a matter of nature that the richest men will have the greatest political power ("empire," rather than "authority" in Harrington's terminology).[173] As a result, in an unequal commonwealth, a nobility rendered idle and luxurious by corrupt *ordini* is left to rule, and the government of excellent men (i.e. reason) is lost. The solution to this moral crisis is the equal commonwealth: "the eminence acquired by suffrage of the people in a commonwealth, especially if it be popular and equal, can be ascended by no other steps than the universal acknowledgement of virtue."[174] Harrington's view can, thus, be

---

[166] *Timaeus* 87e. Aristotle gives a similar image in *Politics* 1284b (III.8) in his defense of ostracism. Describing the dangers of disproportionate power, he writes that "a painter would not let his animal have a foot of disproportionately large size [τὸν ὑπερβάλλοντα πόδα τῆς συμμετρίας], even though it was an exceptionally beautiful foot . . . " Nonetheless, it seems clear that Harrington (who mentions neither painter nor animal) is working from Plato here.

[167] *Political Works*, p. 238.

[168] *Republic* 421e. Plato's discussion of the decay caused by excessive wealth and poverty (quoted in the previous chapter) is found at 421d–422a.

[169] *Political Works*, p. 272.   [170] Ibid., p. 238.   [171] Ibid., p. 234.

[172] See, for example, ibid., p. 405.   [173] See, for example, ibid., p. 163.

[174] Ibid., p. 182. This should also answer Macpherson's argument that Harrington should be regarded as a theorist of class identity (see, for example, *Possessive Individualism*, p. 268). Harrington did not argue, as Macpherson suggests, that the equal agrarian was sustainable because it satisfied the interests to two (or three) distinct economic classes through its embrace of "bourgeois" market relations. He argued rather that the agrarian would actually eliminate "classes." Only when disproportionate wealth enters the state, on Harrington's account, do people begin to see themselves as members of sub-groups whose interests are distinct from the common good (this, remember, is the substance of his critique of Machiavelli). If wealth is kept proportionate, Harrington argues, then all citizens

summarized as follows: the state has a soul which is modeled on the soul of the cosmos and the soul of man; souls are ordered justly when they are arranged according to reason; in the case of the state, extremes in wealth corrupt character, and, as a result, produce rulers who administer the state according to the passions, rather than reason – that is to say, unjustly; when the state maintains an equal distribution of wealth, however, virtue becomes the sole recognized claim to political power and the soul of the state is, thus, governed according to reason. The republic may then become "perfect and immortal" like the cosmos itself. This, in sum, is Harrington's response to the claim that his agrarian law violates the spirit of *iustitia*. He is able to embrace such a comprehensively anti-Roman proposal because he supports it with a Greek rather than a Roman conception of holistic justice (δικαιοσύνη) – one very similar to the "justice" of *Utopia*.[175] This is the cosmic edifice he constructs to house his Machiavellian analysis of wealth and dependence. As he puts it, "we have wandered the earth to find out the balance of power; but to find out that of authority we must ascend, as I said, nearer heaven, or to the image of God which is the soul of man."[176]

will have the same interest: the common good, defined as the rule of reason and virtue. Much the same could be said about Gary Remer's claim that Harrington placed the power of "resolving" in the popular assembly because his "natural aristocracy" was wise, but not virtuous enough to protect the interests of the people. Once again, Harrington's point is rather that excessive power, like excessive wealth, corrupts. When confined to the sphere of guiding the commonwealth, the natural aristocracy seeks the common good. See Gary Remer, "James Harrington's New Deliberative Rhetoric: Reflection of an Anticlassical Republicanism" in *History of Political Thought* 16 (1995), esp. 537.

[175] Blitzer's claim that Harrington's rationale for the agrarian was "economic," rather than "moral" neglects the connections among wealth, character, reason, and justice that I have established (Blitzer, *Immortal Commonwealth*, p. 233)

[176] *Political Works*, p. 169. But Harrington's notion of justice, while polemically un-Roman, also allows him to arrive at a great moment of Graeco-Roman synthesis, as he argues that the dethroning of reason brought about by passion leads to the destruction of *libertas*. In short, Harrington wants to argue that people are rendered unfree in a Roman sense when the state is not ordered according to Platonic principles. He achieves this by claiming that a disordered, unjust soul leaves states open to enslavement by "the one," "the few," or a foreign power. The corruption of the Platonic soul becomes the catalyst for Polybian transformation; the warping of popular character through disproportionate wealth is what opens the door to tyranny. Harrington makes this point explicit in *The Art of Lawgiving*: "a commonwealth, by her natural ways of frugality, of fattening and cockering up of the people, is apt to bring estates unto such excess in some hands, as eating out the rest, boweth the neck of a free state or city unto the yoke, and exposeth her to the goad of a lord and master" (p. 687). Harrington claims that this happened in the case of the Romans, when they "let in the sink of luxury, and forfeited the inestimable treasure of liberty for themselves and posterity" (p. 188). When luxury replaces temperance, Harrington claims, "servitude" is sure to replace "freedom" (p. 202).

The Greek tradition would never be the same after Harrington. Throughout the late seventeenth and eighteenth centuries, political thinkers of all persuasions carefully consulted his works, and it was often from *Oceana* that they received the bulk of their exposure to Greek political theory. The version of the Greek story they encountered there was unique in its formulation and emphasis. It stressed the intrinsic connection between wealth and rulership, and argued that only when fortunes were relatively equal could the rule of virtue (i.e. justice) be instituted. This incarnation of the Greek tradition represented a substantial modification of the Morean view that preceded it. As has already been noted, Harrington bluntly rejected *Utopia*'s abolition of private property, guaranteeing that his disciples would follow him in advocating an egalitarian distribution of wealth, rather than its outright elimination. Moreover, Harrington constructed his Greek schema around Machiavelli's singular analysis of wealth and dependence, with the result that *Oceana* reshaped not only the Greek tradition but the legacy of the *Discorsi* as well. For while Harrington had freely used the Machiavellian vocabulary of *virtù, corruzione, servitù, gentiluomini, modi privati*, and *equalità*, he had embedded them within a Greek theoretical context which dramatically transformed the nature of their referents. For example, Harrington agreed with Machiavelli that *equalità* was a necessary condition of *virtù*, but his "virtue" was Plato's, not Machiavelli's – it was the result of a justly balanced soul aligned with the cosmos through contemplation, not the preparedness to do whatever is necessary to achieve *grandezza* (Harrington, as we have seen, was no theorist of the *vita activa*). In short, Harrington bequeathed to the eighteenth century a Greek tradition transformed by Machiavelli and a Machiavelli transformed by the Greek tradition.

However, in claiming that Harrington arrived at a new, systematic vision of the Greek tradition colored by his reading of Machiavelli, I do not intend to minimize the genuine eclecticism of Harrington's thought nor to suggest that all of *Oceana* can be reduced to a defense of this synthesis. Harrington wrote all his political works in the four-year period between 1656 and the Restoration. Because of the nature of that turbulent time, his writings have a sense of immediacy not found in, for example, More's *Utopia*. He was fighting desperately for the survival of the English commonwealth in its most perilous hour, while trying to persuade its leaders to institute genuine republican government in lieu of the Cromwellian Protectorate. Harrington did not have the luxury of being a purist; he had to draw from a wide variety of sources and authors in order to construct a model for English government that could be embraced and, ultimately, enacted. What is, therefore, most surprising about Harrington is that, while eclectic, he was not haphazard. He knitted together a disparate set of materials, and achieved a powerful new perspective on the Greek case. Despite the urgent demands of history, he chose to "weigh the world again."

CHAPTER 4

"Prolem cum matre creatam"
The background to Montesquieu

I

In his 1808 commentary on *De l'esprit des lois*, later translated into English under the supervision of Thomas Jefferson, the political economist Antoine-Louis-Claude Destutt de Tracy attacks what he considers a central, but bizarre aspect of Montesquieu's thought. He insists that the "democratic republics" whose parameters the President sketches in the early books of his great treatise must be rejected as irretrievably nostalgic and perverse:

[Montesquieu] chooses the most austere rules, and those most likely to uproot in individuals all human feeling. In order to achieve his end, he permits without restriction that one should take the most violent measures, like those of equally dividing all lands, of never allowing one man to join together two estates, of forcing a father to leave his inheritance to one of his sons, and to have the others adopted by citizens without children, of not giving more than a middling dowry to girls, and when they are heiresses, to force them to marry their nearest relation, or even to require that the rich take in marriage, without dowry, the daughter of a poor citizen, and give a rich dowry to their own daughter to marry a poor citizen, etc., etc. He adds to this the deepest respect for everything that is ancient . . .[1]

---

[1] A.-L.-C. Destutt de Tracy, *Commentaire sur l'Esprit des lois de Montesquieu* (Geneva: Slatkine Reprints, 1970), p. 48. All translations are my own, unless otherwise indicated. "il choisit [les règles] les plus austères et les plus propres à déraciner dans les individus tout sentiment humain. Pour atteindre à ce but, il approuve sans restriction que l'on prenne les mesures les plus violentes, comme celles de partager toutes les terres également, de ne jamais permettre qu'un seul homme réunisse deux portions, d'obliger un père à laisser sa portion à un de ses fils, et à faire adopter les autres par des citoyens sans enfants, de ne donner qu'une très-faible dot aux filles, et quand elles sont héritières, de les forcer à épouser leur plus proche parent, ou même d'exiger que les riches prennent, sans dot, en marriage, la fille d'un citoyen pauvre, et donnent une riche dot à la leur, pour épouser un citoyen pauvre, etc., etc. Il ajoute à tout cela le plus profond respect pour tout ce qui est ancien . . ." In fact, while Montesquieu does praise the Platonic statute which forces parents to select one child to inherit, and to have the others adopted, he does not favor the imbalance in dowries between rich and poor that Destutt de Tracy describes here. See Montesquieu, *The Spirit of the Laws*, ed. and trans. Anne Cohler, Basia Miller, and Harold Stone (Cambridge University Press, 1989), p. 46.

Elsewhere, Destutt de Tracy simply concludes that Montesquieu endorses "certain measures clearly contrary to distributive justice and to the sentiments natural to man,"[2] and attributes this endorsement to a bewildering admiration for "many of the institutions of the ancients . . . an admiration of which I cannot partake, and which I am surprised to see in a man who has studied so widely."[3]

Leaving aside for a moment Destutt de Tracy's evident assumption that Montesquieu admires rather than merely describes the practices of his *républiques* in *De l'esprit des lois*[4] – a proposition which has attracted the attention of numerous Montesquieu scholars[5] – his characterization of Montesquieu's comments is extremely astute. It has perhaps not been sufficiently noted that the institutional arrangements Destutt de Tracy finds so objectionable do indeed constitute the fundamental apparatus of Montesquieu's republics, and that this apparatus owes its rudiments to ancient sources. Yet Destutt de Tracy's account stands in need of development. Montesquieu does not draw his republican theory from "ancient sources" in general, but rather from almost exclusively Greek sources. John Adams observed as much when he characterized Montesquieu's republican ideas as "imaginations of his own, derived from the contemplation of the reveries of Xenophon and Plato, concerning equality of goods, and community of wives and children, in their delirious ideas of a perfect commonwealth."[6] Adams might have added that Montesquieu's republican paradigm is clearly indebted to the series of early-modern political philosophers studied above: those whose commonwealth theories can be said to follow in a Greek tradition. In this chapter I will attempt to flesh out Destutt de Tracy's trenchant observations, identifying what is significant in the pedigree of Montesquieu's republicanism, and thereby placing the President in a particular political tradition.

---

[2] Ibid., p. 222. "quelques mesures évidemment contraires à la justice distributive et aux sentiments naturels à l'homme."

[3] Ibid., p. 27. "beaucoup d'institutions des anciens . . . une admiration que je ne puis partager, et que je suis bien surpris de voir dans un homme qui a autant réflechi."

[4] Destutt de Tracy believed that Montesquieu had portrayed republican government as "insupportable et presque aussi absurde [as despotism], tout en lui prodiguant son admiration" (ibid., p. 31).

[5] See, for example, David Carrithers, "Not So Virtuous Republics: Montesquieu, Venice, and the Theory of Aristocratic Republicanism" in *Journal of the History of Ideas* 52 (1991), 245–68; Nannerl O. Keohane, "Virtuous Republics and Glorious Monarchies: Two Models in Montesquieu's Political Thought" in *Political Studies* 20 (1972), 383–96; David Lowenthal, "Montesquieu and the Classics: Republican Government in *The Spirit of the Laws*" in *Ancients and Moderns: Essays on the Tradition of Political Philosophy in Honor of Leo Strauss*, ed. Joseph Cropsey (New York: Basic Books, 1964), pp. 258–87.

[6] *The Works of John Adams, Second President of the United States*, ed. Charles Francis Adams, vol. VI (Boston: Charles C. Little and James Brown, 1851), p. 211.

II

It is perhaps heresy to search for the intellectual forebears of an author who prefaced his greatest work with the phrase "prolem sine matre creatam,"[7] but in order to understand Montesquieu's relationship to Greek republican theory we must first study his interaction with two broadly influential eighteenth-century ideologies. It is a mark of Montesquieu's cosmopolitan complexity that one of these ideologies is exclusively English. His three-year stay in England (1729–31), his association with Bolingbroke through the Club d'Entresol in Paris, and his abiding fascination with English politics make it hardly surprising that English "Country" opposition thought should have colored his relationship to republican political theory, but the extent of the influence is truly remarkable.[8] J. G. A. Pocock memorably dubbed the political principles of the late seventeenth-century Whig politicians and pamphleteers "neo-Harringtonianism" in order to underscore the Whig "Country" party's intense concern over court patronage and the rise of a standing army.[9] Pocock's analysis is ingenious and complex, and there is no room here for an extended discussion of the relationship between Harrington and the English Whigs. My interest is simply to show that Harrington's analysis of the interplay between property, political structures, and virtue in general, and his historical account of the agrarian laws in particular, survived the Restoration and passed intact into the eighteenth century, where, I believe, they played an essential role in the articulation of Montesquieu's republican theory.[10]

The first protagonist in the story of Harringtonian transmission is Henry Neville, the man whom Thomas Hobbes suspected of being directly

---

[7] "An offspring created without a mother." The phrase is from Ovid, *Metamorphoses* II.553.

[8] See, for example, Robert Shackleton, "Montesquieu, Bolingbroke, and the Separation of Powers" in *Essays on Montesquieu and the Enlightenment*, ed. David Gilson and Martin Smith (Oxford: The Voltaire Foundation, 1988), pp. 3–16; Michel Baridon, "Rome et l'Angleterre dans les Considérations" in *Storia e ragione: le* Considérations *sur les causes de la grandeur des Romains et de leur décadence di Montesquieu nel 250° della pubblicazione. Atti del Convegno internazionale organizato dall'Instituto Universitario Orientale e dalla Società italiana di studi sul secolo XVIII*, ed. Alberto Postigliola (Naples: Liguori Editore, 1987), pp. 292–309; and Lando Landi, *L'Inghilterra e il Pensiero Politico di Montesquieu* (Padua: CEDAM, 1981).

[9] J. G. A. Pocock, *The Machiavellian Moment: Florentine Political Thought and the Atlantic Republican Tradition* (Princeton University Press, 1975), pp. 406–7.

[10] The positive attitude toward the Gracchi exhibited by several authors in the Whig historiographical tradition is excellently discussed in M. Raskolnikoff, "Caius Gracchus ou la révolution introuvable: historiographie d'une 'révolution'" in *Demokratia et Aristokratia à propos de Caius Gracchus: mots grecs et réalités romaines*, ed. Claude Nicolet (Paris: Publication de la Sorbonne, 1983), pp. 117–34. Although Raskolnikoff's summary is necessarily cursory and incomplete (and although she does not notice the explicit Harringtonian turn from Roman to Greek sources, or the ideology behind that turn), I am indebted to her insight.

complicit in the authorship of *Oceana*.[11] Neville's first major attempt to popularize Harrington's theory of property came innocuously enough in his 1675 edition of the *The Workes of the Famous Nicolas Machiavel*. In Neville's translation of the *Discorsi* we find an unremarked, but systematic rewriting of Machiavelli's comments on wealth and property designed to bring them into conformity with Harrington's doctrine of "balance" and, not incidentally, to make them more palatable to Neville's Whig audience. Edward Dacres, whose 1636 translation of the *Discorsi* held sway in England for forty years, had brought a cold honesty to the task of rendering Machiavelli's Italian. In the crucial chapter on the agrarian laws (1.37), Dacres declined to soften Machiavelli's insistence on keeping the state rich and the citizens poor. He writes dutifully that from the discord between the patricians and the plebs "grew that disease, that brought forth the quarrell touching the *Agrarian* law. And in conclusion, caus'd the destruction of the Roman Republique. And because Commonwealths well ordered are to maintaine the publique wealthy, and the particulars poore, it is likely there was in Rome some defect in this law..."[12] In contrast, Neville expurgates Machiavelli's paean to poverty at the expense of sense and coherence:

And because it is necessary in every well order'd State, that respect be had rather to the enrichment of the Publick, than particular Citizens, the people of Rome could not (in what belong'd to this Law) but erre against the Fundamentals of their Government, if they were so constituted, that process of time could give no occassion of difference, unless we will rather affirm that at first all things were so well, that it was beyond the power of time to disorder them.[13]

In Neville's hands, Machiavelli's insistence on poverty becomes a vague injunction that public wealth should be considered before private wealth.

On Neville's reading, Machiavelli had preached universal poverty, while Harrington had preached only proportionality. Indeed, Harrington clearly did not attack wealth *per se* (recall that he allowed his citizens to own land yielding up to £2,000 in annual revenue); he worried about disproportionate wealth, a level of luxury that could corrupt souls, topple the balance

[11] John Aubrey reports that "Mr. T. Hobbes was wont to say that Henry Nevill had a finger in that pye [i.e. *Oceana*]; and 'tis like enough." See John Aubrey, *Brief Lives*, ed. Oliver Lawson Dick (London: Secker and Warburg, 1949), p. 124. Raskolnikoff neglects to mention Neville in her summary account.

[12] E. Dacres, *Machiavels Discourses. Upon the first Decade of T. Livius translated out of the Italian; With some animadversions noting and taxing his errours* (London, 1636), p. 152.

[13] Henry Neville, *The Workes of the Famous Nicolas Machiavel, Citizen and Secretary of Florence* (London, 1675), p. 303.

of property on which the popular regime rested, and scuttle the rule of the wise. Neville was anxious to vindicate Harrington on this point, and assiduously turned Machiavelli into a proto-Harringtonian. Accordingly, while Dacres faithfully reports Machiavelli's observation in III.25 that "wee have otherwhere discoursed, that the most profitable ordinance that can be made in a free State, is that the Citizens be kept bare and poore,"[14] Neville writes "We have said elsewhere, that nothing is of more importance to the conservation of the liberty of a State, than to keep the Citizens low, and from being two [sic] wealthy."[15] A similar instance occurs at III.16, where Machiavelli argues that keeping the citizens poor (*mantenere i cittadini poveri*) is one way of forestalling the rise of rich, unworthy men to offices claimed by *gli uomini grandi e rari* – a major source of resentment. Here Dacres translates accurately, "And devising what might bee the remedyes hereof [i.e. to the problem of resentment], wee had two; the one to keepe the Citizens always poore, to the end that riches without vertue should not be able to corrupt."[16] Neville, on the other hand, has: "and thinking sometimes with my self what remedies were most proper, I could light on but two, one was to keep the Citizens from growing too rich, that wealth without virtue might not be sufficient to advance any man."[17] The goal, for Neville, is not to keep the citizens "poor," but to keep them from "growing too rich."

In 1681 Neville would expand on this analysis and offer a full-fledged defense of the Harringtonian program in *Plato Redivivus*. That Neville's dialogue owed a great debt to *Oceana* none of his contemporaries doubted. The publisher of *Plato Redivivus* appended a letter to the first edition in which he expressed his concern that "a considerable part of this treatise being a repetition of a great many principles and positions out of *Oceana*, the author would be discredited for borrowing from another and the sale of the book hindered."[18] Indeed, Neville shows his cards early in the second dialogue; he declares that "there is no maxim more infallible and holding in any science, than this is in politics; that empire is founded in property. Force or fraud may alter a government; but it is property that must found and eternize it."[19] He continues by paraphrasing Harrington's analysis of England's property distribution from the first "Preliminary" to *Oceana*. Neville agrees that, as a result of the policies of former kings (in particular

---

[14] Dacres, *Machiavels Discourses*, p. 561.   [15] Neville, *Machiavel*, p. 410.
[16] Dacres, *Machiavels Discourses*, p. 529.   [17] Neville, *Machiavel*, p. 401.
[18] *Two English Republican Tracts*, ed. Caroline Robbins (Cambridge University Press, 1969), p. 68. Cited hereafter as *Two Tracts*.
[19] Ibid., p. 87.

Henry VII, whom Harrington, following Francis Bacon, had particularly singled out),[20] "entails have been suffered to be cut off; and so two parts in ten of all those vast estates [of the nobility], as well as manors and demenses, by the luxury and folly of their owners, have been within these two hundred years purchased by the lesser gentry and the commons," creating a popular balance and rendering "the country scarce governable by monarchy."

Neville then turns to consider the examples of the ancient republics and how they fared at cultivating the equal distribution of property so necessary to republican government. His maxim, as his translation of Machiavelli would lead us to expect, is that it is not "dangerous to a city to have their people rich, but to have such a power in the governing part of the empire, as should make those who managed the affairs of the commonwealth depend upon them."[21] The deep concern is disproportionate wealth; nonetheless Neville notes approvingly that "Moses, Theseus, and Romulus, founders of democracies, divided the land equally"[22] and adds that "Lycurgus, the greatest politician that ever founded any government, took a sure way to fix property, by confounding it and bringing it all into common."[23] The Athenians, however, "for want of some constitutions to fix property as Theseus placed it, were in danger of utter ruin." Solon came to the rescue, however, and "that city grew and continued long the greatest, the justest, the most virtuous, learned and renowned, of all in that age," as described "in Plutarch, and other authors."[24] Rome, however, was a different story: "The Romans, having omitted in their institution to provide for the fixing of property, and so the nobility (called *patricii*) beginning to take to themselves a greater share in the conquered lands than had been usual (for in the first times of the commonwealth under Romulus, and even after, it was always practised to divide the lands equally amongst the tribes)," Licinius Stolo was prompted to introduce his measure restricting landholding to 500 *iugera* per citizen.[25] The law was finally instituted, Neville continues, "and if this law had been strictly observed to the last, that glorious commonwealth might have subsisted to this day, for aught we know."

But Rome did not maintain the Licinian law, and instead ended up creating a class of excessively rich individuals which "came afterward to be

[20] See, for example, *The Political Works of James Harrington*, ed. J. G. A. Pocock (Cambridge University Press, 1977), p. 197. Harrington directly quotes Bacon's *History of the Reign of King Henry VII*, and his general comments on the danger of a hegemonic nobility in *Of the true Greatness of Kings and Estates*. See *The Works of Francis Bacon*, ed. James Spedding, Robert Leslie Ellis, and Douglas Denon Heath, vol. VI (London: 1858), pp. 93–95, pp. 444–52.
[21] Neville, *Two Tracts*, p. 99.   [22] Ibid., p. 94.   [23] Ibid., p. 95.   [24] Ibid., p. 96.   [25] Ibid.

that which ruined [Roman] liberty, and which the Gracchi endeavoured to prevent when it was too late."[26]

For those illustrious persons [the Gracchi], seeing the disorder that was then in the commonwealth, and rightly comprehending the reason, which was the intermission of the Agrarian, and by consequence the great purchases which were made by the men of Rome (who had enriched themselves in Asia and other provinces) . . . began to harangue the people, in hopes to persuade them to admit of the right remedy; which was to confirm the Agrarian law with a retrospect; which although they carried, yet the difficulties in the execution proved so great, that it never took effect: by reason that the common people whose interest it was to have their lands restored, yet having long lived as clients and dependents of the great ones . . . were prevailed with rather to join (for the most part) with the oppressors of themselves and their country, and to cut the throats of their redeemers, than to employ their just resentment against the covetous violators of their government and property.

Neville concludes, "so perished the two renowned Gracchi . . . not for any crime, but for having endeavoured to preserve and restore their commonwealth." This account is instantly recognizable as an almost exact recapitulation of Harrington's discussion of the Roman agrarian movement in the second "Preliminary." Once again, Neville's description of the "just resentment" of the commons against the "covetous violators" of their property, and his vindication of the Gracchi and their agrarian program as the "right remedy" (despite Machiavelli's belief to the contrary) reveal a thoroughly anti-Roman set of sensibilities.

Indeed, Neville's auxiliary source for this account was Harrington's primary source: the Greek historian Plutarch. He reveals as much when he continues by having his "Noble Venetian" respond to his "English Gentleman," "Sir, I approve what you say in all things; and in confirmation of it, shall further allege the two famous princes of Sparta, Agis and Cleomenes: which I couple together, since Plutarch does so."[27] Plutarch's lives of Agis and Cleomenes, as we have seen, are the "parallels" to his lives of the Gracchi. By adducing them here Neville is simply following Plutarch's own logic. Neville argues, as we might expect from a devotee of Harrington and Plutarch, that these Spartan heroes, "finding the corruption of their commonwealth, and the decay of their ancient virtue, to proceed from the neglect and inobservance of their founder's rules, and a breach of that equality which was first instituted," tried to "restore the laws of Lycurgus, and divide the territory anew." Both men perished from "treachery" and

---

[26] Ibid., p. 99.   [27] Ibid., p. 100.

the "baseness and wickedness of the people," Neville explains (ventriloquizing Plutarch), since "where the policy is corrupted, there must necessarily be a corruption and depravation of manners; and an utter abolition of all faith, justice, honour, and morality." He concludes that all changes in regime "have turned upon this hinge of property," and that only the institution and maintenance of agrarian laws can "make a commonwealth immortal."

In short, in Neville's *Plato Redivivus* Harrington's fundamentally Greek account of agrarian laws and their history survives intact. Agrarian laws are praised because they preserve popular government, without which justice is lost. Likewise, in the crucial case of ancient Rome, Neville agrees with Harrington (and his Greek sources) that the Gracchi were heroes and that it was the lack of an agrarian law which caused the fall of the republic. Neville bequeathed this perspective on the history of the agrarian movement to a new generation of Whig intellectuals.[28] Among these disciples was Neville's younger contemporary Walter Moyle, who would become a crucial conduit of Whig ideology and historiography for the young Montesquieu. Moyle, a lawyer and one-time member of Parliament, became one of the most widely influential Whig pamphleteers of the early eighteenth century. A devotee of "Old Mr. *Henry Nevil*, whom you know they call *Plato* . . . from his being Author of an excellent Treatise intitled *Plato Redivivus*,"[29] Moyle spent much of his career applying Neville's Harringtonian insights to ancient examples. In 1698 he sent his friend Anthony Hammond *An Essay on the Lacedaemonian Government*, which the latter ultimately published in 1727 in an edition of Moyle's collected works. The essay owes much to its namesake, Xenophon's *Politeia of the Lacedaemonians*,[30] and to Plutarch's *Lycurgus*, but its overt reliance on Harrington and Neville is perhaps its most striking feature. Moyle opens his discussion by attributing to Lycurgus an awareness that Sparta needed "security from laws, which may create such

---

[28] Interestingly, Algernon Sidney does not replicate this Harringtonian focus on the agrarian laws. In the *Discourses* he does record that "*Rome* in its foundations" exhibited several defects, among them the fact that the Romans "did not think . . . of setting limits to the proportion of Land that one man might enjoy, till the avarice of a few had so far succeeded, that their Riches were grown formidable, and many by the poverty to which they were reduc'd became useless to the City" (Sidney, *Discourses on Government*, 2nd edn. [London, 1704], p. 103). This is, to be sure, a thoroughly Plutarchan thought. Yet, Sidney argues that the "inconveniences" arising from such disorders "were by degrees discover'd and remedi'd," and he does not give agrarian laws a central place in his theory.

[29] Walter Moyle, *The Whole Works*, ed. Anthony Hammond (London, 1727), p. 73.

[30] Moyle took from Xenophon his emphasis on the fact that Lycurgus had made "the freedom of the city" (ἐλευθερία) the basis of all his laws (*Lac.* VII. 2). See Xenophon, *Scripta minora*, ed. and trans. E. C. Marchant, Loeb Classical Library (London: William Heinemann, 1925). Moyle also translated Xenophon's *Discourse upon Improving the Revenue of the State of Athens* (1697).

a Temperament in the Constitution of the Government, that a due Ballance in Property, Power and Dominion is formed by it."[31] This "ballance," he continues, received its name from "*modern Politicks*," but "it was *ancient Prudence* taught us the Thing."[32] Moyle had indeed read his Harrington.

He proceeds to summarize the ideological thrust of the Spartan constitution in an obvious, but unattributed paraphrase of a central passage from Plutarch (*Lycurgus* VIII). This lengthy analysis contains an archetypal statement of the "Greek view" as we have come to know it:

> Lycurgus, when he first begun to give a new Model to the Common-wealth, found the greatest Part of the People to be wretchedly and desperately poor, and some few extremely rich; his Intention and Design was to banish on the one Side Envy, Fraud and Violence; and on the other, Insolence, Luxury and Oppression; and together with these, Riches and Poverty, each of them, when in Extreams, Diseases dangerous to the Tranquility of a Commonwealth; upon this he persuaded them to come into a new and equal Division of Lands, and that for time to come none should aim at Priority and Precedency in any thing, but in private and public Merit; that all should live upon equal Terms with one another, declaring there ought to be no difference between Man and Man, but what arises from just Praise of Virtue, and necessary Reproach of Vice.[33]

The rather un-Lycurgan argument that wealth and poverty are dangerous "Diseases" only "when in Extreams" is, predictably enough, Moyle's own Harringtonian contribution. But, for the rest, Moyle faithfully reproduces Plutarch's analysis: Lycurgus instituted an equal distribution of land in order to secure the rule of the best men. Only when fortunes are equal can virtue be given its due (Moyle adds the significant detail that this is "just").[34]

At the outset, according to Moyle, the Lycurgan system was an unqualified success. He writes that "the Crimes which are perpetually committed out of the Love of Money, did of themselves soon cease."[35] But eventually "this *Golden Age* at Sparta, where Gold it self was of little Worth or Esteem, declined" and luxury entered the state. The results were predictable: "Some time after the equal distribution of lands (the *Agrarian* Law) was shaken, though this was judged to be the immovable Basis of the Common-wealth." Once the agrarian was toppled, corruption, envy, and luxury reemerged, and the "ballance" of the Spartan constitution collapsed. From all of this,

---

[31] Moyle, *The Whole Works*, p. 50.   [32] Ibid., p. 51.   [33] Ibid., p. 51.
[34] At *Lycurgus* VIII.2, Plutarch simply has καλῶν ἔπαινος ("praise for good deeds"). See Plutarch, *Lives*, ed. and trans. Bernadotte Perrin, vol. I, Loeb Classical Library (Harvard University Press, 1914).
[35] Moyle, *The Whole Works*, p. 52.

Moyle draws the expected Harringtonian conclusion: it is the want of effective agrarian laws that dooms republics. But Moyle does not stop at the suggestion that Sparta represents a helpful case study for illuminating Harringtonian principles; he goes one step further and argues that Harrington drew his constitutional proposals directly from the Spartan example:

> From the *Lacedaemonian* Government *Harrington* formed his Definition, which is the basis of his *Oceana*. 'An equal Commonwealth, *says that excellent author*, is a Government established upon an equal *Agrarian*, arising into the Superstructures, or three Orders, the Senate debating and proposing, the People resolving, and the magistracy executing by an equal Rotation through the Suffrage of the People given by the Ballot.' How nearly this is drawn from *Lycurgus's* Institution you may read with Pleasure in his Life writ by Plutarch . . .[36]

Moyle's Harrington is a disciple of the Greek Lycurgus, and his equal agrarian both derives from and finds justification in the Spartan example.

Having applied the theoretical models of Harrington and Neville to Spartan history, the logical next step for Moyle was to turn his attention to ancient Rome. Accordingly, he penned *An Essay on the Constitution and Government of the Roman State* in 1699, and although it was not published until 1726, Moyle's *Essay* arrived on the scene in time to influence Montesquieu's 1734 *Considérations sur les causes de la grandeur des Romains et de leur décadence*. Contemporaries noticed Montesquieu's debt to Moyle and discussed it openly. In a preface to the 1801 French translation of Moyle's essay, Bertrand Barère writes that "it is no mean encomium for a work to have inspired a genius as great and profound as that of Montesquieu, and this praise is merited by the Essay Walter Moyle published in London in 1726."[37] Nor, Barère insists, should Montesquieu's debt to Moyle diminish the President's reputation; just as his intellect had drawn passages from Tacitus and Plutarch, "why could it not have found in the English work, the chief ideas which inspired the treatise about *The Causes of the Grandeur and Decadence of the Romans?*" Barère fervently denies "any attempt to belittle the great fame of the author of *The Causes*. . . in publishing a work translated from English, which prepared or inspired the profound thought of this worthy admirer of a great people." He thus deftly tries to avoid the appearance of taking the part of an English intellectual against a French one; but he makes absolutely clear that Montesquieu's view of Roman history was deeply influenced by Moyle's – and, as we shall see, Moyle's was explicitly derived from Harrington's.

[36] Ibid., p. 73.   [37] Quoted in *Two Tracts*, p. 206.

From the outset of his *Essay* Moyle advertises his unabashedly Harringtonian outlook:

It appears that land is the true centre of power, and that the balance of dominion changes with the balance of property; as the needle in the compass shifts its points just as the great magnet in the earth changes its place. This is an eternal truth, and confirmed by the experience of all ages and governments; and so fully demonstrated by the great Harrington in his *Oceana*, that it is as difficult to find out new arguments for it, as to resist the cogency of the old.[38]

Indeed, the bulk of Moyle's case rests once again on a straightforward repetition of Harrington's argument that changes in regime result exclusively from changes in the balance of property. Moyle writes that the "periods and revolutions of empires are the natural transmigrations of dominion, from one form of government to another: and make the common circle in the generation and corruption of all states."[39] He continues by offering a Harringtonian critique of Polybius' account of ἀνακύκλωσις: "the succession of these changes Polybius knew from experience, but not from their true natural causes." Polybius, Moyle argues, "plainly derives these alterations from moral reasons; such as vices and corruptions . . . and not from the change of the only true ground and foundation of power, property." Moyle then submits Rome as the perfect example of this principle in action. At the very birth of the state, Romulus "made an equal distribution among the people of the territory belonging to Rome . . . and as he grew greater, divided all the conquered lands among the multitude." This practice, according to Moyle, was a "false step" from Romulus' point of view, in that it fatally undermined Rome's status as a monarchy. There is after all the "eternal principle, that equality of possession makes equality of power." As a result, "whenever the balance of property sways to the people, the monarchy naturally resolves into a popular government."[40] Moyle adds that, after Romulus, Servius Tullius "gave the finishing stroke to the ruin of the monarchy, by dispossessing the patricians of all the public lands they had engrossed, and distributing them to the people . . . Thus Tullius plainly inclined the balance of power and property from the nobility to the commons."[41]

Rome duly became a popular state, and Moyle proceeds to "examine upon what laws and orders the popular frame of government was erected."[42] "The first blow given to the aristocracy," Moyle argues, "was the recision of the debts to the commons, which weakened the interest of the nobility, by taking off the great dependence of the inferior rank of the people upon

---

[38] Ibid., p. 232.　　[39] Ibid., p. 231.　　[40] Ibid., p. 228.　　[41] Ibid., p. 230.　　[42] Ibid., p. 236.

them." Also prominent among these initial measures was "the Agrarian Law; which though the people never perfectly obtained, yet they got large shares of the conquered lands into their possession . . . which confirmed and kept up the popular balance against the encroachments of the nobility."[43] Here Moyle once again deploys the standard Harringtonian terminology in order to defend the Roman agrarian as an essential measure – a bulwark for the preservation of the popular balance. He is even more emphatic in his discussion of the Licinian Law. After the plebs had secured their tribunal rights and other political concessions, "the next care of the people was to secure the present settlement, by making timely provision, that no single man, or order of men, by their riches, possessions, or authority, should so over-balance the rest of the community, as to aspire to absolute dominion."[44] Foremost among their new proposals was "the Licinian Law, which limited the possessions of all private men to five hundred acres of land; which established the great balance of the commonwealth, and would have rendered it immortal, had the law been effectually put into execution." This verdict on the Licinian Law is likely taken directly from *Plato Redivivus*, where, as we have already seen, Neville insists that "if this law had been strictly observed to the last, that glorious commonwealth might have subsisted to this day, for aught we know."[45]

As we shall see, and as Barère confirmed, Montesquieu did indeed thoroughly absorb Moyle's Harringtonian reading of Roman history.[46] But

---

[43] Ibid., p. 237.   [44] Ibid., p. 238.

[45] The exactitude with which this Whig analysis of Roman history is reproduced throughout the late seventeenth and early eighteenth centuries makes it somewhat surprising that agrarian laws do not figure at all in J. A. W. Gunn's discussion of Roman paradigms in Whig pamphlets. See J. A. W. Gunn, *Beyond Liberty and Property: the Process of Self-Recognition in Eighteenth-Century Political Thought* (Kingston and Montreal: McGill-Queen's University Press, 1983), pp. 7–42. Likewise, Alfred Heuss omits the Whigs from his account of the European reception of agrarian laws. See Alfred Heuss, *Barthold Georg Niebuhrs wissenschaftliche Anfänge: Untersuchungen und Mitteilungen über die Kopenhagener Manuscripte und zur europäische Tradition der lex agraria (loi agraire)* (Göttingen: Vandenhoeck & Ruprecht, 1981).

[46] It is essential to recognize that this socioeconomic narrative of the fall of Rome would have been available to Montesquieu only from English sources. An awareness of this connection would have improved Joseph Dedieu's analysis. See Joseph Dedieu, *Montesquieu et la tradition politique anglaise en France* (Paris: Librairie Victor Lecoffre, 1909). There were, to be sure, several important French historians in the late seventeenth and early eighteenth centuries who began to rewrite the story of the Roman *tumulti* along Plutarchan lines. The émigré Sieur de Saint-Evremond offered a relatively charitable characterization of the Gracchi (*Reflexions sur les divers genies du peuple romain, dans les divers temps de la Republique* in *Œuvres melées de M. De Saint Evremond* [Paris, 1693]). On Saint-Evremond, see Joseph M. Levine, *Between the Ancients and the Moderns: Baroque Culture in Restoration England* (Yale University Press, 1999), part 3. Other important examples include the Abbé de Saint-Réal, whose *Conjuration des Gracques* was published posthumously in 1695 (see *Histoire de la conjuration des Gracques* in *Œuvres de M. L'Abbé de Saint-Real*, vol. 1 [Paris, 1724], p. 88), and the Abbé de Vertot, writing in the *Histoire des révolutions de la République romaine*, 3 vols. (Paris, 1719).

there is one more Whig text to which I must turn in order to round out the picture of the President's Harringtonian inheritance. During the same period in which he penned his study of the Spartan constitution, Moyle collaborated with his friend and ally John Trenchard in writing *An Argument shewing that a Standing Army is inconsistent with a Free Government, and absolutely destructive to the Constitution of the English Monarchy*. This tract became the most frequently reprinted pamphlet of the eighteenth century and launched Trenchard's career as a Whig propagandist. That career culminated in his collaboration with Thomas Gordon, with whom he produced *The Independent Whig* (1720–21) and, more importantly for present purposes, *Cato's Letters*. Serialized from November 1720 through July 1723 in the *London Journal*, these letters were composed for the ostensible purpose of attacking the financiers and ministers behind the bursting of the South Sea Bubble. Trenchard and Gordon suspected that the directors of the South Sea Company had conspired with government ministers to manipulate the price of South Sea stock, thus precipitating a financial meltdown.[47] The issue unsurprisingly developed into a classic "court/country" debate, with the Country party identifying the crisis as an instance of "corruption" (that is, a case where government ministers, unchecked by Parliament, had assaulted the common interest for private gain). But only twenty of the 138 letters in the collection deal explicitly with the South Sea Bubble; the rest address the full panoply of contemporary social, political, and philosophical concerns with astonishing insightfulness and elegance, accounting for their subsequent importance.[48]

In John Ozell's 1720 translation, de Vertot announces that "after the Extinction of the Monarchy, the Nobles and Patricians . . . did under various Pretences, appropriate to themselves the best part of those conquered lands . . . thus enlarging their own Revenues to the Diminution of those of the Republic: Or else under borrowed Names, they caused those Portions which were allotted for the subsistence of the poor Citizens, to be adjudged to themselves at inconsiderable Rents. They afterwards lay'd them into their other Lands, without Distinction; and a few yeers Possession, and their own great Credit, covered these Usurpations" (vol. i, p. 38). However, de Vertot is less Plutarchan when he argues that "the two *Gracchi*, by renewing Proposals, just in all Appearance, but not at all convenient in the present state of the Republick, kindled the first sparks of the Civil Wars" (vol. ii, p. 92). See *The History of the Revolutions that happened in the Government of the Roman Republic. Written in French by the Abbot de Vertot*, trans. John Ozell et al., 2 vols. (London, 1720). Yet none of these French historians ever once draws the Harringtonian conclusion: Rome fell because the decay of the agrarian laws destroyed the popular balance of property, and created an aristocratic regime.

47 A similar market collapse resulted from John Law's "Mississippi system," which Montesquieu attacks on similar grounds in *Les Lettres persanes* (see, for example, Letters 132, 135, 138, 142, 143, and 146). Montesquieu published the *Lettres persanes* in 1721 – year two of Cato's serialization.

48 The *Lettres* were reprinted at least six times before 1754. See Caroline Robbins, *The Eighteenth-Century Commonwealthman: Studies in the Transmission, Development and Circumstance of English Liberal Thought from the Restoration of Charles II until the War with the Thirteen Colonies* (Harvard University Press, 1959), pp. 392–93.

The *Letters* burst onto the scene as a subject of scholarly interest with Caroline Robbins's classic study of the eighteenth-century "commonwealthmen" (1959), and subsequently played a central role in Bernard Bailyn's *The Ideological Origins of the American Revolution* (1967).[49] But the most influential modern treatment of the letters appears in Pocock's *The Machiavellian Moment*, and, while his analysis is illuminating, my own examination of the text must begin by addressing a misleading element in his discussion. For Pocock, Trenchard and Gordon are straightforwardly "republicans." He writes that Cato "specifically declares that England (or Britain) is a republic, of that peculiarly happy kind which has a king as its chief magistrate,"[50] and cites letter thirty-seven as evidence. But this letter, written by Gordon and entitled "Character of a good and of an evil Magistrate, quoted from Algernon Sidney, Esq.," is not so simple, and must be viewed within the broader context provided by the rest of the letters.

Gordon begins by acknowledging that his quotation from Sidney might prove objectionable on the grounds that "he [Sidney] is a republican; and it is dishonestly suggested that I am a republican, because I commend him as an excellent writer."[51] He insists, however, that "the passages which I take from him are not republican passages, unless virtue and truth be republicans," and continues, in the passage which attracts Pocock's attention, that, republicanism aside, Sidney's book is "agreeable to our own constitution, which is the best republick in the world, with a prince at the head of it." In short, Gordon argues that he is not a "republican," and he identifies England as a "non-republican republic."

Clearly, part of what is happening here is a play on words; Cato is suggesting that, if "republic" denotes a "virtuous" and "true" state, then England is the most "republican" of all, though governed by a prince. But even granting that Gordon uses the term "republick" here to indicate a "good, mixed regime," I have found no other occasion in the letters where the word "republic" (or the phrase "republican form of government") is not used as a synonym for "commonwealth," and sharply contrasted to England's mixed monarchy. Indeed, Gordon continues in letter thirty-seven by observing that England is "nearer a-kin to a commonwealth . . . than it is to absolute monarchy." That is, England is neither of these: it is a "limited

<hr>

[49] See ibid., esp. pp. 115–25; and Bernard Bailyn, *The Ideological Origins of the American Revolution* (Cambridge: Belknap Press, 1967), esp. pp. 35–36, 48–49.

[50] Pocock, *Machiavellian Moment* p. 468.

[51] John Trenchard and Thomas Gordon, *Cato's Letters, or Essays on Liberty, Civil and Religious, and Other Important Subjects*, ed. Ronald Hamowy, vol. 1 (Indianapolis: Liberty Fund, 1995), p. 262.

monarchy," and very different indeed from, say, the "republick" of the Netherlands.[52] Within the broader structure of Cato's analysis, there are key reasons why this is so.

England cannot have "a republican form of government," Trenchard argues in letter eighty-five, because of its distribution of property:

It proceeds from a consummate ignorance in politicks, to think that a number of men agreeing together can make and hold a commonwealth, before nature has prepared the way; for she alone must do it. An equality of estate will give an equality of power; and an equality of power is a commonwealth, or democracy; An agrarian law, or something equivalent to it, must make or find a suitable disposition of property; and when that comes to be the case, there is no hindering a popular form of government, unless sudden violence take away all liberty, and, to preserve itself, alters the distribution of property again. I hope that no one amongst us has a head so wrong turned, as to imagine that any man, or number of men, in the present situation of affairs, can ever get power enough to turn all the possessions of England topsy-turvy, and throw them into average, especially any who can have a will and interest in doing it; and without all this it is impossible to settle a commonwealth here . . .[53]

Here we have a return to the standard Harringtonian analysis: a popular government requires a popular "balance" of property.[54] In order for England to become a republic, it would have to "throw" all property into "average." As it is, Cato insists, England can "preserve liberty by no other establishment than what we have," namely that of a "well poised monarchy" (which, he argues in terms Montesquieu would echo, may well preserve pure liberty better than most republics). He notes that "the distribution of property in England is adapted to our present establishment," observing that "the nobility and gentry have great possessions; and the former have great privileges and distinctions by the constitution." In short, England's property structure (with its balance between king, lords, and commons)

---

[52] Ibid., vol. II, p. 613. Pocock recognizes that, in several passages, Cato distinguishes England from a "pure republic," but insists that these passages appear in a "later stage in the argument" – letter eighty-five in particular (Pocock, *Machiavellian Moment*, p. 473). Yet, as we now see, Cato's description of England as a "republick" in letter thirty-seven (a unique instance in the *Letters*, itself the result of wordplay) appears alongside this very clear identification of England as a "limited monarchy" (i.e. not a "commonwealth").

[53] *Cato's Letters*, p. 614.

[54] Ronald Hamowy's conclusion that Cato is a Lockean who appropriates very little of the "classical republican" case relies on Pocock's definition of republicanism as a theory of active civic participation and scorn for commerce. But Cato's republicanism is indebted to Harrington, whose republicanism is, as we have seen, of a very different sort. See Ronald Hamowy, "*Cato's Letters*, John Locke, and the Republican Paradigm" in *History of Political Thought* II (1990), 273–94.

fits it for limited monarchy, and "the phantom of a commonwealth must vanish, and never appear again but in distorted brains."[55]

But while Cato argues that England is not a republic, and that liberty can be secured by non-republican governments, he is clear that liberty in any regime requires the absence of disproportionate wealth in individuals.[56] That is, whenever the balance of property shifts to one man or a very few men, liberty is lost. Mixed monarchy has a "democratic part" (the Commons) which must be maintained.[57] In letter ninety-one, for example, Trenchard writes as follows:

Very great riches in private men are always dangerous to states, because they create greater dependence than can be consistent with the security of any sort of government whatsoever; they place subjects upon too near a level with their sovereigns; make the nobility stand upon too great an inequality in respect of one another; destroy amongst the Commons, that balance of property and power, which is necessary to democracy, or the democratic part of any government, overthrow the poise of it, and indeed alter its nature, though not its name.[58]

Trenchard then goes on to describe the methods different regimes employ to halt the spread of disruptive wealth. Princes use extraordinary, often illicit means to "cut off those excrescent members and rivals of their authority"; aristocracies put dangerous men "upon expensive embassies, or load them with honorary and chargeable employments at home, to drain and exhaust their superfluous and dangerous wealth"; and popular governments "provide against this evil, by the division of the estates of particulars after their death amongst their children or relations in equal degree." This last is the substance of the Harringtonian agrarian – as it would be of Montesquieu's. Here Cato argues that every non-despotic regime must take steps to restrict truly disproportionate wealth. As he puts it in letter three, "a free people are kept so, by no other means than an equal distribution of property . . . and the first seeds of anarchy are produced from hence, that some are ungovernably rich, and many more are miserably poor; that is, some are masters of all means of oppression, and others want all the means of self-defence."[59] Free monarchies, Cato argues, can no better survive "stock-jobbers" than republics can.

This reading receives support from a central passage in letter thirty-five, written by Gordon. Here Cato repeats his argument that liberty in a mixed

---

[55] Trenchard and Gordon, *Cato's Letters*, p. 616.
[56] Robbins makes this point clearly, as does Pocock. See Robbins, *Eighteenth-Century Commonwealthman*, p. 125; Pocock, *Machiavellian Moment*, p. 468.
[57] *Cato's Letters*, vol. II, p. 649.　　[58] Ibid., p. 648.　　[59] Ibid., vol. I, p. 44.

regime requires the absence of inordinate wealth, and turns to a familiar analysis of Roman history to make his point:

> As liberty can never subsist without equality, nor equality be long preserved without an agrarian law, or something like it; so when men's riches are become immeasurably or surprizingly great, a people, who regard their own security, ought to make a strict enquiry how they came by them, and oblige them to take down their own size, for fear of terrifying the community, or mastering it. In every country, and under every government, particular men may be too rich. If the Romans had well observed the agrarian law, by which the extent of every citizen's estate was ascertained, some citizens could never have risen so high as they did above others; and consequently, one man would never have been set above the rest, and have established, as Caesar did at last, a tyranny in that great and glorious state . . . But, will some say, is it a crime to be rich? Yes certainly, at the publick expense, or to the danger of the publick. A man may be too rich for a subject; even the revenues of kings may be too large.[60]

Like Harrington, Neville, and Moyle before him, Cato endorses the view that it was the want of an adequate agrarian that doomed Rome to tyranny and enslavement. Rome allowed a few men to achieve disproportionate wealth (which, on this reading, was a "crime," and, hence, unjust) and, thus, to amass dictatorial power. What is important to remember here is that Rome is submitted, not as a republic *per se*, but as a simple state. Cato's argument, once again, is that any state which presumes to offer its citizens liberty must be on guard against excessive wealth.[61]

Cato's basic aim, in short, is to deploy Harrington's republican analysis in support of mixed monarchy. Disagreeing implicitly with Harrington (who had argued that England's property structure made "Gothic" mixed monarchy impracticable), Cato insists that England's distribution of property lends itself only to mixed monarchy, and that this mixed regime, if tended, will secure its citizens' liberty. But, this disagreement aside, Cato

---

[60] Ibid., p. 254.

[61] Bolingbroke takes precisely the same approach to the Roman example in his *Dissertation upon Parties*, written a full decade after *Cato's Letters*: "These two orders or estates [the patricians and the plebs] had very frequent contests, and well they might, since they had very opposite interests. Agrarian laws, for instance, began to be promulgated . . . and continued to the end of the commonwealth to produce the same disorders. How inconsistent, indeed, was that plan of government, which required so much hard service of the people, left them so little property in the distribution of property? Such an inequality of property, and of the means of acquiring it, cannot subsist in an equal commonwealth; and I much apprehend that any near approaches to a monopoly of property, would not be long endured even in a monarchy"; see Henry St. John, Viscount Bolingbroke, *Political Writings*, ed. David Armitage (Cambridge University Press, 1997), p. 131. While the lack of an equal agrarian will certainly doom an "equal commonwealth," a monopoly of property will doom liberty in any form of government.

accepts the central, descriptive Harringtonian premise: the balance of property produces the balance of power. He also endorses the interpretation of the Roman agrarian laws – passed from Harrington to Neville and Moyle – which justifies and encourages the egalitarian distribution of property in order to secure liberty and the rule of virtue.

Thus, Harrington's rendition of Roman history and his account of the interplay between wealth, popular states, and virtue thrived in the Whig tracts of the late seventeenth and eighteenth centuries, ensuring that Montesquieu would have ready access to them.[62] However, we do not find, by and large, in these Harringtonian writers the Platonist metaphysics that had so comprehensively grounded Harrington's theory. Property must be equalized, Harrington had argued, so that the rule of reason can be established, rendering the state "just" and virtuous, and bringing it into agreement with the natural order of the cosmos. To be sure, I have cited passages from Neville and Moyle which emphasize the decidedly Greek argument that disproportionate wealth topples the rule of the virtuous (i.e. justice). Nor do we find any shortage of such passages in *Cato's Letters*.[63] But however

---

[62] Although the focus now shifts to the French scene, we should note the remarkable longevity of this tradition in England itself. In 1759, for example, Edward Wortley Montagu published his *Reflections on the Rise and Fall of the Antient Republicks*, a text which unambiguously endorses the Harringtonian view we have been following. See Edward Wortley Montagu, *Reflections on the Rise and Fall of the Antient Republicks. Adapted to the Present State of Great Britain* (London, 1760). See also Jonathan Curling, *Edward Wortley Montagu 1713–1776: the Man in the Iron Wig* (London: Andrew Melrose, 1954). Although the subject of Gibbon's famous history (published from 1776–88) is the decline of the Roman principate, it nonetheless contains several revealing comments on the earlier agrarian movement. In chapter thirty-one, for example, Gibbon records that "the lands of Italy, which had been originally divided among the families of free and indigent proprietors, were insensibly purchased, or usurped, by the avarice of the nobles; and in the age which preceded the fall of the republic, it was computed that only two thousand citizens were possessed of any independent substance." See Edward Gibbon, *The History of the Decline and Fall of the Roman Empire*, ed. David Womersley, vol. III (Harmondsworth: Allen Lane, The Penguin Press, 1994), p. 182.

[63] In letter seventeen, for example, Trenchard warns against disproportionate wealth on the familiar grounds that excessive wealth and poverty corrupt both rich and poor, making it inevitable that the rich (corrupted by their wealth), rather than the virtuous, will come to rule: "[Corrupt men] will be ever contriving and forming wicked and dangerous projects, to make the people poor, and themselves rich; well-knowing that dominion follows property; that where there are wealth and power, there will be always crowds of servile dependants; and that, on the contrary, poverty dejects the mind, fashions it to slavery, and renders it unequal to any generous undertaking, and incapable of opposing any bold usurpation." Moreover, the corrupt rich will "prefer worthless and wicked men, and not suffer a man of knowledge or honesty to come near them, or enjoy a post under them. They will disgrace men of virtue, and ridicule virtue itself, and laugh at publick spirit." They will "put men into employment, without any regard to the qualification for those employments, or indeed any qualifications at all, but as they contribute to their designs . . ." And perhaps most regrettably, "they will promote luxury, idleness, and expence, and a general depravation of manners, by their own example, as well as by connivance and publick encouragement" (*Cato's Letters*, p. 126). My overall thought is that there is more to *Cato's Letters* than what Pocock calls the "neo-Harringtonian" program (J. G. A. Pocock, "The Varieties of Whiggism from Exclusion to Reform" in *Virtue, Commerce, and History: Essays on*

sincerely Cato and the other Whig writers with whom we have been concerned worried about the effects of disproportionate wealth on ruler-ship, they rarely if ever allowed themselves to adduce Harrington's broadly Platonist worldview in support of their observations and proposals. Indeed, it was not primarily through the English Harringtonians that the Platonist foundations of Harrington's case survived into the eighteenth century. They survived rather in the works of a series of theorists, both Continental and English, who employed Plato's metaphysics in order to attack the legal positivism of Hobbes, and to assert the natural sociability of man.

III

The sources for Montesquieu's mature reflections on natural law and the objectivity of moral facts have received a significant amount of scholarly attention. In 1975 Sheila Mason published *Montesquieu's Idea of Justice*, in which she attributed the President's belief in the immanence of moral principles in nature to the influence of the eighteenth-century French "rationalists," such as Malebranche and Bossuet.[64] In a recent study C. P. Courtney disagrees with Mason, and instead stresses Montesquieu's affini-ties with Grotius, Pufendorf, Barbeyrac and the other natural law jurists.[65] Both arguments have much to recommend them. For the purposes of this study, however, I have only to account for Montesquieu's interaction with a particular tradition of eighteenth-century Platonist metaphysics, and this is easily accomplished by a short look at two essential thinkers with whom he was deeply conversant: Gottfried Wilhelm Leibniz and Anthony Ashley Cooper, third Earl of Shaftesbury.[66]

Political Thought and History, Chiefly in the Eighteenth Century [Cambridge University Press, 1985], p. 241). There is also a faithful reading of Harrington himself, complete with the notion that property must be equalized for the sake of moral survival.

[64] Sheila M. Mason, *Montesquieu's Idea of Justice* (The Hague: Martinus Nijhoff, 1975).

[65] C. P. Courtney, "Montesquieu and Natural Law" in *Montesquieu's Science of Politics: Essays on The Spirit of the Laws*, ed. David W. Carrithers, Michael A. Mosher, and Paul A. Rahe (Lanham, MD: Rowman & Littlefield, 2001), pp. 41–67.

[66] While adducing Shaftesbury as an essential source of Montesquieu's metaphysics is standard practice, the inclusion of Leibniz here may require a brief explanation. Leibniz was certainly less central to Montesquieu's education than, say, Malebranche, but, as A. S. Crisafulli noticed as early as 1937, Montesquieu's definition of justice as a "rapport de convenance" in the *Lettres persanes* is drawn directly from Leibniz's *Théodicée*. In addition, Mason points out that Montesquieu owned a copy of Leibniz's works, along with P. Desmaizeux's *Recueil de diverses pièces sur la philosophie*, which contains Leibniz's laudatory review of Shaftesbury's *Characteristicks* (discussed below). See A. S. Crisafulli, "Parallels to Ideas in the *Lettres persanes*," in *Modern Language Association of America* (1937), pp. 773ff.; see also Mason, *Montesquieu's Idea of Justice*, p. 22n.

Leibniz turned to Plato principally in order to attack Hobbes. In his early works and then ultimately in the *Leviathan* of 1651, Hobbes had articulated a theory of the radical unsociability of man. The state of nature, he argued, was a state of war in which life was rendered so uncertain and intolerable that men were exhorted by the law of nature to seek peace by instituting an absolute sovereign.[67] In this state of nature there was no "mine" and "thine," and no "just" and "unjust." Our ability to use these terms, on Hobbes's account, derives from the political covenant; the duly instituted sovereign promulgates laws, and those laws become the measure of what is "just" and "unjust." To speak of an "unjust law" is, therefore, to speak nonsense. Leibniz found this brand of legal positivism wholly unacceptable.[68] He noted as much in a letter he wrote to Hobbes in 1670; here he rather coyly suggests that Hobbes's readers have been "misusing" his philosophical pronouncements "for bad purposes." Surely, he continues, Hobbes would not deny that "given the existence of a ruler of the world, men cannot live in a pure state of nature outside all republics, since God is the common monarch of all men."[69] But Leibniz would later make clear that, on his reading, Hobbes had denied precisely this.

Accordingly, Leibniz dedicated a substantial portion of his life's work to the refutation of Hobbes. In his 1706 critique of Pufendorf he identifies

---

[67] See Thomas Hobbes, *Leviathan*, ed. Richard Tuck, rev. edn. (Cambridge University Press, 1996), chaps. 13–14.

[68] I use the term "positivism" advisedly in this context. As Noel Malcolm has stressed in an important recent study, it is high time for us to part with our caricature of the purely "positivist" Hobbes (Malcolm, *Aspects of Hobbes* [Oxford: Clarendon Press, 2002], pp. 432–56). Hobbes is in earnest when he writes that "the Lawes of Nature are Immutable and Eternall," and that "the true Doctrine of the Lawes of Nature, is the true Morall Philosophie" (Hobbes, *Leviathan*, p. 111). The conflict with the rationalists arises because Hobbes has a deeply idiosyncratic understanding of what grounds "morality." For Hobbes, morality is the "Science of what is *Good*, and *Evil*," and "good" is simply a term we use to describe those things we want. Although all human beings want different things, they must all want to preserve their lives – because being alive is the minimum necessary condition for the fulfillment of any additional desires. Accordingly, even in the state of nature there are standards of morality, namely rules we must follow if we intend to avoid death and seek what for us is "good." There is, for example, a law of nature which exhorts us to fulfill our covenants, and adherence to that imperative is called "justice." However, Hobbes makes clear that it is not unjust to break a covenant so long as one fears that the other party might shirk his obligations. As a result, only after the creation of the state (the power which enforces obligations) does it become "unjust" to break covenants. Hobbes's theory of "morality" rests on his epistemology, which insists that it is impossible for human beings to infer anything about the nature of God (i.e. what is objectively "good") from the nature of the world. And since, on Hobbes's account, all of our knowledge comes from sense impressions, even if moral principles had independent existence, we would not be able to know them. This was what Leibniz found so unacceptable.

[69] Letter 189, July 1670. *The Correspondence of Thomas Hobbes*, ed. Noel Malcolm, vol. II (Oxford: Clarendon Press, 1994), p. 716. "neque diffiteris supposito Mundi Rectore nullum esse posse hominum statum [>pure] naturalem extra omnem Rempublicam, cum Deus sit omnium Monarcha communis." Hobbes's reply to this letter (if he wrote one at all) does not survive.

Hobbes as the source of the "command theory" of law, insisting that "this paradox, brought out by Hobbes above all, who seemed to deny to the state of nature, that is [a condition] in which there are no superiors, all binding justice whatsoever (although even he is inconsistent), is a view to which I am astonished that anyone could have adhered."[70] In his *Méditation sur la notion commune de la justice* (1702–3) Leibniz offers a revealing comparison:

> Plato in his dialogues introduces and refutes a certain Thrasymachus, who, wishing to explain what justice is, gives a definition which would strongly recommend the position we are combating, if it were acceptable: for that is just (he says) which is agreeable or pleasant to the most powerful. If that were true, there would never be a sentence of a sovereign court, nor of a supreme judge, which would be unjust, nor would an evil but powerful man ever be blameworthy. And what is more, the same action could be just or unjust, depending on the judges who decide, which is ridiculous. It is one thing to be just and another to pass for it, and to take the place of justice.[71]

Leibniz adds that "a celebrated English philosopher named Hobbes, who is noted for his paradoxes, has wished to uphold almost the same thing as Thrasymachus."[72]

Leibniz offers a solidly Platonic rebuttal to Hobbes/Thrasymachus, one that extends beyond arguments about the pre-political existence of moral facts to include an attack on the voluntarist assumption that the word of God is "just" simply because God willed it. Hobbes "wants God to have the right to do everything, because he is all-powerful. This is a failure to distinguish between right and fact. For what one can do is one thing,

---

[70] Gottfried Wilhelm Leibniz, *Monita quaedam ad Samuelis Puffendorfii* [sic] *principia* in *Gothofredi Guillelmi Leibnitii opera omnia,* ed. Louis Dutens, vol. IV (Geneva, 1768). "Quae paradoxa ab *Hobbio* potissimum prodita, qui in statu quem vocat naturali, id est, superiores exsorte, omnem justitiam obligantem tollere visus est (etsi ipse variet) miror a quoquam adoptari potuisse" (p. 279). In quoting Leibniz, I have used Riley's translations. See Leibniz, *Political Writings,* ed. and trans. Patrick Riley, 2nd edn. (Cambridge University Press, 1988), p. 70.

[71] *Political Writings,* p. 46. Leibniz, *Méditation sur la notion commune de la justice* in *Rechtsphilosophisches aus Leibnizens Ungedruckten Schriften,* ed. Georg Mollat (Leipzig, 1885), p. 57. "Platon dans ses dialogues introduit et refute un Certain Thrasymaque, qui voulant expliquer ce que c'est que la justice, donne une definition qui autoriseroit fort le parti que nous combattons, si elle estoit recevable: Car juste (dit-il) est ce qui convient ou plait au plus puissant. Si cela estoit, jamais sentence d'une cour souveraine, ou du dernier juge seroit injuste, jamais mechant homme mais puissant seroit blamable. Et qui plus est, une même action pourroit estre juste et injuste, selon qu'elle trouveroit des juges, ce qui est ridicule. Autre chose est estre juste et autre chose est passer pour tel, et tenir lieu de justice."

[72] *Political Writings,* p. 46. "Un philosophe Anglois celebre, nommé Hobbes qui s'est signalé par ses paradoxes, a voulu soûtenir presque la même chose, que Thrasymaque." My reflections on Leibniz's conflation of Hobbes and Thrasymachus were stimulated by a paper given by Professor Riley at the "Britons Abroad, Strangers at Home" conference at Wolfson College, Cambridge, sponsored by the Cambridge Committee on Seventeenth-Century History (January, 2001).

what one should do, another."[73] To argue, as Hobbes and his ilk do, that any duly promulgated law is just "is nothing else than saying that there is no certain and determined justice," and this is "to change the nature of terms and to speak a language different from other men."[74] Leibniz wants to argue for another "language"; he takes Plato's view in the *Euthyphro* that there are moral facts immanent in the world – abstract relations like mathematical formulae – by which both God and man can be judged.[75] As he puts it in his critique of Pufendorf, "justice follows certain rules of equality and of proportion no less founded in the immutable nature of things, and in the divine ideas, than are the principles of arithmetic and geometry."[76] He writes similarly in the *Meditation* that, just as one would find it ridiculous to argue that 1, 4, 9, 16, 25 and so on are square numbers only for men and "that it is not thus for God and the angels,"[77] we should find it equally ridiculous when people make similar arguments about moral relations. We must understand the "difference which there is between necessary and eternal truths which must be the same everywhere, and that which is contingent and changeable or arbitrary."[78] Justice is not arbitrary; it is a universal, "intelligible" notion which could be consulted even "if there were no law in the world."[79]

After putting forward this argument, Leibniz does not have far to go in order to assert the basic sociability of man. In the preface to his *Codex iuris gentium diplomaticus* (1693), he begins a discussion of moral objectivity by stating that "by moral I mean that which is equivalent to 'natural' for a good man."[80] He continues that "a good man is one who loves everybody in so

---

[73] Ibid., p. 47. "car il veut que Dieu est en droit de tout faire, parce qu'il est tout puissant. C'est ne pas distinguer le droit et le fait. Car autre chose est, ce qui se peut, autre chose ce qui se doit."

[74] Ibid. ". . . n'est d'autre chose que de dire qu'il n'y a point de justice certaine et determinée . . . c'est en effet changer la nature des termes et parler un language different de celui des autres hommes" (*Méditation*, ed. Mollat, p. 58).

[75] For the Platonic sources of Leibniz's metaphysics and epistemology, see Christia Mercer, *Leibniz's Metaphysics: Its Origins and Development* (Cambridge University Press, 2001), esp. pp. 173–205, 243–52.

[76] *Political Writings*, p. 71. "Et vero justitia servat quasdam aequalitatis proportionalitatisque leges, non minus in natura rerum immutabili divinisque fundatas ideis, quam sunt principia Arithmeticae & Geometriae" (*Opera*, ed. Dutens, vol. IV, p. 280).

[77] *Political Writings*, p. 49. "n'est pas ainsi chez Dieu et chez les anges" (*Méditation*, ed. Mollat, p. 61).

[78] Ibid. "La difference qu'il y a entre les verités eternelles et necessaires qui doivent estre les mêmes par tout, et entre ce qui est contingent et changeable ou arbitraire."

[79] *Political Writings*, p. 50. "quand il n'y auroit point de Loy au monde" (*Méditation*, ed. Mollat, p. 61).

[80] Ibid., p. 171. The Latin text is taken from *Die Werke von Leibniz*, ed. Onno Klopp, vol. VI (Hanover, 1872). "*Moralem* autem intelligo, quae apud Virum bonum aequipollet naturali . . . *Vir bonus* autem est, qui amat omnes quantum ratio permittit. *Justitiam* igitur, quae virtus est huius affectus rectrix, quem φιλανθρωπίαν Graeci vocant, commodissime, ni fallor, definiemus *Caritatem sapientis*" (p. 469).

far as reason permits. Justice, then, which is the virtue that regulates that affection which the Greeks call φιλανθρωπία [the love of mankind], will be most conveniently defined, if I am not in error, as the charity of the wise man." For Leibniz, "charity is a universal benevolence, and benevolence the habit of loving or of willing the good."[81] Man by nature loves his fellow man, and nature is an immutable moral compass.

Late in life, Leibniz found support for his moral convictions in the writings of a younger English contemporary, the Earl of Shaftesbury. In 1712 Leibniz penned his *Jugement sur les œuvres de M. le Comte de Shaftesbury*, in which he heaped particular praise on Shaftesbury's characterization of "natural man." Shaftesbury "refutes with reason . . . those who believe that there is no obligation at all in the state of nature, and outside of government."[82] Also praised is his argument that "the affections which nature has given us bring us, not only to seek our own good, but also to achieve that of our relations and even of society; and that one is happy when he acts according to his natural affections."[83] "It seems to me," Leibniz continued, "that I could reconcile this quite easily with my language and opinions. In fact, our natural affections produce our contentment: and the more natural one is, the more he is led to find his pleasure in the good of others, which is the foundation of universal benevolence, of charity, of justice."[84] Leibniz's observation was astute: Shaftesbury shared his broadly Platonist orientation and emerged with a recognizably similar program. Montesquieu would declare in the *Pensées* that "milord Shaftesbury" should rank with Plato among the "great poet" philosophers,[85] a recognition that the Englishman's *Characteristicks of Men, Manners, Opinions, Times* (1711) represented the single most important contemporary English endorsement of Platonic idealism.[86] Indeed, the essays contained in the *Characteristicks* make explicit

---

[81] Ibid. "*Caritas* est benevolentia universalis, et *benevolentia* amandi sive diligendi habitus."

[82] *Political Writings*, p. 196. "Notre illustre Auteur réfute avec raison . . . ceux qui croyent qu'il n'y a point d'obligation dans l'état de la Nature, & hors du Gouvernement." *Gothofredi Guillelmi Leibnitii opera omnia*, ed. Louis Dutens, vol. v (Geneva, 1768), p. 41.

[83] *Political Writings*, p. 199. "Les affections que la nature nous a données, nous portent, non-seulement à chercher notre propre bien, mais encore à procurer celui de nos rélations [*sic*] & même de la societé; & qu'on est heureux quand on agit suivant ses affections naturellesn" (*Opera*, ed. Dutens, vol. v, p. 44).

[84] *Political Writings*, p. 199. "Il me semble que je reconcilierois cela fort aisément avec mom language & mes sentimens. En effet, nos affections naturelles sont notre contentement: & plus on est dans le naturel, plus on est porté à trouver son plaisir dans le bien d'autrui; le qui est le fondement de la bienveillance universelle, de la charité, de la justice" (*Opera*, ed. Dutens, vol. v, p. 44).

[85] Montesquieu, *Œuvres complètes*, ed. Daniel Oster (Paris: Editions du Seuil, 1964), p. 1073.

[86] See Mason's excellent discussion of Shaftesbury's influence on Montesquieu (*Montesquieu's Idea of Justice*, pp. 78–82). My own discussion will focus more specifically on Shaftesbury's ideas of "common sense" and "interest," and on how they relate to the broader Whig intellectual landscape with which

(to a degree that even Leibniz did not) the political implications of taking a broadly Platonist view of nature and society.[87]

To begin with, in *An Inquiry Concerning Virtue, or Merit*, Shaftesbury offers a strictly Platonic, aesthetic account of the way in which the order of nature inspires the human mind to virtue through contemplation:[88]

> In the meanest Subjects of the World, the Appearance of *Order* gains upon the Mind, and draws the Affection towards it. But if *the Order of the World it-self* appears just and beautiful; the Admiration and Esteem of *Order* must run higher, and the elegant Passion or Love of Beauty, which is so advantageous to Virtue, must be the more improv'd by its Exercise in so ample and magnificent a Subject. For 'tis impossible that such a *Divine Order* should be contemplated without Extasy and Rapture; since in the common Subjects of Science, and the liberal Arts, whatever is according to just Harmony and Proportion, is so transporting to those who have any Knowledge or Practice in the kind.[89]

As in Plato's *Timaeus*, we have here the argument that, through contemplation of the beauty and order of the universe, the individual soul is able to pattern itself on the cosmic model, thus achieving virtue. Furthermore, the beauty, harmony, and proportionality of the cosmos (and the soul) constitute "justice."

Shaftesbury makes clear that this Platonist logic affects his view of the state in profound ways, leading, as he himself observes, to a sharp break with Hobbes and the broader contractarian tradition. For Shaftesbury, civil society is no cold compact, but rather the inevitable result of this process of harmonic patterning. "This too is certain; that the Admiration and Love of Order, Harmony, and Proportion, in whatever kind, is naturally improving to the Temper, advantageous to social Affection, and highly assistant to *Virtue*; which is it-self no other than the Love of Order and

Montesquieu was deeply involved. The most recent full-length study of Shaftesbury's thought is Lawrence E. Klein, *Shaftesbury and the Culture of Politeness: Moral Discourse and Cultural Politics in Early Eighteenth-Century England* (Cambridge University Press, 1994). See also Iain Hampsher-Monk, "From Virtue to Politeness" in *Republicanism: a Shared European Heritage*, vol. II, ed. Quentin Skinner and Martin Van Gelderen (Cambridge University Press, 2002), pp. 85–105.

[87] Caroline Robbins provides an insightful discussion of Shaftesbury "the Real Whig" in her *The Eighteenth-Century Commonwealthman*, pp. 128–33. Anxious as she is to place Shaftesbury in a "liberal" tradition, however, she slights his extensive and essential Platonism.

[88] In his study of the Cambridge Platonists, Ernst Cassirer notes the deep influence of Ralph Cudworth and Henry More (in particular the former's *True Intellectual System of the Universe* and the latter's *Enchiridion ethicum*) on Shaftesbury's education and subsequent development, and observes that Shaftesbury's philosophical project can be viewed in part as a continuation of the Cambridge enterprise. See Ernst Cassirer, *The Platonic Renaissance in England*, trans. James. P. Pettegrove (Austin: University of Texas Press, 1953), pp. 157–67.

[89] Anthony Ashley Cooper, 3rd Earl of Shaftesbury, *Characteristicks of Men, Manners, Opinions, Times*, ed. Philip Ayres, vol. I (Oxford: Clarendon Press, 1999), p. 225.

Beauty in Society.">[90] Shaftesbury amplifies this Platonist commitment in *The Moralists*, expounding in full the contemplative, aesthetic links among soul, state, and cosmos:

> ... *well-knowing* and experienc'd in all the Degrees and Orders of Beauty, in all the mysterious Charms or the particular Forms; you rise to what is more general; and with a larger Heart, and Mind more comprehensive, you generously seek that which is highest in the kind. Not captivated by the Lineaments of a fair Face, or the well-drawn Proportions of a human Body, you view *the Life* it-self, and embrace rather the *Mind* which adds the Lustre, and renders chiefly amiable. Nor is the Enjoyment of such a single Beauty sufficient to satisfy such an aspiring Soul. It seeks how to combine more Beautys, and by what Coalition of these, to form a beautiful Society. It views Communitys, Friendships, Relations, Dutys; and considers by what Harmony of particular Minds the general Harmony is compos'd, and *Common-weal* establish'd.[91]

The commonwealth, when ordered correctly (i.e. justly), is a microcosm of the perfectly harmonic universe.

Thus far Shaftesbury is more or less ventriloquizing Plato. But his notion that virtue is (for Platonic reasons) simply "the Love of Order and Beauty in Society" would allow him to wield this Platonist program as a powerful weapon against "private interest" – already the obsession of the "Country" party defended by his grandfather (the 1st Earl of Shaftesbury) and later famously embraced by Bolingbroke (and, thus, a significant factor in Montesquieu's analysis).[92] For Shaftesbury, men achieve virtue when they can see themselves as part of a whole. Their contemplation of the cosmos reveals that they too are a component of an overall harmony, and "virtue" is their desire to play their given role.[93] In the *Inquiry* Shaftesbury observes that "when we reflect on any ordinary Frame or Constitution either of Art or of Nature; and consider how hard it is to give the least account of a particular *Part* without a competent Knowledg of *the Whole*; we need not wonder to find our-selves at a loss in many things relating to the Constitution and

---

[90] Ibid.   [91] Ibid., vol. II, p. 17.

[92] As noted above, Montesquieu attended the Club d'Entresol, which Bolingbroke joined during his French exile, and was deeply influenced by Bolingbroke's analysis of the English constitution (and his "separation of powers" argument). See *The Spirit of the Laws*, pp. xvii–xx. More generally, the debate over "private interest" between the Government and the opposition provided the political context for Montesquieu's English experience.

[93] Montesquieu would have also found this idea amplified in Bolingbroke's *On the Spirit of Patriotism*. In that essay Bolingbroke argues that "reason collects the will of God from the constitution of things" and that "all men are directed by the general constitution of human nature, to submit to government; and that some men are in a particular manner designed to take care of that government on which the common happiness depends." These men suited by nature to rule must assume their role "to preserve the moral system of the world." See Bolingbroke, *Political Writings*, pp. 195–97.

Frame of *Nature* her-self."[94] Nonetheless, he argues that "to what End the many Proportions and various Shapes of Parts in many Creatures actually serve; we are able, by the help of Study and Observation, to demonstrate, with great exactness." Likewise in the ethical realm, "we know that every Creature has a private Good and Interest of his own" and that every creature has a "right and a wrong State" (where the "right-one is by Nature forwarded"). If "any thing either in his Appetites, Passions, or Affections" diverts him from this "right state," then it is "ill" for him. But what if "by the natural Constitution of any rational Creature, the same Irregularitys of Appetite which make him ill to *Others*, make him ill also *to Himself* "? In that case, his "goodness" is good for others, and his "illness" is ill for others. Thus, "*Virtue* and *Interest* may be found at last to agree," because we now realize that the harmony of each part produces the harmony of the whole.

For Shaftesbury, therefore, the most politically relevant fact about virtue is that it alerts people to the larger reality of the social whole, and their status as "parts" within it. It is in this sense that his "virtue" *is* a commitment to the common interest. A well-ordered society is one in which everyone "gets the message" that private interest is properly understood as the common interest:

Thus in *a civil* State or Publick, we see that a virtuous Administration, and an equal and just Distribution of Rewards and Punishments, is of the highest service; not only by restraining the Vicious, and forcing them to act usefully to Society; but by making Virtue to be apparently the Interest of every-one, so as to remove all Prejudices against it, create a fair reception for it, and lead Men into that path which afterwards they cannot easily quit.[95]

Shaftesbury adds later that "whatsoever is the occasion or means of more affectionately uniting a rational Creature to his PART in Society, and causes him to prosecute the Public Good . . . is undoubtedly the Cause of more than ordinary Virtue in such a Person,"[96] and remarks again that "to be well affected towards the *Publick Interest* and *one's own*, is not only consistent, but inseparable: and that moral Rectitude, or *Virtue*, must accordingly be the Advantage, and Vice the Injury and Disadvantage of every Creature."[97]

This reasoning provides the basis for Shaftesbury's pun in the title of his essay *Sensus Communis*. The title refers to "common sense" (i.e. ordinary reasoning ability), but also to "*common* sense," a sense of the "common," the social whole. Shaftesbury insists that this sort of "common sense" cannot be had by "those who scarcely know an *Equal*, nor consider themselves subject

---

[94] Shaftesbury, *Characteristicks*, vol. 1, p. 196.   [95] Ibid., p. 219.   [96] Ibid., p. 225.
[97] Ibid., p. 229.

to any Law of *Fellowship* or *Community*" (those living under "Absolute Power").[98] Observing that "Morality and good Government go together," he writes that "there is no real Love of Virtue, without the Knowledg of the *Publick Good*" – and for there to be a "public good" there must be a "PUBLICK." Those living in despotic states cannot see themselves as part of a whole, either political or cosmic: "*Publick Good*, according to their Apprehension, is as little the Measure or Rule of Government in *the Universe*, as in *the State*." They have no concept of what is "Good or Just" apart from arbitrary "*Will* and *Power*." In England, however, the case is different:

As for us BRITONS, thank Heaven, we have a better *Sense* of Government deliver'd to us from our Ancestors. We have the Notion of A PUBLIC and A CONSTITUTION; how *a Legislative*, and how *an Executive* is model'd. We understand Weight and Measure in this kind, and can reason justly on the *Ballance of Power* and *Property*. The Maxims we draw from hence, are as evident as those in *Mathematics*. Our increasing Knowledg shews us every day, more and more, what COMMON SENSE is in Politicks: And this must of necessity lead us to understand a like *Sense* in Morals; which is the Foundation.[99]

A man in society sees himself as part of an overall whole which must be harmonized using the same, almost "mathematical" principles which harmonize the heavens. There must be a "ballance" of the elements of the state analogous to the balance of the cosmos (and that of the individual soul), one which can only be achieved if citizens attain the holistic perspective of virtue: that is, *common* sense.

In Shaftesbury, then, we find a significant eighteenth-century restatement of the metaphysical program underlying the Greek tradition. We do not, however, find the Greek account proper. As we have seen, in the *Inquiry* Shaftesbury notes the need for a "ballance" in "property," and, later, argues against the indolence and luxury encouraged by wealth on the familiar grounds that "Nature works by a just Order and Regulation as well in the Passions and Affections, as in the Limbs and Organs which she forms,"[100] and that sloth topples this order. He even quotes Harrington's dictum that "*Dominion* must naturally follow *Property*" in the *Miscellaneous Reflections*,[101] as part of his analysis of the rise of the ancient Egyptian priesthood. But despite his periodic nods to property concerns and his frequent protestations against valuing wealth and power above virtue, Shaftesbury never articulates the basic claim of the Greek tradition: that unregulated private property inevitably causes the wealthy (who have been

---

[98] Ibid., p. 60. [99] Ibid., p. 61. [100] Ibid., p. 255. [101] Ibid., vol. II, p. 152.

corrupted by their wealth) to rule, thus undermining the rule of reason (i.e. justice) – and that it is therefore just to resort to coercive means in order to prevent this state of affairs from coming to pass. Property, indeed, plays no significant role in Shaftesbury's system; and Leibniz, while he prefers universal "friendship" and the community of possessions, endorses the Roman standard of distributive justice.[102] Just as Harrington's Platonist metaphysics was largely absent from the Whig account of property and agrarian laws, his analysis of property was missing from the philosophical treatises of the early eighteenth-century Platonists. Montesquieu would re-unite these disparate elements, and emerge with a solidly Greek analysis of republican government. He would argue that only republics have virtue as their "principle," and he would define virtue, with Shaftesbury, as the love of order and beauty in society. But, most importantly, he would insist that, because republics are entirely reliant upon virtue, they must secure an equal distribution of property in order to survive.

[102] See, for example, Leibniz, *Political Writings*, pp. 64, 98.

CHAPTER 5

Montesquieu's Greek republics

I

From the outset of his career, Montesquieu found himself obsessed with the uneasy relationship between wealth, virtue, and justice. In the *Lettres persanes*, published anonymously in 1721 when their author was only thirty-two, Montesquieu's *porte-parole* Usbek emphatically asserts the objective reality of justice and attacks the pretensions of the positivists. "Justice," he announces, "is a relation of suitability, which actually exists between two things. This relationship is always the same, by whatever being it is perceived, whether by God, or by an angel, or finally by man."[1] Indeed, "justice is eternal, and does not depend on human conventions;"[2] like Leibniz before him, Montesquieu makes clear that it even exists independently of the will of God himself. Usbek continues that "it is true that men do not see these relationships all the time. Often, indeed, when they do not see them, they turn away from them, and what they see best is always their self-interest. Justice raises its voice, but has difficulty in making itself heard amongst the tumult of the passions."[3] Justice is, then, a fixed, eternal *rapport de convenance* (Montesquieu took the phrase from Leibniz's *Théodicée*)[4] which towers above the abundant variety of human laws, but finds itself obscured by human passions. The chief agent responsible for promoting the passions at the expense of justice turns out to be wealth.

[1] English translations from *Les Lettres persanes* are taken from Montesquieu, *Persian Letters*, ed. and trans. C. J. Betts (London: Penguin Books, 1973); all French texts of Montesquieu's works, unless otherwise noted, are taken from Montesquieu, *Œuvres complètes*, ed. Daniel Oster (Paris: Editions du Seuil, 1964). This passage is from Letter 83 (p. 162). "La Justice est un rapport de convenance, qui se trouve réellement entre deux choses; ce rapport est toujours le même, quelque être qui le considère, soit que ce soit Dieu, soit que ce soit un ange, ou enfin que ce soit un homme."

[2] "la Justice est éternelle et ne dépend point des conventions humaines."

[3] "Il est vrai que les hommes ne voient pas toujours ces rapports; souvent même, lorsqu'ils les voient, ils s'en éloignent; et leur intérêt est toujours ce qu'ils voient le mieux. La Justice élève sa voix; mais elle a peine à se faire entendre dans le tumulte des passions."

[4] On this, see Sheila M. Mason, *Montesquieu's Idea of Justice* (The Hague: Martinus Nijhoff, 1975), pp. 178ff.

Montesquieu explores this theme in Letters 11 through 14 of the *Lettres persanes*, in which he describes the fanciful republic of the Troglodytes. The generic features of this narrative alone furnish a powerful indication of the direction of Montesquieu's thoughts. Like More and Harrington before him, Montesquieu gives his fictional Arabian people a Greek name (τρωγλοδύται, the Ethiopian "cave dwellers" of Book IV of Herodotus' *Histories*),[5] and, recalling both More's *Utopia* and Fénelon's more recent *Télémaque* (1699), places his account in the mouth of a traveler, Usbek. The similarities increase as we move from form to content. Montesquieu's Troglodytes, having turned away from the barbarism, isolation, and vigilantism of their forbearers, have built a virtuous community that acts (like Plato's *politeia*, More's Utopia, Harrington's Oceana, and Fénelon's *Bétique*) "as a single family" (*une seule famille*),[6] and has banished envy by allowing each man only what he needs. It has, in short, rendered its people "happy" (*heureux*) by teaching them virtue (which it defines, in terms almost identical to Shaftesbury's, as the understanding that "the individual's self-interest is always to be found in the common interest").

But in Letter 14 the Troglodytes, like the children of Israel in *I Samuel*, beseech one of their brethren to accept a crown. Their nominee bemoans the decision, realizing that his countrymen seek only a respite from the demanding regimen of virtue which republican government necessitates (and which, as Montesquieu would explain at great length in *De l'esprit des lois*, is not required in a well-ordered monarchy). The Troglodytes, their nominee concludes, merely desire an excuse to "satisfy [their] ambitions, accumulate wealth, and live idly in degrading luxury"[7] – in short, to live "under the rule of something other than virtue" (*sous un autre joug que celui de la Vertu*).

That is where Montesquieu leaves the Troglodytes in *Les Lettres persanes*, but he had written one further installment in their story which survives in one of the notebooks later edited as the *Pensées*. In this scene the first king has died, and the Troglodytes (living in what seems to be less a monarchy than a republic which has fallen from grace) choose the wisest man in his family to succeed him. During this second king's reign – and quite predictably given what we learned in Letter 14 – the Troglodytes decide

---

[5] IV.183. See Herodotus, *Histories*, ed. and trans. A. D. Godley, vol. II, Loeb Classical Library (London: William Heinemann, 1921).

[6] In *De l'esprit des lois*, Montesquieu would insist that republics can only exist "in a small state, where one can educate the general populace and raise a whole people like a family" (IV.7). English translations from *De l'esprit des lois* are taken from *The Spirit of the Laws*, ed. and trans. Anne Cohler, Basia Miller, and Harold Stone (Cambridge University Press, 1989).

[7] "vous pourrez contenter votre ambition, acquérir des richesses et languir dans une lache volupté."

to "institute trade and commerce among them."[8] In response, their king asks the fateful question: "Do you now want to have wealth rather than your virtue?" (*Voudriez-vous préférer aujourd'hui les richesses à votre vertu?*). The answer given by the people's representative deserves to be quoted at length, as it sets out the basic terms in which Montesquieu would discuss republicanism for the rest of his life:

it will be you alone who decides whether wealth is or is not to be harmful to your people. If they see you would rather have wealth than virtue, they will soon fall into the same habit; in this manner your attitude will determine theirs. If you raise a man to an important post, or bring him into your confidence, merely because he is rich, you may be sure that you have struck a mortal blow at his virtue... The foundation of your people's virtue, sir, as you know, is their education. Change this education, and those who are not bold enough to be criminals will soon be ashamed of being virtuous. There are two things that we have to do: to make both meanness and extravagance equally shameful. Everyone must be accountable to the state for the administration of his property, and the man who ignobly demeans himself, by denying himself a reasonable standard of living, must be judged as harshly as the man who squanders his children's patrimony. Each citizen must spend his own wealth as equitably as if it belonged to someone else.

The king responds forlornly:

Troglodytes, you are about to acquire the use of riches; but I declare to you that if you are not virtuous you will be one of the unhappiest nations on earth. As things are at present, all that is required is for me to be juster than you: it is the sign of my royal authority, and no other that I could find would be more illustrious. If you seek to distinguish yourself only by riches, which in themselves are nothing, I shall certainly have to distinguish myself by the same means... At present it is within myself that I find all my riches.[9]

---

[8] Montesquieu, *Persian Letters*, p. 286 (appendix); reproduced in *Œuvres*, p. 863. "d'établir chez les Troglodytes le commerce et les arts."

[9] "Ce sera vous seul qui déciderez si les richesses seront pernicieuses à votre peuple, ou non. S'ils voient que vous les préférez à la vertu, ils s'accoutumeront bientôt à en faire de même, et, en cela, votre goût réglera le leur. Si vous élevez dans les emplois ou que vous approchiez de votre confiance un homme par cela seul qu'il est riche, comptez que ce sera un coup mortel que vous porterez à sa vertu... Vous connoissez, Seigneur, la base sur quoi est fondée la vertu de votre peuple: c'est sur l'éducation. Changez cette éducation, et celui qui n'étoit pas assez hardi pour être criminel rougira bientôt d'être vertueux. Nous avons deux choses à faire: c'est de flétrir également l'avarice et la prodigalité. Il faut que chacun soit comptable à l'État de l'administration de ses biens et que le lâche qui s'abaissera jusqu' à se dérober une honnête subsistance ne soit pas jugé moins sévèrement que celui qui dissipera le patrimoine de ses enfants. Il faut que chaque citoyen soit équitable dispensateur de son propre bien, comme il le seroit de celui d'un autre" (*Œuvres complètes*, ed. Roger Caillois [Paris: Librairie Gallimard, 1949], pp. 378–79).

"Troglodytes, dit le Roi, les richesses vont entrer chez vous mais je vous déclare que, si vous n'êtes pas vertueux, vous serez un des peuples les plus malheureux de la Terre. Dans l'état où vous êtes, je n'ai besoin que d'être plus juste que vous: c'est la marque de mon autorité royale, et je n'en saurois

The great fear about wealth in this passage is that it will compete with virtue in order to become the criterion which determines the distribution of political power.[10] Before the advent of riches, Troglodyte kings attained their office by being more virtuous than the rest of the citizens (an arrangement which is "just" in the Greek sense, since the rule of the best men corresponds to a rational *rapport de convenance*). But wealth might come to replace virtue as the political coin of the realm in two ways: either the king might begin appointing the wealthy, rather than the virtuous to important state positions, thus setting a devastating example for his people, or the people might themselves come to place more stock in wealth than virtue, and might therefore begin to seek wealthy rather than virtuous kings. If either should happen, both people and king agree, the Troglodyte republic would lose its virtue (its conformity to objective moral facts) and its people would be rendered *malheureux*, "unhappy."[11] Their proposed solution is to empower the state to regulate the *use* of property, and to enforce moderation.

It is worth noticing that, on this account, the introduction of commerce and money provides an opportunity for wealth to gain ascendancy over virtue, but it does not *guarantee* that outcome. Indeed, Montesquieu's fable does not embrace determinism: given the introduction of wealth, and even in the absence of fixed limits on the amount of property that individuals may possess, virtue can still win the day. Later, however, Montesquieu would lose faith in the notion that virtue can survive if the state merely regulates the ways in which people use their property; he would come to

---

trouver de plus auguste. Si vous ne cherchez à vous distinguer que par des richesses, qui ne sont rien en elles-mêmes, il faudra bien que je me distingue par les mêmes moyens . . . Je trouve à présent toutes mes richesses dans moi-même" (*Œuvres complètes*, ed. Caillois, p. 379).

There is a helpful summary of the Troglodyte episode in Nannerl O. Keohane, "Virtuous Republics and Glorious Monarchies: Two Models in Montesquieu's Political Thought" in *Political Studies* 20 (1972), 385–87. Keohane does not, however, connect Montesquieu's anxiety about wealth and virtue to the tradition we have been following. She does mention Montesquieu's general indebtedness to Plato, but discusses only structural, generic similarities. She also attributes to Montesquieu a belief that Plato's Republic is "difficult to introduce" and "impossible to maintain," despite Montesquieu's clear statements to the contrary (which will be discussed shortly).

[10] This is, I believe, the central feature of the Troglodyte story that Richard B. Sher neglects in his otherwise excellent essay. See Richard B. Sher, "From Troglodytes to Americans: Montesquieu and the Scottish Enlightenment on Liberty, Virtue, and Commerce" in *Republicanism, Liberty, and Commercial Society, 1649–1776*, ed. David Wootton (Stanford University Press, 1994), pp. 368–402.

[11] *Œuvres*, p. 864. Donald Desserud provides a helpful discussion of what Montesquieu means by calling the Troglodytes' life of virtue "natural," although I disagree with his broader conclusions. See Donald A. Desserud, "Virtue, Commerce and Moderation in the 'Tale of the Troglodytes': Montesquieu's *Persian Letters*" in *History of Political Thought* 12 (1991), 605–26.

believe that it must regulate the *amount* of property they have to begin with. Only if property is distributed in an egalitarian manner, he would argue, could wealth be prevented from thrashing virtue in the political arena, and thus rendering the state unjust. On this later account disproportionate wealth corrupts its possessors, causing them to lose sight of the social whole and their proper place within it; and when they come to rule, virtue is lost. Already in the *Lettres persanes*, Montesquieu gestures at that conviction. In Letter 122 Usbek insists that "equality between citizens, which usually produces an equal distribution of wealth, itself conveys prosperity and life to the body politic and scatters it throughout,"[12] and in Letter 119 he attacks the "unjust law of primogeniture" which "destroys the equality between citizens, on which their prosperity entirely depends."[13] But Montesquieu's major reorientation on the subject would come, unsurprisingly, in his confrontation with Roman history.

As Bertrand Barère noted, Montesquieu's 1734 *Considérations sur les causes de la grandeur des Romains et de leur décadence* bears the mark of Moyle's *An Essay on the Constitution and Government of the Roman State*, and, as we would expect given that provenance, it endorses the substance of the Harringtonian analysis of Roman decline.[14] Early in his treatise

---

[12] *Persian Letters*, p. 220. "L'égalité même des citoyens, qui produit ordinairement de l'égalité dans les fortunes, porte l'abondance et la vie dans toutes les parties du corps politique et la répand partout." I have substituted my own translation here.

[13] Ibid., p. 215. "l'injuste droit d'aînesse . . . en ce qu'il détruit l'égalité des citoyens, qui en fait toute l'opulence."

[14] Machiavelli is also a major influence, and occasionally Montesquieu sides with him against Harrington (for example, Montesquieu refuses to condemn the tumults in Rome [*Œuvres*, p. 453], although, unlike Machiavelli, he treats them as a necessary evil, rather than an intrinsically beneficial part of civic life). On the crucial issue of the agrarian, however, Montesquieu is firmly within the Harringtonian camp. See Robert Shackleton, "Montesquieu and Machiavelli: a reappraisal" in *Essays on Montesquieu and the Enlightenment*, ed. David Gilson and Martin Smith (Oxford: The Voltaire Foundation, 1988), pp. 117–32. The role of the agrarian laws in the *Considérations* is often entirely passed over, as in Richard Meyers, "Montesquieu on the Causes of Roman Greatness" in *History of Political Thought* 16 (1995), 37–47; and Georges Benrekassa, "Le problème des sources dans les *Considérations*: questions de méthode" in *Storia e ragione: le* Considérations sur les causes de la grandeur des Romains et de leur décadence *di Montesquieu nel 250° della pubblicazione. Atti del Convegno internazionale organizato dall'Instituto Universitario Orientale e dalla Società italiana di studi sul secolo XVIII*, ed. Alberto Postigliola (Naples: Liguori Editore, 1987), pp. 33–46. A notable exception is an article by Luciano Guerci, in which he discusses the philo-Gracchan position in the *Considérations*, and sets it in the broader context of eighteenth-century Francophone Roman historiography. He does not, however, trace this strand of Roman historiography to its rightful source: Harrington and the English Whigs (Luciano Guerci, "La *République romaine* di Louis de Beaufort e la discussione con Montesquieu" in *Storia e ragione*, pp. 421–53). Much the same could be said of Alfred Heuss's analysis. See Alfred Heuss, *Barthold Georg Niebuhrs wissenschaftliche Anfänge: Untersuchungen und Mitteilungen über die Kopenhagener Manuscripte und zur europäische Tradition der lex agraria (loi agraire)* (Göttingen: Vandenhoeck & Ruprecht, 1981), pp. 289–93. Translations from the *Considérations* are my own.

Montesquieu unequivocally asserts the centrality of the Roman agrarian law, both for civic health and for military prowess: "The founders of ancient republics divided the lands equally: this alone produced a powerful people, that is a well-ordered society; it also produced a good army, each one having an equal interest – and a great one at that – to defend his country."[15] Rome was not founded as a republic, but Montesquieu follows Moyle in arguing that the decision of the Roman kings to empower and enrich the people made monarchy untenable and inevitably yielded republican government.[16] The comparison he draws is instructive: "Just as Henry VII, the king of England, augmented the power of the commons in order to debase the great, Servius Tullius before him had extended the privileges of the people in order to diminish the senate. But the people, having become more powerful, overturned both monarchies."[17] The parallel between Henry VII and Servius Tullius is, as we have seen, a staple of the Harringtonian account.[18]

Montesquieu records that the equality of possessions in Rome was maintained by the state's treatment of conquered lands and the spoils of war. It was standard practice that, after a Roman victory, "the spoils were held in common,"[19] and equally divided amongst the soldiers. Conquered *ager publicus*, in turn, was divided in two: "one part was sold for the profit of the public, and the other was distributed among the poor citizens, in return for rent paid to the republic."[20] Montesquieu summarizes his position neatly: "It was the equal division of lands that rendered Rome capable of

---

[15] Montesquieu, *Œuvres*, p. 439. "Les fondateurs des anciennes républiques avaient également partagé les terres: cela seul faisait un peuple puissant, c'est à dire une société bien réglée; cela faisait aussi une bonne armée, chacun ayant un égal intérêt, et très grand, à défendre sa patrie."

[16] See note 153 in the *Dossier des Considérations* (*Œuvres*, p. 215).

[17] "Comme Henri VII, roi d'Angleterre, augmenta le pouvoir des communes pour avilir les grands, Servius Tullius, avant lui, avoit étendu les privilèges du peuple pour abaisser le sénat. Mais le peuple, devenu d'abord plus hardi, renversa l'une et l'autre monarchie." (*Œuvres*, p. 436).

[18] Servius Tullius is also given a central role in the institution of the first agrarian law by Giambattista Vico in his *Scienza Nuova*. See Vico, *The New Science*, ed. Thomas Goddard Bergin and Max Harold Fisch (Cornell University Press, 1976), esp. 107, 420, 613, 619, 620. This argument of Vico's puzzled Momigliano: "Where did Vico get this extraordinary idea of transforming the Servian constitution and the alleged nucleus of the XII Tables into two agrarian laws? My researches on the study of Roman agrarian laws in the seventeenth century... have yielded no results. So far I have been unable to discover any predecessors to Vico in this theory." Moyle was such a predecessor. See Arnaldo Momigliano, "Vico's *Scienza Nuova*: Roman 'Bestioni' and Roman 'Eroi'" in *Essays in Ancient and Modern Historiography* (Oxford: Basil Blackwell, 1977), p. 268. I am grateful to Richard Serjeantson for this reference.

[19] "Le butin était mis en commun, et on le distribuait aux soldats" (*Œuvres*, p. 436).

[20] Ibid. "On confisquait une partie des terres du peuple vaincu, dont on faisait deux parts: l'une se vendait au profit public; l'autre étoit distribuée aux pauvres citoyens, sous la charge d'une rente en faveur de la république."

escaping from its abasement; and it felt this well when it was corrupted."[21] Like the Harringtonians, he traces the cause of Roman corruption to the rejection of the agrarian law: "When the laws were not rigidly observed, things returned to the point where they are presently among us: the avarice of some individuals, and the prodigality of others caused parcels of land to pass into few hands; and for the first time arts introduced themselves, for the mutual needs of rich and poor."[22] No longer was it the case that "in Rome public offices could not be achieved but by virtue, and gave no reward besides honor."[23] Decline came fast and furious. In a familiar line of reasoning, Montesquieu argues that Sparta met the same fate for the same reasons:

The kings Agis and Cleomenes, seeing that in the place of the nine thousand citizens who lived in Sparta at the time of Lycurgus there were now no more than seven hundred, of whom perhaps one hundred possessed lands, and that the rest were nothing but a populace without courage, they endeavored to reestablish the laws in this regard; and Sparta recovered its former power, and one again became formidable to all the Greeks.[24]

This account (duly adduced by each and every Harringtonian author), Montesquieu tells us, can be found easily in Plutarch's life of Agis and Cleomenes.[25] That he concludes this chapter by quoting the speech which Appian gives to Tiberius Gracchus should establish beyond question the ideological thrust of his thoughts (and should explain his emphasis on the depletion of Roman manpower caused by the lapse of the agrarian).[26]

We should note, however, that Montesquieu did not by any means argue that the original Roman agrarian laws were flawless. On the contrary, in a passage from the *Pensées*, he comments: "the laws of the Romans were not as wise as those of Plato, and they permitted (or reluctantly allowed) the citizens, under assumed names, to acquire the inheritances of other

---

[21] Ibid., p. 440. "Ce fut le partage égal des terres qui rendit Rome capable de sortir d'abord de son abaissement; et cela se sentit bien, quand elle fut corrompue."

[22] Ibid., p. 439. "Quand les lois n'étaient plus rigidement observées, les choses revenaient au point ou elles sont à présent parmi nous: l'avarice de quelques particuliers, et la prodigalité des autres, faisaient passer les fonds de terre dans peu de mains; et d'abord les arts s'introduisaient, pour les besoins mutuels des riches et des pauvres."

[23] Ibid., p. 440. "à Rome les emplois publics ne s'obtenoient que par la vertu, et ne donnoient d'utilité que l'honneur . . ."

[24] Ibid. "Les rois Agis et Cleomènes, voyant qu'au lieu de neuf mille citoyens qui étoient à Sparte de temps de Lycurge, il n'y en avoit plus que sept cents, dont à peine cent possédoient des terres, et que tout le reste n'étoit qu'une populace sans courage, ils enterprirent de rétablir les lois à cet égard; et Lacédémone reprit sa première puissance, et redevint formidable à tous les Grecs."

[25] Ibid., note.

[26] Montesquieu remained interested in the effects of agrarian laws on population (a point of view he passed on to Rousseau). See, for example, *The Spirit of the Laws* (ed. Cohler et al.) XXIII.15 (p. 436).

citizens, which was to elude the law. But if this law had not been eluded, Rome would not have fallen into corruption."²⁷ Later in *De l'esprit des lois*, he observes that "the laws of the first Romans concerning inheritances thought only to observe the spirit of the division of lands; they did not sufficiently restrict the wealth of women, and thereby left a door open to luxury, which is always inseparable from this wealth."²⁸ He adds:

the indefinite permission to make testaments, granted among the Romans, gradually ruined the political provision on the sharing of lands; more than anything else it introduced the ominous difference between wealth and poverty; many shares were brought together in the same person; some citizens had too much, an infinity of others had nothing. Thus, the people, continually deprived of their share, constantly asked for a new distribution of lands.²⁹

Nonetheless, Montesquieu did believe that the ancient Roman agrarian was the sound bedrock of Roman virtue and power, and he attributed the republic's collapse to lax observance. In one passage of the *Considérations*, for example, he explains that, after the plebs had finished undermining patrician authority – which had been based on "wisdom, justice, and the love the senate inspired for the fatherland"³⁰ – inequalities in wealth led to a disastrous, but familiar outcome:

Over the course of time, after the plebs had so debased the patricians that this familial distinction was empty, and both groups were indifferently elevated to honors, there were new disputes between the lowly people, spurred on by their tribunes, and the principal patrician and plebeian families, which one called the "nobles," and who had for themselves the senate, which was composed of them. But, since the ancient mores [with respect to land] were no more, and certain individuals had immense wealth, and since it is impossible that riches will not secure power, the nobles resisted with more force than the patricians ever had; it was this that caused the death of the Gracchi and several others of those who worked in their ranks.³¹

---

²⁷ Montesquieu, *Œuvres*, p. 893. "Les lois des Romains ne furent pas si sages que celles de Platon, et elles permirent (ou l'on souffrit) que des citoyens, sous des noms empruntés, acquissent les héritages propres des citoyens, ce qui était éluder la loi. Mais, si cette loi n'avaient pas été éludée, Rome n'aurait pas tombé dans la corruption." This passage was left out of *De l'esprit des lois*.

²⁸ *The Spirit of the Laws*, p. 525.   ²⁹ Ibid., p. 523.

³⁰ *Œuvres*, p. 451. "Le sénat se défendoit par sa sagesse, sa justice et l'amour qu'il inspiroit pour la patrie."

³¹ Ibid. "Dans la suite de temps, lorsque les plébéiens eurent tellement abaissé les patriciens, que cette distinction de famille devint vaine, et que les unes et les autres furent indifféremment élevées aux honneurs, il y eut de nouvelles disputes entre le base peuple, agité par ses tribuns et les principales familles patriciennes ou plébéiennes, qu'on appela les Nobles, et qui avaient pour elles le sénat, qui en était composé. Mais, comme les mœurs anciennes n'étaient plus, que des particuliers avaient des richesses immenses, et qu'il est impossible que les richesses ne donnent du pouvoir, les nobles

In this telling, the Gracchi, defenders of the "ancient mores," end their lives overwhelmed by a regime in which Montesquieu's nightmare has come to pass: deference to the virtue of the patricians is replaced by the usurpation of wealthy and corrupt men. The republic is undermined, and virtue banished. Thus Rome fell.[32] In short, for Montesquieu, as for Harrington and his English disciples, Rome had to be analyzed in Greek terms. With his embrace of this account of Roman collapse in the *Considérations*, the stage was set for Montesquieu's mature account of republican government.

II

Montesquieu's readers have tended to take one of two general approaches to the task of interpreting *De l'esprit des lois*. Some have assumed that Montesquieu meant to endorse one of the regimes he describes in the treatise, and they have accordingly concentrated their efforts on identifying the object of his praise.[33] Others, however, have seen Montesquieu as an empirical proto-sociologist who responsibly analyzes each regime without playing favorites.[34] On this view, the quest for Montesquieu's "preferred regime" is badly conceived. At first glance, the sociological approach has much to recommend it. In the preface to *De l'esprit des lois*, Montesquieu announces: "I do not write to censure that which is established in any country whatsoever. Each nation will find here the reason for its maxims, and the consequence will naturally be drawn from them that changes can be proposed only by those who are born fortunate enough to fathom by a stroke of genius the whole of a state's constitution."[35] Indeed, Montesquieu makes clear that his primary purpose is to elucidate the principles that make sense of the great variety of human laws and institutions – not to explain away or attack that variety. As he puts it, "I began by examining men, and

résistèrent avec plus de force que les patriciens n'avaient fait; ce qui fut cause de la mort des Gracques et de plusieurs de ceux qui travaillèrent sur leur plan."

[32] Roger Oake neglects to discuss this aspect of Montesquieu's writings on Rome. See Roger Oake, "Montesquieu's Analysis of Roman History" in *Journal of the History of Ideas* 16 (1955), 44–59.

[33] I include in this category scholars who have sought to establish Montesquieu's preference for "moderate" regimes. See, for example, Lando Landi, *L'Inghilterra e il Pensiero Politico di Montesquieu* (Padua: CEDAM, 1981).

[34] For a helpful exposition of these two positions in the literature, see Sara MacDonald, "Problems with Principles: Montesquieu's Theory of Natural Justice" in *History of Political Thought* 24 (2003), 109–11.

[35] *The Spirit of the Laws* (preface), p. xliv. "Je n'écris point pour censurer ce qui est établi dans quelque pays que ce soit. Chaque nation trouvera ici les raisons de ses maximes; et on en tirera naturellement cette conséquence, qu'il n'appartient de proposer des changements, qu'à ceux qui sont assez heureusement nés pour pénétrer, d'un coup de génie, toute la Constitution d'un Etat."

I believed that, amidst the infinite diversity of laws and mores, they were not led by their fancies alone."[36] The diversity of regimes is neither random nor senseless, but results from nature itself. Accordingly, multiple forms of government can "make sense," and there is no one form of government which suits all people in all places and times. On the contrary, "it is better to say that the government most in conformity with nature is the one whose particular arrangement best relates to the disposition of the people for whom it is established."[37]

In reading the first book of *De l'esprit des lois*, however, it becomes readily apparent that Montesquieu uses the word "natural" in two radically different senses. To begin with, there are natural laws – "necessary relations deriving from the nature of things"[38] – which govern the material world. These laws cannot be "disobeyed": "Between one moving body and another moving body, it is in accord with relations of mass and velocity that all motions are received, increased, diminished, or lost; every diversity is *uniformity*, every change is *consistency*."[39] But there are also moral laws embedded in nature. Montesquieu repeats his definition of objective moral relations from the *Lettres persanes*: "Before laws were made, there were possible relations of justice. To say that there is nothing just or unjust but what positive laws ordain or prohibit is to say that before a circle was drawn, all its radii were not equal."[40]

Therefore, one must admit that there are relations of fairness prior to the positive law that establishes them, so that, for example, assuming that there were societies of men, it would be just to conform to their laws; so that, if there were intelligent beings that had received some kindness from another being, they ought to be grateful for it; so that, if one intelligent being had created another intelligent being, the created one ought to remain in its original dependency; so that one intelligent being who has done harm to another intelligent being deserves the same harm in return, and so forth.[41]

---

[36] Ibid., p. xliii. "J'ai d'abord examiné les hommes; et j'ai cru que, dans cette infinie diversité de lois et de mœurs, ils n'étaient pas uniquement conduits par leurs fantasies."

[37] Ibid. 1.3 (p. 8). "Il vaut mieux dire que le gouvernement le plus conforme à la nature est celui dont la disposition particulière se rapporte mieux à la disposition du peuple pour lequel il est établi."

[38] Ibid. 1.1 (p. 3). "les rapports nécessaires qui dérivent de la nature des choses."

[39] Ibid. "Entre un corps mu et un autre corps mu, c'est suivant les rapport [*sic*] de la masse et de la vitesse que tous les mouvements sont reçus, augmentés, diminués, perdus; chaque diversité est *uniformité*, chaque changement est *constance*."

[40] Ibid., p. 4. "Avant qu'il eût des lois faites, il y avait des rapports de justice possibles. Dire qu'il n'y a rien de juste ni d'injuste que ce qu'ordonnent ou défendent les lois positives, c'est dire qu'avant qu'on eût tracé de cercle, tous les rayons n'étaient pas égaux."

[41] Ibid. "Il faut donc avouer des rapports d'équité antérieurs à la loi positive qui les établit: comme par exemple, que, supposé qu'il y eût des sociétés d'hommes, il serait juste de se conformer à leur lois;

These laws are objective and natural "relations," but they differ from physical laws in that they can be ignored – and frequently are. While the "intelligent world also has laws that are invariable by their nature, unlike the physical world, it does not follow its laws consistently."[42] Montesquieu concludes that "man, as a physical being, is governed by invariable laws like other bodies" but "as an intelligent being, he constantly violates the laws god has established."[43] He is in constant need of being recalled to his natural duties by divine revelation and by philosophers, who have "reminded him of himself by the laws of morality."[44] Something can, thus, be "natural" in the sense of following logically from the nature of the material world, and still be "unnatural" in the moral sense.

Advocates of the sociological approach are right to stress that Montesquieu's most original contribution to political thought lies in two connected areas. The first is his attribution of the variety of regimes to a cluster of factors (climatological, geographical, demographic, economic, etc.) which produce different sorts of societies by physical necessity (for example, a republic cannot exist in a large geographical area). The second is his similarly empirical analysis of what kinds of laws and institutions effectively support different regimes. In this sense, every regime that Montesquieu describes is indeed "natural" under certain circumstances (that is, can follow naturally from those circumstances), and a government can be said to be "perfect" or "imperfect" based on the extent to which it embraces the laws and apparatus which – as a matter of material necessity – tend to produce and support its particular type of regime. But Montesquieu also retains a different idea of "nature" which asserts the independent existence of abstract moral principles. On this definition of "nature," some regimes may be said to be intrinsically more "natural" than others. "The law of nature," he explains, "makes everything tend toward the preservation of the species," while the "law of natural enlightenment" encourages us "to do to others what we would want done to us."[45] All governments

---

que, s'il y avait des êtres intelligents qui eussent reçu quelque bienfait d'un autre être, ils devraient en avoir de la reconnaissance; que, si un être intelligent avait créé un être intelligent, le crée devrait rester dans la dépendance qu'il a eue dès son origine; qu'un être intelligent qui a fait du mal à un être intelligent mérite de recevoir le même mal; et ainsi du reste."

[42] Ibid. "Car, quoique celui-là [le monde intelligent] ait aussi des lois qui par leur nature sont invariables, il ne les suit constamment comme le monde physique suit les siennes."

[43] Ibid., p. 5. "L'homme, comme être physique, est, ainsi que les autres corps, gouverné par des lois invariables. Comme être intelligent, il viole sans cesse les lois que Dieu a établies . . . "

[44] Ibid. "Un tel être pouvait à tous les instants s'oublier lui-même; les philosophes l'ont averti par les lois de la morale."

[45] Ibid. x.3 (p. 139). "la loi de la nature, qui fait que tout tend à la conservation des espèces; la loi de la lumière naturelle, qui veut que nous fassions à autrui ce que nous voudrions qu'on nous fît."

will necessarily be driven by the first law, but few will observe the second. Indeed, Montesquieu gives us substantial grounds for believing that only republics will maximize human virtue and create a morally "natural" life for human beings. Montesquieu's republics may no longer be possible or "natural" in the physical sense given the circumstances of modernity, but he makes clear that they still "astonish our small souls"[46] and stand at the summit of regimes for extremely Greek reasons.

In Book 11 of *De l'esprit des lois* Montesquieu divides all governments into republics, monarchies, and despotisms. Each of these, he explains, has a dominant "principle" (a "spring" which sets it in motion), and in the case of republics that principle is "virtue." What exactly Montesquieu means by "virtue" in this context has divided and preoccupied generations of scholars. The source of the confusion is Montesquieu's "Avertissement de l'auteur" at the outset of the text. "In order to understand the first four books," Montesquieu writes, "one must note that what I call *virtue* in a republic is love of the homeland, that is love of equality. It is not a moral virtue or a Christian virtue; it is *political* virtue, and is the spring that makes republican government move . . ."[47] Montesquieu offers this clarification in order to mollify critics who had protested that he appeared to grant republican government an unwarranted monopoly on virtue:[48] do we not find moral and Christian virtue in monarchies as well, they asked? Indeed we do, Montesquieu replied, but this particular *vertu politique*, while it may be present in other regimes, is the essential motive force in republics.

It has become increasingly popular to cite this "avertissement" as evidence that Montesquieu's *vertu politique* is not only wholly unrelated to moral virtue, but even inherently hostile to it. If substantiated, this argument would have the obvious effect of disconnecting the "virtue" of Montesquieu's republics from the immanent moral relations of Book 1, thus refuting the suggestion that his republics give human beings the best chance of fulfilling their moral natures. Thomas Pangle makes this argument, and

---

[46] Ibid. IV.4 (p. 35). "qui étonnent nos petites âmes."

[47] Ibid., p. xli. "Pour l'intelligence des quatres premiers livres de cet ouvrage, il faut observer que ce que j'appelle la *vertu* dans la république, est l'amour de la patrie, c'est-à-dire, l'amour de l'égalité. Ce n'est point une vertu morale, ni une vertu chrétienne; c'est la vertu *politique*; et celle-ci est le ressort qui fait mouvoir le gouvernement républicain . . . "

[48] See, for example, Montesquieu's comments in the *Eclaircissements sur l'esprit des lois* (*Œuvres*, p. 822). See also Nannerl O. Keohane, *Philosophy and the State in France: the Renaissance to the Enlightenment* (Princeton University Press, 1980), pp. 415–19. Keohane provides a helpful discussion of Montesquieu's view of *vertu politique*, but does not take an explicit position on this quality's relationship to the moral *rapports* of Book 1.

his reasoning is developed by Paul Rahe in a recent study.[49] Rahe argues that when Montesquieu discusses virtue, "he has in mind the fostering of an irrational, unreasoning passion for equality" which "in no way depends on, gives rise to, or is subordinate to anything resembling moral, Christian, or even philosophical virtue."[50] Such claims seem difficult to reconcile with Montesquieu's insistence that "one can define virtue as love of the laws and the homeland. This love, requiring a continuous preference of the public interest over one's own, produces all the individual virtues; they are only that preference."[51] Montesquieu writes similarly that "political virtue" *is* "moral virtue in the sense in which it points toward the general good,"[52] and that "love of the homeland leads to good mores, and goodness in mores leads to love of the homeland. The less we can satisfy our particular passions, the more we give ourselves up to passions for the general order [i.e. virtue]."

True, Montesquieu is clear that while "political virtue" engenders the moral virtues, it does not follow that it is impossible for moral virtues to exist in its absence (although he does suggest that monarchies cannot exhibit moral virtue to as great a degree as republics[53]). He also stresses the difference between virtue proper and "that virtue which relates to revealed truths" (nor is he the first classicizing philosopher to draw such a distinction).[54] However, none of this diminishes Montesquieu's conviction that *vertu politique* is the quality which causes men to love the common interest and accept their given place within the organic whole.[55] It is, in short, the characteristic possessed by virtuous people that is most relevant to political

[49] See Thomas Pangle, *Montesquieu's Philosophy of Liberalism* (University of Chicago Press, 1973), pp. 54–65, and Paul A. Rahe, "Forms of Government: Structure, Principle, Object, and Aim" in *Montesquieu's Science of Politics: Essays on The Spirit of the Laws*, ed. David W. Carrithers, Michael A. Mosher, and Paul A. Rahe (Lanham, MD: Rowman & Littlefield, 2001), pp. 69–108.

[50] Ibid., p. 73.

[51] David Carrithers stresses this point in "Democratic and Aristocratic Republics: Ancient and Modern" in *Montesquieu's Science of Politics*, p. 117. However, he is promptly overcome by the desire to place Montesquieu on the side of the "moderns" against the "ancients" when it comes to virtue.

[52] III.5. *The Spirit of the Laws*, p. 25n. "Je parle ici de la vertu politique, qui est la vertu morale, dans le sens qu'elle se dirige au bien général." This point is made nicely in Franco Venturi, *Utopia and Reform in the Enlightenment* (Cambridge University Press, 1971), p. 44.

[53] In monarchies, "one judges men's actions not as good but as fine, not as just but as great; not as reasonable but as extraordinary" (*The Spirit of the Laws*, p. 32). See also p. 25: "in a monarchy it is very difficult for the people to be virtuous." Likewise, in commercial states citizens are taught "ius strictum," not those "moral virtues that make it so that one does not always discuss one's own interests alone" (p. 339).

[54] Consider, *inter alia*, the distinction between moral and theological virtues in Catholic theology.

[55] See *The Spirit of Laws*, pp. 36, 42. This explains why Montesquieu advocates such restrictive measures in his republics in order to secure and defend the moral virtues: they are inextricably linked to political virtue. See esp. pp. 56–60.

life in republics; that is its utility in Montesquieu's scheme. In republics, where the people must uphold laws to which they themselves are subject, this is a necessary quality.[56] But *vertu politique* is not devoid of normative significance: it brings the moral virtues – those *rapports de convenance* – in its wake and, in turn, is undermined by their absence. Indeed, Montesquieu insists that "when that virtue ceases, ambition enters those hearts that can admit it, and avarice enters them all," and the fatal process of παραδιαστολή (rhetorical redescription) so feared by Thucydides and Aristotle takes hold:[57] "What was a *maxim* is now called *severity*; what was a *rule* is now called *constraint*; what was *vigilance* is now called *fear*. There, frugality, not the desire to possess, is avarice."[58]

This notion that a public or political kind of virtue brings the moral virtues in its train was quite prevalent during the period. Consider, for example, a passage from Fénelon's essay *Sur le pur amour* (first published in 1718):

All these [ancient] legislators and philosophers who reasoned about laws presupposed that the fundamental principle of political society was that of preferring the public to the self – not through hope of serving one's own interests, but through the simple, pure, disinterested love of the political order, which is beauty, justice, and virtue itself.[59]

Likewise, a passage from *Cato's Letters* seems to anticipate Montesquieu's comments directly. In letter thirty-five Gordon discusses what he calls *publick spirit*, or "the love of one's country." In tyrannical regimes, Gordon observes, public spirit might encourage citizens to be "blind slaves to the blind will of the prince." In "free countries," however, "publick spirit is another thing; it is to combat force and delusion; it is to reconcile the true interests of the governed and the governors":

This is publick spirit; which contains in it every laudable passion, and takes in parents, kindred, friends, neighbours, and every thing dear to mankind; it is the

---

[56] Ibid., p. 22.

[57] For an account of the role of rhetorical redescription in classical and early-modern thought, see Quentin Skinner, *Reason and Rhetoric in the Philosophy of Hobbes* (Cambridge University Press, 1996), pp. 138–80.

[58] *The Spirit of the Laws* III.3 (p. 23). "Lorsque cette vertu cesse, l'ambition entre dans les cœurs qui peuvent la recevoir, et l'avarice entre dans tous . . . Ce qui était *maxime*, on l'appelle *rigueur*; ce qui était *règle*, on l'appelle *gêne*; ce qui était *attention*, on l'appelle *crainte*. C'est la frugalité qui y est l'avarice, et non pas le désir d'avoir."

[59] Fénelon, *Œuvres*, vol. 1 (Paris: Gallimard, 1983), p. 668. "Tous les législateurs et tous les philosophes qui ont raisonné sur les lois ont supposé comme un principe fondamental de la societé dans la patrie, qu'il faut préférer le public à soi, non par espérance de quelque intérêt, mais par le seul amour désintéressé de l'ordre, qui est la beauté, la justice et la vertue même." The translation is taken from Fénelon, *Telmachus*, ed. and trans. Patrick Riley (Cambridge University Press, 1994), p. xxi.

highest virtue, and contains in it almost all others; steadfastness to good purposes, fidelity to one's trust, resolution in difficulties, defiance of danger, contempt of death, and impartial benevolence to all mankind. It is a passion to promote the universal good, with personal pain, loss and peril: It is one man's care for many, and the concern of every man for all.[60]

This notion of "publick spirit" is uncannily similar to Montesquieu's "vertu politique."

Indeed, it is also tempting to see in *Cato* the antecedent to Montesquieu's theory of the dominant "principles" (or "springs" – *ressorts*) of government:

Government is political, as a human body is natural, mechanism: both have proper springs, wheels, and a peculiar organization to qualify them for suitable motions, and can have no other than that organization enables them to perform; and when those springs or principles are destroyed by accident or violence, or are worn out by time, they must suffer a natural or political demise.[61]

For both Cato and Montesquieu, "political virtue" is the root of free government. This most politically relevant passion is not hostile or antithetical to the moral virtues; rather, by inculcating a deep reverence for the common whole, it gives rise to moral virtue. As Montesquieu has it, all the constituent virtues are only expressions of a fundamental commitment to the common interest.

So while political virtue is "natural" to republican government in the material sense (i.e. it makes republics tick), it also produces a society which conforms to "nature" in the moral sense. In order to understand Montesquieu's account of how all of this works, it is necessary to appreciate how deeply indebted the President was to ancient Greek models. In the second volume of his *Pensées* Montesquieu makes a remarkable statement:

I am not to be numbered among those who view the Republic of Plato as something ideal and purely imaginary, and the institution of which would be impossible. My reason is that the Republic of Lycurgus seemed every bit as difficult to institute as that of Plato, and, meanwhile, it was so well instituted that it endured as long as any republic that one knows of in its power and splendor.[62]

---

[60] John Trenchard and Thomas Gordon, *Cato's Letters, or Essays on Liberty, Civil and Religious, and Other Important Subjects*, ed. Ronald Hamowy (Indianapolis: Liberty Fund, 1995), vol. I, p. 251.

[61] Ibid., vol. II, p. 607.

[62] Montesquieu, *Œuvres*, p. 1036. "Je ne suis pas du nombre de ceux qui regardent la République de Platon comme une chose idéale et purement imaginaire, et dont l'exécution serait impossible. Ma raison est que la République de Lycurge paraît d'une exécution tout aussi difficile que celle de Platon, et que, cependant, elle a été si bien exécutée qu'elle a duré autant qu'aucune république que l'on connaise, dans sa force et sa splendeur." This passage is identified as Pensée 1811 in the standard Bordeaux edition, which organizes Montesquieu's material thematically rather than chronologically. It actually appears in volume II of the manuscript, which places it between the years 1734 and

Written several years before David Hume would declare in his *Idea of a Perfect Commonwealth* that Plato's *politeia* was "plainly imaginary" and unattainable,[63] this is an observation of some significance. Indeed, Montesquieu goes even farther than Plato himself, who, we might recall, has Socrates admit at the end of *Republic* IX that his *politeia* can be found nowhere on earth, but is rather a pattern "laid up in heaven for him who wishes to contemplate it, and so beholding to constitute himself its citizen."[64] Montesquieu, however, takes Plato's work as a practical political handbook and regards it as very much in keeping with the mainstream of ancient Greek political life. In another section of the *Pensées*, he insists that "one must reflect upon the *Politics* of Aristotle and upon the two republics of Plato [i.e. the *Republic* and the *Laws*] if one wants to get a good idea of the laws and mores of the Greeks."[65] As the passage just quoted suggests, Montesquieu associated Plato's philosophy with the operational principles of an actual Greek republic, namely that of Sparta. In Book IV of *De l'esprit des lois*, Montesquieu praises the laws of Lycurgus, but exalts Plato's as their "correction."[66] Lycurgus' laws, we learn, aimed at making citizens "plus guerriers,"[67] while Plato's sought to transform them into "honnêtes gens." Montesquieu's regard for Plato as an authoritative political guide appears to be unequalled. Plato is everywhere in *De l'esprit des lois*, and his presence shapes the text extensively.[68]

1754 (volume I begins in 1720 and ends *c.* 1728, while volume III begins in 1754 and ends with Montesquieu's death). As the development of Montesquieu's thoughts over time is significant for this project, all items from the *Pensées* will be listed according to volume. All volume references are drawn from Montesquieu, *Œuvres complètes*, ed. Caillois.

[63] David Hume, "Idea of a Perfect Commonwealth" in *Utopias of the British Enlightenment*, ed. Gregory Claeys (Cambridge University Press, 1994), p. 58.

[64] Quotations from Plato in English are taken from *Plato: the Collected Dialogues, including the Letters*, ed. Edith Hamilton, Huntington Cairns, Bollingen Series 71 (Princeton University Press, 1989). Greek texts are taken from *Platonis opera*, ed. John Burnet, 5 vols., Oxford Classical Texts, 2nd edn. (Oxford: Clarendon Press, 1963). This reference is found in *Collected Dialogues*, p. 819 (Republic 592b). 'Ἀλλ', ἦν δ' ἐγώ, ἐν οὐρανῷ ἴσως παράδειγμα ἀνάκειται τῷ βουλομένῳ ὁρᾶν καὶ ὁρῶντι ἑαυτὸν κατοικίζειν."

[65] Montesquieu, *Œuvres*, p. 1007. "Il faut réfléchir sur *la Politique* d'Aristote et sur les deux Républiques de Platon, si l'on veut avoir une juste idée des lois et des mœurs des Grecs." This passage appears in volume II.

[66] Montesquieu, *The Spirit of the Laws* IV.6 (p. 36). See Plutarch, *Lycurgus* XXXI.

[67] Montesquieu, *Œuvres*, p. 1044.

[68] The most astute analysis of Montesquieu's Platonism undoubtedly remains that of Badreddine Kassem in *Décadence et absolutisme dans l'œuvre de Montesquieu* (Geneva: Librairie E. Droz, 1960), pp. 89–103. But even as Kassem notes that "c'est pour que les citoyens ne soient pas détournés, par la recherche des richesses, des devoirs que leur impose le patriotisme, qu'ils puissent concourir à qui rendra le plus de services au pays, que Montesquieu, exige, dans les la république, la médiocrité et l'égalité des fortunes" (p. 98), she neglects to connect this preoccupation to Plato or to trace Montesquieu's regulations to those recommended in the *Laws* (and coopted by the likes of More

But, as Montesquieu himself points out, Plato had written about "deux républiques," and when it comes to the problem of wealth and virtue, the *Republic* and the *Laws* agree in their diagnosis but prescribe very different treatments. In order to prevent wealth from undermining virtue as the criterion that determines the distribution of political power, the *Republic* institutes the complete abolition of private property among the guardians, a proposal enthusiastically taken up by another "législateur" whom Montesquieu associates with Plato in the quest for "honnêteté": Sir Thomas More.[69] Indeed, in Book xxix of *De l'esprit des lois*, when we learn that Thomas More "wanted to govern all states with the simplicity of a Greek city" – an objective which, as we have just seen, Montesquieu did not dismiss as "utopian" – the city we are surely meant to think of is Plato's *politeia*. In *Utopia* More follows the *Republic* in arguing that, once we admit private property, it is simply inevitable that the wealthy will appropriate public offices "which ought to go to the wise."[70] But, as his *porte-parole* Hythloday informs us, because all their property is held in common, the Utopians are able to favor the most excellent members of society – those who should rule by nature. Montesquieu is by no means unsympathetic to this approach. In Book iv he argues that those who wish to emulate the "extraordinary" institutions of the Greeks "will establish the community of goods of Plato's *Republic*" and "will proscribe silver, whose effect is to fatten the fortune of men beyond the limits nature has set for it, to teach men to preserve vainly what has been amassed vainly, to multiply desires infinitely and to supplement nature, which has given us very limited means to excite our passions and to corrupt one another."[71] Here we have the standard Platonic argument that wealth causes men to lose sight of their own nature, and should accordingly be abolished. But, as a general matter,

and Harrington). Most importantly, she misses the opportunity to connect these measures to a theory of justice – although, unlike many, she does stress Montesquieu's reliance on Platonic holism. David Lowenthal's "Montesquieu and the Classics" in *Ancients and Moderns*, ed. Joseph Cropsey (New York: Basic Books, 1964) also contains an insightful discussion of Montesquieu's Platonism, but he and I part company when he describes *De l'esprit des lois* as an ironic critique of the *Republic* (pp. 278–80). Thomas Pangle also seems to be sympathetic to this view. See Pangle, *Montesquieu's Philosophy*, p. 65.

[69] Montesquieu, *Œuvres*, p. 1044. This passage appears in volume ii.

[70] Thomas More, *Utopia*, ed. George M. Logan, Robert M. Adams, and Clarence H. Miller (Cambridge University Press, 1995), p. 103.

[71] *The Spirit of the Laws* iv.6 (p. 38). "Ceux qui voudront faire des institutions pareilles établiront la communauté de biens de la république de Platon . . . Ils proscriront l'argent, dont l'effet est de grossir la fortune des hommes au-delà des bornes que la nature y avait mises, d'apprendre à conserver inutilement ce qu'on avait amassé de même, de multiplier à l'infini les désirs, et de suppléer à la nature, qui nous avait donné des moyens très bornés d'irriter nos passions, et de nous corrompre les uns les autres."

Montesquieu places more stock in the solution advanced in Plato's *Laws* – and, not at all coincidentally, also in Harrington's *Oceana*.[72]

In the *Laws* private property is not abolished, but intricately regulated in such a way as to equalize holdings. Recall that Plato had advocated a city composed of 5,040 citizens, in which no one could possess more than four times the standard land allotment, and in which dowries were banned and inheritances sharply regulated. Montesquieu makes clear in Book VII that he takes the *Laws* as his model for dealing with questions of luxury, wealth, and inheritance. He records:

> in the republic of Plato [by which he means the *Laws*], it was possible to calculate luxury accurately. Four levels of census were established. The first was set at precisely the point where poverty ended; the second at double the first, the third triple, and the fourth quadruple. In the first census, luxury was equal to *zero*: it was equal to one in the second, to two in the third, to three in the fourth; and it followed arithmetic proportion accordingly.[73]

Montesquieu agrees with Plato's Athenian, and with Harrington, that the central problem for republics is luxury, the existence of disproportionate wealth. For him, the republican watchword is "frugality," a quality which must be established by laws.[74] "If wealth is equally divided in a state," he observes, "there will be no luxury," so the state should maintain an equal distribution of wealth by giving "each man only the physical necessities."[75]

---

[72] Landi makes this point nicely (Landi, *Montesquieu*, p. 44). Montesquieu does not have much to say about Harrington directly. He criticizes him once on the question of "political liberty" (i.e. the separation of powers), claiming that the Englishman sought liberty "only after misunderstanding it" (*The Spirit of the Laws*, p. 166), and praises him once as a thinker who "saw only the republic of England, while a crowd of writers found disorder wherever they did not see a crown" (p. 618). But, like Harrington, Montesquieu comes to base his republicanism explicitly on a rigid, meticulously developed agrarian law, and does so for precisely the same reasons. Giuseppe Cambiano deserves credit for being the only contemporary scholar even to allude to the Harringtonian influence on Montesquieu's agrarian proposals – although I disagree with his ultimate characterizations of both Harrington and Montesquieu. His statement that we find in Montesquieu's account of extreme equality "echi platonici ed aristotelici" which have been fused with the altogether different "temi del discorso di Harrington e della tradizione repubblicana inglese" calls attention to the fact that, throughout his essay, he neglects to see Harrington himself (and Montesquieu) in the context of what I have called the Greek tradition. See Giuseppe Cambiano, "Montesquieu e le antiche repubbliche greche" in *Rivista di Filosofia*, 65 (1974), esp. 114–20. Montesquieu owned a copy of the first edition of *Oceana* (Shackleton, "Montesquieu and Machiavelli," p. 126).

[73] *The Spirit of the Laws* VII.1 (p. 96). "Dans la république de Platon, le luxe aurait pu se calculer au juste. Il y avait quatre sortes de cens établis. Le premier était précisément le terme où finissait la pauvreté, le second était double, le troisième triple, le quatrième quadruple du premier. Dans le premier cens, le luxe était égal à zero; il était égal à un dans le second, à deux dans le troisième, à trois dans le quatrième; et il suivait ainsi la proportion arithmétique."

[74] Ibid. V.4 (p. 44).

[75] Ibid. VII.1 (p. 96). "Si, dans un Etat, les richesses sont également partagées, il n'y aura point de luxe . . . il faut que la loi ne donne à chacun que le nécessaire physique."

Accordingly, Montesquieu notes with approval that "some legislators of ancient times, like Lycurgus and Romulus, divided the lands equally."[76] But he insists that "if the legislator who makes such a division does not give laws to maintain it, his is only a transitory constitution; inequality will enter . . . and the republic will be lost."[77] His own solution should sound rather familiar:

One must, therefore, regulate to this end dowries, gifts, inheritance, testaments, in sum, all the kinds of contracts. For if it were permitted to give one's goods to whomever one wanted and as one wanted, each individual bequest would disturb the disposition of the fundamental laws . . . It suffices to establish a census that reduces differences or fixes them at a certain point; after which, it is the task of the particular laws to equalize inequalities, so to speak, by the burdens they impose on the rich and the relief they afford to the poor.[78]

Solon, who is praised for approving the cancellation of debts, is then criticized for allowing "one to leave one's goods to whomever one wanted by testament provided one had no children,"[79] while the Athenian law "that forbade one to have two inheritances" is praised for being consistent with "the equal divisions of lands and portions given to each citizen" in ancient times.[80] Even in "aristocratic republics" (republics in which sovereignty resides in only a part of the citizenry), where moderation, rather than virtue, is the motive principle, Montesquieu insists that "the laws should remove the right of primogeniture from the nobles so that fortunes are always restored to equality by the continual divisions of inheritances."[81] He also writes, in what is in effect a quotation of the Harringtonian position,

---

[76] Ibid. v.5 (p. 44). "Quelques législateurs anciens, comme Lycurge et Romulus, partagèrent également les terres." Montesquieu adds that land allotments should be small in addition to being equal; they should create self-sufficient yeoman farmers. Any excess will invite commerce, which (almost always) leads to luxury and decay. Ibid., p. 47.

[77] Ibid., p. 45. "Si lorsque le législateur fait un pareil partage, il ne donne pas des lois pour le maintenir, il ne fait qu'une constitution passagère; l'inégalité entrera . . . et la république sera perdue."

[78] Ibid. (I have replaced Cohler's "will" with "bequest" for the sake of clarity.) "Il faut donc que l'on règle, dans cet objet, les dots des femmes, les donations, les successions, les testaments; enfin, toutes les manières de contracter. Car, s'il était permis de donner son bien à qui on voudrait, chaque volonté particulière troublerait la disposition de la loi fondamentale."

[79] Ibid. "Solon, qui permittait à Athènes de laisser son bien à qui on voulait par testament, pourvu qu'on n'eût point d'enfants . . . "

[80] Ibid. "C'était une bonne loi, pour la démocratie, que celle qui défendait d'avoir deux hérédités. Elle prenait son origine du partage égal des terres et des portions donées à chaque citoyen."

[81] Ibid. v.8 (p. 54). "Les lois doivent ôter le droit d'aînesse entre les nobles; afin que, par le partage continuel des successions, les fortunes se remettent toujours dans l'égalité." These aristocratic republics have been a subject of some confusion. Carrithers is surely correct, however, when he states that Montesquieu's attitude toward these states was negative ("Democratic and Aristocratic Republics," p. 263), a claim born out by Montesquieu's insistence that aristocratic republics function better the more they resemble "democratic republics" (*The Spirit of the Laws*, p. 17).

that "laws dividing fields anew, demanded with such insistence in certain republics, were salutary by their nature. They are dangerous only as a sudden action."[82] Also like Harrington (whose agrarian law does not require the actual confiscation of property unless citizens acquire illicit levels of land after the institution of the law), Montesquieu retains a visceral distaste for violent, coercive action in the here-and-now. The source of his distaste is not surprising. In Book xxvi (although no longer discussing republics) he records that "Cicero held that the agrarian laws were deadly because the city was established only in order for each one to preserve his goods."[83] Accordingly, Montesquieu lays it down as a general principle that the "public good" should never be interpreted to authorize a capricious assault on the property of the rich. Even in the midst of this strongly Greek edifice, the Ciceronian theory of justice continues to haunt the President.

Yet Montesquieu, like Harrington, nonetheless places agrarian laws at the very center of the republican project. In the *Pensées* he begins one of his lengthy discussions by announcing "here are the laws that I believe are the most effective for causing a republic or colony to flourish" (*voici les lois que je croirais les plus propres à rendre une république ou une colonie florissante*).[84] What follows is nothing but a string of marriage and inheritance laws:

All goods should be equally distributed among the male children, save that the mother and father may bestow an extra portion of their holdings on the one of their male children they believe most worthy of it . . . In the distribution of the goods of an inheritance, one should not acknowledge any distinction of goods, movable and immovable, original goods, acquisitions and winnings, goods given as dowries, goods brought by a spouse over and above the dowry, noble or plebeian goods . . . Those who have no children should not be able to make wills: their goods should pass to the nearest relation, preferably male . . . Unmarried males should be unable to inherit or bequeath by will, if they are above twenty-five years of age . . . All places of honor should be marked in church and other places according to the number of children [one has] . . . Those who have seven children,

---

[82] *The Spirit of the Laws* VII.2 (p. 98). "Les lois du nouveau partage des champs, demandées avec tant d'instance dans quelques républiques, étaient salutaires par leur natures. Elles sont dangereuses que comme action subite."

[83] Ibid. XXVI.15 (p. 510). "Cicéron soutenait que les lois agraires étaient funestes, parce que la cité n'était établie que pour que chacun conservât ses biens."

[84] Montesquieu, *Œuvres*, p. 1051. This passage appears in volume 1, which, as noted earlier, places it in the early portion of Montesquieu's career (*c.* 1720–28). But, given how closely the reasoning behind it resembles his reasoning in *De l'esprit des lois*, I see no reason to discount it as "immature."

alive or killed in war, will be exempt from all assessments; those who have six will pay none except the tithe... [85]

All of these meticulous laws have one aim in common: to encourage the fragmentation of estates, and, as a result, the equalization of holdings. Parents must divide their estates among their children, and they are encouraged to have as many children as possible – and sharply stigmatized if they have few or no children. That these laws are submitted and singled out as "les plus propres" for republican government speaks volumes about how comprehensively Montesquieu internalized the tradition we have been following.

Montesquieu also agrees with his predecessors in the Greek tradition that republics alone are characterized by the rule of the best men, and that the introduction of excessive wealth and poverty topples this government of virtue. As he makes clear in Book v, when "frugality"[86] reigns in a republic and it is state policy that each citizen "should have the same happiness and the same advantages, each should taste the same pleasures and form the same expectations,"[87] all distinctions in the republic will derive from "the principle of equality, even when equality seems to be erased by successful services or superior talents"[88] – that is, men will only achieve disproportionate power if they are more virtuous, not more wealthy, than their fellow citizens. Otherwise, as Montesquieu puts it later, "the one who has silver is always the master of the one without."[89] And we should not be surprised that, in order to express the danger of applying this principle to government, the President turns to Plato: "Plato cannot endure such venality. 'It is,' he says, 'as if, on a ship, one made someone a pilot or a

---

[85] Ibid. "Tout les biens seront partagés également entre les enfants mâles, sans que les pères et mères puissent avantager que d'un tiers de leur bien celui de leurs enfants mâles qu'ils en croiront le plus digne... Dans le partage des biens d'une succession, on n'admettra aucune distinction de biens, meubles et immeubles, propres, acquêts et conquêtes, dotaux ou paraphernaux, nobles ou roturiers... Ceux qui n'auront point d'enfants ne pourront faire de testaments: leurs biens passeront aux plus proches, les mâles préférés... Mâles non mariés seront incapables de donner et de recevoir par testament, s'ils sont âgés de vingt-cinq ans. Gens non mariés succéderont pourtant à leurs père et mère comme les autres enfants; ne pourront posséder aucune charge de judicature, être temoins en matière civile. Toutes places d'honneur seront marquées dans les églises et autres lieux par rapport au nombre d'enfants... Ceux qui auront sept enfants vivants ou morts à la guerre seront exempts de toutes sortes de tributs; ceux qui en auront six n'en payeront que la moitié..."

[86] Pocock has a fine discussion of this term's entrée into political discourse. See Pocock, *The Machiavellian Moment: Florentine Political Thought and the Atlantic Republican Tradition* (Princeton University Press, 1975), pp. 445–46.

[87] *The Spirit of the Laws* v.3 (p. 43). "Chacun devant y avoir le même bonheur et les mêmes avantages, y doit goûter les mêmes plaisirs, et former les mêmes espérances."

[88] Ibid. "Ainsi les distinctions y naissent du principe de l'égalité, lors même qu'elle paraît ôtée par des services heureux, ou par des talents supérieurs."

[89] Ibid. XIII.19 (p. 226). "celui qui a l'argent est toujours le maître de l'autre."

sailor for his silver. Is it possible that the rule is good only for guiding a republic, and bad in all other life employments?'"⁹⁰ In frugal republics (and only there) "magistracies are testimonies to virtue."⁹¹ But when republics become corrupt, the spirit of "extreme equality" is embraced, and "each one wants to be the equal of those chosen to command."⁹² The natural order is then utterly subverted:

> Then there can no longer be virtue in the republic. The people want to perform the magistrates' functions; therefore, the magistrates are no longer respected. The senate's deliberations no longer carry weight; therefore, there is no longer consideration for senators or, consequently, for elders. And if there is no respect for elders, neither will there be any for fathers; husbands no longer merit deference nor masters submission. Everyone will come to love this license . . . There will no longer be mores or love of order, and finally, there will no longer be virtue.⁹³

Montesquieu's republics were, indeed, as Greek as they come.⁹⁴

III

Montesquieu's *De l'esprit des lois*, more than any other text, provided the ideological structure for eighteenth-century French republicanism.⁹⁵ As a result, the basic Hellenism of that tradition should serve as a continuing reminder of Montesquieu's own Greek scale of values. Consider, for example,

---

⁹⁰ Ibid. v.19 (p. 70). "Platon ne peut souffrir cette vénalité. 'C'est, dit-il, comme si, dans un navire, on faisait quelqu'un pilote ou matelot pour son argent. Serait-il possible que la règle fût mauvaise dans quelque autre emploi que ce fût de la vie, et bonne seulement pour conduire une république?'"

⁹¹ Ibid., p. 68. "Dans le premier [le gouvernement républicain] les magistratures sont des témoignages de vertu."

⁹² Ibid. vIII.2 (p. 112). "chacun veut être égal à ceux qu'il choisit pour lui commander."

⁹³ Ibid. "Il ne peut plus y avoir de vertu dans la république. Le peuple veut faire les fonctions des magistrats: on ne les respecte donc plus. Les délibérations du sénat n'ont plus de poids: on n'a donc plus d'égard pour les sénateurs, et par conséquent pour les vieillards. Que si l'on n'a pas du respect pour les vieillards, on n'en aura pas non plus pour les pères: les maris ne méritent pas plus de déférence, ni les matres plus de soumission. Tout le monde parviendra à aimer ce libertinage . . . Il n'y aura plus de mœurs, plus de l'amour de l'ordre, enfin plus de vertu." Note that Montesquieu considered slavery "unnatural" in a moral sense, and also mechanically unnatural for republics, since slavery introduces luxury (xv.1).

⁹⁴ This is by no means to suggest, however, that Montesquieu's relationship to the Greek tradition was wholly uncritical. For one thing, he expressed no affection for the contemplative life, and insisted that republics must force their citizens to accept public offices (*The Spirit of the Laws*, p. 68). However, even here, his emphasis (like Bolingbroke's) is on the fact that, in republics, "magistracies are testimonies to virtue," and not on a claim about liberty. He also leaves room at the civic table for glory, although defined in an extremely idiosyncratic manner. On the whole, however, his republics do indeed seem to derive their form from the Greek tradition that I have analyzed.

⁹⁵ It also ensured that late eighteenth-century French histories of Rome would retain their decidedly Whig character. See, for example, Louis de Beaufort, *La Republique romaine, ou Plan général de l'ancien gouvernement de Rome* (Paris, 1766).

the republican writings of his younger contemporary, Gabriel Bonnot de Mably.[96] Mably began his scholarly life as a committed monarchist, and his first work, the *Parallèle des Romains et des François, par rapport au gouvernement* (1740), celebrates this commitment. Later in the decade, however, he found himself persuaded of the merits of republican government, and dedicated his remaining years to defending a popular regime. In 1819 Benjamin Constant classed Mably as a chief exponent of "la liberté des anciens" as against that of the "modernes," which accounts for Mably's continued attractiveness to contemporary scholars.[97] For present purposes, however, the essential fact about Mably is the explicitly Greek character of his republican theory. Indeed, it is not insignificant that he unveiled his republican program in 1749 (one year after the publication of *De l'esprit des lois*) with his *Observations sur les Grecs*, later republished under the title *Observations sur l'histoire de la Grèce* (1764). The hero of his story – and the hero of his entire political theory – is the Spartan legislator Lycurgus. After instituting a mixed constitution for Sparta which secured a dynamic balance of monarchy, aristocracy, and democracy, Lycurgus realized that he still had work to do:

What would have been, in effect, the benefit of the order he had established in order to render the laws the only powers and the only sovereigns, if riches and luxury, always linked together, and always followed by depravity of mores, inequality among citizens, and, as a result, tyranny and servitude, had again taught the Spartans to disdain or elude their new laws? The people, enfeebled by misery, would have soon been incapable of conserving its dignity; it would have sold its

---

[96] For a recent study of Mably's life and thought, see Johnson Kent Wright, *A Classical Republican in Eighteenth-Century France: the Political Thought of Mably* (Stanford University Press, 1997). Wright's analysis is nuanced and learned, but his acceptance of Pocock's account of "classical republicanism" causes him to discount the possibility that some of the idiosyncrasies he notices in Mably might be attributable to different republican principles. He notices, for example, that Mably's "laconomania" leads him into open rebellion against the neo-Roman Machiavelli, but fails to attribute this fissure to Mably's embrace of a fundamentally different political theory (Wright's reflections on Mably's "laconomania" are clearly indebted to Elizabeth Rawson, *The Spartan Tradition in European Thought* [Oxford: Clarendon Press, 1991], esp. pp. 245–51). Likewise, Wright notices that Mably's view of property puts him at odds with Locke and Cicero, but does not connect this fact to his equally trenchant observation that eighteenth-century French republicanism was characterized by a "shift of attention from Roman models to the more 'primitive' Greek city-states" (*A Classical Republican*, p. 208). See also Keith Michael Baker, *Inventing the French Revolution: Essays on French Political Culture in the Eighteenth Century* (Cambridge University Press, 1990), chap. 4; Heuss, *Barthold Georg Niebuhrs wissenschaftliche Anfänge*, pp. 301–8; R. B. Rose, "The 'Red Scare' of the 1790s: the French Revolution and the 'Agrarian Law'" in *Past and Present* 103 (1984), esp. 117–18; and Jennifer Tolbert Roberts, *Athens on Trial: the Antidemocratic Tradition in Western Thought* (Princeton University Press, 1994), pp. 162–66.

[97] Benjamin Consant, "De la liberté des anciens comparée à celle des modernes" in *De la liberté chez les modernes: écrits politiques*, ed. Marcel Gauchet (Paris: Librairie Générale Française, 1980), pp. 493–515.

votes, its rights, and its liberty to the highest bidder. The senate, whose seats were only intended to honor the most virtuous men, would not have been open except to the richest.[98]

As we would expect from a theorist in the Greek tradition, Mably emphasizes the effects of wealth on rulership (and, thus, justice): disproportionate wealth corrupts and gives political power to the rich, rather than the virtuous. In order to prevent this state of affairs from developing amongst his citizens, Lycurgus "established a perfect equality in their fortunes."[99] Indeed, "he did not stop at instituting a new distribution of lands. Since nature certainly did not give all the Spartans the same passions, or the same industriousness in cultivating their inheritances, he [Lycurgus] feared that avarice would soon accumulate possessions."[100] Accordingly, "so that Sparta would not enjoy a merely temporary reform, he descended, so to speak, right down to the bottom of the heart of his citizens, and extinguished the germ of the love of riches."[101] He "forbade the use of gold and silver," and it came to pass that "riches, having become useless, seemed contemptible, and Sparta became a fortress inaccessible to corruption."[102]

Just as More had dismissed laws decreeing that "no one should own more than a certain amount of land or receive more than a certain income" as the equivalents of "poultices continually applied to sick bodies that are past cure,"[103] Mably attributes to Lycurgus an understanding that only the outright elimination of gold and luxury could bring health to his state. Nonetheless, he never doubts for a moment the significance of the Spartan agrarian laws. He takes his account of Sparta's descent into corruption from

---

[98] Gabriel Bonnot de Mably, *Collection complète des œuvres*, vol. IV (Paris, 1794), p. 20. "Quel eût été en effet le fruit de l'ordre qu'il avoit établi pour rendre les lois seules puissantes et seules souveraines, si les richesses et le luxe, toujours liés ensemble, et toujours suivis de la dépravation des mœurs, de l'inégalité des citoyens, et par conséquent de la tyrannie et de la servitude, eussent encore appris aux Spartiates à mépriser ou à éluder leurs nouvelles lois? Le peuple, avili par la misère, auroit bientôt été incapable de conserver sa dignité; il eût vendu ses suffrages, ses droits et sa liberté au plus offrant. Le sénat, dont les places n'etoient destinées qu'à honorer les hommes les plus vertueux, n'auroit été ouvert qu'aux plus riches."

[99] Ibid., p. 22. "établit une parfaite égalité dans leur fortune."

[100] Ibid. "Il ne se borna point à faire un nouveau partage des terres. La nature ne donnant pas sans doutes à tous les Lacédémoniens les mêmes passions, ni la même industrie à faire valoir leur héritage, il [Lycurgus] craignit que l'avarice n'accumulât bientôt les possessions."

[101] Ibid. "Pour que Sparte ne jouît pas d'une réforme passagère, il descendit, pour ainsi dire, jusque dans le fond du cœur des citoyens, et y étouffa le germe de l'amour des richesses."

[102] Ibid. "proscrivit l'usage de l'or et de l'argent les richesses devenues inutiles parurent méprisables . . . et Sparte devint une forteresse inaccessible à la corruption."

[103] More, *Utopia*, p. 103.

the same passage of Plutarch's *Agis* that Harrington and his followers had appropriated so enthusiastically:

The Spartans, again defeated by the Thebans at Mantinea, fell into the most shameful degradation, from the time that the ephor Epitadeus, giving free rein to avarice, had proposed a law according to which he was permitted to sell his possessions, and to dispose of them by will. The desire for riches invaded all of Laconia, and the citizens without patrimony begged their favor in a servile manner, or stirred up seditions to recover the goods they had lost. The hands of the Spartans, which Lycurgus had intended only for the sword, the lance, and the shield, were dishonored amongst the instruments of the arts which luxury introduced into Laconia unawares.[104]

The repeal of Lycurgus' ban on the sale of property and on the making of wills resulted in the rise of disproportionate wealth and poverty, and doomed the Spartan commonwealth.

Later in his career, Mably would expand on this analysis and offer a systematic summary of his Greek political theory in *Des droits et des devoirs du citoyen* (1758). The author's interlocutor – initially named "Harrington" when Mably circulated the text in manuscript form[105] – joins Montesquieu and the rationalists in rejecting legal positivism, insisting that "the idea of good and evil necessarily preceded the establishment of society," and that political life ought to be based upon "those luminous, fixed, and immutable principles that nature has given us in order to seek out and secure our own happiness."[106] More specifically, "the laws and the whole machinery of political government were only devised to come to the aid of our reason, almost always powerless against our passions."[107] Earlier, in his *Entretiens de Phocion, sur le rapport de la morale avec la politique* (1763), he made

---

[104] Mably, *Œuvres*, vol. IV, p. 123. "Les Lacédémoniens, encore défaits à Mantinée par les Thébains, tombèrent dans l'avilissement le plus honteux, dès que l'éphore Epitadeus, ouvrant une libre carrière à l'avarice, eût porté une loi par laquelle il étoit permis de vendre ses possessions, et d'en disposer par testament. L'avidité des riches envahit toute la Laconie, et les citoyens sans patrimoine mendièrent servilement leur faveur, ou excitèrent des séditions pour recouvrer les biens qu'ils avoient perdus. Les mains des Spartiates que Lycurge avoit destinées à ne manier que l'épée, la lance et le bouclier, se deshonorèrent parmi les instruments des arts que le luxe introduisit dans la Laconie étonnée."

[105] See Michael Sonenscher, "Republicanism, State Finances and the Emergence of Commerical Society in Eighteenth-Century France – or from Royal to Ancient Republicanism and Back" in *Republicanism: a Shared European Heritage*, vol. II, ed. Quentin Skinner and Martin van Gelderen (Cambridge University Press, 2002), p. 278.

[106] Mably, *Œuvres*, vol. XI, p. 270. "l'idée du bien et du mal a nécessairement précédé l'établissement de la société." The second passage is quoted using Wright's translation (see Wright, *A Classical Republican*, p. 83).

[107] Mably, *Œuvres*, vol. XI, p. 271. "les lois et toute la machine du gouvernement politique n'ont été imaginées que pour venir au secours de notre raison, presque toujours impuissante contre nos passions."

clear that, in instituting the laws of Sparta, Lycurgus had consulted this transcendent blueprint:

Instead of consulting [his people's] prejudices, Lycurgus only consulted their nature. He descended into the tortuous depths of the human heart, and penetrated the secrets of Providence. His laws, made to repress our passions, only tended to develop and affirm the same laws which the Author of nature prescribed for us through the agency of the rational faculty he endowed us with, and which is the supreme and only infallible magistrate for men.[108]

The Lycurgan system was in conformity with reason, which is natural and just.[109] But, looking around him at the state of his own government, Mably (like Montesquieu) despairs: "How the baseness of our mores has degraded our souls and our laws! The virtue which Solon desired in Athens would be regarded today as the crime of a rabble-rouser."[110] The way out of this morass of corruption, Mably insists, is to institute republican government: "the republican citizen, so proud in his bearing for wanting to obey only the laws, naturally has a soul that is upright, just, elevated, and courageous."[111] Republics, animated by "l'amour de la liberté," make their citizens just and reasonable.

But Mably argues passionately that republics cannot produce virtuous citizens where there are extremes of wealth and poverty; indeed, his ideal is the abolition of private property.[112] He asks, "what is the principle source of all the evils which afflict humanity? The private ownership of goods":[113]

We who see the infinite evils which arise from this fatal Pandora's Box, if the least ray of hope struck our reason, should we not aspire to that happy community of

---

[108] Ibid., vol. x, p. 47. "Au lieu de consulter leurs préjugés, il [Lycurgus] ne consulte que la nature. Il descendit dans les profondeurs tortueuses du cœur humain, et pénétra les secrets de la Providence. Ses lois, faites pour réprimer nos passions, ne tendirent qu'à développer et affermir les lois mêmes que l'Auteur de la nature nous prescrit par le ministère de la raison dont il nous a doués, et qui est le magistrat suprême et seul infaillible des hommes."

[109] Wright makes this point very forcefully (Wright, *A Classical Republican*, pp. 83–84).

[110] Mably, *Œuvres*, vol. xi, p. 351. "Que la bassesse de nos mœurs a avili nos âmes et nos lois! La vertu que Solon désiroit dans Athènes seroit regardée aujourd'hui comme le crime d'un séditieux."

[111] Ibid., p. 372. "Un républicain assez fier de sa dignité pour ne vouloir obéir qu'aux lois, a naturellement l'âme droite, juste, élevée et courageuse."

[112] There is not space here for a full account of Mably's advocacy of a "communauté des biens." He discusses the issue at length in *De l'étude de l'histoire*, *De la législation*, and *Doutes proposées aux philosophes économistes*. See also the informative discussion in Wright, *A Classical Republican*, pp. 95–109.

[113] Mably, *Œuvres*, vol. xi, p. 379. "quelle est la principale source de tous les malheurs qui affligent l'humanité? C'est la propriété des biens . . . Nous qui voyons les maux infinis qui sont sortis de cette boîte funeste de Pandore, si le moindre rayon d'espérance frappoit notre raison, ne devrions-nous pas aspirer à cette heureuse communauté de biens, tant louée, tant regrettée par les poètes, que Lycurge avoit établie à Lacédémone, que Platon vouloit faire revivre dans sa république, et qui, grâce à la dépravation des mœurs, ne peut plus être qu'une chimère dans le monde?"

goods, so praised, so mourned by the poets, which Lycurgus established in Sparta, which Plato wanted to revive in his republic, and which, thanks to the depravity in manners, cannot be anything but a chimera in the world?

Once again, Mably insists that "with whatever equality one distributes the goods of a republic in the beginning, be sure . . . that the equality will not prevail amongst the citizens in the third generation."[114] Imagine, he explains, that one person has only one son whom he has reared to be virtuous and industrious, while another, less virtuous person has three or four sons, all of them slaves of vice. The first person's estate will grow and be passed on intact, while the second's will be diminished and divided three or four ways. Inequality then arises, and "it is not possible that the rich, once they are esteemed and looked up to for their fortunes, will not band together and claim to form an order separate from the multitude. With the best faith in the world, they will believe that they merit the place which is due only to virtue and talents."[115] Mably amplifies this concern in the *Entretiens*, where Phocion observes of the Athenians that "hardly had we begun to esteem voluptuousness, elegance, and riches, and to respect great fortunes, when we were punished, in seeing charms, pomp, luxury and riches take the place of talents, and become themselves titles for being elevated to the magistracy."[116] Wealth replaces virtue as the criterion which determines the distribution of political power, and the state is rendered unjust. In case the Greek character of this argument is not sufficiently clear, Mably includes a footnote explaining that "Plato admirably describes, in Book VIII of his Republic, the progress, and if I may speak this way, the generation of vices in a city which possesses superfluous riches."[117] Once this corruption has infiltrated the city, Mably continues, "do not even hope that the public good will be the first interest of the citizen: his property and the distinctions which his pride acquires for him are for him goods more precious than the fatherland."[118]

---

[114] Ibid., p. 380. "avec quelque égalité qu'on partage d'abord les biens d'une république, soyez sûr . . . que l'égalité ne régnera plus entre les citoyens à la troisième génération."

[115] Ibid. "Il n'est pas possible que les riches, dès qu'ils seront estimés et considérés par leur fortune, ne se liguent et ne prétendent former un ordre séparé de la multitude. De la meilleure foi du monde, ils croiront mériter la place qui n'est due qu'à la vertu et aux talens."

[116] Ibid., vol. x, p. 71. "à peine, en un mot, avons-nous estimé la volupté, l'élégance, les richesses, et respecté les grandes fortunes, que nous en avons été punis, en voyant les grâces, le faste, le luxe et les richesses tenir lieu de talens, et devenir autant de titres pour s'élever aux magistratures."

[117] Ibid., note. "Platon peint admirablement dans sa *république*, livre 8, les progrès, et si je puis parler ainsi, la génération des vices dans une ville qui possède des richesses superflues."

[118] Ibid. "n'espérez plus que le bien public soit le premier intérêt du citoyen: sa propriété et les distinctions que son orgueil s'est acquises, sont pour lui des biens plus précieux que la patrie."

Mably is led by these convictions about the intrinsic dangers of property to carry out the same thought experiment as Plato and More, his two great predecessors. Indeed, later, in his *De la manière d'écrire l'histoire* (1783), Mably would have Théodon, his interlocutor, respond in shock and disbelief to the suggestion that "it was important to study seriously the follies of Plato, of Thomas More, and of however many other dreamers who only talk about a kind of politics which has possibly never been known to exist."[119] But Mably answers that "I do not only insist that the historian should know about those things you call reveries; I condemn him to meditating on them thoroughly so that they seem to him to be so many incontestable truths."[120] In his treatise on rights and duties, however, he himself becomes the *rêveur*:

> Never do I read of some deserted island where the sky is serene and the waters are healthy without being seized by the desire of going there to establish a republic, where all are equal, all rich, all poor, all free, all brothers, and our first law would be not to possess anything individually. We would carry the fruits of our labors to public stores; there it would be the treasure and patrimony of every citizen. Every year the fathers of each family would elect those in charge of distributing necessary things for the needs of each individual, assigning him the work task which the community has ordained for him, and maintaining good mores in the state.[121]

Whereas property invariably creates a situation in which "little by little virtues and talents lose as much of their reputation as riches acquire" and men "persuade themselves that riches can take the place of merit, and from then on they [the riches] begin to give a certain reputation to their possessors,"[122] in Mably's utopia, as in More's, "virtuti pretium sit" – virtue has its just recognition. "The most intelligent men" are at long last able to play their rightful role in society, namely "to make up for the incapacity of others, and to guide them just as a father directs and guides his child,

---

[119] Ibid., vol. XII, p. 380. "il faudra s'occuper sérieusement des folies de Platon, de Thomas Morus, et de je ne sais combien d'autres rêveurs qui ne parlent que d'une politique qui n'a peut-être jamais été connue."

[120] Ibid. "Je n'exige pas seulement que l'historien connoisse ce que vous appellez des rêveries; je le condamne à les mediter assez pour qu'elles lui paroissent autant de vérités incontestables."

[121] Ibid., vol. XI, p. 283. "Jamais je ne lis de quelque île déserte dont le ciel est serein et les eaux salubres, qu'il me prenne envie d'y aller établir une république, où tous égaux, tous riches, tous pauvres, tous libres, tous frères, notre première loi seroit de ne rien posséder en propre. Nous porterions dans les magasins publics les fruits de nos travaux; ce seroit-là le trésor de l'état et le patrimoine de chaque citoyen. Tous les ans les pères de famille éliroient des économes chargés de distribuer les choses nécessaires au besoin de chaque particulier, de lui assigner la tâche de travail qu'en exigeroit la communauté, et d'entretenir les bonnes mœurs dans l'etat."

[122] Ibid., vol. X, p. 76. "peu à peu les vertus et les talens perdirent autant de leur crédit que les richesses en acquirent . . . se persuadèrent que les richesses pourroient tenir lieu de mérite, et dès-lors elles commencèrent à donner quelque considération à leurs possesseurs."

when the child's reason is not yet developed."[123] "Contempt for riches," he explains, "is always accompanied by the love of order and justice."[124]

Mably's republics, thus, bear a striking resemblance to those of Montesquieu, though their contours are more obvious for not being couched in the detached, descriptive tone of *De l'esprit des lois*. Mably's republics, like Montesquieu's, require *vertu politique* and its moral offspring in order to survive, and both theorists insist that virtue and justice cannot be engendered or preserved without the equality of fortunes or the outright abolition of private property. They agree that political virtue – a reverence for the organic whole – leads citizens to embrace the rule of reason in the persons of the most excellent men (which is justice). This just balance of elements, in turn, gives rise to the individual moral virtues and, through them, the happiness of the commonwealth.

But, in addition to Mably, Constant also listed a second eighteenth-century political theorist among the advocates of the "liberté des anciens": Jean-Jacques Rousseau. Accordingly, I ought to say a word about where the author of the second *Discours* and *Du Contrat social* fits into this story. There are, to begin with, plausible reasons for thinking that Rousseau does not fit in at all. If we take the substance of the Greek case to rest upon the notion that men achieve their greatest happiness and fulfillment when they are part of a rationally ordered state in which the best men rule, then Rousseau must at first glance seem difficult to assimilate to this mold. Certainly, the Rousseau of the *Discours sur l'inégalité* (1755) paints a very different picture. He invites us to imagine that men enjoy their greatest felicity, freedom, and innocence in the state of nature, isolated and alone, free from the grip of *amour propre*, and susceptible to the benign force of disinterested pity. Man in his original state is "good," not in the sense of "virtuous" or "just" (categories of thought which would not yet exist), but in the sense that his natural sentiment of pity draws him to aid others when doing so will not adversely affect his own condition. Moreover, because he is self-sufficient and free from vainglory, such disinterested assistance will rarely compromise him.[125]

The path toward civil society, on the other hand, is one of degradation and corruption. The progress of "enlightenment" produces enormous

---

[123] Ibid., p. 374. "Les hommes les plus intelligents . . . suppléer à l'incapacité des autres, et les conduire, de même qu'un père dirige et conduit son enfant dont la raison n'est pas encore developpée."

[124] Ibid., p. 111. "Le mépris des richesses est toujours accompagné de l'amour de l'ordre et de la justice."

[125] Jean-Jacques Rousseau, *Discours sur l'origine et les fondemens de l'inégalité parmi les hommes* in *Œuvres complètes de Jean-Jacques Rousseau*, ed. Bernard Gagnebin and Marcel Raymond, vol. III (Paris: Gallimard, 1964).

"moral" inequalities out of relatively modest "physical" inequalities, establishing extreme wealth and poverty, servitude and rulership, and the rise of *amour propre* (the powerful tendency, both destructive and constructive, to measure ourselves against our fellows). The formation of the state appears as a ruse conceived by the rich to legitimize their usurpations as "private property." Within the state, to be sure, man first learns virtue, justice, and enlightened reason, but the reader is left with the distinct impression that he is not better off. After concluding this account of the rise of the state, Rousseau summarizes:

> Such was, or might have been, the origin of Society and of Laws, which gave the weak new fetters and the rich new forces, irreversibly destroyed natural freedom, forever fixed the Law of property and inequality, transformed a skillful usurpation into an irrevocable right, and for the profit of a few ambitious men henceforth subjugated the whole of Mankind to labor, servitude and misery.[126]

In a fragment on the state of nature, written during the same period as the second *Discours*, Rousseau is even more emphatic. "All the noble words of society," he writes, "justice, laws, mutual defense, assistance to the weak, philosophy, and the progress of reason, are only lures . . . the pure state of nature is the one of all the others where men would be the least wicked, the happiest, and the most numerous on earth."[127]

This view of the state would indeed have the effect of distancing Rousseau quite considerably from the Greek tradition, but, as is well known, he soon modifies and tempers it. Even in the "political fragments" of the 1750s, Rousseau announces that, however attractive the state of nature may be, man can only realize his true self in the civil state: "It is only by becoming sociable that he becomes a moral being, a reasonable animal, the king of

---

[126] English text is taken from Rousseau, *The* Discourses *and other early political writings*, ed. and trans. Victor Gourevitch (Cambridge University Press, 1997), p. 173. "Telle fut, ou dut être l'origine de la Societé et des Loix, qui donnérent de nouvelles entraves au foible et de nouvelles forces aux riche, détruisirent sans retour la liberté naturelle, fixérent pour jamais la Loi de la propriété et de l'inégalité, d'une adroite usurpation firent un droit irrévocable, et pour le profit de quelques ambitieux assujétirent désormais tout le Genre-humain au travail, à la servitude et à la misère" (*Œuvres*, vol. III, p. 178).

[127] Rousseau, *Fragments politiques* in *Œuvres Complètes de Jean-Jacques Rousseau*, ed. Bernard Gagnebin and Marcel Raymond, vol. III (Paris: Gallimard, 1964). "tous ces grands mots de société, de justice, de lois, de défense mutuelle, d'assistance des faibles, de philosophie et de progrès de la raison, ne sont que leures inventés . . . le pur état de nature est celui de tous où les hommes seroient le moins méchants, le plus heureux, et en plus grand nombre sur la terre" (p. 475). English text is taken from *The Collected Writings of Rousseau*, ed. Roger D. Masters and Christopher Kelly, trans. Judith R. Bush, Roger D. Masters and Christopher Kelly, vol. IV (Hanover, NH, and London: University Press of New England, 1994).

the other animals, and the image of God on earth."[128] Rousseau elaborates on this view in a classic passage from Book 1, chapter eight of the *Contrat social* (1762):

This passage from the state of nature to the civil state produces a remarkable change in man, by substituting justice for instinct in his behavior and giving his actions the morality they previously lacked. Only then, when the voice of duty replaces physical impulse and right replaces appetite, does man, who until that time only considered himself, find himself forced to act upon other principles and to consult his reason before heeding his inclinations. Although in the state he deprives himself of several advantages given him by nature, he gains such great ones, his faculties are exercised and developed, his ideas broadened, his feelings ennobled, his whole soul elevated to such a point that if the abuses of this new condition did not often degrade him beneath the condition he left, he ought ceaselessly to bless the happy moment that tore him away from it forever, and changed him from a stupid, limited animal into an intelligent being and a man.[129]

The state of nature is certainly to be preferred to the degraded, corrupt condition of many states and regimes, but the rationally ordered state would allow man a fulfillment even surpassing the one he achieved in his isolated innocence.

Thus, Rousseau eventually embraces a vision of the state which allows for real dialogue with Montesquieu and Mably. But even here, an absolutely sweeping departure presents itself. Rousseau agrees with the theorists we have been following in locating man's most complete realization of his own nature in the rationally ordered state; he does not, however, follow the Greek tradition in locating the basic rationality of the state in the rule of the best men. For Rousseau, the governing reason of the state is to be found rather in the *volonté générale*, the collective judgment of the people as Sovereign. As described in the *Contrat social* and in the *Discours*

---

[128] *Collected Writings*, p. 19. "En un mot, ce n'est qu'en devenant sociable qu'il devient un être moral, un animal raisonnable, le roi des autres animaux, et l'image de Dieu sur la terre" (*Œuvres*, vol. III, p. 477).

[129] English text from *the Contrat social* is taken from *Collected Writings* (ed. Masters et al.), vol. IV. "Ce passage de l'état de nature à l'état civil produit dans l'homme un changement très rémarquable, en substituant dans sa conduite la justice à l'instinct, et donnant à ses actions la moralité qui leur manquoit auparavant. C'est alors seulement que la voix du devoir succédant à l'impulsion physique et le droit à l'appetit, l'homme, qui jusques là n'avoit regardé que lui-même, se voit forcé d'agir sur d'autres principes, et de consulter sa raison avant d'écouter ses penchans. Quoiqu'il se prive dans cet état de plusieurs avantages qu'il tient de la nature, il en regagne de si grands, ses facultés s'exercent et se développent, ses idées s'étendent, ses sentiments s'ennoblissent, son âme toute entiere s'éleve à tel point, que si les abus de cette nouvelle condition ne le dégradoient souvent au dessous de celle dont il est sorti, il devroit bénir sans cesse l'instant heureux qui l'en arracha pour jamais, et qui, d'un animal stupide et borné, fit un être intelligent et un homme" (*Œuvres*, vol. III, p. 364).

sur l'économie politique (1755), this *volonté générale* is emphatically not the sum of the *volontés particulières*, the individual opinions of all the citizens. It is rather an occult, abstracted expression of the common good – an idealized projection of what each citizen's "higher self" would choose when untethered from his private desires. To be sure, as Rousseau puts it in the *Contrat social,* while "the general will is always right and always tends toward the public utility," it is not the case that "the people's deliberations have the same rectitude."[130] Indeed, "one always wants what is good for oneself, but one does not always see it. The people is never corrupted, but it is often deceived, and only then does it appear to want what is bad."[131]

In unmistakably Platonic terms, Rousseau insists that the *volonté générale* represents what the people would choose if not "deceived"; when they choose something wicked, it is never an intentional act. The *volonté générale* is not what the aggregated citizens actually want; it is what they should want. It is, therefore, reason itself insofar as it identifies the common good, an almost mystical guide which is accessible when particularity and private passions have not yet overwhelmed the individual citizen. Accordingly, in the *Economie politique,* Rousseau seeks the union of the general and particular wills, and states unambiguously that "virtue is nothing but this conformity of the particular will to the general one."[132] Virtue is, indeed, a gift of the social condition. Only when we have the opportunity to make the general will our own can we learn what virtue is. Moreover, the *volonté générale,* "which always tends toward the conservation and the well-being of the whole and of every part, and which is the source of the laws," is also "the measure of just and unjust."[133] Rousseau goes so far as to suggest that "the most general will is also always the most just, and that the voice of the people is in effect the voice of God."[134]

We are left, then, with a view which, like its Greek antecedents, stresses the reconstitutive potential of the state. Only within the rationally ordered

[130] *Collected Writings,* vol. IV, p. 147. "Il s'ensuit de ce qui procède que la volonté générale est toujours droite et tend toujours à l'utilité publique: mais il ne s'ensuit pas que les déliberations du peuple aient toujours la même rectitude" (*Œuvres,* vol. III, p. 371).

[131] *Collected Writings,* vol. IV, p. 147. "On veut toujours son bien, mais on ne le voit pas toujours: Jamais on ne corrompt le peuple, mais souvent on le trompe, et c'est allors seulement qu'il paroit vouloir ce qui est mal." My translation of "tromper" as "to deceive," rather than "to fool," departs from the printed translation.

[132] "la vertu n'est que cette conformité de la volonté particulière à la générale" (*Œuvres,* vol. III, p. 252). English translations from this text are my own.

[133] "cette volonté générale, qui tend toûjours à la conservation et au bien-être du tout et de chacque partie, et qui est la source des lois, est pour tous les membres de l'état par rapport à eux et à lui, la regle de juste et injuste" (*Œuvres,* vol. III, p. 245).

[134] "la volonté la plus générale est aussi toûjours la plus juste, et que la voix du peuple est en effet la voix de Dieu" (ibid., p. 246).

state can men learn virtue and live according to justice. The catch is that, in the Rousseauian state, the people as an idealized whole are the locus of rationality – not a small number of wise and virtuous men. This is not to say that Rousseau does not leave room in his theory for a more conventional attachment to the "natural aristocracy." Even in the second *Discours*, he insists that merit "confers a Natural Ascendancy"[135] whose legitimacy is contrasted to the unnatural ascendancy of wealth and power.[136] Indeed, he ends the *Discours* with the observation that nothing could be more contrary to natural right than "for an imbecile to lead a wise man,"[137] and observes in his *Preface to "Narcissus"* that "in a well-constituted State" one gains precedence only "for being the best."[138]

Rousseau's most extensive discussion of this theme, however, appears in Book III of the *Contrat social*, where he turns to consider the various advantages and disadvantages of different governments. First considering democracy, Rousseau follows Montesquieu's lead in identifying its range of important (and rare) prerequisites:

First, a very small State where the people is easily assembled and where each citizen can easily know all the others. Second, great simplicity of morals, which prevents a multitude of business and knotty discussions. Next, a great equality of ranks and of fortunes, without which equality of rights and authority could not subsist for long. Finally, little or no luxury, because either luxury is the result of wealth, or it makes wealth necessary. It corrupts both rich and poor, the one by possessing, the other by coveting. It sells out the fatherland to indolence and vanity; it deprives the State of all its Citizens by enslaving some of them to others and all of them to opinion.[139]

Even without these moral and logistical problems, however, pure democracies, on Rousseau's account, have never existed. It is, he writes, "contrary to

---

[135] *Discourses* (ed. Gourevitch), p. 181. "mérite . . . qui donne un Ascendant Naturel" (*Œuvres*, vol. III, p. 245).

[136] *Œuvres*, vol. III, p. 188.

[137] *Discourses*, p. 188. "qu'un imbécille conduise un homme sage" (*Œuvres*, vol. III, p. 194).

[138] Compare with *Projet de constitution pour la Corse*, p. 910. "L'état ne doit accorder des distinctions qu'au mérite, aux vertus, aux services rendus à la patrie . . ." See also *Projet*, p. 939: "La puissance civile s'exerce de deux manières: l'une légitime par l'autorité, l'autre abusive par les richesses."

[139] *Collected Writings*, vol. IV, pp. 173–74. "Premierement un Etat très petit où le peuple soit facile à rassembler et où chaque citoyen puisse aisément connoitre tous les autres: secondement une grande simplicité de mœurs qui prévienne la multitude d'affaires et les discussions épineuses: Ensuite beaucoup d'égalité dans les rangs et dans les fortunes, sans quoi l'égalité ne sauroit subsister longtems dans les droits et l'autorité; Enfin peu ou point de luxe: car, ou le luxe est l'effet des richesses, ou il les rend nécessaires; il corrompt à la fois le riche et le pauvre, l'un par la possession l'autre par la convoitise; il vend la patrie à la molesse à la vanité; il ôte à l'Etat tous ses Citoyens pour asservir les uns aux autres, et tous à l'opinion" (*Œuvres*, vol. III, p. 405).

the natural order that the majority govern and the minority be governed."[140]
Far preferable is an elective aristocracy: "It is the best and most natural order
for the wisest to govern the multitude, as long as it is certain that they govern for its benefit and not their own."[141] All of this sounds quite Greek, but
it is essential to remember the distinction in Rousseau's account between
Legislation and Government. The governors of a Rousseauian state play an
exclusively executive role: they enforce the laws in particular cases. They
are not, however, the source of the laws, nor, indeed, are they the source of
the rational principle that sets the state in motion. The Legislator is always
the people, and the laws result from the *volonté générale*. This is Rousseau's
great departure.

Yet Rousseau's conviction that reason is to be found in the *volonté générale*,
rather than in the persons of the wise, does not prevent him from applying the principles of the Greek tradition to his own idiosyncratic circumstances. In order for men to live according to their (higher) nature, they
must be governed by the *volonté générale*. A state so ordered will be "just."
However, when particularity and private interests begin to predominate,
the *volonté générale* becomes inaccessible. The chief factor in the rise of
volontés particulières is disproportionate wealth, and, as a result, Rousseau
is as committed as Harrington to the proposition that only an egalitarian
distribution of property will allow a just regime. Indeed, Rousseau makes
this case throughout his life. In the second *Discours* he insists that unnatural
moral inequalities should not be temporized with, but, rather, that a good
lawgiver would "begin by purging the threshing floor and setting aside all
the old materials, as Lycurgus did in Sparta, in order afterwards to erect a
good Building."[142] In the *Economie politique* he writes that "the greatest evil
is already done when there are poor people to defend and rich people to
appease. It is on middling fortunes alone that the force of the laws can exert
itself. They are equally impotent against the treasures of the rich and the
misery of the poor."[143] It is, therefore, "one of the most important tasks of
government to prevent extreme inequalities in wealth, not by confiscating
treasures from their owners, but by removing from everyone the means

---

[140] *Collected Writings*, vol. IV, p. 173. "Il est contre l'ordre naturel que le grand nombre gouverne et que
le petit soit gouverné" (*Œuvres*, vol. III, p. 404).

[141] *Collected Writings* vol. IV, p. 175. "c'est l'ordre le meilleur et le plus naturel que les plus sages
gouvernent la multitude, quand on est sûr qu'ils la gouverneront pour son profit et non pour la
leur" (*Œuvres*, vol. III, p. 407).

[142] *Discourses*, p. 175. "qu'il eut fallu commencer par nettoyer l'aire et écarter tous les vieux matériaux,
comme fit Licurgue à Sparte, pour élever un bon Edifice" (*Œuvres*, vol. III, p. 180).

[143] "le plus grand mal est déja fait, quand on a des pauvres à défendre et des riches à contentir. C'est
sur la médiocrité seule que s'exerce toute la force des lois; elles sont également impuissantes contre
les thrésors du riche et contre le misère du pauvre . . ." (*Œuvres*, vol. III, p. 258).

to accumulate them . . . in order to maintain, together with good mores, respect for the laws, love of the fatherland, and the strength of the general will."[144] Likewise, in the *Contrat social* Rousseau warns that "with regard to wealth, no citizen should be so opulent that he can buy another, and none so poor that he is constrained to sell himself,"[145] and adds in a celebrated footnote that wealth and poverty "are equally fatal to the common good."[146]

In all of this, however, Rousseau does not discuss agrarian laws. In the *Economie politique*, his prescription for the elimination of wealth and poverty rests upon the taxation of luxury goods, not upon the breakup of large estates. "It is by means of such taxes," he insists, "which relieve poverty and charge wealth, that one should prevent the continual increase of the inequality of fortunes."[147] It is little wonder, then, that the American colonists whom I am shortly to consider did not cite Rousseau in their defenses of the agrarian movement.[148] Had they known of Rousseau's unpublished *Projet de constitution pour la Corse*, however, they would have had every reason to list him with Harrington and Montesquieu. Rousseau

---

[144] "une des plus importantes affaires du gouvernement, de prévenir l'extrême inégalité des fortunes, non en enlevant les thrésors à leurs possesseurs, mais en ôtant à tous les moyens d'en accumuler . . . pour maintenir avec les bonnes mœurs le respect pour les lois, l'amour de la patrie, et la vigeur de la volonté générale" (ibid.). Rousseau, indeed, has quite elevated words for the right to private property. See *Economie Politique*, p. 263; *Political Fragments*, p. 22.

[145] *Collected Writings*, vol. IV, p. 162. "quant à la richesse, que nul citoyen ne soit assez opulent pour en pouvoir acheter un autre, et nul assez pauvre pour être contraint de se vendre" (*Œuvres*, vol. III, p. 391). Here is the more neo-Roman version of the argument: the great worry is dependence. But Rousseau argues that wealth endangers freedom for two distinct reasons. On the one hand (and this is the Roman point), the wealthy can in effect buy the poor, thereby rendering the latter dependent and, hence, unfree. On the other hand, extremes of wealth and poverty imperil freedom by fostering particularity, private interest, and the subjugation of the *volonté générale*. Cut off from the moral dictates of the general will, man is a slave to his impulses and private passions; he does things which his higher self would not choose to do, and he is therefore unfree. A lack of attention to this second anxiety about wealth is, it seems to me, the shortcoming in John O'Neal's analysis. See John C. O'Neal, "Rousseau's Theory of Wealth" in *History of European Ideas* 7 (1986), 453–67.

[146] *Collected Writings*, vol. IV, p. 163. "Ces deux états . . . sont également funestes au bien commun" (*Œuvres*, vol. III, p. 392n.). Rousseau also developed these themes in an unpublished *Discours sur les richesses*. On this, see Charles E. Ellison, "The Moral Economy of the Modern City: Reading Rousseau's *Discourse on Wealth*" in *History of Political Thought* 12 (1991), 253–61.

[147] "C'est par tels impôts qui soulagent la pauvreté et charge la richesse, qu'il faut prévenir l'augmentation continuelle de l'inégalité des fortunes" (*Œuvres*, vol. III, p. 276).

[148] An exception may be Jonathan Jackson's *Thoughts upon the Political Situation of the United States of America* (Worcester, MA, 1788). Jackson defends the abolition of primogeniture and entails on the grounds that such measures scuttle the aristocracy of wealth and clear a path for the "natural aristocracy." Such a situation is desirable because "the happiness of a free government consists in obtaining the wisest and best general will of the community, and in being sure of having it conformed to. Mankind are abundantly happier, when obliged to conform strictly to rules, if they are wise ones; as the children of the same family are, to those of a well regulated house, than where each one may do as he pleases" (pp. 56–58). This may well be Rousseauian language.

wrote the *Projet* in 1765 while living in Prussian Neuchâtel, where he had fled to after the condemnation of the *Contrat social* and *Emile* in 1762. He had by then already recorded a special admiration for Corsica (which had recently revolted against centuries of Genoese rule) in the *Contrat social*:[149] in Book II he observes that "in Europe there is still one country capable of legislation; it is the Island of Corsica. The valor and perseverance with which this courageous people was able to recover and defend its freedom would well deserve that some wise man should teach them how to preserve it."[150] Matthieu Buttafoco, a Corsican noble and officer, took the hint, and wrote to Rousseau in August of 1764, declaring that his comments "gave the nation reason to hope that you would want to be that wise man who could obtain the means to conserve this liberty which cost so much blood to acquire."[151] Rousseau took on the task, but seems to have abandoned any intention of publishing his proposals after Corsica was united to France in the Versailles treaty of 1768. His notes for the *Projet* were found at his death, and were finally published in 1861.

Rousseau recommends the life of agrarian democracy for Corsica, and hopes to create an institutional arrangement which will favor virtue and justice.[152] As he puts it, "I will not preach morality to them, nor will I direct them to have virtues, but I will rather put them in a position such that they will have the virtues without knowing the word, and will be good and just without really knowing what justice and goodness are."[153] In order to secure this goal, Rousseau emphasizes the importance of a uniform, equal citizenry, evenly distributed over the various provinces of the island, and free from extremes in wealth and poverty. His intention, as he phrases it, is "not completely to destroy private property, since this is impossible, but to enclose it within more narrow boundaries, to give it a measure, a rule,

---

[149] For Rousseau and Corsica, see Venturi, *Utopia and Reform*, pp. 88–90.

[150] *Collected Writings*, vol. IV, p. 162. "Il est encore en Europe un pays capable de législation; c'est l'Isle de Corse. La valeur et la constance avec laquelle ce brave peuple a su recouvrer et défendre sa liberté, mériteroit bien que quelque homme sage lui apprît à la conserver. J'ai quelque pressentiment qu'un jour cette petite Isle étonnera l'Europe" (*Œuvres*, vol. III, p. 391).

[151] Quoted in *Œuvres*, vol. III, p. ccii. "a fait souhaiter à la nation que vous vouloussiez être cet homme sage qui pourrait procurer les moyens de conserver cette liberté qui a coûté tant de sang à acquérir."

[152] For a defense of the view that Rousseau regarded the proposals in his "practical" writings as realistic blueprints, rather than purely "utopian" musings, see Ethan Putterman, "Realism and Reform in Rousseau's Constitutional Projects for Poland and Corsica" in *Political Studies* 49 (2001), 481–94.

[153] "Je ne leur précherai pas la morale, je ne leur ordonnerai pas d'avoir des vertus mais je les mettrai dans une position telle qu'ils auront des vertus sans en connoitre le mot; et qu'ils seront bons et justes sans trop savoir ce que c'est que justice et bonté" (*Œuvres*, vol. III, p. 948). English translations from the *Projet* are my own.

a bridle which restrains it, which directs it, which subdues it, and always keeps it subordinate to the public good."[154]

In this spirit, Rousseau proposes the creation of extensive public lands "which could even increase in a few years through the order that will be discussed in the law of successions,"[155] and the enforcement of sumptuary laws. But his central proposal is for a Corsican agrarian law. He observes that, "when there is simplicity in mores, agrarian laws are necessary, because then the rich man, not being able to put his wealth anywhere else, hoards his possessions."[156] In other words, since sumptuary laws prevent the wealthy from spending their money on luxury goods, they open the doors wide to massive accumulations of wealth. Because the republic cannot tolerate such fortunes, limits must be placed on the size of estates. Accordingly, Rousseau sketches out a familiar, although preliminary framework: "No one will be able to own lands outside his district. No one will be able to own more than [Rousseau left the number blank] acres of land. He who has such a quantity will be able to acquire equivalent quantities through exchange, but not greater quantities, even of inferior lands, and all gifts, all bequests which could be made to him in lands will be nullified . . . No young man will be able to make a will, but rather all his goods will pass to the community."[157] Once again, the rationale behind such laws could not be clearer. As Rousseau has it, "all the laws concerning succession must tend to return circumstances to equality, so that each person should have something, and no one should have anything excessive."[158]

That said, Rousseau (like Harrington) makes clear that agrarian laws should not tamper with existing holdings; they should simply prevent further accumulation and use inheritance laws to advance their redistributionary goals.[159] He insists that "neither agrarian laws nor any other

[154] "n'est pas de détruire absolument la propriété particulière parce que cela est impossible mais de la renfermer dans les plus étroites bornes, de lui donner une mesure, [une] règle, un frein qui la contienne, qui la dirige, qui la subjugue et la tienne toujours subordonnée au bien public" (ibid., p. 931)

[155] "qui pourront même augmenter en peu d'années par l'ordre dont il sera parlé dans la loi des successions" (ibid., p. 926).

[156] "Quand il y a de la simplicité dans les mœurs, les lois agraires sont necessaires, parce qu'alors le riche ne pouvant placer sa richesse en autre chose accumule ses possessions" (ibid., p. 936).

[157] "Nul ne pourra posséder des terres hors de sa piéve. Nul ne pourra posséder plus de [ ] de terres. Celui qui en aura cette quantité pourra par échanges acquerir des quantités pareilles, mais non plus grandes même de terres moins bonnes et tous dons, tous legs qui lui pourroient être faits en terres seront nuls . . . Nul h(omme) garçon ne pourra tester, mais tout son bien passera à la communauté" (ibid., p. 942).

[158] "Les Loix concernant les successions doivent toutes tendre à ramener les choses à l'égalité, en sorte que chacun ait quelque chose et que personne n'ait rien de trop" (ibid., p. 945).

[159] Rousseau states emphatically in the *Economie politique* that property rights end with death. Thus, redistributionary inheritance laws involve no violations of right (*Œuvres*, vol. III, p. 263). At this point

laws can ever have a retroactive effect, and one cannot confiscate any lands acquired legitimately, no matter their quantity, by virtue of a later law which forbids having so much."[160] Indeed, "no law can despoil any particular person of any portion of his goods. The law can only prevent him from acquiring more; then if he breaks the law, he deserves punishment and the illegally acquired surplus can be confiscated."[161] Unsurprisingly, Rousseau draws this lesson from a discussion of Roman history:

> The Romans saw the necessity of agrarian laws when it was already too late to establish them, and for want of the distinction that I have just made, they finally destroyed the Republic by a method which should have saved it: the Gracchi wanted to take away the existing landholdings of the Patricians, whereas they should have prevented them from acquiring more.[162]

It is of course true that "later on these same Patricians acquired more lands in spite of the law, but this is because the evil was already very deep-rooted when the law was carried, and there was not enough time to remedy it."[163] The Roman agrarian laws were necessary and would have been salutary, had they simply forbidden the growth of existing estates and used inheritance laws to redistribute land and wealth. They would then, without the least appearance of inequity, have safeguarded the rule of virtue and the rational order of the state. Once these comments have been taken into account,

---

it is perhaps worth correcting a statement by O'Neal. He argues that Rousseau, unlike Plato, More, and Bodin, was unwilling to abrogate the right to property in order to achieve equality. In making this argument, he claims to be endorsing an observation by Robert Derathé. Yet Derathé quite clearly (and correctly) includes only Plato and More among those who were willing to part with property rights. As we have seen, Bodin certainly does not belong in this company; indeed, Rousseau's own analysis may well have owed something to the *Six Livres*. Compare O'Neal, "Rousseau's Theory of Wealth," 465n. to Robert Derathé, "La Place et l'importance de la notion d'égalité dans la doctrine politique de Jean-Jacques Rousseau" in *Rousseau after Two Hundred Years: Proceedings of the Cambridge Bicentennial Colloquium*, ed. R. A. Leigh (Cambridge University Press, 1982), pp. 55–63.

[160] "si [*sic*] les loix agraires ni aucunes loix ne peuvent jamais avoir d'effet rétroactif et l'on ne peut confisquer nulles terres acquises légitimement en quelque quantité qu'elles puissent être en vertu d'une loi postérieure qui defende d'en avoir tant" (*Œuvres*, vol. III, p. 936).

[161] "Aucune loi ne peut dépouiller aucun particulier d'aucune portion de son bien. La loi peut seulement l'empêcher d'en acquérir davantage; alors, s'il enfreint la loi il mérite le châtiment et le surplus illegitimement acquis peut et droit être confisqué" (ibid.).

[162] "Les Romains virent la nécessité des loix agraires quand il n'étoit plus tems de les établir, et faute de la distinction que je viens de faire ils detruisirent enfin la Republique par un moyen qui l'eut du conserver: les Gracques voulurent oter aux Patricians leures terres; il eut fallu les empecher de les acquérir" (ibid., p. 937).

[163] "dans la suite ces mêmes Patriciens en acquerint encore malgré la loi mais c'est que le mal étoit invéteré quand elle fut portée et qu'il n'étoit plus tems d'y remedier" (ibid.).

Rousseau's place in the story that I have been telling becomes much more clear.

IV

It is, then, a helpful exercise to look back at Montesquieu through the eyes of his early French acolytes. Both Mably and Rousseau followed him in insisting that republics alone can guarantee the rule of reason, that such regimes cannot survive without virtue, and that extremes in wealth and poverty will warp the just arrangement of the commonwealth. As we have seen, some scholars have tried to avoid the implications of this analysis for Montesquieu's overall thought by stressing the supposedly amoral character of his *vertu politique*: if his republics are kept in motion by something other than "virtue proper," they reason, the purely descriptive character of his analysis remains intact. The republic is, then, merely an equal among equals, or is even surpassed by the "political liberty" of the British constitution. But if Montesquieu's republics, alone among regimes, produce truly virtuous citizens and a life that accords with reason and nature, then something decidedly normative has crept into Montesquieu's analysis. That the President (like Mably) makes clear that his Greek republics cannot be brought into being in "the dregs and corruption of modern times"[164] does not negate his basic point. True, the "political men" who lived in ancient Greece "recognized no other force to sustain [the city] than virtue" while "those of today speak to us only of manufacturing, commerce, finance, wealth, and even luxury."[165] But that disparity only reinforces Montesquieu's conviction that republics alone gave men the chance to live in accordance with their true natures.

This message was received loud and clear by many of the President's early readers – Bertrand Barère among them[166] – who saw Montesquieu as a straightforward republican partisan, and took his advice on how to

---

[164] *The Spirit of the Laws* IV.6 (p. 37). In this passage Montesquieu notes that there are occasional examples of classical republican virtue in the modern world. William Penn, for example, is styled a "true Lycurgus," a characterization that Voltaire disputed in his *Commentaire sur l'esprit des lois*: "Je ne sais rien de plus contraire à Lycurge qu'un législateur et un peuple qui ont toute guerre en horreur" (*Œuvres complètes de Voltaire*, vol. XXX [Paris: Garnier Frères, 1880], p. 419). In general, however, Montesquieu believed that the world of the ancient republics was unavailable to modernity.

[165] *The Spirit of the Laws* III.3 (p. 22).

[166] See, for example, Bertrand Barère, *Montesquieu peint d'après ses ouvrages* (Paris, 1797). That said, it must be remembered that it was the same Barère who, in 1793, proposed the death penalty "for anyone who shall propose the agrarian law" (See Rose, "French Revolution," 111).

constitute and preserve republican government extremely seriously. One of those early readers, Thomas Jefferson, wrote a letter to John Adams in 1813 in which he outlined the difference between the "natural aristocracy" and the "pseudo-aristocracy" of wealth. In this connection, Jefferson reminds his old friend of an important measure adopted by the Virginia legislature during the American Revolution:

At the first session of our legislature after the Declaration of Independence, we passed a law abolishing entails. And this was followed by one abolishing the privilege of Primogeniture, and dividing the lands of intestates equally among all their children, or other representatives. These laws, drawn by myself, laid the axe to the root of the Pseudo-aristocracy. And had another which I prepared been adopted by the legislature, our work would have been compleat. It was a Bill for the more general diffusion of learning . . . Worth and genius would thus have been sought out from every condition of life, and compleatly prepared by education for defeating the competition of wealth and birth for public trusts.[167]

It is difficult not to see the hand of Montesquieu in this pattern of thought.[168] Indeed, Montesquieu deserves much of the credit for transporting the Greek tradition to the New World.

[167] *The Adams–Jefferson Letters*, ed. Lester J. Cappon (Chapel Hill: University of North Carolina Press, 1959), p. 390.

[168] For a helpful summary of Jefferson's reading of Montesquieu, see David Carrithers, "Montesquieu, Jefferson and the Fundamentals of Eighteenth-Century Republican Theory" in *The French-American Review* 6 (1982), 160–88.

CHAPTER 6

The Greek tradition and the American Founding

I

Taking the story of the Greek tradition forward into the period of the American Founding necessarily involves an intervention in one of the most vitriolic historiographical debates of the last thirty years. Beginning with the release of Bernard Bailyn's *Ideological Origins of the American Revolution* (1967) and Gordon S. Wood's *Creation of the American Republic* (1969), a distinguished group of American historians began to question the scholarly consensus that had placed the political theory of John Locke at the center of American revolutionary and constitutional thought.[1] These historians stressed instead the reliance of the Founders on eighteenth-century British opposition writers and, by implication, on the "classical republicanism" sketched out in the postwar period by Zera Fink and Caroline Robbins.[2] The new "republican synthesis," as Robert Shalhope dubbed it in 1972,[3] received perhaps its most crucial defense from J. G. A. Pocock's *The Machiavellian Moment* (1975), which, as we have seen, presents the American Revolution as the apotheosis of a tradition of republican thought stretching back to the writings of Aristotle and Polybius.[4] The controversy

[1] Bernard Bailyn, *The Ideological Origins of the American Revolution* (Harvard University Press, 1967); Gordon S. Wood, *The Creation of the American Republic: 1776–1787* (Chapel Hill: University of North Carolina Press, 1969). Joining Bailyn and Wood were, among others, Lance Banning, *The Jeffersonian Persuasion: Evolution of a Party Ideology* (Cornell University Press, 1978), and Drew R. McCoy, *The Elusive Republic: Political Economy in Jeffersonian America* (Chapel Hill: University of North Carolina Press, 1980). The classic postwar statement of the Lockean case was Louis Hartz, *The Liberal Tradition in America: an Interpretation of American Political Thought since the Revolution* (New York, 1955).

[2] Zera S. Fink, *The Classical Republicans: an Essay in the Recovery of a Pattern of Thought in Seventeenth-Century England* (Evanston: Northwestern University Press, 1945); Caroline Robbins, *The Eighteenth-Century Commonwealthman: Studies in the Transmission, Development and Circumstance of English Liberal Thought from the Restoration of Charles II until the War with the Thirteen Colonies* (Harvard University Press, 1959).

[3] Robert E. Shalhope, "Toward a Republican Synthesis: the Emergence of an Understanding of Republicanism in American Historiography" in *The William and Mary Quarterly* 29 (1972), 49–80.

[4] J. G. A. Pocock, *The Machiavellian Moment: Florentine Political Thought and the Atlantic Republican Tradition* (Princeton University Press, 1975).

generated by this new wave of republican historiography has been very extensive. Literally dozens of historians on both sides of the Atlantic have responded to Pocock and his followers by attempting to reclaim center stage for Locke and "liberalism."[5] After decades of conflict, however, it has become increasingly clear to a new generation of historians that Locke's influence in eighteenth-century America is unlikely to have been either complete or completely absent, and, accordingly, these younger scholars have advocated a *rapprochement* between the two warring factions based on mutual recognition of the complexity and heterogeneity of the intellectual landscape at the Founding.[6]

Apart from its unpleasantness, the most obvious deficiency of the "republicanism–liberalism" debate has been the almost unquestioned assumption by all its participants that Pocock's account of the history and content of "classical republicanism" or "civic humanism" is unimpeachably correct. While they disagree on almost everything else, scholars as diverse as Lance Banning and Joyce Appleby will both accept that "classical republicanism" was an ideology, or conceptual cluster, rooted in the Aristotelian belief that political participation is essential for the constituting of human virtue, and expressing itself characteristically in a deep anxiety about the corrupting effects of luxury and commerce.[7] There has been precious little effort among early Americanists to come to terms with the revisionist

---

[5] See, among many others, Joyce Appleby, *Liberalism and Republicanism in the Historical Imagination* (Harvard University Press, 1992); Appleby, "Commercial Farming and the 'Agrarian Myth' in the Early Republic" in *Journal of American History* 68 (1982), 833–49; Appleby, "Republicanism in Old and New Contexts" in *The William and Mary Quarterly* 43 (1986), 20–34; John Patrick Diggins, *The Lost Soul of American Politics: Virtue, Self-Interest, and the Foundations of Liberalism* (University of Chicago Press, 1986); Isaac Kramnick, "Republican Revisionism Revisited" in *American Historical Review* 87 (1982), 629–64; Jennifer Nedelsky, *Private Property and the Limits of American Constitutionalism: the Madisonian Framework and Its Legacy* (Chicago, 1990).

[6] The trajectory of the debate is admirably summarized in Alan Gibson, "Ancients, Moderns and Americans: the Republicanism–Liberalism Debate Revisited" in *History of Political Thought* 21 (2000), 261–80. The consensus-builders have included, among many others, Jeffrey C. Isaac, "Republicanism vs. Liberalism? A Reconsideration" in *History of Political Thought* 9 (1988), 349–77; James T. Kloppenberg, "The Virtues of Liberalism: Christianity, Republicanism, and Ethics in Early American Political Discourse" in *Journal of American History* 74 (1987), 9–33; and Michael Zuckert, *The Natural Rights Republic: Studies in the Foundations of the American Political Tradition* (Notre Dame, IN, 1996). Some scholars of the previous generation have also come to embrace the consensus view. See Lance Banning, "Jeffersonian Ideology Revisited: Liberal and Classical Ideas in the New American Republic" in *The William and Mary Quarterly* 42 (1987), 11–19; Isaac Kramnick, *Republicanism and Bourgeois Radicalism: Political Ideology in Late 18th Century England and America* (Cornell University Press, 1990); J. G. A. Pocock, "Communications" in *The William and Mary Quarterly* 45 (1988), 817; Gordon S. Wood, "Afterword" in *The Republican Synthesis Revisited: Essays in Honor of George Athan Billias*, ed. Milton M. Klein, Richard D. Brown, John B. Hench (Worcester, MA: American Antiquarian Society, 1992), pp. 143–51.

[7] See Appleby, *Liberalism and Republicanism*, p. 20; Banning, *The Jeffersonian Persuasion*, p. 31; and also Diggins, *American Politics*, p. 10. Banning, like Pocock, recruits Harrington for his "classical

historiography of the last twenty years that has challenged Pocock's representation of both the classical inheritance itself and the *fortuna* of classical texts in the Renaissance and early-modern period. In short, the "republicanism–liberalism" debate has been reduced to a controversy over the extent to which Pocock's template can be applied to the political theory of the Founding; neither side has brought critical scrutiny to bear on the template itself.[8]

The most immediate casualty of this confusion has been, perhaps unsurprisingly, the persuasiveness of the "republican synthesis" (or, as Banning prefers, the "republican hypothesis"). Its advocates have, *inter alia*, found themselves wedded to Pocock's argument for the centrality of Aristotelian political participation in republican thought. This commitment has proven especially inconvenient, since the notion that people cannot be fully human unless they participate in politics is largely absent from the literature of the period.[9] Political participation tended, instead, to be lauded as a bulwark against tyranny and oligarchy – an instrumentality, rather than a good in itself. But the most severe damage has been done, not to the partisans of Locke or Machiavelli, but to those scholars who have been trying assiduously to map out the possible points of contact between liberalism

republican" story by locating in *Oceana* "an Aristotelian concept of the citizen as independent man, whose virtue is expressed both in the government and in a citizen militia." Although Wood does not stress this idea in his *Creation of the American Republic*, he certainly does so later on: "According to the classical republican tradition, man was by nature a political being, a citizen who achieved his greatest moral fulfillment by participating in a self-governing republic." See Gordon S. Wood, *The Radicalism of the American Revolution* (New York: Vintage Books, 1991), p. 104.

[8] Mark Jurdjevic makes this point quite nicely in his recent article, "Virtue, Commerce, and the Enduring Florentine Moment: Reintegrating Italy into the Atlantic Republican Debate" in *Journal of the History of Ideas* 62 (2001), 721–43. A good example of the phenomenon in question is Daniel T. Rodgers, "Republicanism: the Career of a Concept" in *Journal of American History* 79 (1992), esp. 16–17. I am bound to say that I find Rodgers's sharp distinction between Pocock and Wood overdrawn (p. 19). For a notable, if lonely exception to this general rule, see J. R. Pole, *Political Representation in England and the Origins of the American Republic* (New York: Macmillan, 1966), esp. pp. 3–13. Alone among scholars of the Founding, Pole noticed Pocock's over-reliance on Harrington's Machiavellian inheritance. Aristotle, Pole recognized, far more than Machiavelli, influenced Harrington's defense of the equal agrarian.

[9] Pocock's Straussian critics have made this point with some enthusiasm. See, for example, Paul Rahe, *Republics Ancient and Modern*, vol. III (Chapel Hill: University of North Carolina Press, 1994), p. 28. This is also an important reason for Diggins's skepticism about the "republican synthesis" (see Diggins, *American Politics*, p. 19). However, the contrary position persists. See, for example, Ralph Ketcham, "Publius: Sustaining the Republican Principle" in *The William and Mary Quarterly* 44 (1987), esp. 578–79; Kramnick, *Republicanism and Bourgeois Radicalism*, 164–65; and Hon. Stephen Breyer, "Our Democratic Constitution," The Fall 2001 James Madison Lecture, New York University Law School, esp. pp. 1–4. This view has particularly significant consequences for Breyer, an associate justice of the US Supreme Court, in that it suggests to him that constitutional courts should weigh the protection of this participatory liberty against the provisions of the Constitution that enshrine "negative" liberty. However, once the constitutional preoccupation with self-government is regarded instead as a further expression of a theory of negative liberty, Breyer's argument becomes considerably less convincing.

and republicanism. It has long been a commonplace in the literature that the Founders perceived no conflict between authors such as Cicero and Locke (i.e. between republicans and natural-rights theorists), but there has been little effort to determine in what respects that perception might have been justified.[10] On the crucial issue of property rights, for example, there would be no confrontation between readers of Cicero and readers of Locke, between neo-Romans and liberals.[11] Both agree on the inviolability of private property and both accept the maxim that governments are constituted primarily to preserve and protect the property of their citizens. It is only with the Greeks that liberals would quarrel when it comes to property.

Another way of saying the same thing is that simply looking for anxiety about "luxury" and "corruption" (or *encomia* of "virtue," for that matter) might not be a good litmus test for identifying "anti-Lockean" thought in eighteenth-century America. As we have seen repeatedly, neo-Roman writers, Lockean jurisprudential theorists, and thinkers in the Greek tradition (to say nothing of evangelical Calvinists) could all express intense concern over the social effects of disproportionate wealth. But liberals and neo-Romans will disagree with the Greeks both as to precisely *why* such wealth is harmful and over what tools the state may justly employ to deal with the problem. William Moore Smith captured the dilemma facing both Lockeans and neo-Romans in a 1775 commencement address to the College of Philadelphia.[12] Lycurgus, he argued, "seems not to have reflected that there can be no true liberty without security of property; and where property is secure, industry begets wealth; and wealth is often productive of a train of evils naturally destructive to virtue and freedom!"[13] Smith identified the following "sad dilemma in politics": if states "exclude *wealth*,

---

[10] Lance Banning concluded that although "liberalism" and "classical republicanism" were "ultimately irreconcilable philosophies," we cannot suppose that "the analytical distinctions we detect were evident to those we study . . . Logically, it may be inconsistent to be simultaneously liberal and classical. Historically it was not" (Banning, "Republican Ideology and the Triumph of the Constitution" in *The William and Mary Quarterly* 31 [1974], 179).

[11] David Armitage notes something similar when he observes that the neo-Roman idiom was perfectly compatible with the discourse of "political economy" in eighteenth-century Britain. See David Armitage, *The Ideological Origins of the British Empire* (Cambridge University Press, 2000), p. 168. This is also one of Jeffrey Isaac's primary grounds for arguing for the compatibility of republican and natural-rights languages. Although I strongly disagree with his "liberalizing" characterization of Harrington, Isaac should receive credit for noticing that certain kinds of republican discourse could be reconciled very easily with natural-rights arguments (Isaac, "Republicanism vs. Liberalism?," 349–77).

[12] Wood's claim that Smith offered these remarks in a speech to the Continental Congress is mistaken. G. S. Wood, *Creation of the American Republic*, p. 64.

[13] William Moore Smith, "On the Fall of Empires," *Dunlap's Pennsylvania Packet, or, the General Advertiser* (Philadelphia), vol. IV, no. 188, May 29, 1775.

it must be by regulations intrenching too far upon civil liberty."[14] Commenting on this speech, Wood suggests that Smith "perceived the inherent conflict between individual liberty and traditional republican theory," by which Wood clearly means the quarrel between "liberalism" and "republicanism."[15] But this is precisely the same dilemma that Guicciardini, a republican in the neo-Roman tradition, had identified in the *Discorso di Logrogno* two centuries before. Smith is actually expressing the shared perspective of liberalism and the neo-Roman tradition: that the principle of justice (*cuique tribuere ius suum*) sharply restricts the state's range of possible responses to the problems of luxury and corruption, and, as a result, confines the state to the Polybian cycle. The dissenting view does not come from "republicanism" *per se*, but from the particular strand of republican thought we have been following.

The Greek tradition, with its distinctive insistence on the necessity of using the coercive power of government to maintain an egalitarian distribution of property (for the sake of preserving justice, defined as the rule of the best men), was indeed a vibrant force in the intellectual landscape of the American Revolution and the debates over the ratification of the Constitution. The arch-Federalist Fisher Ames noticed as much when he wrote in 1787 that, for many of his countrymen, the Revolution had represented an opportunity "to reduce to practice the schemes, which Plato and Harrington had only sketched upon paper," and to forge a republic truly "perfect and perpetual."[16] Those who embraced this view were not restricted to any one party or faction; they included Northerners and Southerners, Federalists and Antifederalists, Jeffersonians and their opponents, and, taken collectively, they represent a powerful current of thought which has been neglected and misunderstood. In studying the influence of this Greek tradition on the Founding, I have steered clear of totalizing claims, and have intentionally declined to take a position on the relative importance of "republicanism" or "liberalism" during the period. I hope simply that, by adopting a more complex and nuanced understanding of the varieties of republican thought available in late eighteenth-century America, it may be possible to shed new light on the intellectual roots of the world's most powerful republic.

---

[14] Smith offers the following solution: "The grand object then of modern legislation, has been to regulate the use of wealth, but not to exclude it. And to this end, all systems of education, all laws, all the efforts of patriotism, ought to be directed."

[15] G. S. Wood, *Creation of the American Republic*, p. 64.

[16] Fisher Ames, "Camillus IV" in *The Independent Chronicle*, March 8, 1787. Reproduced in *Works of Fisher Ames*, ed. W. B. Allen, vol. II (Indianapolis: Liberty *Classics*, 1983), p. 82.

II

Writing to each other late in life, John Adams and Thomas Jefferson recorded their mutual hatred for Plato. In an 1814 letter to his old friend and rival, Jefferson wrote that, presented with ample leisure, "I amused myself with reading seriously Plato's republic," an enterprise he absolutely detested.[17] "While wading thro' the whimsies, the puerilities, and unintelligible jargon of this work, I laid it down often to ask myself how it could have been that the world should have so long consented to give reputation to such nonsense as this... how could the Roman good sense do it? And particularly how could Cicero bestow such eulogies on Plato?" Jefferson blamed Plato's continued popularity on elitist schoolmasters and superstitious Christians, without whose enthusiastic support the Athenian's "foggy mind" could never have "procured him immortality of fame and reverence." He adds in conclusion that "it is fortunate for us that Platonic republicanism has not obtained the same favor as Platonic Christianity; or we should now have been all living, men, women and children, pell mell together, like beasts of the field and forest."

In his reply Adams could hardly contain his enthusiastic agreement: "I am very glad you have seriously read Plato: and still more rejoiced to find that your reflections upon him so perfectly harmonize with mine."[18] Thirty years before, Adams continues, he had gone through Plato's works in the original Greek, and "my disappointment was very great, my Astonishment was greater and my disgust was shocking." In particular, he attacks Plato and his disciples (among whom, interestingly, he numbers Rousseau and Tom Paine) for failing to realize that "nothing can be conceived more destructive of human happiness; more infallibly contrived to transform Men and Women into Brutes, Yahoos, or Daemons than a Community of Wives and Property" (the allusion to Swift here is revealing). He insists that he gleaned only two useful pieces of information from his reading of Plato's dialogues: "1. that Franklins Ideas of exempting Husbandmen and Mariners etc. from the depredations of War were borrowed from him. 2. that Sneezing is a cure for the Hickups. Accordingly I have cured myself and

---

[17] *The Adams–Jefferson Letters*, ed. Lester J. Cappon (Chapel Hill: University of North Carolina Press, 1959), p. 432. For a useful corrective to the widespread view that the founders had little classical training, and gained their familiarity with ancient sources by reading second-hand accounts in the writings of English Whigs, see Carl J. Richard, *The Founders and the Classics: Greece, Rome, and the American Enlightenment* (Harvard University Press, 1994), esp. chaps. 1 and 7. Richard provides a useful description of classical education in eighteenth-century America, but is, I feel, rather less successful in delineating the role of classical ideologies in the period of the Founding.

[18] *The Adams–Jefferson Letters*, p. 437.

all my Friends of that provoking disorder, for thirty Years with a Pinch of Snuff."

Adams's recollections of his earlier encounters with Plato are, to be sure, of dubious reliability. In his 1787 *Defence of the Constitutions of Government of the United States*, for example, Adams had included a lengthy discussion of how Plato's theory of mixed government coincided exactly with his own.[19] That said, this exchange between Jefferson and Adams hardly leaves the impression that Plato could have been a significant influence on the formation of either man's political theory. Yet, as we have seen, by the end of the eighteenth century the Greek tradition had passed through so many incarnations that an endorsement of its basic claims no longer necessarily implied an affinity for Plato, or even Harrington for that matter. The language of agrarian laws, the republican regulation of inheritances, the impossibility of achieving the rule of the best men in the midst of disproportionate wealth and poverty, had entered the common intellectual culture. And it should come as no surprise that, his disdain for Plato notwithstanding, Thomas Jefferson in particular emerged as a champion of the tradition we have been following.

In every piece of autobiographical writing that Jefferson ever composed he insisted that one of the proudest moments of his public career occurred on October 14, 1776. On that day he introduced a bill in the Virginia legislature abolishing the practice of entails (his bill to abolish primogeniture finally came before the legislature on October 31, 1785, and was passed in November).[20] In his 1821 *Autobiography* Jefferson observes that "in the

---

[19] John Adams, *Defence of the Constitutions of Government of the United States of America* in *Works*, ed. Charles Francis Adams, vol. IV (Boston, 1851), pp. 448–63.

[20] *An act directing the course of descents* in *The Statutes at Large: Being a Collection of all the Laws of Virginia, from the First Session of the Legislature, in the Year 1619*, ed. William Waller Hening, vol. XII (Richmond, 1823), pp. 138–40. On October 15, 1776, the Virginia legislature approved "An act for the revision of laws," championed by Jefferson, under which a select committee was entrusted with the task of revising the legislative code in accordance with republican principles. Jefferson was the moving force on this committee, which submitted its full report on June 18, 1779. Most of the proposed bills, including the bill abolishing primogeniture, came up for consideration at the October 1785 session of the legislature. On this complex procedure, see the very thorough account in *The Papers of Thomas Jefferson*, vol. II, ed. Julian P. Boyd, Lyman H. Butterfield, and Mina R. Bryan (Princeton University Press, 1950), pp. 305–24. See also Dumas Malone, *Jefferson and His Time: Jefferson the Virginian* (London: Eyre and Spottiswoode, 1948), pp. 251–57. It is important to stress, however, that the inheritance laws under consideration in this chapter concerned only intestates (i.e. those who did not leave a will). Prior to the Revolutionary period, most states had enacted that, in the absence of a will, the eldest son should receive a double share of the deceased's estate, while some (such as New York and New Jersey) practiced full-fledged primogeniture. Jefferson and the others whom I will be discussing sought to repeal this practice, although they did not attempt to curtail testamentary freedom in this respect: a will could still override the new standard of partible inheritance. These thinkers did, however, propose an outright ban on the practice of entails – and

earlier times of the colony when lands were to be obtained for little or nothing, some provident individuals procured large grants, and desirous of founding great families for themselves, settled them on their descendants in fee-tail."[21] Jefferson argues that "the transmission of this property from generation to generation in the same name raised up a distinct set of families who, being privileged by law in the perpetuation of their wealth were thus formed into a Patrician order." He then adds, in a passage which reveals how the Greek view could furnish a defense of revolution, that "from this order too the king habitually selected his Counsellors of State, the hope of which distinction devoted the whole corps to the interest & will of the crown."

Jefferson loathed the *status quo* and made its elimination his first priority after the adoption of the Declaration of Independence:

To annul this privilege, and instead of an aristocracy of wealth, of more harm and danger, than benefit to society, to make an opening for the aristocracy of virtue and talent, which nature has wisely provided for the direction of the interests of society, & scattered with equal hand through all it's [sic] conditions, was deemed essential to a well-ordered republic. To effect it no violence was necessary, no deprivation of natural right, but rather an enlargement of it by a repeal of the law. For this would authorize the present holder to divide the property among his children equally, as his affections were divided; and would place them, by natural generation on the level of their fellow citizens.[22]

The restatement of the Greek case could hardly have been more precise: the presence of disproportionate wealth produces an environment in which

---

even on the question of primogeniture, their rhetoric often seems to reach beyond intestates. For a summary of the evolution of inheritance laws in America during the colonial and Revolutionary periods, see Carole Shammas, Marylynn Salmon, and Michel Dahlin, *Inheritance in America from Colonial Times to the Present* (New Brunswick, NJ: Rutgers University Press, 1987), pp. 30–67. See also Toby L. Ditz, *Property and Kinship: Inheritance in Early Connecticut, 1750–1820* (Princeton University Press, 1986), esp. chap. 3.

[21] Thomas Jefferson, *Autobiography* in *Writings*, ed. Merrill D. Peterson (New York: Library of America, 1984), p. 32.

[22] It is worth pointing out here that primogeniture could be attacked from a wide variety of perspectives. In chapter IX of his *First Treatise of Government*, Locke asserts the right of each child to subsistence from his father: "Since every one [of Adam's children] having a Right of Inheritance to his Portion, they might enjoy their Inheritance, or any part of it in common, or share it, or some parts of it by Division, as best liked them. But no one could pretend to the whole Inheritance, or any Sovereignty supposed to accompany it, since a Right of Inheritance gave every one of the rest, as well as any one, a Title to share in the Goods of his Father." Accordingly, "Primogeniture" can have no "Pretence to a Right of solely Inheriting either *Property* or *Power*" (See John Locke, *Two Treatises of Government*, ed. Peter Laslett [Cambridge University Press, 1967], pp. 227–30). Locke's comments remind us that primogeniture could be attacked from within the natural-rights tradition, and its abolition could be understood as a defense of property rights. However – and this is the essential point – it was *not* on these grounds that Jefferson defended his bill.

money, not virtue, is the criterion according to which political power is assigned. In order to make sure that the "natural aristocracy" rules, therefore, the republic must adopt a series of inheritance laws designed to break up large estates (a practice which, Jefferson is at pains to insist, does not violate the "natural right" to property). It is important to note here that Jefferson's rationale for breaking up large estates is *not*, contrary to frequent scholarly claims, the need for an independent yeomanry free from "exploitation."[23] It is, rather, the moral necessity of the rule of the best men (who, on this account, can come from any segment of society). He announces the provenance of his ideas even more clearly later in the text when he summarizes the four bills which "a foundation laid for a government truly republican." He notes that "the repeal of laws of entail would prevent the accumulation and perpetuation of wealth in select families" and that "the abolition of primogeniture, and equal partition of inheritances removed the feudal and unnatural distinctions which made one member of every family rich, and all the rest poor, substituting equal partition, the best of all Agrarian laws."[24]

As we have already seen, Jefferson repeats this account almost verbatim in an 1813 letter to Adams:

At the first session of our legislature after the Declaration of Independence, we passed a law abolishing entails. And this was followed by one abolishing the privilege of Primogeniture, and dividing the lands of intestates equally among all their children, or other representatives. These laws, drawn by myself, laid the axe to the root of the Pseudo-aristocracy. And had another which I prepared been adopted by the legislature, our work would have been compleat. It was a Bill for the more general diffusion of learning . . . Worth and genius would thus have been sought out from every condition of life, and compleatly prepared by education for defeating the competition of wealth and birth for public trusts.[25]

The addition here is extremely important. Jefferson envisioned the institution of republican inheritance laws as the first part of a two-part process; the second was the provision of a good education to all citizens in whatever station of life. The logical connection between the two proposals resonated quite powerfully with many of the Founders: if political power should be

---

[23] See, for example, Richard K. Matthews, *The Radical Politics of Thomas Jefferson: a Revisionist View* (Lawrence, KA: University Press of Kansas, 1984), and Drew McCoy, *The Elusive Republic*, p. 68.
[24] Jefferson, *Writings*, p. 44. The Virginia law against entails read in part: "Every estate in lands or slaves, which on the seventh day of October, in the year of our Lord one thousand seven hundred and seventy-six, was an estate in fee-tail, shall be deemed from that time to have been, and from thence forward to continue, an estate in fee simple; and every estate in lands, which since hath been limited, or hereafter shall be limited, so that as the law aforetime was, such estate would have been an estate tail, shall also be deemed to have been and to continue an estate in fee simple." See *An act for regulating conveyances* in *The Statutes at Large*, vol. XII, p. 156.
[25] *The Adams–Jefferson Letters*, p. 390.

assigned on the basis of virtue, not wealth, then it was necessary both to eliminate disproportionate wealth *and* to cultivate virtue wherever it could be found. "That form of government is the best," according to Jefferson, "which provides the most effectually for a pure selection of these natural aristoi into the offices of government." Or, as he had put it in the preamble to his *Bill for the More General Diffusion of Knowledge* (1778), since "the people will be happiest" when "those who form and administer [laws] are wise and honest," it is necessary "for promoting the publick happiness that those persons, whom nature hath endowed with genius and virtue, should be rendered by liberal education worthy . . . to be called to that charge [public service] without regard to wealth, birth or other accidental condition or circumstance."[26]

It is worth pointing out that Jefferson's intense concern over the question of inheritance laws and the distribution of land was not simply retrojected into his past in old age; it was clearly present throughout his public career. A fascinating glimpse into Jefferson's early thought on the subject can be found in his "Common-Place Book," compiled in the several years before 1776. Here he transcribed a series of quotations from Montesquieu's *De l'esprit des lois*, inserting a substantial piece of his own English commentary on Book v:

In a democracy equality & frugality should be promoted by the laws, as they nurse the amor patriae. To do this, a census is advisable, discriminating the people according to their possessions; after which, particular laws may equalise them in some degree by laying burthens on the richer classes, & encouraging the poorer ones. – In a commercial republic, where great wealth will be amassed by individuals, inheritances should be divided among all the children.[27]

But perhaps Jefferson's most pronounced statement on the redistribution of wealth appears in a 1785 letter to James Madison which he composed while serving in France as US ambassador. In the context of a diatribe against wealthy landowners (of whom, of course, he was one) for allowing large tracts of their land to remain uncultivated, Jefferson makes the following remarkable statement:

I am conscious that an equal division of property is impracticable, but the consequences of this enormous inequality producing so much misery to the bulk of

---

[26] Jefferson, *Writings*, p. 365. The relationship between Jefferson's idea of a "natural aristocracy" and his education proposals is discussed briefly in Bernard Bailyn, *To Begin the World Anew: the Genius and Ambiguities of the American Founders* (New York: Alfred A. Knopf, 2003), pp. 55–56.

[27] *Pensées choisies de Montesquieu tirées du "Common-Place Book" de Thomas Jefferson*, ed. Gilbert Chinard (Paris, 1925), p. 33. Jefferson also quotes at length Montesquieu's analysis of the effects of agrarian laws on population growth (p. 72).

mankind, legislators cannot invent too many devices for subdividing property, only taking care to let their subdivisions go hand in hand with the natural affections of the human mind. The descent of property of every kind therefore to all the children, or to all the brothers and sisters, or other relations in equal degree, is a politic measure and a practicable one. Another means of silently lessening the inequality of property is to exempt all from taxation below a certain point, and to tax the higher portions or property in geometrical progression as they rise. Whenever there are in any country uncultivated lands and unemployed poor, it is clear that the laws of property have been so far extended as to violate natural right. The earth is given as a common stock for man to labor and live on ... It is too soon yet in our country to say that every man who cannot find employment, but who can find uncultivated land, shall be at liberty to cultivate it, paying a moderate rent. But it is not too soon to provide by every possible means that as few as possible shall be without a little portion of land. The small landholders are the most precious part of a state.[28]

Here the very same Jefferson who, in old age, was careful to insist that his Revolutionary inheritance laws had been consonant with property rights actually contemplates new federal inheritance laws, a progressive tax scheme, and the outright confiscation of land in order to eliminate excessive wealth and poverty.

The second half of this passage also represents a unique moment in the Jeffersonian corpus, in that it dresses arguments for the redistribution of property, not so much in the language of the Greek tradition, as in the language of rights. Jefferson is clearly thinking here of Locke's classic argument in chapter five of the *Second Treatise of Government*.[29] Locke had

---

[28] Jefferson, *Writings*, p. 841. Jefferson sings the praises of yeoman farmers most famously in his *Notes on the State of Virginia*, Query XIX. "Those who labour in the earth are the chosen people of God, if ever he had a chosen people, whose breasts he has made his peculiar deposit for substantial and genuine virtue. It is the focus in which he keeps alive that sacred fire, which otherwise might escape from the face of the earth. Corruption of morals in the mass of cultivators is a phaenomenon of which no age nor nation has furnished an example. It is the mark set on those, who not looking up to heaven, to their own soil and industry, as does the husbandman, for their subsistance, depend for it on the casualties and caprice of customers. Dependence begets subservience and venality, suffocates the germ of virtue, and prepares fit tools for the designs of ambition ... It is the manners and spirit of a people which preserve a republic in vigor. A degeneracy in these is a canker which soon eats to the heart of its laws and constitution" (*Writings*, pp. 290–91). This is Jefferson at his most Roman, emphasizing the moral toll of dependence. It differs sharply from his explicitly Greek defense of agrarian laws – perhaps because only the Greek account could justify state intervention in the distribution of property. See also Benjamin Franklin's panegyric of agricultural life in *Positions to Be Examined Concerning National Wealth* (1769) in *Selected Works of Benjamin Franklin*, vol. II (London: William Pickering, 1996).

[29] Jefferson's image of the indigent pauper who is permitted to farm uncultivated land recalls Locke's example of the Spanish farmers: "Nay, the extent of *Ground* is of so little value, *without labour*, that I have heard it affirmed, that in *Spain* it self, a Man may be permitted to plough, sow, and reap,

made the case that, since "God gave the World to Men in Common,"[30] in the state of nature "Men had a Right to appropriate, by their Labour, each one of himself, as much of the things of Nature, as he could use," and no more.[31] "Nothing was made by God for Man to spoil or destroy," so no man had a right in the state of nature to claim more land than he himself could cultivate and use.[32] But Locke had argued that, through the tacit consent whereby money was created, and through the explicit consent of all citizens to "settle" property at the moment of contract, men renounced their common right to the earth and confirmed the right of individuals to "disproportionate and unequal Possession" – the right to amass surplus lands and goods.[33] In departing from Locke's argument in this respect, Jefferson's letter is perhaps the only genuinely proto-socialist statement to issue from the pen of an American founding father.

Madison's reply to this letter may seem surprising, coming as it does from the man who declared only two years later in *Federalist* 10 that the "first object of government" is the "protection of different and unequal faculties of acquiring property," from which derives "the possession of different degrees and kinds of property," and who thundered against "a rage for paper money, for an abolition of debts, for an equal division of property."[34] But, although Madison cautions that population density rather than any particular inheritance scheme may lie at the root of popular misery in France, he agrees with Jefferson that "the misery of the lower classes will be found to abate wherever the Government assumes a freer aspect, and the laws favor subdivision of property."[35] He adds that "from a more equal partition of property must result a greater simplicity of manners, consequently less consumption of manufactured superfluities, and a less proportion of idle proprietors and domestics." Such a situation will yield a "juster government," which, in turn, will have "less need of soldiers either for defence against dangers from without or disturbances from within." Madison developed this line of reasoning some years later in a 1792 essay for the *National Gazette* on "Parties." He

---

without being disturbed, upon Land he has no other Title to, but only his making use of it" (Locke, *Two Treatises*, p. 311). That said, Locke offers this example to reinforce his view that land without labor is of very little value; he does not commit himself to the position that such farmers cultivate waste land by natural right.

[30] Ibid., p. 309.   [31] Ibid., p. 312.   [32] Ibid., p. 308.   [33] Ibid., pp. 316–20.

[34] Alexander Hamilton, James Madison, John Jay, *The Federalist Papers*, ed. Clinton Rossiter (New York: NAL Penguin, 1961), p. 84.

[35] *The Papers of Thomas Jefferson*, vol. IX, ed. Julian P. Boyd and Mina R. Bryan (Princeton University Press, 1954), p. 660.

notes the inevitable presence of parties in political associations, but insists that

the great object should be to combat the evil: 1. By establishing political equality among all. 2. By withholding *unnecessary* opportunities from a few, to increase the inequality of property, by an immoderate, and especially an unmerited, accumulation of wealth. 3. By the silent operation of laws, which, without violating the rights of property, reduce extreme wealth to a state of mediocrity, and raise extreme indigence towards a state of comfort.[36]

Jefferson's and Madison's conviction that the breakup of large estates and the mass availability of land would prove economically salutary was entirely consonant with Adam Smith's argument in his *Inquiry into the Nature and Causes of the Wealth of Nations* (1776) – a work which Jefferson characterized as the "best book extant" on "political oeconomy."[37] Smith had insisted that primogeniture was "founded upon the most absurd of all suppositions, the supposition that every successive generation of men have not an equal right to the earth, and to all that it possesses; but that the property of the present generation should be restrained and regulated according to the fancy of those who died perhaps five hundred years ago" (III.2).[38] He argues that, under primogeniture, "the small quantity of land . . . which is brought to market, and the high price of what is brought thither, prevents a great number of capitals from being employed in its cultivation and improvement which would otherwise have taken that direction" (III.4).[39] However, "if landed estates . . . were divided equally among all the children, upon the death of any proprietor who left a numerous family, the estate would generally be sold. So much land would come to market, that it could no longer sell at a monopoly price." Land could then be more generally dispersed, a state of affairs which would promote economic dynamism since, on Smith's view, small proprietors are "of all improvers the most industrious." It is not coincidental that Smith found his great example of this efficient system in the northern colonies of British North America,

---

[36] "Parties" in the *National Gazette*, January 23, 1792. *The Papers of James Madison*, vol. xiv, ed. Robert A. Rutland and Thomas A. Mason (Charlottesville: University Press of Virginia, 1983), p. 197.

[37] Letter from Jefferson to Thomas Mann Randolph, May 30, 1790. *The Papers of Thomas Jefferson*, vol. xvi, ed. Julian P. Boyd, Alfred L. Bush, and Lucius Wilmerding (Princeton University Press, 1961), p. 449.

[38] Adam Smith, *An Inquiry into the Nature and Causes of the Wealth of Nations*, ed. R. H. Campbell, A. S. Skinner, and W. B. Todd, vol. i (Oxford: Clarendon Press, 1976), p. 384.

[39] Ibid., p. 423.

where "there is no right of primogeniture, and lands, like moveables, are divided equally among all the children of the family" (IV.7).[40]

But both Madison and Jefferson go further than Smith. They argue not only that a more egalitarian distribution of property would be economically desirable, but that it would create a "juster government" and a revolution in morals and rulership particularly suited to republican life. They were each prepared to consider government action in pursuit of that egalitarian distribution, and both placed enormous faith in the power of inheritance laws to secure the agrarian. Indeed, the extent of that faith may seem puzzling in retrospect: the practice of entails, for example, was quite rare in the early Republic, so it seems odd that such significance was attached to its abolition.[41] Part of the explanation must surely be that a ban on entails (like its twin, the elimination of primogeniture) did not in any ostentatious sense constitute an attack on property rights (although John Randolph of Roanoke could still call Jefferson a "leveller"[42]). Like so many others in the 1780s, Jefferson and Madison were forced to maneuver between two poles: their conviction that justice required the rule of the wise, and the universal belief that it required the protection of *ius*. Since neither principle could be sacrificed completely, all efforts were directed at identifying the mean. Some authors felt that inheritance laws alone could secure the equal agrarian, and,

---

[40] Ibid., vol. II, p. 572. Smith turns to an analysis of the Roman agrarian laws at the start of Book IV, chapter 7, in a section entitled "Of the Motives for establishing new Colonies." He begins by observing, quite like Montesquieu in the *Considérations*, that "Rome, like most of the other ancient republicks, was originally founded upon an Agrarian law, which divided the publick territory in a certain proportion among the different citizens who composed the state" (IV.vii.3). But "the course of human affairs, by marriage, by succession, and by alienation, necessarily deranged this original division, and frequently threw the lands, which had been allotted for the maintenance of many different families into the possession of a single person." Smith continues, "To remedy this disorder, for such it was supposed to be, a law was made, restricting the quantity of land which any citizen could possess to be five hundred jugera . . . " This law, however, was "neglected and evaded" and "the inequality of fortunes went on continually increasing." The resulting state of affairs left the poor wholly dependent on "the bounties of the candidates at the annual elections," who "when they had a mind to animate the people against the rich and great, put them in mind of the antient division of lands, and represented the law which restricted this sort of private property as the fundamental law of the republick." For a discussion of Smith's attitude toward disproportionate wealth, see Donald Winch, "Commercial Realities, Republican Principles" in *Republicanism: a Shared European Heritage*, vol. II, ed. Quentin Skinner and Martin van Gelderen (Cambridge University Press, 2002), pp. 293–310. Winch does not, however, raise the issue of the Roman agrarian laws.

[41] See Bernard Bailyn, *Faces of the American Revolution: Personalities and Themes in the Struggle for American Independence* (New York: Vintage Books, 1992), pp. 191–92; and James T. Schleifer, "Jefferson and Tocqueville" in *Interpreting Tocqueville's Democracy in America*, ed. Ken Masugi (Savage, MD: Rowman and Littlefield, 1991), p. 178n. That said, Holly Brewer makes a strong case for the importance of entails in tidewater Virginia (and even in the western counties). See Holly Brewer, "Entailing Aristocracy in Colonial Virginia: 'Ancient Feudal Restraints' and Revolutionary Reform" in *The William and Mary Quarterly* 54 (1997), 307–46.

[42] Hugh A. Garland, *The Life of John Randolph of Roanoke*, vol. I (New York, 1860), pp. 18–19.

accordingly, saw no need to contemplate more intrusive proposals. Others disagreed, and found themselves forced to consider outright bans on the accumulation of property past a certain level. But this set of questions did not arrive suddenly on the scene in the 1780s; it was a significant feature of the political writings of the Revolutionary decade, and it is to that series of texts that I now turn.

III

If the appearance of Greek sensibilities in the writings of Madison and Jefferson is startling, such beliefs might seem even more out of place in the papers of John Adams. Adams had not only enthusiastically participated in Jefferson's geriatric jousts with Plato, but he was America's first (and last) Federalist president and Jefferson's unfortunate opponent in the bitter election of 1800. Yet on May 26, 1776, it was a younger John Adams who had written to James Sullivan on the shape of the new republic. His comments on that occasion seem so completely at odds with our inherited view of his life and beliefs that they deserve quotation in full:

> Harrington has shown that power always follows property. This I believe to be as infallible a maxim in politics, as that action and reaction are equal, is in mechanics. Nay, I believe we may advance one step farther, and affirm that the balance of power in a society, accompanies the balance of property in land. The only possible way, then, of preserving the balance of power on the side of equal liberty and public virtue, is to make the acquisition of land easy to every member of society; to make a division of land into small quantities, so that the multitude may be possessed of landed estates. If the multitude is possessed of the balance of real estates, the multitude will have the balance of power, and in that case the multitude will take care of the liberty, virtue, and interest of the multitude, in all acts of government.[43]

Here the farmer from Braintree endorses the Harringtonian case in its entirety, and insists that the government must "make a division of land into small quantities" in order to secure liberty and virtue.

In making this argument, Adams spoke not simply for himself, but for a cross-section of learned opinion that had been making this case in British North America since the early 1760s.[44] As far back as 1764, James Otis had observed in *The Rights of the British Colonies Asserted and Proved* that "it

---

[43] J. Adams, *Works*, vol. IX, p. 376.
[44] The classic discussion of Harrington's influence on American colonial charters and Revolutionary thought is H. F. Russell Smith, *Harrington and His Oceana: a Study of a 17th Century Utopia and Its Influence in America* (Cambridge University Press, 1914), chaps. 7 and 8. Russell Smith includes an especially fascinating account of William Penn's Harringtonianism (pp. 161–83), which, however, lies outside the scope of this discussion. While I make a very different case about the nature

is true in fact and *experience*, as the great, the incomparable *Harrington* has most abundantly demonstrated in his Oceana and other divine writings, that empire follows the balance of property."[45] Otis continued by lamenting that "'tis also certain that property in fact generally confers power, though the possessor of it may not have much more wit than a mole or a mugwash: and this is too often the cause that riches are sought after without the least concern for the right application of them." That same year Oxenbridge Thacher, writing in *The Sentiments of a British North American*, had bemoaned the luxury and corruption imported by Britain into the colonies, arguing that the Crown had intentionally "repealed two or or three sumptuary laws made in the colonies for restraining that luxury" for its own profit.[46] The notion that Britain was responsible for the failure of virtuous sumptuary laws to take hold in the colonies proved a durable force. In a 1778 oration commemorating the outbreak of the Revolutionary War, David Ramsay insisted that "it was the interest of Great Britain to encourage our dissipation and extravagance, for the two-fold purpose of *increasing the sale of her manufactures*, and of *perpetuating our subordination*."[47] He continues by describing how "in vain we sought to check the growth of luxury, by sumptuary laws; every wholesome restraint of this kind was sure to meet with the royal negative ... If, therefore, we had continued dependent, our frugality, industry, and simplicity of manners, would have been lost in an imitation of British extravagance, idleness, and false refinements."

Bailyn and Wood both notice that the fight against British luxury was an essential component of American Revolutionary ideology. What is more important in this context, however, is that political actors in the founding generation were prepared to endorse coercive government measures (such as sumptuary laws) in order to maintain a Harringtonian distribution of wealth – and on wholly Harringtonian grounds. In a 1778 sermon Phillips Payson lists those "circumstances much in favor of a free government and public liberty," and highlights the benefits to be derived "especially if there is a general distribution of property, and the landed interest not engrossed by a few, but possessed by the inhabitants in general through the state."[48] He

of Harrington's influence in the Revolutionary period, I am, like all scholars of early-American intellectual history, deeply indebted to this work.

[45] *Pamphlets of the American Revolution: 1750–1776*, ed. Bernard Bailyn (Cambridge, MA: Belknap, 1965), p. 423.

[46] Ibid., p. 496.

[47] *Principles and Acts of the Revolution in America*, ed. H. Niles (New York, 1822), p. 64.

[48] *American Political Writing during the Founding Era: 1760–1805*, ed. Charles S. Hyneman, and Donald S. Lutz, vol. 1 (Indianapolis: Liberty Press, 1983), p. 531.

defends this claim by insisting that "the exorbitant wealth of individuals has a most baneful influence on public virtue, and therefore should be carefully guarded against."[49] "A wicked rich man," he continues, "soon corrupts a whole neighborhood, and a few of them will poison the morals of a whole community." The best defense against this process of corruption is, as we have come to expect, "the general diffusion of knowledge" (note that Jefferson employed precisely the same terminology), which would "beget and increase that public virtue, which, under God, will prove, like the promise of the gospel, an impregnable bulwark to the state."

Payson's case is explored and developed more comprehensively in an anonymous tract entitled *Rudiments of Law and Government Deduced from the Law of Nature*, published in Charleston in 1783. In the section "On Property" the author explains that "Natural law imparts an equality of property; which however is liable to alteration from the difference of acquisition by different talents and industry." Yet, he continues, "from some fortunate circumstances, however, America has not yet departed far from the rule of right, which ought as much as possible to be observed, not only as the law of God pointed out to us, but as a just law, and as productive of happiness and safety."[50] He adds that "its efficiency with respect to the last consideration [i.e. the achievement of happiness and safety] may be evinced from the following observations," and proceeds to quote *Cato's* Harringtonian observation that "men in moderate circumstances, are most virtuous. An equality of estate, will give an equality of power; and equality of power is a natural commonwealth."

"Anonymous" then makes the key statement: "the eagerness to obtain large fortunes, arises frequently from emulation. Equality must be borne with; but superiority from incidental circumstances, not annexed to merit is galling and insufferable." The great fear in the Greek tradition is nothing other than "superiority from incidental circumstances." The author adds that "equality, or submission only to magistrates, age, and superior knowledge and wisdom, should be the prevailing disposition, and compose the spirit that pervades the whole state system. When, with the extent of property permitted, every just honour is attainable; the mind must be warped indeed, that is still dissatisfied." Yet, "how is this balance to be

---

[49] Benjamin Franklin makes a similar point in his *The Internal State of America*: "Whoever has travelled thro' the various Parts of Europe, and observed how small is the Proportion of People in Affluence or easy circumstances there, compar'd with those in Poverty and Misery . . . and views here the happy Mediocrity, that so generally prevails throughout these States, where the cultivator works for himself, and supports his family in decent Plenty, will . . . be convinc'd that no Nation that is known to us enjoys a greater Share of human Felicity" (Franklin, *Selected Writings*, vol. II, p. 123).

[50] *American Political Writing*, vol. I, p. 577.

moderately maintained?" The answer: "by ceasing to be unjust." "The reason of ordaining title by primogeniture, or to men in preference to women, arose solely from the intent of feudal tenures," and, since the reason for the practice is no more, the law should change:

A just and equal succession will diffuse property in portions not greatly dissimilar. But should this measure not have all the effect desired, real estates might be made unalienable, without particular permission. And if this won't do, further increase of property must be positively restricted.[51]

In the event that inheritance laws fail to maintain an egalitarian distribution of wealth – and thus fail to extirpate the dreaded "superiority from incidental circumstances" – the author, like Harrington and so many others in the Greek tradition, is willing to insist that the accumulation of property should be "positively restricted." One of the policies the state may adopt in this respect, as he makes clear, is the use of punitive taxes and sumptuary laws to stem the "inundation of riches."[52]

Later in the treatise, in the section entitled "Of Political Consequences," the author repeats his earlier conclusions, and like Payson, Jefferson, and so many others, ties his claims about an equal distribution of property to an argument for the "general diffusion of knowledge." He begins his discussion with a recapitulation: "The ill effect of superfluous riches has been already taken notice of: To maintain a mediocrity and equipoise, not only some must be prevented from soaring too high, but others must be encouraged to elevate their ideas, and not be permitted to consider themselves as a grovelling, distinct species, uninterested in the general welfare."[53] "Anonymous" concludes that, "for the latter defect (i.e. the dejection of the poor), education is the natural remedy. With this view schools should be established in every parish or petty district, to initiate children in learning." He argues that "by means of such seminaries of learning, many will emerge from obscurity and become shining members of the community, who would otherwise, from confinements to occupations not suited to their

---

[51] Ibid., p. 579. This passage provides a helpful reminder that those who favored the use of inheritance laws to secure an equal agrarian did not necessarily agree among themselves on exactly which measures to enact. One could, for example, argue against entails, on the grounds that they allow one nuclear family's wealth to pass intact to another nuclear family, thereby avoiding division and producing ever larger estates. But the reverse could also be argued: that only by requiring that each patrilineal family's estate remain within that family could one guard against the consolidation of different patrimonies. Likewise, one could argue (as Montesquieu does) that women should not inherit property, on the grounds that their fortunes will combine with those of their husbands and produce immoderate estates. Or one might argue that they should inherit property, since that would mean that each nuclear family's fortune would be divided in as many parts as possible.
[52] Ibid., p. 595.   [53] Ibid., p. 581.

capacities, be lost to their country and themselves."[54] The author has no doubt that, through such a program, "our country will be enriched; our manners will be polished; our minds will be illuminated."

This strand of political thought relating the rule of the best men to an equal distribution of wealth was so widespread during the period of the Revolution that in Pennsylvania in 1776 "it was debated for some time in the Convention, whether the future legislatures of this State should have the power of lessening property when it became excessive in individuals."[55] Indeed, an early draft of the state's *Declaration of Rights* included a clause arguing that, since "an enormous Proportion of Property vested in a few individuals is dangerous to the Rights, and destructive of the Common Happiness of Mankind," the legislature should make laws preventing it.[56] In commenting on this development, Wood notes that "such agrarian laws were known to be an aspect of classical Whig republicanism and were sporadically suggested by Americans throughout the Revolution." But he insists that the Pennsylvania legislature's brief flirtation with Whig political theory in 1776 represented the last gasp of these laws in early America. From then onward, "their eventual abandonment by even the most radical Whigs . . . indicates that Americans were willing to trust more to opportunity than in such legislation to bring about a general leveling."[57]

The flaw in Wood's otherwise brilliant analysis is his failure to recognize that the inheritance laws proposed successfully by Jefferson and praised throughout the literature of the period *were themselves* understood to be the most archetypal agrarian laws imaginable, prescribed by every authority in the Greek tradition from Plato to Montesquieu – as Jefferson's own comments in retrospect make clear. And while it is certainly true that the sorts of highly coercive measures endorsed by "Anonymous" and contemplated by the Pennsylvania Convention were not enacted during the early Republic, the theory underlying them was far stronger during the Ratification debates of the late 1780s than it had been during the Revolutionary decade.

IV

Noah Webster, the staunch Federalist, scholar, and lexicographer, produced *An Examination into the leading principles of the Federal Constitution* in 1787,

---

[54] Ibid., p. 582. [55] *Dunlap's Pennsylvania Packet*, Nov. 26, 1776.
[56] *An Essay of a Declaration of Rights* (Philadelphia, 1776), Article 16.
[57] Wood, *Creation of the American Republic*, p. 89.

shortly after the Philadelphia Convention had concluded its business. This text is fascinating for several reasons, but for present purposes its chief attraction lies in its status as the most forceful and influential presentation of the Greek case published in the 1780s. Webster sets out to allay Antifederalist concerns that assigning the proposed Federal government the right to tax and maintain standing armies would clear a path through the wilderness for tyranny. Such measures pose no significant threat, Webster insists, because "the source of power is in the *people* of this country, and cannot for ages, and probably never will, be removed."[58] He defends this statement by asking, "In what then does *real* power consist? The answer is short and plain – in *property*." Webster elaborates, unsurprisingly given the conventional accoutrements of the case we have been following, by reproducing the classic Harringtonian interpretation of Roman history:

> Rome exhibited a demonstrative proof of the inseparable connexion between property and dominion. The first form of its government was an elective monarchy – its second, an aristocracy; but these forms could not be permanent, because they were not supported by property. The kings at first and afterwards the patricians had nominally most of the power; but the people, possessing most of the lands, never ceased to assert their privileges, till they established a commonwealth.

Like Harrington, Neville, and Moyle before him, Webster argues that the Roman monarchy and aristocracy yielded a commonwealth because of the balance of property. Indeed, he continues by reproducing an extensive quotation from Moyle's *Essay*:

> "Thus this weak constitution of government," says Mr. Moyle, speaking of the aristocracy of Rome, "not founded on the true center of dominion, land, nor on any standing foundation of authority, nor rivetted in the esteem and affections of the people; and being attacked by strong passion, general interest and the joint forces of the people, mouldered away of course, and pined of a lingering consumption, till it was totally swallowed up by the prevailing faction, and the nobility were moulded into the mass of the people."

Rome's first two regimes were, on this view, mere apparitions without solid foundations.

The Roman republic, then, was founded on the actual distribution of property in the Roman state. As Webster has it, "by acquiring the property of the plebeians, the nobility, several times, held most of the power of the state; but the people, by reducing the interest of money, abolishing debts, or by forcing other advantages from the patricians, generally held the power of

---

[58] *Pamphlets on the Constitution of the United States*, ed. Paul L. Ford (New York: Da Capo Press, 1968), p. 57.

governing in their own hands."[59] Indeed, Webster particularly praises one very familiar measure secured by the tribunes of the plebs: "The Licinian law limited all possessions to five hundred acres of land; which, had it been fully executed, would have secured the commonwealth." Webster amplifies this view in his 1790 *Miscellaneous Remarks on Divisions of Property*. Just as, in the beginning, Rome had been a monarchy only in name, after the failure of the Licinian law, it became a republic only in name:

The causes which destroyed the ancient republics were numerous; but in Rome, one principal cause waz, the vast inequality of fortunes, occasioned partly by the stratagems of the patricians and partly by the spoils of their enemies, or the exaction of tribute in their conquered provinces. Rome, with the name of a republic, waz several ages loozing the Spirit and principle. The Gracchi endeavored to check the growing evil by an agrarian law; but were not successful.[60]

Here, by repeating Plutarch's endorsement of the Roman agrarian laws (and his reverent praise for the Gracchi), Webster makes his debts explicit.

In the *Examination* Webster then proceeds by using these principles to analyze the potential for republican government in England. He writes that "whenever the right of primogeniture is established, property must accumulate and remain in families. Thus the landed property in England will never be sufficiently distributed, to give the powers of government wholly into the hands of the people." In America, however, as he would later put it (in a stunning anticipation of Tocqueville), "a republican or free government, necessarily springs from the state of society, manners, and property in the United States."[61] His prescription for maintaining that state of affairs is both clear and predictable:

Wherever we cast our eyes, we see this truth, that *property* is the basis of *power*; and this, being established as a cardinal point, directs us to the means of preserving our freedom. Make laws, irrevocable laws in every state, destroying and barring entailments; leave real estates to revolve from hand to hand, as time and accident may direct; and no family influence can be acquired and established for a series of generations – no man can obtain dominion over a large territory – the laborious and saving, who are generally the best citizens, will possess each his share of property and power, and thus the balance of wealth and power will continue where it is, in the *body of the people*.

---

[59] Ibid., p. 58.
[60] Noah Webster, *A Collection of Essays and Fugitiv Writings, on Moral, Historical, Political and Literary Subjects* (Boston, 1790), p. 331.
[61] Webster, "An Oration on the Anniversary of the Declaration of Independence" in *American Political Writing*, vol. II, p. 1236.

Emboldened by the Harringtonian analysis of Roman history, Webster endorses the standard package of agrarian laws, and concludes that "*a general and tolerably equal distribution of landed property is the whole basis of national freedom.*" Indeed, he takes his principle one step further, insisting that "the system of the great Montesquieu will ever be erroneous, till the words *property or lands in fee simple* are substituted for *virtue*, throughout his *Spirit of Laws.*"

This last statement has attracted the attention of several scholars, some of whom have assumed that, in suggesting that "lands in fee simple" should replace "virtue" as the principle of republics, Webster was furthering a broader Federalist "turn" from "virtue" to "interest." Bailyn, for example, concludes that Webster intended to suggest that "abstract virtue – absolutely disinterested love of country – is unreal and has nothing to do with the matter."[62] But this is not straightforwardly the case. What Webster is suggesting (based, arguably, on a serious misreading of his source) is that Montesquieu conceived of political virtue as being in a sense logically prior to the equal distribution of land in republican government. Webster takes himself to be inverting this hierarchy, arguing instead that virtue is flimsy and cannot secure a commonwealth in the absence of an equal agrarian. As he puts it in a footnote, "these principles [of political virtue] are never permanent – they decay with refinement, intercourse with other nations and increase of wealth. No wonder then that these [ancient] republics declined, for they were not founded on fixed principles."[63] Harrington had made precisely the same case, as (*pace* Webster) had Montesquieu. Webster continues:

Virtue, patriotism, or love of country, never was and never will be, till mens' natures are changed a fixed, permanent principle and support of government. But in an agricultural country, a general possession of land in fee simple, may be rendered perpetual, and the inequalities introduced by commerce, are too fluctuating to endanger government. An equality of property, with a necessity of alienation, constantly operating to destroy combinations of powerful families, is the very *soul of a republic* – While this continues, the people will inevitably possess both *power* and *freedom*; when this is lost, power departs, liberty expires, and a commonwealth will inevitably assume some other form.[64]

Webster is certain that it is the equal distribution of wealth, and not virtue (certainly not what he takes to be Montesquieu's militaristic brand

---

[62] Bernard Bailyn, *Faces of the American Revolution*, p. 264. It seems that Bailyn may have inadvertently projected the late Webster onto the early Webster. Late in life, especially after his conversion to Evangelical Protestantism in 1808, Webster did indeed despair of cultivating virtue through political institutions – a transition reflected in several interesting entries in his dictionary. On this, see Diggins, *American Politics*, pp. 170–72.

[63] Webster, *Examination*, p. 61.   [64] Ibid., p. 59.

of virtue), that ultimately *produces* republican government ("*property*," he writes, "is considered as the *basis* of the freedom of the American yeomanry"). He elaborates the next year in his letter *To the Dissenting Members of the late Convention of Pennsylvania* that "*Love of country* is a powerful auxiliary motive to patriotic actions; but rarely or ever operates against *interest*."[65] Since a republic cannot withstand the pressure of wildly divergent interests produced by excessive wealth, the trick is "to connect the interest of the *Governors* with that of the *governed*" by barring "all perpetuities of estates." Webster's claim here is about the relative force of virtue and interest; not their relative value.

Indeed, virtue does not by any means drop out of the theory; as with Harrington, it furnishes the chief grounds for *preferring* republican government. As Webster puts it in his 1802 *Oration on the Anniversary of the Declaration of Independence*, "if by virtue, writers mean *pure morals*, we shall all agree that such virtue is the true, safe, and permanent foundation of a republic."[66] But Webster makes his case most passionately, as we might expect given what we have already seen of the Greek tradition in America, in his 1788 essay *On the Education of Youth in America*. Here he opens with a dramatic statement:

Two regulations are essential to the continuance of republican governments: 1. Such a distribution of lands and such principles of descent and alienation, as shall give every citizen a power of acquiring what his industry merits. 2. Such a system of education as gives every citizen an opportunity of acquiring knowledge and fitting himself for places of trust. These are fundamental articles: the *sine qua non* of the existence of the American republics.[67]

The notion that, once property levels have been equalized, general education is required in order for the state to gather the best men from every station of life is once again the classic vision expounded by Jefferson. Webster suggests as much when he observes in regard to the curriculum that "the *virtues* of men are of more consequence to society than their *abilities*: and for this reason, the *heart* should be cultivated with more assiduity than the head." The general priority remains the cultivation of a virtuous, natural aristocracy, whose existence is imperiled by the development of disproportionate wealth.

Webster makes this point at some length in his *Oration*. Equality of rights, he argues, is an essential republican value, but "if by equality, writers

---

[65] *The Documentary History of the Ratification of the Constitution*, ed. John P. Kaminski and Gaspare J. Saladino, vol. xv (Madison: State Historical Society of Wisconsin, 1984), p. 195.
[66] *American Political Writing*, vol. ii, p. 1226.   [67] Webster, *A Collection of Essays*, p. 24.

understand an equal share of talents and bodily powers; in these senses all men are not equal."[68] "Such an equality," he argues, "would be inconsistent with the whole economy of nature." There are "distinctions among men . . . they are established by nature, as well as by social relations. Age, talents, virtue, public services, the possession of office and certain natural relations, carry with them claims to distinction, to influence and authority."[69] Palpably absent from this list of claims to authority is wealth. Webster's passionate commitment to general education is predicated on the adoption of agrarian laws which eliminate the "pseudo-aristocracy" of money and property. In a clear echo of Montesquieu, Webster exclaims, "miserable, indeed, would be the condition of men, if the son could disengage himself from the authority of his father; the apprentice from the command of his master; and the citizen from the dominion of the law and magistrate."

There is, however, a second thought expressed in this passage from *On the Education of Youth in America* which is less familiar. Webster justifies the equal distribution of property on the grounds that it will "give every citizen a power of acquiring what his industry merits." He touches on a related theme in his 1790 *Miscellaneous Remarks*:

The basis of a democratic and republican form of government, iz, a fundamental law favoring an equal or rather a general distribution of property. It is not necessary nor possible that every citizen should hav exactly an equal portion of lands and goods, but the laws of such a state should require an equal distribution of intestate estates, and bar all perpetuities. Such laws occasion constant revolutions of property, and thus hold out to all men equal motivs to vigilance and industry.[70]

Webster had commented similarly in his 1787 *Remarks on the Manners, Government, and Debt of the United States* that "America is a young country, with small inequalities of property, and without manufactures. Few people

---

[68] *American Political Writing*, vol. II, p. 1229.

[69] In a review of Jonathan Jackson's *Thoughts upon the Political Situation of the United States* (discussed below) Webster reaffirms that "there are in all societies some men, who are superior to their fellow citizens in abilities and respectability," and that these men "constitute the *natural aristocracy* mentioned by Dr. Adams" (Adams had listed wealth among the defining characteristics of this group – a move Webster does not follow). However, Webster does not believe that the election of these men to political office can be required by the Constitution: "The truth is, such declarations are empty things, as they require that to be done which cannot be *defined*, much less *enforced*." This observation is part of a pattern in Webster's thought. He frequently rejects the idea that an edict on a piece of paper can have any real force (e.g. a bill of rights). If such an edict is consistent with the circumstances of the country, then it is unnecessary; if it is inconsistent with those circumstances, then it is futile. See Webster, "Review" of *Thoughts upon the Political Situation of the United States* in *American Magazine* ([New York, 1787–88]; Ann Arbor, MI: University Microfilms International, 1942), pp. 747, 804.

[70] Webster, *A Collection of Essays*, p. 326.

are here dependent on the rich, for every man has an opportunity of becoming rich himself."[71] Some states had secured this good fortune with
agrarian laws, so that, for example, "the people of New England enjoy an
equality of condition unknown in any other part of the world."[72] Beneath
this set of comments there seems to be a new ideology forming: only when
levels of property are kept temperate does the bulk of the citizenry have the
opportunity to use industry to acquire property. Furthermore, a situation
in which every man has that share of goods to which his industry entitles
him is in some sense just. This is indeed quite different from the view we
found in Jefferson and in "Anonymous." They stressed the theory of justice
which gives to every man that share of rulership to which his virtue entitles
him. But the version of the Greek case that Webster hints at would become
a powerful force, and would ultimately attract the attention of Alexis de
Tocqueville.

In the meantime, however, a second Federalist who made the full Greek
case with remarkable specificity was Jonathan Jackson of Massachusetts. In
his 1788 *Thoughts upon the Political Situation of the United States of America*
Jackson begins his discussion by praising the republican balance of property
that has taken hold in North America.

When we consider the small inequality of fortune throughout the country, compared with others which we know . . . that in most of the states the laws of primogeniture are gone or going, out of use – that landed property is in general held in
small portions, even in the southern states, compared with the manors, parks and
royal demesnes of most countries – that without the establishment of entails, it is
almost impossible for estates to grow to alarming size, or even to continue long in
the same families . . . the period must be distant, very far distant, when there can
be such a monopoly of landed estates, as to throw the suffrages or even influence of
electors into few hands . . . where is the risk of an *aristocracy* dangerous to liberty?[73]

Having disposed of the danger of a pernicious, hereditary aristocracy,
Jackson then turns to a more likely, salutary possibility. Speaking of the
American people, he writes, "if they will admit the aristocracy of experience, and of the best understandings to guide their measures, it is as much
as they will be persuaded to do . . . What I shall aim at, will be to draw
out this natural aristocracy, if it must be called so, and bring it into use,
disarmed of its malignity; endeavouring to make it a source of the greatest
publick good, by conveying authority to those, and those only, who by
nature, education, and general dispositions, are qualified for government."

[71] Ibid., p. 88.   [72] Ibid., p. 331.
[73] Jonathan Jackson, *Thoughts upon the Political Situation of the United States of America* (Worcester,
   MA, 1788), p. 56.

The rule of such men is, for Jackson, a moral requirement. "I had rather wise men to govern me," he writes, "even though at times they should be severe, than fools." He continues in the language of Rousseau:

The happiness of a free government consists in obtaining the wisest and best general will of the community, and in being sure of having it conformed to. Mankind are abundantly happier, when obliged to conform strictly to rules, if they are wise ones; as the children of the same family are, to those of a well regulated house, than where each one may do as he pleases.[74]

He adds, in regard to the natural aristocracy, "I care not where they come from, so they be men of sense and experience; let them be taken from the plough, from the mechanick's bench, or from behind the counter."[75] Here we have the Greek case set out in meticulous detail, complete with the telltale comparison of citizens to children who are benignly governed by their natural superiors (no neo-Roman theorist would ever use such language, as children are not *sui iuris*).

But this analysis of the new republic did not simply surface in an incidental way in Federalist discussion; in a very real sense it provided the foundation and justification for key elements of the Federalist case. The chief worry of the Antifederalists, after all, was that the proposed Constitution would create a massively powerful, centralized authority whose members would, in effect, become an American aristocracy.[76] The Federalists could respond using the classic Harringtonian account of the balance of power: America's agrarian, they argued, was simply too equal to accommodate an aristocratic regime. As a result, the Antifederalists had nothing to fear from the concentration of power in the new federal government. In making this case, the Federalists were identifying some essential common ground they shared with their opponents. Indeed, while it became commonplace for Federalists to accuse Antifederalists of "flattering" the people with "a Community of Goods, & a general Release of Debts,"[77] in point of fact most Antifederalists advocated exactly the same sort of egalitarian, but not equal division of property championed by Webster. The quarrel, rather, was over how best to achieve and secure it.

---

[74] Ibid., p. 58.   [75] Ibid., p. 71.

[76] It was precisely because of this anxiety that Antifederalists almost never spoke approvingly of the "natural aristocracy." They viewed this term as a pernicious Federalist disguise for an old-fashioned landed aristocracy. On this, see G. S. Wood, *Creation of the American Republic*, pp. 513–16. Wood is, however, perhaps overly anxious to accept the Anti-Federalist characterization of Federalist proposals.

[77] Letter from Charles Nisbet to the Earl of Buchan (Dec. 25, 1787) in *Documentary History*, vol. xv, p. 88.

The first in the series of letters published in Philadelphia by the Antifederalist Samuel Bryan ("Centinel") in October 1787 takes it as an axiom that

a republican, or free government, can only exist where the body of the people are virtuous, and where property is pretty equally divided; in such a government the people are the sovereign and their sense or opinion is the criterion of every public measure; for when this ceases to be the case, the nature of the government is changed, and an aristocracy, monarchy or despotism will rise on its ruin.[78]

In the 1788 *Observations of The Federal Farmer*, widely regarded as the most substantial and influential of Antifederalist pamphlets, the author (sometimes supposed to be Richard Henry Lee of Virginia) alludes to Webster's argument that because "the yeomanry of the country possess the lands, the weight of property, possess arms, and are too strong a body of men to be openly offended . . . they will take care of themselves, that men who shall govern will not dare pay any disrespect to their opinions."[79] Thus, Webster had argued, standing armies and the power of taxation could not pose a threat. The Farmer, however, insists that, without a popular veto on congressional laws, the people may "in twenty or thirty years be by means imperceptible to them, totally deprived of their boasted weight and strength."

The Farmer understood only too well the weight that Federalists such as Webster had placed on the equal agrarian. The broad and equitable distribution of land in America had served, in their arguments, as a justification for the accumulation of federal power. Such power, they contended, could not disturb the republican foundations of the state while the current distribution of land remained in place. The Farmer agreed with that assessment, but departed from his interlocutor in arguing that an unchecked Congress could undermine the vaunted balance and topple the republican regime before anyone noticed what was happening. He formulates his case quite elegantly in the fifth letter:

Instead of checks in the formation of the government, to secure the rights of the people against the usurpations of those they appoint to govern, we are to understand the equal division of lands among our people, and the strong arm furnished them by nature and situation, are to secure them against those usurpations. If there are

---

[78] *The Anti-Federalist: Writings by Opponents of the Constitution*, ed. Herbert J. Storing (University of Chicago Press, 1981), p. 16.

[79] Ibid., p. 51. This argument also appears nearly verbatim in "'The Republican' to the People," *Connecticut Courant* (Hartford), January 7, 1788. See *The Debate on the Constitution: Federalist and Antifederalist Speeches, Articles, and Letters During the Struggle over Ratification*, vol. 1, ed. Bernard Bailyn (New York: Library of America, 1993), p. 712.

advantages in the equal division of our lands, and the strong and manly habit of our people, we ought to establish governments calculated to give duration to them, and not governments which can never work naturally, till that equality of property, and those free and manly habits shall be destroyed; these evidently are not the natural basis of the proposed constitution.[80]

Standing on strong Harringtonian ground, the Farmer insists that the proposed Constitution is aristocratic, and, as such, cannot truly take hold until an aristocratic balance of property replaces the current republican one. It is, the Farmer suggests, therefore in the evident interest of the federal government to topple the equal agrarian (an arrangement he sharply differentiated from the equal distribution advocated by the "levellers, Shayites, etc.").[81]

At the moment, the Farmer rhapsodizes, America presents the spectacle of "a numerous people settled in a fertile and extensive country, possessing equality, and few or none of them oppressed with riches or wants." Americans are therefore virtuous, and "a virtuous people make just laws, and good laws tend to preserve unchanged a virtuous people."[82] A fellow Antifederalist, Melancthon Smith, would echo and develop this thought in a speech of the same year to the New York State Convention:

Those in middling circumstances, have less temptation – they are inclined by habit and the company with whom they associate, to set bounds to their passions and appetites – if this is not sufficient, the want of means to gratify them will be a restraint – they are obliged to employ their time in their respective callings – hence the substantial yeomanry of the country are more temperate, of better morals and less ambition than the great.[83]

But, as the Farmer was desperate to point out, "a virtuous and happy people by laws uncongenial to their characters, may easily be gradually changed into servile and depraved creatures."[84] Many Antifederalists were convinced that the proposed Constitution represented exactly the sort of "uncongenial" law envisioned in this warning.

---

[80] Ibid., p. 60.

[81] Ibid., p. 62. I pass over Shays's Rebellion of 1786 because its instigators did not justify their call for monetary intervention on the grounds that it would secure the rule of the wise. The reaction to the revolt does, however, furnish an important example of how strong the Ciceronian view of agrarian laws remained in America during the confederation. Although the Shayites never called for a general redistribution of wealth, Henry Knox wrote to George Washington that the agitators were "determined to annihilate all debts public and private and have agrarian laws." Benjamin Lincoln concurred that the rebels were after an "agrarian law" to equalize all holdings. For these observers, "agrarian laws" were synonymous with "unjust expropriations of property." See David P. Szatmary, *Shays' Rebellion: the Making of an Agrarian Insurrection* (Amherst, MA: University of Massachusetts Press, 1980), p. 72.

[82] *The Anti-Federalist*, p. 75.　　　[83] Ibid., p. 341.　　　[84] Ibid., p. 75.

Federalists, in turn, were quick to try to allay this particular concern. Some, like David Ramsay, simply repeated the old mantra:

In a country like our's, abounding with free men all of one rank, where property is equally diffused, where estates are held in fee simple, the press free, and the means of information common; tyranny cannot readily find admission under any form of government; but its admission is next to impossible, under one where the people are the source of all power, and elect either mediately by representatives, or immediately by themselves the whole of their rulers.[85]

Others, however, tried to engage the Antifederalists more creatively. In January 1788 the second letter from "A Freeman" appeared in the *Pennsylvania Gazette*. It set out to show how state governments would remain a vital, irreplaceable force in the new dual-sovereignty system. The author lists a series of powers retained for the states, and spends a considerable amount of time discussing one in particular:

4thly. Regulating the law of descents, and forbidding the entail of landed estates, are exclusively in the power of the state legislatures. A perfect equality, at least among the males, and possibly among the females, should be established, not only in the strict line of descent, but in the most remote collateral branches. If a man *omits* to make a will, the public should distribute his property *equally* among those who have *equal* pretensions, and who are able to render *equal* services to the community. By these means, poverty and extreme riches would be avoided, and a republican spirit would be given to our laws, not only without a violation of private rights, but consistently with the principles of justice and sound policy. This power... if exercised with wisdom and virtue, will preserve the freedom of the states beyond any other means.[86]

This passage is clearly meant to answer precisely the sort of criticism lodged by the Farmer. Antifederalists need not fear "uncongenial" federal laws affecting the balance of property, the Freeman suggests, because the all-important inheritance laws are left to the discretion of the individual states.

Almost exactly the same argument appears in a refutation of the Farmer prepared by Timothy Pickering for Charles Tillinghast in December 1787. Pickering rejects the Farmer's suggestion that "the leading men in the convention were of aristocratic principles & seized the opportunity of laying the foundation for one general *aristocratic* government for the United States."[87] After all, he argues, "if a man has virtue & abilities, tho' not worth a

---

[85] David Ramsay, "Civis: To the Citizens of South Carolina" in *Documentary History*, vol. XVI, p. 26.
[86] *Documentary History*, vol. XV, p. 509.   [87] *The Debate on the Constitution*, p. 290.

shilling, he may be the president of the United States. Does this savour of ARISTOCRACY?" "On the contrary," he continues, "does it not manifest the marked regard of the Convention to the equal rights of the people, without suffering mere *wealth* to hold the smallest preeminence over *poverty* attended with *virtue* and *abilities*." Pickering concludes that, if a pseudo-aristocracy should arise in America, it will not be the fault of the federal government:

> If great *hereditary estates*, the foundation of *nobility*, are suffered to *continue* or to be *created* by entails it will be the fault, of the individual states, and not of the general government of the union. The laws of most, if not all, of the states admit the distribution of the property of a deceased citizen among all his children; and no *entails* ought to be permitted. And when existing entails shall be broken, & future ones forbidden, we may make ourselves easy about aristocratic ambition. Great accumulations of wealth will then be rare, of short continuance, and consequently never dangerous.[88]

The equal agrarian lies in the hands of the states, and, as a result, federal power need not be feared. The natural *aristoi* will be harvested efficiently from every corner and stratum of society. Once again, a Harringtonian analysis becomes the basis for the Federalist case.

In the last analysis, perhaps the best measure of this tradition's impact on Federalist thought is the extent to which its logic was accepted even by those who had no patience for its policy recommendations. The ideal example in this respect is Alexander Hamilton. Famous for his attachment to "the interests and opinions of men" rather than the "speculative parchment provisions" of republican writers,[89] Hamilton nonetheless declared his agreement with the descriptive claims of the Greek tradition in important remarks to the New York State Convention:

> While property continues to be pretty equally divided, and a considerable share of information pervades the community, the tendency of the people's suffrage will be to elevate merit even from obscurity. As riches increase and accumulate in a few hands, as luxury prevails in society, virtue will be in greater degree considered only as a graceful appendage of wealth, and the tendency of things will be to depart from the republican standard.[90]

The difference is that, on Hamilton's view, this process is inevitable; it is, quite simply, the American destiny. "This is the real disposition of human

---

[88] Ibid., p. 291.
[89] *The Debates in the Several State Conventions on the Adoption of the Federal Constitution*, ed. Jonathan Elliot, vol. ii (Philadelphia: J. B. Lippincott Co., 1907), p. 251.
[90] Ibid., p. 256.

nature," he writes, "it is what neither the honorable member [Melancthon Smith, to whom he is replying] nor myself can correct; it is a common misfortune, that awaits our state constitution as well as others." The problem can only be somewhat mitigated by the incorporation of a large, federal system in which "the corruption of electors is much more difficult." Even a stalwart of "interest" such as Hamilton, it would seem, was drawn to the language of the Greek tradition.

I cannot, however, leave the present analysis of this tradition during the fight for ratification without taking a moment to consider the curious example of John Adams. Recall that Adams, a committed Federalist, had endorsed the Harringtonian case in the 1770s; he reaffirmed his sympathies in his 1776 *Thoughts on Government*, where he went so far as to embrace wartime sumptuary laws:

> The very mention of sumptuary laws will excite a smile. Whether our countrymen have wisdom and virtue enough to submit to them, I know not; but the happiness of the people might be greatly promoted by them, and a revenue saved sufficient to carry on this war [i.e. the Revolutionary War] forever. Frugality is a great revenue, besides curing us of vanities, levities, and fopperies, which are real antidotes to all great, manly, and warlike virtues.[91]

Later in life, however, Adams had developed an idiosyncratic political theory which distinguished him sharply from those discussed above. In particular, he endorsed an understanding of the term "natural aristocracy" which was quite different from Jefferson's or from that of any other North American of the period with Greek sensibilities. For Adams, the natural aristocracy was not to be contrasted with the "pseudo-aristocracy" of wealth. Indeed, he writes in an 1813 letter to Jefferson that "your distinction between natural and artificial Aristocracy does not appear to me well founded."[92] For Adams, any faculty or asset which, in the natural course of things, tends to attract followers and power to a given individual makes its holder a "natural aristocrat." He offers a partial list of such characteristics: "Education, Wealth, Strength, Beauty, Stature, Birth, Marriage, graceful Attitudes and Motions, Gait, Air, Complexion, Physiognomy . . . as well as Genius and Science and Learning."[93] The bearers of these traits represent *de facto* a separate caste of men, with separate interests, who have to be accommodated in a separate house of the legislature. With an analysis such as this one, Adams had certainly parted company with the Greek tradition. Indeed, one of the central claims of that tradition is precisely that, given a temperate distribution of wealth, and a prudential allocation of political power, the natural aristocrats

---

[91] J. Adams, *Works*, vol. IV, p. 199.   [92] *Adams–Jefferson Letters*, p. 400.   [93] Ibid., p. 398.

will *not* have different interests from those of the rest of the citizens. All will simply seek the common good.

But Adams retains enough of a commitment to the normative idea of a "natural aristocracy" (as Harrington and Jefferson use the term) to incorporate the full range of Harringtonian terminology and topoi into his political writings. In the 1787 *Defence of the Constitutions of Government of the United States,* he agrees with Harrington that there is a "natural aristocracy, diffused by God throughout the whole body of mankind, to this end and purpose [i.e. to guide the commonwealth]; and, therefore, such as the people have not only a natural, but a positive obligation to make use of as their guides."[94] Although he fumes openly about those who seek to undermine the sanctity of private property, exclaiming "is it not an insult to common sense, for a people with the same breath to cry *liberty,* an *abolition of debts,* and *division of goods?*," he can also place a massive paraphrase of Harrington's argument about the dangers of disproportionate wealth at the center of the first volume of the *Defence.* Adams recalls his mentor's admonition that "riches will hold the first place, in civilized societies, at least, among the principles of power, and will often prevail, not only over all the principles of authority, but over all the advantages of birth, knowledge, and fame."[95] Harrington discovered that "empire follows the balance of property, whether lodged in one, a few, or many hands"; this is "a noble discovery, of which the honor solely belongs to [Harrington], as much as the circulation of the blood to Harvey . . ." (Harrington himself had suggested this comparison).[96]

Applying this principle to the American example, Adams reaches the predictable Federalist conclusions. "In America, the right of sovereignty resides indisputably in the body of the people, and they have the whole property of land. There are no nobles or patricians; all are equal by law and by birth."[97] Later on, Adams notes similarly that

the agrarian in America is divided among the common people in every state, in such a manner, that nineteen twentieths of the property would be in the hands of the commons, let them appoint whom they could for chief magistrate and senators. The sovereignty then, in fact, as well as morality, must reside in the whole body of the people.[98]

A hereditary order of legislators or magistrates, Adams argues, could not come into being in America "until great quantities of property shall get

[94] J. Adams, *Works,* vol. IV, p. 412.   [95] Ibid., p. 427.   [96] Ibid., p. 428.   [97] Ibid., p. 309.
[98] Ibid., p. 359.

into few hands." Indeed, Adams goes so far as to attribute victory in the American Revolution to the popular balance of property. Harrington, he points out, had insisted that even force could not in the long run impose a government that runs counter to the balance of property in a given state. In America, Adams continues, "the balance of land, especially in New England, where the force was first applied, was neither in the king nor a nobility, but immensely in favor of the people. The intention of the British politicians was to alter this balance . . . We have seen the effects. The balance destroyed that which opposed it."[99]

In Adams, then, we find a notoriously complex case. Passionately committed to the defense of private property, and often accused (unjustly) in his own lifetime of having aristocratic proclivities, he remained committed to the Harringtonian balance. This tension spills out most dramatically in the contrast between Adams's two accounts of the Roman agrarian movement in the *Defence*. The first appears in volume I in the context of Adams's survey of the historical experiences of the various ancient republics. In this instance, he takes his account of Roman history directly from Adam Ferguson's *History of the Progress and Termination of the Roman Republic*, a text which largely follows the ancient Roman sources in their disdain for the agrarian movement.[100] Adams quotes Ferguson directly when he writes that, after the Coriolanus episode, a dispute arose "which served to the last hour of the republic as an object of popular zeal, and furnished a specious pretense to ambitious and deigning men to captivate the ears of the populace – an equal division of land, known by the name of an agrarian law."[101] Adams editorializes here in adding that "by this was by no means meant a community of goods and lands, or an equal division of all the lands and goods; the Roman people had too much sense and honesty ever to think of introducing into practice such an absurd figment of the brain." On the contrary, Adams explains quoting Ferguson, the lands in question were tracts of *ager publicus* that had been allowed to "pass by connivance, occupancy, or purchase into the hands of powerful citizens."

At this point, Adams continues *in propria persona*, "Spurius Cassius, the consul, who was in favor with the people, and affected still farther popularity by flattering the passions of the inferior classes" announced his

---

[99] Ibid., p. 430.

[100] Adam Ferguson, *The History of the Progress and Termination of the Roman Republic* (London, 1837), esp. chap. 2.

[101] J. Adams, *Works*, vol. IV, pp. 526–27. Ferguson's text is slightly different (*Roman Republic*, p. 10).

intention to redivide the recently conquered lands among the plebs. Paraphrasing Ferguson, Adams explains that Spurius Cassius then made a grave error:

The patricians were alarmed; but Cassius had numbers on his side, and was so confident of success, that he betrayed too soon his ambitious design, by offering the freedom of the city to aliens, who, at his invitation, crowded from all parts to vote in the assemblies of the Roman people. This convinced all parties that his views were, by the means of alien and indigent citizens, to usurp the government. All parties combined against him, and he was condemned for treason.[102]

This is in every sense the account of the Roman agrarian movement we would expect from a careful reader of Livy and Cicero (as Ferguson certainly was). Here, Spurius Cassius is judged to have advanced a destructive, seditious law in order to "flatter" the people and achieve an "ambitious design." Later in this section Adams uncritically quotes Ferguson's account of the Gracchan laws, in which Tiberius Gracchus is said to have "formed a project in itself extremely alarming, and in its consequences dangerous to the peace of the republic."[103]

In the third volume of the *Defence*, however, Adams presents a very different account of the same episode. By this stage in the work, he had turned to a critical analysis of famous republican authors, and had arrived at last at Marchamont Nedham. Adams spends a considerable amount of time rebutting Nedham's Machiavellian suggestion that the people are admirable guardians of their own liberty, and that, accordingly, there was nothing to be feared from a single, sovereign popular assembly. Adams, who dreaded "simple democracy" as much as he feared "simple aristocracy," championed a mixed regime. Accordingly, in this section of the *Defence*, he provides a series of examples of popular stupidity and ingratitude designed to undermine Nedham's case. One of these, oddly enough, is the case of Spurius Cassius. For the sake of perspective, it is important to recall that even *within* the Greek tradition, Spurius Cassius had always been dismissed as an opportunist who had tried to use the noble agrarian cause to achieve dictatorial powers. Authors in the Greek tradition beginning with Plutarch had lionized the Gracchi, not Spurius Cassius. From John Adams in 1787 we receive, as far as I am aware, the very first *apologia* for Spurius Cassius in the history of Western political thought.

---

[102] J. Adams, *Works*, vol. IV, p. 527.
[103] Ibid., p. 539. Cf. Ferguson, *Roman Republic*, p. 84.

Adams recounts how Spurius Cassius proposed the agrarian law to the senate, and offers the following commentary:

This law, which had at least a great appearance of equity, would have relieved the misery of the people, and no doubt rendered Cassius popular. The Romans never granted peace to their enemies until they had taken some of their territory from them. Part of such conquests were sold to defray the expense of the war; another portion was distributed among the poor plebeians. Some cantons were farmed out for the public; rapacious patricians, solely intent upon enriching themselves, took possession of some; and these lands, unjustly usurped by the rich, Cassius was for having distributed anew in favor of the plebeians.[104]

In response to this proposal, "the aristocratical pride, avarice, and ambition, were all incensed, and the senators greatly alarmed." Accordingly they decided that "some device or other must be invented to dupe the people and ruin their leader," and resolved to accept the law only on the condition that it be restricted to Romans, and not extended to Latins. "This distinction," Adams continues, "without the least appearance of equity, was addressed simply to the popular hatred between the Romans and the Latins, and the bait was greedily swallowed." The Romans were encouraged to suspect Spurius Cassius of including the Latins in his proposals in order to amass absolute power. When "he continued his friendly intentions towards the people and proposed in the senate to reimburse, as it was but just, out of the public treasury, the money which poor citizens had paid for the corn [during the recent shortage]," the people took this as further evidence of personal ambition. The result: "the agrarian law was opposed in the senate . . . and evaded by the appointment of ten commissioners to survey the lands." Spurius Cassius, for his part, was accused of attempting to subvert the republic, and was mercilessly killed. "So ignorant, so unjust, so ungrateful, and so stupid, were that very body of plebeians who were continually suffering the cruel tyranny of patricians, and continually soliciting protectors against it!"[105]

It is tempting here to accuse Adams of trying to be more Greek than the Greeks. Spurius Cassius is described as a disinterested great man, whose laws were designed to correct palpable injustices in the state, and who ended up a victim of patrician rapaciousness and plebeian gullibility. Reconciling this picture of the agrarian movement with the one Adams had been content to paste into the first volume is no easy task. In a sense, a *rapprochement* should not even be attempted. Adams wrote the three volumes of the *Defence* in two months in 1787, giving the work, as its first editor remarked,

---

[104] J. Adams, *Works*, vol. VI, p. 40.   [105] Ibid., p. 42.

a decidedly scattered and inconsistent feel. There is therefore little reason
to suppose that all of its disparate elements should cohere into a single
argument. Perhaps we are fortunate that the text was produced under such
harried conditions. In its current form, it preserves a snapshot of the deep
ideological ambivalence of its author, a man who never quite reconciled his
deep attachment to private property with his Greek sensibilities.

v

In the years following the ratification of the Constitution, and throughout
the first decade of the new federal republic, the Greek tradition remained
a vibrant force in American political theory. A sermon Perez Fobes delivered in Boston in 1795 makes the point nicely. Confronting the frighten-
ing prospect of "exorbitant wealth in the hands of individuals,"[106] Fobes
declared straightforwardly that "*national wealth, especially when carefully
accumulated in the hands of a few individuals, is dangerous in the extreme to
human liberty.*" Opulence, Fobes argued, "is the common parent of idleness,
luxury and dissipation &c. The reflection of a moment will convince us,
that wealth is both the object and principal cause of avarice and ambition."
Moreover, wealth's "influence on civic elections is still more pernicious.
Money is frequently the most forcible logic, and he that carries the longest
purse, will often carry the most votes." Having raised the classic Greek objection that disproportionate wealth ensures that money rather than virtue
will determine the distribution of power, Fobes then addressed it in indisputably Greek terms: "In this view of wealth, we see and admire the policy
as well as the justice of a late act of our legislature, which rescinded an old
fragment of monarchy too long worn as the right of primogeniture." Fobes
added that "we feel also, and revere the wisdom of GOD in the appointment
of a jubilee, as an essential article in the Jewish policy. This, it is probable,
was the great palladium of liberty to that people. A similar institution perhaps may be the only method in which liberty can be perpetuated among
selfish, degenerate beings in every government under heaven." Once again
the repeal of primogeniture, and, indeed, the rescission of debts, is lauded,
both in its "policy" and its "justice," on the familiar grounds that it will
allow virtue to have its day.

For a similar example, we might look to an 1801 sermon of Jeremiah
Atwater delivered in Middlebury, Vermont. In his paean to American government and culture Atwater stressed that "property, in this country, is

---

[106] *American Political Writing*, vol. II, p. 1000.

pretty equally divided among the people, and the principles of a just and equal distribution are recognized and established by the laws, which regulate the descent of estates."[107] He was grateful that "an ocean of three thousand miles has separated us from the vices of an old and corrupt world. With a soil, not so spontaneously productive as to encourage idleness, but sufficiently fertile to repay the annual loan of industry, the innocent employments of an agricultural life have blessed us with health and happiness." Atwater continued in ringing tones:

> The feudal distinctions of tenant and lord are here unknown. In most European countries, the dependence of the peasants on the rich, produces, on the one side, idleness and pride, and on the other, depression and humiliating debasement. The dependence of our citizens is only on each other, for the supply of mutual wants; which produces mutual confidence and good-will in the interchange of kind offices.[108]

Atwater, like Fobes, focused attention on the deleterious effects of extreme wealth and poverty on both rich and poor, and praised the "just and equal distribution" of wealth that the American agrarian laws had secured.

These two texts, taken together, raise an interesting possibility. It has long been supposed that the path recommended by "classical republicanism" or "radical Whig thought" was "the road not taken" in late eighteenth-century America. Numerous scholars, following the trajectory sketched out by Gordon Wood, have argued that, if the Revolution signaled in large measure the apotheosis of classical political theory, then the Constitution signaled its final and conclusive rejection. Interest was put forward to replace virtue, massive scale was preferred to small communities of civic brotherhood, and the distinguished notion of a mixed constitution reflecting a balance of social types was finally put to rest. Each of these claims is compelling. But Perez Fobes and Jeremiah Atwater could look back on the upheavals of the 1770s and 1780s and conclude that what we have called the Greek tradition had emerged victorious. Through the sorts of laws recommended by Plato, Harrington, and Montesquieu, America had secured an "equal agrarian."

By the turn of the century, as James Kent reported in his 1840 *Commentaries on American Law*, laws repealing primogeniture and guaranteeing the equal division of estates among lineal descendants had been adopted in almost every state in the Union.[109] Those legislators who drafted the

---

[107] Ibid., p. 1178.   [108] Ibid.

[109] James Kent, *Commentaries on American Law*, vol. IV (New York, 1844), p. 374. The exceptions were Connecticut (which continued to grant the eldest son a double share of intestate estates) and New

state laws abolishing entails and primogeniture left little doubt as to their motivation. The preamble of the 1784 North Carolina bill reads in part:

WHEREAS it will tend to promote that equality of property which is of the spirit and principle of a genuine republic, that the real estates of persons dying intestate should undergo a more general and equal distribution than has hitherto prevailed in this state ... And whereas entails of estates tend only to raise the wealth and importance of particular families and individuals, giving them an unequal and undue influence in a republic, and prove in manifold instances the source of great contention and injustice.[110]

Here we have an unambiguously Greek justification of the agrarian program, complete with the Montesquieuan language of *esprit* and *principe*. Similarly, Delaware's 1794 bill abolishing the practice of assigning a double portion of inheritance to the eldest son (the so-called "Jewish" or "Hebrew agrarian") justifies itself in the preamble by observing that "it is the duty and policy of every republican government to preserve equality amongst its citizens, by maintaining the balance of property as far as it is consistent with the rights of individuals."[111] Looking back on measures such as these and

---

Jersey and North Carolina (which mandated the equal division of estates among male children only). All other American states adopted partible inheritance between 1784 and 1798. See Shammas et al., *Inheritance in America*, pp. 64–65. The same policy was adopted for the Northwest Territory in an "Ordinance of Congress" on July 13, 1787. See Kent, *Commentaries*, vol. IV, p. 375.

110 Reproduced in Stanley N. Katz, "Republicanism and the Law of Inheritance in the American Revolutionary Era" in *Michigan Law Review* 76 (1977), 14. See also "A Declaration of Rights" (North Carolina), Secs. 22, 23 in *The Federal and State Constitutions*, ed. Francis Newton Thorpe, vol. V (Washington, DC: Government Printing Office, 1909), p. 2787. Katz deserves a great deal of credit for being the only scholar to consider the Revolutionary inheritance laws in any detail from an ideological point of view. Yet he interprets the rejection of primogeniture and entails during the Revolutionary era as the expression of a rather amorphous egalitarian sensibility, when in fact, as we have seen, it is better understood as an attempt to preserve the rule of the best men – in accordance with a particular theory of justice. In discussing the Revolutionary inheritance laws, Wood quotes Jefferson's comments about the "natural aristocracy," but neglects to connect them to the tradition we have been following, or to assess the extent to which they were representative. See G. S. Wood, *Radicalism of the American Revolution*, p. 184. Shammas, Salmon, and Dahlin supply an important corrective when they note that, even in colonies where inheritance laws favored eldest sons, most testators made a more equitable division of their estates. They also point out that entails were extremely rare in the colonies, with the important exception of tidewater Virginia (p. 56). Such continuities are indeed important, but I do feel that, in arguing against Katz, Shammas, Salmon, and Dahlin make far too little of the ideological impact of the Revolution (pp. 64–67).

111 Katz, "Law of Inheritance," 15. However, not all of the bills establishing partible inheritance among intestates were as explicit about their ideological allegiances. Georgia's bill of 1789, for example, included no preamble of any kind. See *AN ACT To Explain the fifty first Article of the Constitution respecting Intestate Estates and also concerning marriages* in *The Colonial Records of the State of Georgia: Statutes, Colonial and Revolutionary*, ed. Allen D. Chandler, vol. XIX (part 2) (New York: AMS Press, 1970), pp. 455–58. See also *Constitution of Georgia* (1777), Art. 51 (ed. Thorpe, vol. II, p. 784). Likewise, but for a passing reference to the importance of a "just and equal distribution" of intestate property, the Pennsylvania bill of 1794 contained no justificatory prose. See

the ideological fervor that generated them, we can perhaps forgive Fobes and Atwater for believing that America had taken the Greek road after all.

Yet the prevalence of the Greek tradition within the political literature of the Revolution and Ratification Debates provides little in the way of support for those postwar scholars who have attempted to locate a proto-socialist radicalism in the era of the Founding.[112] There is indeed no sense in which the Greek tradition can serve as a foothold for the agenda of the contemporary Left in the pre-history of the Constitution. Jefferson and Webster were certainly prepared to recommend the adoption of redistri-butionary measures, but only in the service of explicitly hierarchical ends. Theorists in the Greek tradition advocated the redistribution of wealth so that they could institute and preserve a particular structure of rulership: a structure in which a few elect, virtuous men rule, and all the rest are ruled. If such a program seems fairly foreign to us, we are bound to smile when we reflect on the ideological origins of our redistributionary schemes.

An ACT directing the descent of intestates' real estates, and distribution of their personal estates, and for other purposes therein mentioned in *Laws of the Commonwealth of Pennsylvania, From the Seventh day of December, one thousand seven hundred and ninety, to the Twentieth Day of April, one thousand seven hundred and ninety-five*, ed. Alexander James Dallas, vol. III (Philadelphia, 1795), pp. 521–33.

[112] See, for example, Sean Wilentz, "America's Lost Egalitarian Tradition" in *Daedalus* (2002), 66–80, as well as William Connell's insightful comments about the communitarian and socialist appropriation of Pocock's "classical republicanism" in William J. Connell, "The Republican Idea" in *Renaissance Civic Humanism: Reappraisals and Reflections*, ed. James Hankins (Cambridge University Press, 2000), esp. pp. 23–24. Bailyn likewise canvases this argument (*Faces of the American Revolution*, p. 187).

Coda: Tocqueville and the Greeks

Alexis de Tocqueville seems at first glance to have no place in a story about Greek republicanism. His greatest work, *Democracy in America*, has been characterized routinely as the first intimation of a fundamentally new age and the unveiling of a new approach to political reasoning. As Tocqueville himself puts it, his study of American democracy exhibits "a new political science for a world completely new."[1] This is a statement worth taking seriously. Tocqueville's belief that mankind no longer faces a choice among different regimes leads him to abandon the standard search for the *optimus status reipublicae*. The rise and global victory of democracy is "fated," he tells us, and nations can only hope to control "whether equality leads them to servitude or liberty, to enlightenment or barbarism, to prosperity or misery."[2] In short, for Tocqueville, political science in the modern world is left with the relatively modest task of identifying the *optimus status democratiae*. But Tocqueville's critique of the republican tradition goes far deeper. Apart from insisting that men of his day have no real choice of regimes, he is clear that no form of government is "best" at all times, or always promotes human flourishing better than all the others. He argues that "the political powers which seem best established have no safeguard of their longevity aside from the opinions of one generation, the interests of one century, or often the life of one man ... There has never been a government which is based on some invariable disposition of the

---

[1] All quotations from *Democracy in America* are taken from Alexis de Tocqueville, *De la démocratie en Amérique*, with a preface by André Jardin, 2 vols. (Paris: Librairie Gallimard, 1986). All translations are my own. "Il faut une science politique nouvelle à un monde tout nouveau" (vol. I, p. 43).

[2] "Les nations de nos jours ne sauraient faire que dans leur sein les conditions ne soient pas égales; mais il dépend d'elles que l'égalité les conduise à la servitude ou à la liberté, aux lumières ou à la barbarie, à la prosperité ou aux misères" (ibid., vol. II, p. 455). On this, see Catherine H. Zuckert, "Political Sociology Versus Speculative Philosophy" in *Interpreting Tocqueville's* Democracy in America, ed. Ken Masugi (Savage, MD: Rowman and Littlefield, 1991).

human heart, nor one which could found itself on an immortal interest."[3] Nature has been replaced by circumstance as the source of political principles.

This deeply historical vision of political society in turn leads Tocqueville to an unabashed appreciation of what Machiavelli called the "effectual truth" (*la verità effettuale*), the "facts on the ground."[4] Different historical moments have different needs, and those needs determine political principles and, to some extent, the moral apparatus that underlies them. For example, Tocqueville ascribes to the Americans a moral philosophy based on "self-interest rightly understood" (*l'intérêt bien entendu*), according to which they perform virtuous actions because they believe those actions will bring them benefits – and that the resulting benefits will outweigh any costs associated with performing the actions. This theory, writes Tocqueville, is not as noble or beautiful as one which recommends virtue for its own sake, nor does "self-interest rightly understood" inspire the great acts of self-sacrifice that have animated other societies. Tocqueville explicitly contrasts this "virtue as interest" approach to a Platonist notion of virtue, in which man "sees that the purpose of God is order; he assimilates himself freely to this grand design, and, in sacrificing his particular interests to this admirable order of all things, he expects no other reward than the pleasure of contemplating it."[5] This Platonist idea of virtue is "sublime," but nonetheless, Tocqueville concludes, "I will not hesitate to say that the doctrine of self-interest rightly understood seems to me, of all the philosophical theories, the most attuned to the needs of men in our time, and I see in it the most powerful safeguard men have left against themselves."[6] He continues by urging contemporary moralists to embrace this theory, though imperfect, because its adoption is "necessary" if virtue is to be preserved in an age of interest. As Arthur Schlesinger, Jr. summarizes Tocqueville's thinking, "the city-state was founded on virtue, the nation-state on interest. The problem

---

[3] "Les puissances politiques qui paraissent le mieux établies n'ont pour garantie de leur durée que les opinions d'une génération, les intérêts d'un siècle, souvent la vie d'un homme...et l'on n'a jamais vu de gouvernement qui se soit appuyé sur une disposition invariable du cœur humain, ni qui ait pu se fonder sur un intérêt immortel" (Tocqueville, *Démocratie*, vol. i, p. 440).

[4] See Niccolò Machiavelli, *Il principe*, in *Opere*, ed. Mario Bonfantini (Milan: Riccardo Ricciardi, 1963), p. 50 (chapter xv).

[5] "il voit que le but de Dieu est l'ordre; il s'associe librement à ce grand dessein; et, tout en sacrifiant ses intérêts particuliers à cet ordre admirable de toutes choses, il n'attend d'autres récompenses que le plaisir de le contempler" (Tocqueville, *Démocratie*, vol. ii, p. 179).

[6] "Je ne craindrai pas dire que la doctrine de l'intérêt bien entendu me semble, de toutes les théories philosophiques, la mieux appropriée aux besoins des hommes de notre temps, et que j'y vois la plus puissante garantie qui leur reste contre eux-mêmes" (ibid., p. 176).

was to make private interest the moral equivalent of public virtue."[7] For Tocqueville, even views of morality must bend to the demands of the age.

Thus, Tocqueville is without question a very different sort of philosopher from those I have been discussing. But, strikingly, it is not Tocqueville's repudiation of a fixed account of human nature which has seemed most novel to scholars, but rather his notion of the *état social*. Several recent students of Tocqueville have seen this aspect of his thought as an innovation which should secure his status as the founder of social science. For Harvey Mansfield, Tocqueville's "social state" was a "new feature" which, for the first time, shattered the "liberal (or Rousseauian) distinction between state and society that derives from a prepolitical, presocial situation called the state of nature."[8] Likewise, for J. G. A. Pocock, it was through this concept of *état social* that "Tocqueville charted the transition from equality in its Machiavellian or Montesquieuan sense – *isonomia* or equality of subjection to the *res publica* – which had been part of the ideal of virtue, to that of *égalité des conditions* which he saw as marking the triumph of democracy in its modern sense, superseding the values of the classical republic."[9] Thus, the "social state" is seen as a fundamentally new notion which allowed Tocqueville to leave behind both the classical-republican and natural-law traditions, and to embark on a new theoretical path.

To be sure, not all scholars have embraced this abstracted view of Tocqueville's *état social*. Aurelian Craiutu, for example, prefers to derive Tocqueville's "social state" from the French *doctrinaires* of the nineteenth century, such as François Guizot, Pierre Royer-Collard, and Charles de Rémusat. He then assigns to these thinkers the credit for having first identified democracy as "a new type of *society*," rather than a "form of government,"[10] and for having espoused "an original *sociological* approach, which stressed the influence of the social order on the functioning of political

---

[7] Arthur Schlesinger, Jr., "Individualism and Apathy in Tocqueville's *Democracy*" in *Reconsidering Tocqueville's Democracy in America*, ed. Abraham S. Eisenstadt (New Brunswick, NJ: Rutgers University Press, 1988), p. 96.

[8] Harvey C. Mansfield and Delba Winthrop, "Introduction" to Alexis de Tocqueville, *Democracy in America*, ed. and trans. Harvey C. Mansfield and Delba Winthrop (University of Chicago Press, 2000), p. xliv.

[9] J. G. A. Pocock, *The Machiavellian Moment: Florentine Political Thought and the Atlantic Republican Tradition* (Princeton University Press, 1975), p. 537.

[10] Aurelian Craiutu, "Tocqueville and the Political Thought of the French Doctrinaires (Guizot, Royer-Collard, Rémusat)" in *History of Political Thought* 20 (1999), 485. See also Georgios Varouxakis, "Guizot's Historical Works and J. S. Mill's Reception of Tocqueville" in *History of Political Thought* 20 (1999), 292–312.

institutions."[11] But in suggesting that the distribution of property shapes mores and determines the distribution and exercise of political power (and is, therefore, in a sense "prior" to political structures), Tocqueville was drawing on a much older line of thought. Indeed, his discussion of the *état social* is very much within the Greek tradition we have been following.

Tocqueville addresses the "social state" of the Americans early in the first volume of *Democracy*. He explains that "equality of conditions" constitutes a "democratic social state" which in turn supports democratic government. What is not often noticed is that this observation had long been a commonplace of early American historiography and political theory. David Ramsay, for example, wrote in his 1789 *History of the American Revolution* that in the American colonies "a sameness of circumstances and occupations created a great sense of equality, and disposed them to union in any common cause, from the success of which, they might expect to partake of equal advantages."[12] Likewise, as we have seen, Noah Webster and others routinely insisted that "a republican or free government, necessarily springs from the state of society, manners, and property in the United States."[13] As a result of this ideological commitment, the American Founders, like Harrington and Montesquieu before them, placed enormous weight on the significance of inheritance laws in bringing about the equal agrarian.

Tocqueville replicates this analysis with remarkable exactitude, making it somewhat strange that this aspect of his thought has received so little scholarly attention:[14]

I am surprised that the ancient and modern writers have not attributed a larger influence in the progress of human affairs to inheritance laws. These laws, it is

---

[11] Craiutu, "Tocqueville," 487.

[12] *American Political Writing during the Founding Era: 1760–1805*, ed. Charles S. Hyneman and Donald S. Lutz, vol. II (Indianapolis: Liberty Press, 1983), p. 725.

[13] Webster, "An Oration on the Anniversary of the Declaration of Independence" in *American Political Writing*, vol. II, p. 1236.

[14] Even Jean-Claude Lamberti, who provides an excellent account of Tocqueville's *état social*, almost wholly neglects this aspect of the subject. See Lamberti, *Tocqueville and the Two Democracies*, trans. Arthur Goldhammer (Harvard University Press, 1989), pp. 15–17, 25–39. In a study of Jefferson's influence on Tocqueville, James Schleifer makes passing reference to the question of inheritance laws, but then adds a remarkable footnote: "Tocqueville failed to realize that Jefferson himself exaggerated the significance of the abolition in Virginia of the laws of primogeniture and entail." If by this he means that the new laws did not have a significant effect on the actual practices of testators, then it is not a point I care to argue (although, see Holly Brewer, "Entailing Aristocracy in Colonial Virginia: 'Ancient Feudal Restraints' and Revolutionary Reform" in *The William and Mary Quarterly* 54 [1997], 307–46). If, however, he means that these laws were not of staggering ideological consequence at the time, he is surely mistaken. See James T. Schleifer, "Jefferson and Tocqueville" in *Interpreting Tocqueville's* Democracy in America, ed. Ken Masugi (Savage, MD: Rowman and Littlefield, 1991), p. 178n.

true, pertain to the civil order, but they must be placed at the head of all political institutions, since they have an incredible influence on the social state of peoples, of which the political laws are a mere expression.[15]

Montesquieu, who had called inheritance laws the mainstay of republican government, could hardly have said it better.[16] Tocqueville adds that "the lawgiver regulates the inheritances of citizens just once, and he can rest for centuries. His work having been put in motion, he can withdraw his hand. The mechanism works by its own forces, and directs itself as if of its own accord toward its appointed goal."[17] He is even more emphatic later in the first volume, where he claims rather grandly that "no great change in human institutions takes place where one does not find inheritance laws among its causes."[18] On Tocqueville's account, these inheritance laws can tend in one of two radically opposed directions. On the one hand, "constituted in a certain manner, the law reunites, concentrates, and groups property – and soon afterwards power – around a single individual. In a way, it causes an aristocracy to sprout out of the soil."[19] Once again we have the standard Harringtonian view: the balance of property determines the balance of power. If property is allowed to accumulate in the hands of a few men, aristocratic government is the result. This, argues Tocqueville, was precisely what transpired in the early years of the American south. The settlers brought with them the English aristocratic inheritance law; wealth quickly began to concentrate in a very few hands, and the resulting wealthy elite gathered to itself the bulk of political power.[20] In a note,

[15] "Je m'étonne que les publicistes anciens et modernes n'aient pas attribué aux lois sur les successions une plus grande influence dans la marche des affaires humaines. Ces lois appartiennent, il est vrai, à l'ordre civil; mais elles devraient être placées en tête de toutes les institutions politiques, car elles influent incroyablement sur l'état social des peuples, dont les lois politiques ne sont que l'expression" (Tocqueville, *Démocratie*, vol. 1, p. 96).

[16] Indeed, the first sentence of the above passage is somewhat unexpected, since Tocqueville was a careful reader of both Plato and Montesquieu and was surely familiar with their intense interest in inheritance laws. Perhaps he saw his own account as building on the interventions of his predecessors, and assigning an even more prominent place to these laws.

[17] "le législateur règle une fois la succession des citoyens, et il se repose pendant des siècles: le mouvement donné à son œuvre, il peut en retirer la main: la machine agit par ses propres forces, et se dirige comme d'elle-même vers un but indiqué d'avance" (Tocqueville, *Démocratie*, vol. 1, p. 96).

[18] "Il ne se fait pas un grand changement dans les institutions humaines sans qu'au milieu des causes de ce changement on ne découvre la loi des successions" (ibid., p. 510). See also Tocqueville's analysis of the distribution of land in *L'Ancien Régime et la Révolution* (II.1). Tocqueville, *The Old Regime and the Revolution*, ed. François Furet and Françoise Mélonio, trans. Alan S. Kahan, vol. 1 (University of Chicago Press, 1998), pp. 112–13.

[19] "Constituée d'une certaine manière, elle réunit, elle concentre, elle groupe autour de quelque tête la propriété, et bientôt après le pouvoir; elle fait jaillir en quelque sorte l'aristocratie du sol" (Tocqueville, *Démocratie*, vol. 1, p. 96).

[20] Ibid., p. 95.

Tocqueville glosses this discussion with a familiar passage from Jefferson's *Autobiography*:

In the earlier times of the colony, when lands were to be obtained for little or nothing, some provident individuals procured large grants, and desirous of founding great families for themselves, settled them or their descendants in fee tail. The transmission of this property from generation to generation, in the same name, raised up a distinct set of families, who, being privileged by law in the perpetuation of their wealth, were thus formed into a Patrician order, distinguished by the splendor and luxury of their establishments. From this order, too, the king habitually selected his councillors of state.[21]

This nascent aristocracy only failed to consolidate its position, Tocqueville argues, because it relied on slavery, rather than landed patronage (i.e. wealthy landholders had slaves, rather than dependent tenants), and lived amongst people already accustomed to the democratic social state.

There was, however, an alternative approach to inheritance laws which Tocqueville insisted was becoming irreversibly dominant:

Driven by other principles, and launched on another path, its action [i.e. the action of an inheritance law] is more rapid still. It divides, parcels out, and disseminates goods and power. It sometimes happens that one is frightened at the speed of its advance; in despair of halting its movement, one tries at least to place before it problems and obstacles. One wants to counterbalance its action by contrary efforts, but all in vain! This law crushes or dashes to pieces everything it finds in its path. It causes things to rise up and fall again onto the soil incessantly, until the point where it no longer presents to view anything other than the fleeting and impalpable dust on which democracy makes its foundation.[22]

With almost no noticeable variation, we have here the Harringtonian and Montesquieuan agrarian. Inheritance laws which insist on the equal division of estates among children (i.e. which have abolished primogeniture and the entail of estates) produce a relative equality of conditions which brings with it democratic government and mores. These democratic inheritance laws, according to Tocqueville, have two immediate effects: first, and more obviously, they continually break up large estates, dividing them into smaller

---

[21] Ibid., p. 615. Jefferson's English is given in Alexis de Tocqueville, *Democracy in America*, ed. J. P. Mayer, trans. George Lawson (New York: Harper & Row, 1966), p. 721.

[22] Conduite par d'autres principes, et lancées dans une autre voie, son action est plus rapide encore; elle divise, elle partage, elle dissémine les biens et la puissance; il arrive quelquefois alors qu'on est effrayé de la rapidité de sa marche; désespérant d'en arrêter le mouvement, on cherche du moins à créer devant elle des difficultés et des obstacles; on veut contrebalancer son action par des efforts contraires; soins inutiles! Elle broie, ou fait voler en éclats tout ce qui se rencontre sur son passage, elle s'élève et retombe incessamment sur le sol, jusqu'à ce qu'il ne présente plus à la vue qu'une poussière mouvante et impalpable, sur laquelle s'assoit la démocratie (Tocqueville, *Démocratie*, vol. 1, p. 97).

parcels and redistributing them. But equally importantly, Tocqueville believes that these laws have a particular psychological effect on wealthy landholders. Since, under such laws, landholders despair of maintaining large
family estates, they lose their sentimental attachment to ancestral lands
and sell them of their own free will, even before the inheritance laws have
a chance to break them up.[23] The wealthy become complicit in the liqui-
dation of their own patrimonies.

This process of agrarian levelling, argues Tocqueville, was the most significant legacy of the American Revolution:

> The English legislation on the transfer of goods was abolished in almost all the states
> during the era of the Revolution. The law of entails was modified in such a way as to
> hinder the free circulation of goods only in the most innocuous manner. The first
> generation passed away, and the lands began to be divided. The pace became more
> and more rapid as time went on. Today, when scarcely sixty years have passed, the
> appearance of society is already unrecognizable. The families of great landowners
> are almost all swallowed up in the midst of the common masses . . . The sons of
> these opulent citizens are today merchants, lawyers, and doctors. Most have fallen
> into deep obscurity. The last trace of ranks and hereditary distinctions is destroyed,
> and the inheritance law has everywhere established its middling level.[24]

In his note Tocqueville reproduces the basic inheritance law almost univer-
sally instituted throughout the United States after the Revolution: "When
a man dies intestate, his goods pass to his heirs in direct line; if he only has
one heir or one heiress, he or she alone receives the entire estate. If there
happen to be several heirs of the same degree, they divide up the estate
equally among themselves with no distinction of sex."[25] Property is thus
continually divided and redistributed, ensuring what Tocqueville calls the
democratic "social state."

---

[23] Ibid., p. 98.
[24] "La législation anglaise sur la transmission des biens fut abolie dans presque tout les Etats à l'époque
de la révolution. La loi sur les substitutions fut modifiée de manière à ne gêner que d'une manière
insensible la libre circulation des biens. La première génération passa; les terres commencèrent à se
diviser. Le mouvement devint de plus en plus rapide à mesure que le temps marchait. Aujourd'hui,
quand soixante ans à peine se sont écoulés, l'aspect de la société est déja méconnaissable; les familles de
grands propriétaires fonciers se sont presque toutes englouties au sein de la masse commune . . . Les
fils de ces opulents citoyens sont aujourd'hui commerçants, avocats, médecins. La plupart sont
tombés dans l'obscurité la plus profonde. La dernière trace des rangs et des distinctions héréditaires
est détruite; la loi des successions a partout passé son niveau" (ibid., p. 101).
[25] "Lorsqu'un homme meurt intestat, son bien passe à ses héritiers en ligne directe; s'il n'y a qu'un
héritier ou une héritière, il ou elle recueille seul toute la succession. S'il existe plusieurs héritiers
du même degré, ils partagent également entre eux la succession, sans distinction de sexe" (ibid.,
p. 615).

It should be noted, however, that Tocqueville does not labor under the misapprehension that such a democratic agrarian will eliminate the classes of "rich" and "poor." On the contrary, he repeatedly insists that rich and poor will exist in any society, and that they certainly exist in America.[26] In America, however, wealth is kept within practicable bounds, and is promptly redistributed after the deaths of wealthy men. As a result, the son of a wealthy man is invariably poorer than his father,[27] and the consolidation of supereminence in particular families becomes impossible. The democratic agrarian, in short, provides that men are never so wealthy that they can "exercise a great influence over their fellow citizens."[28] Furthermore, the mores and intellectual habits produced by the general equality of conditions ensure that, even when average men confront men of significant wealth and (as a result) power, American public opinion "which bases itself on the usual order of things, restores them to a common level and creates between them a sort of imaginary equality, despite the actual inequality of their conditions."[29] Thus, the democratic social state can defend itself against mild and temporary disparities in wealth through the accumulated force of the beliefs it engenders. In Harringtonian terms, there will always be democratic and aristocratic elements in society; the agrarian and its resulting mores make sure that the rich do not "overbalance" the people.

II

Described in this way, Tocqueville seems largely similar to the major figures in the tradition we have been following. But differences abound, and the most significant among them is suggested by a quick look at one of Tocqueville's more innocuous comments. In his appendix concerning inheritance laws Tocqueville notes that the central provisions of the American agrarian (in particular its repudiation of entails) were proposed in Virginia by Jefferson in 1776. As we have seen, Jefferson embraced these democratic inheritance laws out of a conviction that, once the disproportionate wealth of the "Pseudo-aristoi" was eliminated, the natural aristocracy would shine

---

[26] Ibid., p. 101.

[27] Ibid., vol. II, p. 216. This entire discussion clearly recalls Montesquieu's account of how commercial republics can preserve good mores through inheritance laws (*De l'esprit des lois* v.6).

[28] "n'étant plus assez riches ni assez puissants pour exercer une grande influence sur le sort de leurs semblables" (Tocqueville, *Démocratie*, vol. II, p. 145).

[29] "l'opinion publique, qui se fonde sur l'ordre ordinaire des choses, les rapproche du commun niveau et crée entre eux une sorte d'égalité imaginaire, en dépit de l'inégalité réelle de leur conditions" (ibid., p. 253).

forth brightly and the people, forgetting the allure and glamor of riches, would always choose the "real good and wise" to rule – thus satisfying the demands of nature and justice. Tocqueville believes no such thing. He completely rejects the basic Greek notion that, if extremes of wealth and poverty were eliminated, money-loving would cease to be a dominant passion in society. Indeed, he argues the precise opposite: on his view, the equalization of holdings produces a universal tendency toward money-loving. Speaking of the United States with its democratic *état social*, he declares that "I do not know of any country where the love of money holds a larger place in the heart of man."[30] The reason for this perplexing state of affairs, explains Tocqueville, is that, in societies where a non-democratic social state prevails, the rich are tranquil in their wealth, knowing full well that it has always been there and will always be there. As a result, they do not worry or obsess about money, and their bent runs to luxury and sloth.[31] The poor for their part have no hope of acquiring extensive property, so they sensibly decline to give money-making much consideration. In societies where the democratic social state holds sway, however, everyone has a reasonable expectation of being able to make a fortune, and no one is immune from financial concerns.[32]

Once again, for Tocqueville, a key contrast is that between the American North and South. The Southern, patrician, slave-holding class displays no regard for money-making, and exhibits all the vices of habitual indolence.[33] In New England, however, the situation is very different:

Since the equality of fortunes reigns in the North, and slavery does not exist there, man finds himself absorbed with those same material wants which the white man disdains in the South. From childhood, he occupies himself with combating misery, and he learns to place material ease above all the joys of the mind and heart. Focused on the small details of life, his imagination stifles itself, his ideas are less numerous and less general, but they become more practical, more clear, and more precise. Since he directs all the efforts of his intellect only toward the study of well-being, he does not take long to excel at it. He knows admirably to take advantage of nature and men to produce riches.[34]

---

[30] "Je ne connais même pas de pays où l'amour de l'argent tienne une plus large place dans le cœur de l'homme" (ibid., vol. I, p. 101).

[31] Ibid., pp. 546–47.

[32] Ibid., vol. II, p. 336. On this, see also Tocqueville's "Preface" to *L'Ancien Régime* (Tocqueville, *The Old Regime*, p. 87).

[33] This was a standard observation in American political pamphlets of the 1780s. See, for example, the third letter from "Cato" to the *New York Journal* (October 25, 1787) in *The Debate on the Constitution: Federalist and Antifederalist Speeches, Articles, and Letters During the Struggle over Ratification*, vol. I, ed. Bernard Bailyn (New York: Library of America, 1993), p. 217.

[34] "L'égalité des fortunes régnant au Nord, et l'esclavage n'y existant plus, l'homme s'y trouve comme absorbé par ces mêmes soins matériels que le blanc dédaigne au Sud. Depuis son enfance il s'occupe

Because fortunes are middling, all men seek great fortunes.

But Tocqueville goes even further. Not only, he suggests, does the democratic social state condition a population to seek money above all things; it also greatly enhances the prestige of money-making. In direct opposition to the Greek claim that the temperate regulation of property will diminish the status of wealth as a social good, Tocqueville argues that such arrangements have the effect of ennobling it. Indeed, on his view, once the social state has become democratic, wealth asserts itself as the only relevant social distinction:

Men who live in democratic times have many passions, but the majority of their passions either result in the love of riches, or flow from it. This does not come about because their souls are smaller, but because the importance of money in such times is truly greater... Since the prestige which attached itself to things ancient has disappeared, birth, station, and profession no longer distinguish men. Nothing remains but money which creates very visible differences among them and which can place some of them above the common level. The distinction which is born from riches feeds off the disappearance and diminution of all the other distinctions.[35]

Moreover, this unique source of social distinction receives the status of a positive virtue (a fact which greatly concerns Tocqueville) due to the overall circumstances of the American experience:

There are certain tendencies which are deplorable in the eyes of general reason and universal conscience which happen to be consonant with the particular and immediate needs of the American confederation... I mention particularly the love of riches and the secondary tendencies which attach themselves to it. In order to clear, cultivate, and transform this vast, uninhabited continent which is his domain, an American needs the daily support of an energetic passion. That passion cannot be anything other than the love of riches. The passion for riches is therefore not at all condemned in America, and, provided that it does not exceed the limits which

à combattre la misère, et il apprend à placer l'aisance au-dessus de toutes les jouissances de l'esprit et du cœur. Concentrée dans les petits détails de la vie, son imagination s'éteint, ses idées sont moins nombreuses et moins générales, mais elles deviennent plus pratiques, plus claires et plus précises. Comme il dirige vers l'unique étude du bien-être tous les efforts de son intelligence, il ne tarde pas à y exceller; il sait admirablement tirer parti de la nature et des hommes pour produire la richesse" (Tocqueville, *Démocratie*, vol. 1, p. 547).

[35] "Les hommes qui vivent dans les temps démocratiques ont beaucoup de passions; mais la plupart de leurs passions aboutissent à l'amour des richesses ou en sortent. Cela ne vient pas de ce que leurs âmes sont plus petites, mais de ce que l'importance de l'argent est alors réellement plus grande... Le prestige qui s'attachait aux choses anciennes ayant disparu, la naissance, l'état, la profession ne distinguent plus les hommes, ou les distinguent à peine; il ne reste plus guère que l'argent qui crée des différences très visibles entre eux et qui puisse en mettre quelques-uns hors de pair. La distinction qui naît de la richesse s'augmente de la disparition et de la diminution de toutes les autres" (ibid., vol. 11, p. 315).

public order assigns it, it is honored. The American calls noble and estimable ambition that which our fathers of the middle ages called servile cupidity.[36]

Thus, in Tocqueville's opinion, far from banishing wealth from the pantheon of esteemed goods, the temperate distribution of property elevates money-making into a cardinal virtue.

The implication of all this is fairly clear. Tocqueville is led completely to reject the view of Plato, More, Harrington, and their progeny, that the equalization of holdings will result in a more excellent society. On the contrary, he argues that equality of conditions creates a pervasive mediocrity. Middling fortunes produce middling characters, neither disgraceful nor inspirational. Tocqueville explains that "it is not only fortunes which are equal in America: to a certain point, equality reaches intellects themselves. I do not think that there is anywhere on earth where, in proportion to the population, there are as few ignorant men and as few intellectuals as in America."[37] For Tocqueville, this accounts for what he calls the *niveau moyen* of American intellectual life: out of equal conditions and relatively equal education emerges a calcified consensus on major social, economic, political, and philosophical questions, along with a relative absence of dynamic thinking.[38] Nor does the onslaught of mediocrity end with the life of the mind. All of social life is reduced to a palatable, sometimes profitable, but always unexceptional common denominator:

Great riches disappear; the number of small fortunes increases. Desires and enjoyments multiply; there are no longer extraordinary prosperities or miseries without remedy . . . Souls are not energetic, but mores are mild and laws humane. If one finds few great acts of self-sacrifice and few virtues that are very high, very brilliant, and very pure, yet habits are well-ordered, violence is rare, and cruelty almost unknown. The existence of men becomes longer and their property safer. Life is not very ornate, but very easy and very peaceful. There are few very delicate or very

---

[36] "Il y a certains penchants condamnables aux yeux de la raison générale et de la conscience universelle du genre humain, qui se trouvent être d'accord avec les besoins particuliers et momentanés de l'association américaine . . . je citerai particulièrement l'amour des richesses et les penchants secondaires qui s'y rattachent. Pour défrichir, féconder, transformer ce vaste continent inhabité qui est son domaine, il faut à l'Américain l'appui journalier d'une passion énergetique; cette passion ne saurait être que l'amour des richesses; la passion des richesses n'est donc point flétrie en Amérique, et, pourvu qu'elle ne dépasse pas les limites que l'ordre public lui assigne, on l'honore. L'Américain appelle noble et estimable ambition ce que nos pères du moyen âge nommaient cupidité servile" (ibid., p. 325).

[37] "Ce ne sont pas seulement les fortunes qui sont égales en Amérique; l'égalité s'étend jusqu'à un certain point sur les intelligences elles-mêmes. Je ne pense pas qu'il y ait dans le monde où, proportion gardée avec population, il se trouve aussi peu d'ignorants et moins de savants qu'en Amérique" (ibid., vol. I, p. 101).

[38] Ibid., p. 103.

coarse pleasures, little refinement in manners and little brutality in tastes . . . There is less perfection, but a greater proliferation of accomplishments.[39]

Tocqueville may well have believed, as he says, that through such an arrangement "le grand lien de l'humanité se resserre," but he leaves little doubt that such a society is not the most virtuous imaginable (although it is, perhaps, the most virtuous available).

In order to see precisely how revolutionary Tocqueville's model actually is, it is worth comparing it to a theory which appears superficially similar: Aristotle's account of middle-class rule in *Politics* IV. Like Tocqueville, Aristotle argues that middling fortunes tend to produce characters which are in some important sense "middling," and he also agrees with Tocqueville in suggesting that the relative equality of conditions yields a certain kind of fellow-feeling which helps to bind political communities (*Politics* 1295a25 [IV.8]–1296a22 [IV.9]). Aristotle writes as follows:

those who have an excess of fortune's goods, strength, wealth, friends and the like, are not willing to be governed and do not know how to be (and they have acquired this quality even in their boyhood from their home-life, which was so luxurious that they have not got used to submitting to authority even in school), while those who are excessively in need of these things are too humble. Hence the latter class do not know how to govern but know how to submit to government of a servile kind, while the former class do not know how to submit to any government, and only know how to govern in the manner of a master. The result is a state consisting of slaves and masters, not free men, and of one class envious of another and contemptuous of their fellows. (*Politics* 1295b15)[40]

This condition, Aristotle adds, is "very far removed from friendliness, and from political partnership," the essential element of "political" rulership. As a result, he concludes that since "the ideal of the state is to consist as much as possible of persons that are equal and alike, and this similarity is most found in the middle classes," a state dominated by the middle class will be the best readily available state.

But Aristotle insists that the "middling" quality of the middle class *is itself* virtue: moderate property is a "mean" between the extremes of wealth

---

[39] "Les grandes richesses disparaissent; le nombre des petits fortunes s'accroît; les désirs et les jouissances se multiplient; il n'y a plus de prospérités extraordinaires ni de misères irrémédiables . . . Les âmes ne sont pas énergiques; mais les mœurs sont douces et les législations humaines. S'il se rencontre peu de grands dévouements, de vertus très hautes, très brillantes et très pures, les habitudes son rangées, la violence est rare, la cruauté presque inconnue. L'existence des hommes devient plus longue et leur propriété plus sûre. La vie n'est très ornée, mais très aisée et très paisible. Il y a peu de plaisirs très délicats et très grossiers, peu de politesses dans les manières et peu de brutalité dans les goûts . . . Il y a moins de perfection, mais plus de fécondité dans les œuvres" (ibid., vol. II, p. 452).

[40] All quotations from Aristotle are taken from Aristotle, *Politics*, ed. and trans. H. Rackham, Loeb Classical Library (Harvard University Press, 1932). I have used Rackham's translations.

and poverty. Far from "dumbing down" virtue and creating a society of money-lovers, Aristotle's temperate distribution of wealth allows for the broader exercise of virtue and tames the passions of greed and envy:

Since then it is admitted that what is moderate or in the middle is best, it is manifest that the middle amount of all of the good things of fortune is the best amount to possess. For this degree of wealth is the readiest to obey reason, whereas for a person who is exceedingly beautiful or strong or nobly born or rich, or the opposite – exceedingly poor or weak or of very mean station, it is difficult to follow the bidding of reason; for the former turn more to insolence and grand wickedness, and the latter overmuch to malice and petty wickedness, and the motive of all wrongdoing is either insolence or malice. (*Politics* 1295b4)

For Aristotle, disproportionate wealth and poverty create vice, not virtue, and the man with moderate property is the most attentive to the demands of reason. In the political sphere, the chief demand of reason is distributive justice: the distribution of political offices according to desert. Since the state aims at the good life, explains Aristotle, the most virtuous men have the most to contribute to governance, and, accordingly, should be assigned rulership positions. The man of middling property, immune from the influence of greed or envy, will obey the demands of reason in deferring to the rule of the best men.

In Tocqueville's model nothing is further from the truth. States possessing an equal agrarian are by no means governed by the most exceptional men:

Many men in Europe believe without saying, or say without believing, that one of the great advantages of universal suffrage is to call men worthy of public confidence to the management of public affairs. The public does not know how to govern itself, they say, but it always sincerely desires the good of the State, and its instinct does not lack the ability to identify those men who are animated by the same desire and who are the most capable of holding power. For myself – I must say it – what I saw in America does not authorize me at all to think that this is the case. On my arrival in the United States, I was struck with surprise to discover the extent to which merit was common among the governed, and rare among the governors. It is a constant fact that, in our days, in the United States the most remarkable men are rarely called to public offices.[41]

---

[41] "Bien des gens, en Europe, croient sans le dire, ou disent sans le croire, qu'un des grands avantages du vote universel est d'appeler à la direction des affaires des hommes dignes de la confiance publique. Le peuple ne saurait gouverner lui-même, dit-on, mais il veut toujours sincèrement le bien de l'Etat, et son instinct ne manque guère de lui désigner ceux qu'un même désir anime et qui sont les plus capables de tenir en main le pouvoir. Pour moi, je dois le dire, ce que j'ai vu en Amérique ne m'autorise point à penser qu'il en soit ainsi. A mon arrivée aux Etats-Unis, je fus frappé de surprise en découvrant à quel point le mérite était commun parmi les gouvernés, et combien il était peu chez les gouvernants. C'est un fait constant que, de nos jours, aux Etats-Unis, les hommes les plus

There are, according to Tocqueville, several reasons for this state of affairs. First, the desire for money is so pervasive – and the process of electioneering so demeaning – that capable men will seldom pass up their commercial opportunities to pursue public service (a total contradiction of Aristotle's insistence that men of moderate property will neither covet political office unduly, nor shun it for financial reasons [*Politics* 1295b12]).[42] Second, the mediocre education of the populace leaves it susceptible to the seduction of demagogues.[43] But most importantly, the democratic social state makes people resentful of their intellectual superiors, and implants in them a tendency to keep the most exceptional men away from political office:

For the rest, it is not always only the ability to choose men of merit which is lacking in a democracy, but the desire and the taste. It is no use denying that democratic institutions develop the sentiment of envy in the human heart to a very high degree. This is not at all because such institutions offer to each person the means to become equal to others, but because these means constantly fail to achieve that goal for those who use them. Democratic institutions awaken and flatter the passion for equality without ever having the power to satisfy it entirely . . . In that condition [i.e. the state of continually seeking absolute equality, only to be frustrated] anything that surpasses the public seems like an obstacle to its desires, and there is no superiority so legitimate that the sight of it does not tire the public's eyes.[44]

Accordingly, Americans "do not fear great talents, but they have no taste for them. In general, one notices that those who rise on their own without popular support obtain the public's favor later only with great difficulty."[45] This democratic envy which keeps the best men out of power can be tamed somewhat by good mores and education. In New England, for example, the general orientation of society is so deeply meritocratic that "the people, while it has banished all the superiorities which wealth and birth ever created among men, is nonetheless accustomed to respect intellectual and

---

remarquables sont rarement appelés aux fonctions publiques . . ." (Tocqueville, *Démocratie*, vol. 1, p. 299).

[42] See ibid., and pp. 309–10.   [43] Ibid., p. 299.

[44] "Du reste, ce n'est pas toujours la capacité qui manque à la démocratie pour choisir les hommes de mérite, mais le désir et le goût. Il ne faut pas se dissimuler que les institutions démocratiques développent à un très haut degré le sentiment de l'envie dans le cœur humain. Ce n'est point tant parce qu'elles offrent à chacun des moyens d'égaler aux autres, mais parce que ces moyens défaillent sans cesse à ceux qui les emploient. Les institutions démocratiques réveillent et flattent la passion de l'égalité sans pouvoir jamais la satisfaire entièrement . . . Tout ce qui le dépasse par quelque endroit lui paraît alors un obstacle à ses désirs, et il n'y a pas de supériorité si légitime dont la vue ne fatigue ses yeux" (ibid., p. 300).

[45] "[le peuple] ne craint pas les grands talents, mais il les goûte peu. En général, on remarque que tout ce qui s'élève sans appui obtient difficilement sa faveur" (ibid., p. 301).

moral superiorities and to submit to them without displeasure."[46] But the particular circumstances of Puritan New England's founding make it an exceptional case. In general, as far as Tocqueville is concerned, a disinclination to promote excellent men to political office is a very real byproduct of the equality of conditions.

III

We have seen that, while Tocqueville's concept of the *état social* follows closely in the Greek tradition, his account of the social and intellectual consequences of the democratic social state distance him significantly from Plato, Aristotle, Montesquieu, and other authors examined above. Should we then say that Tocqueville's debt to the Greek tradition consists solely in the Harringtonian dictum that "the balance of property produces the balance of power"? Has this descriptive claim simply been abstracted from its traditional normative context? What is perhaps most fascinating about Tocqueville is that this is not the case. While Tocqueville denies that the equality of conditions will clear a path through the wilderness for the natural aristocracy or scuttle the social prestige of wealth, he continues to insist that the temperate distribution of wealth will have ameliorative effects on mores. Although he argues that aristocratic societies will produce a kind of virtue not to be found in democratic societies, he maintains the conviction of the ancients that disproportionate wealth and poverty corrupt. In the case of the poor, he states flatly that "in those places where we find men who are extremely strong and rich, the weak and poor men feel overwhelmed by their baseness. Not discovering any means by which they can regain equality, they despair of themselves completely and let themselves fall beneath the level of human dignity."[47] Likewise, Tocqueville insists that the guarantee of permanent wealth (in particular the sort which lives off slavery) breeds indolence, luxury, and laxity in mores.[48] Equality of conditions, on the other hand, carries with it a robust work ethic, one that survives even the amassing of great fortunes. For if a man develops a large amount of wealth in a democracy, he retains the instincts of temperance and thrift that allowed

[46] "Le peuple, en même temps qu'il échappe à toutes les supériorités que la richesse et la naissance ont jamais crées parmi les hommes, s'est habitué à respecter les supériorités intellectuelles et morales, et à s'y soumettre sans déplaisir" (ibid., p. 303).

[47] "Dans ces lieux, où se rencontrent des hommes si forts et si riches, les faibles et les pauvres se sentent comme accablés de leur bassesse; ne découvrant aucun point par lequel ils puissent reganger l'égalité; ils désespèrent entièrement d'eux-mêmes et se laissent tomber au-dessous de la dignité humaine" (ibid., p. 65).

[48] Ibid., p. 74.

him to amass it in the first place, and his son, though born wealthy, will have less wealth than his father and will take as an example his father's workmanlike manner.[49]

Moreover, Tocqueville is adamant that sexual mores improve under a democratic social state. In an aristocratic society, matches between members of different classes are strictly forbidden, leading star-crossed lovers to seek relief in extra-marital dalliances.[50] The fact of forced marriages, or forcibly prevented marriages, in turn, captures public sympathy and leads to a tolerant, "look the other way" sort of attitude toward infidelity. In a democratic social state, however, anyone may marry anyone else, eliminating the need for clandestine liaisons, and choking public sympathy toward those who engage in them. Furthermore, the active, engaged life of middle-class people simply leaves them less time to make mischief; the idleness that invites vice has no place in democratic society. Man's energy is either taken up by industry, or diverted at an unprecedented level to civic engagement. Indeed, as Roger Boesche and others have observed, Tocqueville is perhaps the last great theorist of the *vita activa*:[51]

In the United States, the fatherland makes itself felt throughout. It is an object of care all the way from the village to the entire Union. The inhabitant attaches himself to each of the interests of his country as if they were his own interests. He feels glorified himself by the glory of the nation; in the success the fatherland obtains, he believes he can recognize his own effort, and it elevates him. He rejoices in the general prosperity through which he himself profits. He has for his country a feeling analogous to that which one feels for one's family . . .[52]

Of course, in Tocqueville's case, the democratic civic renaissance does not take place because temperate wealth inclines its possessors to public virtue, but rather because individual interest gives each person a stake in the success of the whole.[53] Nonetheless, equality of conditions encourages political liberty and participation, which, in Tocqueville's estimation, produce good mores – albeit in a somewhat circuitous manner.

---

[49] Ibid., vol. II, p. 337.   [50] Ibid., p. 283.

[51] See, for example, Roger Boesche, *The Strange Liberalism of Alexis de Tocqueville* (Ithaca: Cornell University Press, 1987), pp. 121–22.

[52] "Aux Etats-Unis, la patrie se fait sentir partout. Elle est un object de solicitude depuis le village jusqu'à l'Union entière. L'habitant s'attache à chacun des intérêts de son pays comme aux siens mêmes. Il se glorifie de la gloire de la nation; dans les succès qu'elle obtient, il croit reconnaître son propre ouvrage, et il s'en élève; il se rejouit de la prospérité générale dont il profite. Il a pour sa patrie un sentiment analogue à celui qu'on éprouve pour sa famille . . ." (Tocqueville, *Démocratie*, vol. I, p. 159).

[53] See ibid., pp. 118, 160.

But, for present purposes, Tocqueville explains the most significant moral effect of the democratic social state early in volume two, in the chapter entitled "Why the example of the Americans does not prove at all that a democratic people could not have an aptitude or taste for the sciences, literature, and the arts."[54] In the first volume, as we have seen, Tocqueville had tried to explain what he perceived as a dearth of artistic and literary achievement in the United States by highlighting the "middling" character of American life. Equal social conditions ensured that citizens received an always tolerable, but never exceptional education, which, in turn, created a breed of thoroughly competent but uncreative people. In this chapter of the second volume, however, Tocqueville qualifies his earlier pronouncement by insisting that democracies can and should produce great scientific and artistic achievements (America simply had not, due to a series of particular circumstances). His reason is extremely significant:

> When there is no longer any hereditary wealth, class privilege, or prerogative of birth, and each man no longer acquires his force from any source outside himself, it becomes apparent that the thing which creates the principal difference between the fortunes of men is intelligence. Everything which serves to strengthen, extend, and adorn intelligence quickly acquires a great value.[55]

Once all distinctions of class and condition have been leveled, the only means of advancement will be intellectual achievement. When the public becomes aware of this fact, it will seek knowledge and improvement above all things in order to advance, and society will have been rendered creative. Thus, while the desire for wealth remains a constant, Tocqueville maintains that when coupled with equality of conditions it becomes an engine for intellectual progress – and ends up assigning to the gifts of the mind pride of place among social goods.

Tocqueville compares this societal condition to a proposal offered by "une secte célèbre" (by which he means Saint-Simon and his colleagues) to concentrate "all goods in the hands of a central power and to charge those who manage it to distribute the goods to individuals according to their merit."[56] Such a mechanism would combat the tendency of democracies

---

[54] "Comment l'exemple des Americains ne prouve point qu'un peuple démocratique ne saurait avoir de l'aptitude et du goût pour les sciences, la littérature et les arts" (ibid., vol. II, p. 55).

[55] "Quand il n'y a plus de richesse héréditaire, de privilèges de classes et de prérogatives de naissance, et que chacun ne tire plus sa force que de lui-même, il devient visible que ce qui fait la principale différence entre la fortune des hommes, c'est l'intelligence. Tout ce qui sert à fortifier, à étendre, à orner l'intelligence, acquiert aussitôt un grand prix" (ibid., p. 60).

[56] "tous les biens dans les mains d'un pouvoir central et charger ceux-là de les distribuer ensuite, suivant le mérite, à tous les particuliers" (ibid., p. 59).

to give equal benefits to unequal people. But Tocqueville comments that there is a less drastic way of accomplishing the same end, a way which is intrinsically built into the structure of democracy itself: simply "to give to everyone equal enlightenment and an equal independence, and to leave each individual to make a place for himself."[57] If this approach is taken, "natural inequality will very soon make itself felt, and wealth will pass of its own accord to the most able men."[58]

The outlines of a new theory – an adaptation of the basic Greek view outlined above – are apparent here. The question is no longer one of rulership, or even of virtue *per se*, but instead concerns the distribution of goods according to merit and desert. In a non-democratic social state where conditions are unequal, hereditary wealth and generational poverty prevent the allocation of a fair share of social goods to the most talented citizens; wealth stays where it is, regardless of how meritorious its proprietors happen to be. In a democratic social state, however, where estates are continually broken into pieces and disproportionate wealth and poverty have been eliminated, the organization of society at last allows merit to have its day. The argument is no longer that property levels must be equalized in order to secure the rule of the best men, and, in so doing, to align society with nature and justice. It has become an argument to maintain a temperate distribution of property in order to protect the "level playing field," a position which remains alive and well in our own time. Tocqueville ends *Democracy in America* by reflecting that "equality is perhaps less elevated, but it is more just – and its justice constitutes its grandeur and beauty."[59] Perhaps that is the signature statement of a thinker who transformed the Greek tradition and prepared it for life in the modern world.

---

[57] "de donner à tous d'égales lumières et une égal indépendance, et de laisser à chacun le soin de marquer lui-même sa place" (ibid.). I have based my translation here on Lawson's (*Democracy in America*, ed. Mayer, p. 457).

[58] "L'inégalité naturelle se fera bientôt jour, et la richesse passera d'elle-même du côté des plus habiles" (Tocqueville, *Démocratie*, vol. ii, p. 59). I have based my translation here on Lawson's (*Democracy in America*, ed. Mayer, p. 457).

[59] "L'égalité est moins élevée peut-être; mais elle est plus juste, et sa justice fait sa grandeur et sa beauté" (Tocqueville, *Démocratie*, vol. ii, p. 453).

Bibliography

PRIMARY SOURCES

An act directing the course of descents in *The Statutes at Large: Being a Collection of all the Laws of Virginia, from the First Session of the Legislature, in the Year 1619,* ed. William Waller Hening. Vol. XII. Richmond, 1823.

An ACT directing the descent of intestates' real estates, and distribution of their personal estates, and for other purposes therein mentioned in *Laws of the Commonwealth of Pennsylvania, From the Seventh day of December, one thousand seven hundred and ninety, to the Twentieth Day of April, one thousand seven hundred and ninety-five,* ed. Alexander James Dallas. Vol. III. Philadelphia, 1795.

An act for regulating conveyances in *The Statutes at Large: Being a Collection of all the Laws of Virginia, from the First Session of the Legislature, in the Year 1619,* ed. William Waller Hening. Vol. XII. Richmond, 1823.

AN ACT To Explain the fifty first Article of the Constitution respecting Intestate Estates and also concerning marriages in *The Colonial Records of the State of Georgia: Statutes, Colonial and Revolutionary,* ed. Allen D. Chandler. Vol. XIX (part II). New York: AMS Press, 1970.

Adams, John. *Defence of the Constitutions of Government of the United States of America* in *The Works of John Adams, Second President of the United States,* ed. Charles Francis Adams. Vols. IV–VI. Boston: Charles C. Little and James Brown, 1851.

 Letters in *The Works of John Adams, Second President of the United States,* ed. Charles Francis Adams. Vol. IX. Boston: Charles C. Little and James Brown, 1851.

 Thoughts on Government in *The Works of John Adams, Second President of the United States,* ed. Charles Francis Adams. Vol. IV. Boston: Charles C. Little and James Brown, 1851.

Adams, John and Jefferson, Thomas. *The Adams–Jefferson Letters,* ed. Lester J. Cappon. Chapel Hill: University of North Carolina Press, 1959.

Ames, Fisher. "Camillus IV" in *Works of Fisher Ames,* ed. W. B. Allen. Vol. II. Indianapolis: Liberty *Classics,* 1983.

Appian. *Roman History,* ed. and trans. Horace White. 4 vols. Loeb Classical Library. London: William Heinemann, 1912–13.

Aristotle. *Nicomachean Ethics*, ed. and trans. H. Rackham. Rev. edn. Loeb Classical Library. London and Cambridge, MA: Harvard University Press, 1934.

Politics, ed. and trans. H. Rackham. Loeb Classical Library. London and Cambridge, MA: Harvard University Press, 1932.

Rhetoric, ed. and trans. John Henry Freese. Loeb Classical Library. London and Cambridge, MA: Harvard University Press, 1926.

Atwater, Jeremiah. *Sermon* in *American Political Writing during the Founding Era: 1760–1805*, ed. Charles S. Hyneman and Donald S. Lutz. Vol. II. Indianapolis: Liberty Press, 1983.

Aubrey, John. *Brief Lives*, ed. Oliver Lawson Dick. London: Secker and Warburg, 1949.

Bacon, Sir Francis. *Essays or Counsels Civil and Moral* in *The Works of Francis Bacon*, 14 vols., ed. James Spedding, Robert Leslie Ellis, and Douglas Denon Heath. Vol. VI. London: 1858.

History of the Reign of King Henry VII in *The Works of Francis Bacon*, 14 vols., ed. James Spedding, Robert Leslie Ellis, and Douglas Denon Heath. Vol. VI. London: 1858.

Barère, Bertrand. *Montesquieu peint d'après ses ouvrages*. Paris, 1797.

Beaufort, Louis de. *La Republique romaine, ou Plan générale de L'ancien gouvernement de Rome*. Paris, 1766.

Boccaccio, Giovanni. *De mulieribus claris*, ed. and trans. Virginia Brown. I Tatti Renaissance Library. Cambridge, MA: Harvard University Press, 2001.

Bodin, Jean. *Les Six Livres de la Republique de I. Bodin Angevin*. 2nd edn. Paris, 1577.

Io. Bodini Andegavensis, De republica libri sex, latine ab autore redditi, multo quam antea locupletiores. Paris, 1586.

The Six Bookes of A Commonweale Written by I. Bodin a famous Lawyer, and a man of great Experience in matters of State, trans. Richard Knolles. London, 1606.

Method for the Easy Comprehension of History, ed. and trans. Beatrice Reynolds. New York: Columbia University Press, 1945.

Six Books of the Commonwealth (abridged), ed. and trans. M. J. Tooley. Oxford: Basil Blackwell, 1955.

Les Six Livres de la République, ed. Christiane Frémont, Marie-Dominique Couzinet, and Henri Rochais. 6 vols. Paris: Fayard, 1986.

Centinel in *The Anti-Federalist: Writings by Opponents of the Constitution*, ed. Herbert J. Storing. Chicago: University of Chicago Press, 1981.

Cicero. *De finibus bonorum et malorum*, ed. and trans. H. Rackham. Loeb Classical Library. London and Cambridge, MA: Harvard University Press, 1967.

De officiis, ed. and trans. Walter Miller. Loeb Classical Library. London and Cambridge, MA: Harvard University Press, 1913.

De republica, De legibus, ed. and trans. C. W. Keyes. Loeb Classical Library. London and Cambridge, MA: Harvard University Press, 1928.

Epistulae ad Atticum, ed. and trans. E. O. Winstedt. Vol. I. Loeb Classical Library. London and Cambridge, MA: Harvard University Press, 1912.

In Catilinam I–IV, Pro Murena, Pro Sulla, Pro Flacco, ed. and trans. C. Macdonald. Loeb Classical Library. London and Cambridge, MA: Harvard University Press, 1977.

Pro Publio Quinctio, Pro Sexto Roscio Amerino, Pro Quinto Roscio Comoedo, De lege agraria, ed. and trans. J. H. Freese. Loeb Classical Library. London and Cambridge, MA: Harvard University Press, 1930.

Tusculanae Disputationes, ed. and trans. J. E. King. Rev. edn. Loeb Classical Library. London and Cambridge, MA: Harvard University Press, 1927.

Ps.-Cicero. *Rhetorica ad Herennium*, ed. and trans. Harry Caplan. Loeb Classical Library. London and Cambridge, MA: Harvard University Press, 1968.

Constant, Benjamin. "De la liberté des anciens comparée à celle des modernes" in *De la liberté chez les modernes: écrits politiques*, ed. Marcel Gauchet. Paris: Librairie Générale Française, 1980.

Constitution of Georgia in *The Federal and State Constitutions, Colonial Charters, and Other Organic Laws*, ed. Francis Newton Thorpe. Vol. v. Washington, DC: Government Printing Office, 1909.

Cooper, Anthony Ashley, 3rd Earl of Shaftesbury. *Characteristicks of Men, Manners, Opinions, Times*, ed. Philip Ayres. 2 vols. Oxford: Clarendon Press, 1999.

Croke, Richard. *Orationes Richardi Croci duae*. Paris, 1520.

Cunaeus, Petrus. *De republica Hebraeorum libri III*. Amsterdam, 1632.

Dante. *La Divina Commedia*, ed. Daniele Mattalia. 3 vols. Milan: Rizzoli, 1960.

The Debate on the Constitution: Federalist and Antifederalist Speeches, Articles, and Letters During the Struggle over Ratification, ed. Bernard Bailyn. 2 vols. New York: Library of America, 1993.

The Debates in the Several State Conventions on the Adoption of the Federal Constitution. ed. Jonathan Elliot. 5 vols. Philadelphia: J. B. Lippincott Company, 1907.

A Declaration of Rights [North Carolina] in *The Federal and State Constitutions, Colonial Charters, and Other Organic Laws*, ed. Francis Newton Thorpe. Vol. v. Washington, DC: Government Printing Office, 1909.

Destutt de Tracy, A. L. C. *Commentaire sur l'Esprit des lois de Montesquieu*. Geneva: Slatkine Reprints, 1970.

Diodorus Siculus. *Diodorus of Sicily*, ed. and trans. Francis R. Walton. 12 vols. Loeb Classical Library. London: William Heinemann; and New York: G. P. Putnam's Sons, 1933.

Diogenes Laertius. *Lives of Eminent Philosophers*, ed. and trans. R. D. Hicks. 2 vols. Loeb Classical Library. London and Cambridge, MA: Harvard University Press, 1965–66.

Dionysius of Halicarnassus. *Roman Antiquities*, ed. and trans. Earnest Cary, based on the version of Edward Spelman. 7 vols. Loeb Classical Library. London: William Heinemann, 1937–50.

Dunlap's Pennsylvania Packet, or, the General Advertiser (Philadelphia). Vol. vi, no. 266, November 26, 1776.

Erasmus, Desiderius. *Dulce bellum inexpertis*. Louvain, 1517.

Opus epistolarum Des. Erasmi Roterodami, ed. P. S. Allen and H. M. Allen. 12 vols. Oxford: Oxford University Press, 1922.

The Praise of Folly, ed. A. H. T. Levi, trans. Betty Radice. Harmondsworth: Penguin Books, 1971.

Moriae encomium in *Opera omnia Desiderii Erasmi Roterodami*, vol. IX, ed. Clarence H. Miller. Amsterdam: Elzevier, 1979.

Ciceronianus in *The Collected Works of Erasmus*, vol. XXVIII, ed. and trans. Betty I. Knott. Toronto: University of Toronto Press, 1986.

Enchiridion militis christiani in *The Collected Works of Erasmus*, vol. LXVI, ed. John W. O'Malley. Toronto: University of Toronto Press, 1988.

Adagia in *Opera omnia Desiderii Erasmi Roterodami*, vol. XX, ed. M. L. van Poll-van de Lisdonk, M. Mann Phillips, and Chr. Robinson. Amsterdam: Elzevier, 1993.

An Essay of a Declaration of Rights. Philadelphia, 1776.

Estienne, Henri II. Θησαυρὸς τῆς Ἑλληνικῆς Γλώσσης (*Thesaurus Graecae Linguae*). Paris, 1842–46.

Fénelon, François de Salignac de La Mothe-. *Œuvres*, ed. Jacques Le Brun. 2 vols. Paris: Gallimard, 1983.

Telemachus, ed. and trans. Patrick Riley. Cambridge: Cambridge University Press, 1994.

Ferguson, Adam. *The History of the Progress and Termination of the Roman Republic*. London, 1837.

Ficino, Marsilio. *Platonis opera omnia*. Venice, 1517.

Theologia Platonica, ed. James Hankins and William Bowen, trans. Michael J. B. Allen and John Warden. I Tatti Renaissance Library. Cambridge, MA: Harvard University Press, 2001.

Florus, L. Annaeus. *Epitome*, ed. and trans. Edward Seymour Forster. Loeb Classical Library. London and Cambridge, MA: Harvard University Press, 1929.

Fobes, Perez. *Sermon* in *American Political Writing during the Founding Era: 1760–1805*, vol. II, ed. Charles S. Hyneman and Donald S. Lutz. Indianapolis: Liberty Press, 1983.

Franklin, Benjamin. *The Internal State of America* in *Selected Writings of Benjamin Franklin*. Vol. II. London: William Pickering, 1996.

Positions to Be Examined Concerning National Wealth in *Selected Writings of Benjamin Franklin*. Vol. II. London: William Pickering, 1996.

Garland, Hugh A. *The Life of John Randolph of Roanoke*. 2 vols. New York, 1860.

Gibbon, Edward. *The History of the Decline and Fall of the Roman Empire*, ed. David Womersley. 6 vols. Harmondsworth: Allen Lane, The Penguin Press, 1994.

Guicciardini, Francesco. *Dialogo del Reggimento di Firenze* in *Opere inedite di Francesco Guicciardini*. Vol. II. Florence, 1858.

Discorso di Logrogno in *Opere inedite di Francesco Guicciardini*. Vol. II. Florence, 1858.

Dialogue on the Government of Florence, ed. and trans. Alison Brown. Cambridge: Cambridge University Press, 1994.

Discorso di Logrogno in *Cambridge Translations of Renaissance Philosophical Texts*, ed. Jill Kraye, trans. Russell Price. Vol 11. Cambridge: Cambridge University Press, 1997.

Hamilton, Alexander, Madison, James, and Jay, John. *The Federalist Papers*, ed. Clinton Rossiter. New York: NAL Penguin, 1961.

Harrington, James. *The Commonwealth of Oceana*. London, 1656.

James Harrington's Oceana, ed. S. B. Liljegren. Heidelberg, 1924.

Aphorisms Political in *The Political Works of James Harrington*, ed. J. G. A. Pocock. Cambridge: Cambridge University Press, 1977.

The Art of Lawgiving in *The Political Works of James Harrington*, ed. J. G. A. Pocock. Cambridge: Cambridge University Press, 1977.

Brief Directions in *The Political Works of James Harrington*, ed. J. G. A. Pocock. Cambridge: Cambridge University Press, 1977.

Oceana in *The Political Works of James Harrington*, ed. J. G. A. Pocock. Cambridge: Cambridge University Press, 1977.

The Prerogative of Popular Government in *The Political Works of James Harrington*, ed. J. G. A. Pocock. Cambridge: Cambridge University Press, 1977.

The Stumbling Block in *The Political Works of James Harrington*, ed. J. G. A. Pocock. Cambridge: Cambridge University Press, 1977.

A System of Politics in *The Political Works of James Harrington*, ed. J. G. A. Pocock. Cambridge: Cambridge University Press, 1977.

An Essay vpon Two of Virgil's Eclogues and Two Books of his Aeneis [London, 1658]. Ann Arbor, MI: University Microfilms International, 1984.

The Commonwealth of Oceana and A System of Politics, ed. J. G. A. Pocock. Cambridge: Cambridge University Press, 1992.

Hartlib, Samuel. *A Description of the Famous Kingdome of Macaria*. London, 1641.

Hegel, G. W. F. *The Philosophy of Right* (*Grundlinien der Philosophie des Rechts*), ed. and trans. T. M. Knox. Oxford: Clarendon Press, 1942.

Lectures on the Philosophy of World History, trans. H. B. Nisbet. with an introduction by Duncan Forbes. Cambridge: Cambridge University Press, 1975.

The Philosophy of History, trans. J. Sibree. New York: Prometheus Books, 1991.

Vorlesungen über die Philosophie der Weltgeschichte, vol. XII, ed. Karl Heinz Ilting, Karl Brehmer, and Hoo Nam Seelmann. Vorlesungen: Ausgewählte Nachschriften und Manuskripte. Hamburg: Felix Meiner Verlag, 1996.

Herodotus. *Histories*, ed. and trans. A. D. Godley. 4 vols. Loeb Classical Library. London: William Heinemann, 1921.

Hesiod. *Hesiodi Theogonia*, ed. Friedrich Solmsen. Oxford Classical Texts. Oxford: Clarendon Press, 1983.

Hobbes, Thomas. *The Correspondence of Thomas Hobbes*, ed. Noel Malcolm. 2 vols. Oxford: Clarendon Press, 1994.

Leviathan, ed. Richard Tuck. Rev. edn. Cambridge: Cambridge University Press, 1996.

Homer. *Homeri opera*, ed. David B. Munro and Thomas W. Allen. 4 vols. Oxford Classical Texts. Oxford: Clarendon Press, 1902.

The Odyssey, ed. W. B. Stanford. London: Bristol Classics Press, 1958.

Horace. *Satires, Epistles, Ars Poetica*, ed. and trans. H. R. Fairclough. Loeb Classical Library. Rev. edn. Cambridge, MA: Harvard University Press, 1929.

Hume, David. *Idea of a Perfect Commonwealth* in *Utopias of the British Enlightenment*, ed. Gregory Claeys. Cambridge: Cambridge University Press, 1994.

Isocrates. *Orations*, ed. and trans. George Norlin. 3 vols. Loeb Classical Library. London and Cambridge, MA: Harvard University Press, 1929.

[Jackson, Jonathan]. *Thoughts upon the Political Situation of the United States of* America, *in which that of* Massachusetts *Is more particularly Considered*. Worcester, MA, 1788.

Jefferson, Thomas, *Pensées choisies de Montesquieu tirées du "Common-Place Book" de Thomas Jefferson*, ed. Gilbert Chinard. Paris, 1925.

The Papers of Thomas Jefferson, vol. 11, ed. Julian P. Boyd, Lyman H. Butterfield, and Mina R. Bryan. Princeton, NJ: Princeton University Press, 1950.

The Papers of Thomas Jefferson, vol. ix, ed. Julian P. Boyd and Mina R. Bryan. Princeton, NJ: Princeton University Press, 1954.

The Papers of Thomas Jefferson, vol. xvi, ed. Julian P. Boyd, Alfred L. Bush, and Lucius Wilmerding. Princeton, NJ: Princeton University Press, 1961.

Autobiography in *Writings*, ed. Merill D. Peterson. New York: Library of America, 1984.

Notes on the State of Virginia in *Writings*, ed. Merill D. Peterson. New York: Library of America, 1984.

Justinian. *The Digest*, ed. Theodor Mommsen and Paul Krueger, trans. Alan Watson. 4 vols. Philadelphia: University of Pennsylvania Press, 1985.

Juvenal. *Satires*, ed. and trans. G. G. Ramsay. Loeb Classical Library. London and Cambridge, MA: Harvard University Press, 1940.

Kaminski, John P. and Saladino, Gaspare J., eds. *The Documentary History of the Ratification of the Constitution*, Vol. xv. Madison: State Historical Society of Wisconsin, 1984.

Kent, James. *Commentaries on American Law*. 4 vols. New York, 1844.

Leibniz, Gottfried Wilhelm. *Jugement sur les œuvres de M. le Comte de Shaftesbury* in *Gothofredi Guillelmi Leibnitii opera omnia*, ed. Louis Dutens. vol. v. Geneva, 1768.

Monita quaedam ad Samuelis Puffendorfii [sic] principia in *Gothofredi Guillelmi Leibnitii opera omnia*, ed. Louis Dutens. Vol. iv Geneva, 1768.

Méditation sur la notion commune de la justice in *Rechtsphilosophisches aus Leibnizens Ungedruckten Schriften*, ed. Georg Mollat. Leipzig, 1885.

Codex iuris gentium diplomaticus in *Die Werke von Leibniz*, ed. Onno Klopp. Vol. vi. Hanover, 1872.

Political Writings, ed. and trans. Patrick Riley. 2nd edn. Cambridge: Cambridge University Press, 1988.

Lilburne, John. *The Upright Mans Vindication: Or, An Epistle writ by JOHN LILBURN Gent. Prisoner in Newgate, August 1. 1653*. London, 1653.

Livy. *History of Rome*, ed. and trans. B. O. Foster et al. 14 vols. Loeb Classical Library. London and Cambridge, MA: Harvard University Press, 1919–59.

Locke, John. *Two Treatises of Government*, ed. Peter Laslett. Rev. edn. Cambridge: Cambridge University Press, 1967.

John Locke: Selected Correspondence, ed. Mark Goldie. Oxford: Oxford University Press, 2002.

Lucan. *The Civil War*, ed. and trans. J. D. Duff. Loeb Classical Library. London: William Heinemann, 1928.

Mably, Gabriel Bonnot de. *Des droits et des devoirs du citoyen* in *Collection complète des œuvres*, ed. Peter Friedemann. Vol. xi. Paris, 1794.

De la manière d'écrire l'histoire in *Collection complète des œuvres*, ed. Peter Friedemann. Vol. xii. Paris, 1794.

Entretiens de Phocion, sur le rapport de la morale avec la politique in *Collection complète des œuvres*, ed. Peter Friedemann. Vol. x. Paris, 1794.

Observations sur les Grecs in *Collection complète des œuvres*, ed. Peter Friedemann. Vol. iv. Paris, 1794–95.

Machiavelli, Niccolò. *Machiavels Discourses. Upon the first Decade of T. Livius translated out of the Italian; With some animadversions noting and taxing his errours*, trans. Edward Dacres. London, 1636.

The Workes of the Famous Nicolas Machiavel, Citizen and Secretary of Florence, trans. Henry Neville. London, 1675.

Discursus florentinarum rerum post mortem iunioris Laurentii Medices in *Il Principe e altri scritti minori*, ed. Michele Scherillo. Milan: Ulrico Hoepli, 1916.

Il Principe in *Il Principe e altri scritti minori*, ed. Michele Scherillo. Milan: Ulrico Hoepli, 1916.

Opere, ed. Mario Bonfantini. Milan: Riccardo Ricciardi, 1963.

Discorsi sopra la prima deca di Tito Livio, ed. Giorgio Inglese. Milan: Rizzoli, 1984.

Florentine Histories, ed. and trans. Laura F. Banfield and Harvey C. Mansfield, Jr. Princeton, NJ: Princeton University Press, 1988.

Discourses on Livy, ed. and trans. Harvey C. Mansfield and Nathan Tarcov. Chicago: University of Chicago Press, 1996.

Madison, James. "Parties" in *National Gazette*. January 23, 1792.

The Papers of James Madison, vol. xiv, ed. Robert A. Rutland and Thomas A. Mason. Charlottesville: University Press of Virginia, 1983.

May, Sir Thomas. *The Reigne of King Henry the Second Written in Seaven Bookes*, ed. Götz Schmitz. Tempe, AZ: Renaissance English Text Society, 1999.

Milton, John. *The readie and easy way to establish a free Commonwealth* in *The Riverside Milton*, ed. Roy Flannagan. New York: Houghton Mifflin, 1998.

Montagu, Edward Wortley. *Reflections on the Rise and Fall of the Antient Republicks. Adapted to the Present State of Great Britain*. London, 1760.

Montesquieu, Charles de Secondat, baron de. *Œuvres complètes*, ed. Roger Caillois. Paris: Librairie Gallimard, 1949.

Considérations sur les causes de la grandeur des Romains et de leur décadence in *Œuvres complètes*, ed. Daniel Oster. Paris: Editions du Seuil, 1964.

Eclaircissements sur l'esprit des lois in *Œuvres complètes*, ed. Daniel Oster. Paris: Editions du Seuil, 1964.

Les Lettres persanes in *Œuvres complètes*, ed. Daniel Oster. Paris: Editions du Seuil, 1964.

Mes pensées in *Œuvres complètes*, ed. Daniel Oster. Paris: Editions du Seuil, 1964.

Persian Letters, ed. and trans. C. J. Betts. Harmondsworth: Penguin Books, 1973.

De l'esprit des lois, ed. Victor Goldschmidt. 2 vols. Paris: Garnie-Flammarion, 1979.

The Spirit of the Laws, ed. and trans. Anne Cohler, Basia Miller, and Harold Stone. Cambridge: Cambridge University Press, 1989.

More, Sir Thomas. *Utopia* in *The Complete Works of St. Thomas More*, vol. IV, ed. Edward Surtz and J. H. Hexter. New Haven, CT: Yale University Press, 1965.

Cynicus in *The Complete Works of St. Thomas More*, vol. III (part 1), ed. Craig R. Thompson. New Haven, CT: Yale University Press, 1974.

Letter to Dorp in *The Complete Works of St. Thomas More*, vol. XV, ed. Daniel Kinney. New Haven, CT: Yale University Press, 1986.

Letter to a Monk in *The Complete Works of St. Thomas More*, vol. XV, ed. Daniel Kinney. New Haven, CT: Yale University Press, 1986.

Letter to Oxford in *The Complete Works of St. Thomas More*, vol. XV, ed. Daniel Kinney. New Haven, Conn.: Yale University Press, 1986.

Life of John Picus in *The Complete Works of St. Thomas More*, vol. II, ed. Anthony S. G. Edwards, Katherine Gardiner Rodgers, and Clarence H. Miller. New Haven, CT: Yale University Press, 1997.

Utopia: Latin Text and English Translation, ed. George M. Logan, Robert M. Adams, and Clarence H. Miller. Cambridge: Cambridge University Press, 1995.

Moyle, Walter. *An Essay on the Constitution and Government of the Roman State* in *The Whole Works*, ed. Anthony Hammond. London, 1727.

An essay on the Lacedaemonian government in *The Whole Works*, ed. Anthony Hammond. London, 1727.

Nedham, Marchamont. *The Excellencie of a Free State*. London, 1767.

The Case of the Commonwealth of England, Stated, ed. Philip A. Knachel. Charlottesville: University Press of Virginia, 1969.

Neville, Henry. *The Workes of the Famous Nicolas Machiavel, Citizen and Secretary of Florence*. London, 1675.

Plato Redivivus in *Two English Republican Tracts*, ed. Caroline Robbins. Cambridge: Cambridge University Press, 1969.

Nietzsche, Friedrich. *Unfashionable Observations*, trans. R. T. Gray. Stanford, CA: Stanford University Press, 1995.

Nozick, Robert. *Anarchy, State, and Utopia*. New York: Basic Books, 1974.

Observations of the Federal Farmer in *The Anti-Federalist: Writings by Opponents of the Constitution*, ed. Herbert J. Storing. Chicago: University of Chicago Press, 1981.

Otis, James. *The Rights of the British Colonies Asserted and Proved* in *Pamphlets of the American Revolution: 1750–1776*, ed. Bernard Bailyn. Cambridge, MA: Belknap, 1965.

Ovid. *Metamorphoses*, ed. and trans. Frank J. Miller. 2 vols. Loeb Classical Library. London and Cambridge, MA: Harvard University Press, 1977.

Pace, Richard. *De fructu qui ex doctrina percipitur*, ed. and trans. Frank Manley and Richard S. Sylvester. Renaissance Texts Series, II. New York: Renaissance Society of America, 1967.

Patrizi, Francesco [of Siena]. *Francisci Patricii Senensis, pontificis Caietani, de institutione reipublicae libri IX. Ad senatum populumque Senesem scripti.* Strasbourg, 1594.

Pausanias. *Description of Greece*, ed. and trans. J. G. Frazer. Loeb Classical Library. London: Macmillan, 1898.

Payson, Phillips. *Sermon* in *American Political Writings during the Founding Era: 1760–1805*, ed. Charles S. Hyneman and Donald S. Lutz. Vol. 1. Indianapolis: Liberty Press, 1983.

Platina [Bartolomeo Sacchi]. *De optimo cive* in *B. Platinae cremonensis de vita & moribus summarum pontificum historia . . . eiusdem de optimo cive.* Cologne, 1529.

    Dialogo de falso et vero bono in *B. Platinae cremonensis de vita & moribus summarum pontificum historia . . . eiusdem de optimo cive.* Cologne, 1529.

Plato. *The Collected Dialogues, including the Letters*, ed. Edith Hamilton, Huntington Cairns. Bollingen Series 71. Princeton, NJ: Princeton University Press, 1989.

    Euthyphro in *Platonis opera*, ed. John Burnet. Vol. 1. 2nd edn. Oxford Classical Texts. Oxford: Clarendon Press, 1963.

    Gorgias in *Platonis opera*, ed. John Burnet. Vol. III. 2nd edn. Oxford Classical Texts. Oxford: Clarendon Press, 1963.

    Laws in *Platonis opera*, ed. John Burnet. Vol. V. 2nd edn. Oxford Classical Texts. Oxford: Clarendon Press, 1963.

    Republic in *Platonis opera*, ed. John Burnet. Vol. IV. 2nd edn. Oxford Classical Texts. Oxford: Clarendon Press, 1963.

    Sophist in *Platonis opera*, ed. John Burnet. Vol. 1. 2nd edn. Oxford Classical Texts. Oxford: Clarendon Press, 1963.

    Statesman in *Platonis opera*, ed. John Burnet. Vol. 1. 2nd edn. Oxford Classical Texts. Oxford: Clarendon Press, 1963.

    Timaeus in *Platonis opera*, ed. John Burnet. Vol. IV. 2nd edn. Oxford Classical Texts. Oxford: Clarendon Press, 1963.

[Ficino, Marsilio]. *Platonis opera omnia.* Venice, 1517.

Plutarch. *Agis and Cleomenes* in *Lives*, ed. and trans. B. Perrin. Vol. X. Loeb Classical Library. London and Cambridge, MA: Harvard University Press, 1914.

    Caius and Tiberius Gracchus in *Lives*, ed. and trans. B. Perrin. Vol. X. Loeb Classical Library. London and Cambridge, MA: Harvard University Press, 1914.

    Coriolanus in *Lives*, ed. and trans. B. Perrin. Vol. VI. Loeb Classical Library. London and Cambridge, MA: Harvard University Press, 1914.

    Lycurgus in *Lives*, ed. and trans. B. Perrin. Vol. 1. Loeb Classical Library. London and Cambridge, MA: Harvard University Press, 1914.

Poggio Bracciolini. *In laudem reipublicae Venetorum* in *Opera omnia*, ed. Riccardo Fubini. Vol. II. Turin: Bottega D'Erasmo, 1966.

In Praise of the Venetian Republic in *Cambridge Translations of Renaissance Philosophical Texts*, ed. Jill Kraye, trans. Martin Davies. Vol. II. Cambridge: Cambridge University Press, 1997.

Polybius. *Histories*, ed. and. trans. W. R. Paton. Loeb Classical Library. London and Cambridge, MA: Harvard University Press, 1923.

Pontano, Giovanni. *Opera omnia soluta oratione composita*. 3 vols. Venice, 1518.

Raleigh, Sir Walter. *A Discourse of the Original and Fundamental Cause of Natural, Arbitrary, Necessary, and Unnatural War* in *The Works of Sir Walter Raleigh, Kt.*, ed. T. Birch and W. Oldys. Vol. VIII. Oxford: Oxford University Press, 1829.

Ramsay, David. *Oration* in *Principles and Acts of the Revolution in America*, ed. H. Niles. New York, 1822.

History of the American Revolution in *American Political Writing during the Founding Era: 1760–1805*, ed. Charles S. Hyneman and Donald S. Lutz. Vol II. Indianapolis: Liberty Press, 1983.

"Civis: To the Citizens of South Carolina" in *The Documentary History of the Ratification of the Constitution*, ed. John P. Kaminski and Gaspare J. Saladino. Vol. XVI. Madison: State Historical Society of Wisconsin, 1984.

Rousseau, Jean-Jacques. *Discours sur l'économie politique* in *Œuvres complètes de Jean-Jacques Rousseau*, ed. Bernard Gagnebin and Marcel Raymond. Vol. III. Paris: Gallimard, 1964.

Discours sur l'origine et les fondemens de l'inégalité parmi les hommes in *Œuvres complètes de Jean-Jacques Rousseau*, ed. Bernard Gagnebin and Marcel Raymond. Vol. III. Paris: Gallimard, 1964.

Du contrat social in *Œuvres complètes de Jean-Jacques Rousseau*, ed. Bernard Gagnebin and Marcel Raymond. Vol. III. Paris: Gallimard, 1964.

Fragments politiques in *Œuvres complètes de Jean-Jacques Rousseau*, ed. Bernard Gagnebin and Marcel Raymond. Vol. III. Paris: Gallimard, 1964.

Projet de constitution pour la Corse in *Œuvres complètes de Jean-Jacques Rousseau*, ed. Bernard Gagnebin and Marcel Raymond. Vol. III. Paris: Gallimard, 1964.

Political Fragments in *The Collected Writings of Rousseau*, ed. Roger D. Masters and Christopher Kelly, trans. Judith R. Bush, Roger D. Masters, and Christopher Kelly. Vol. IV. Hanover, NH, and London: University Press of New England, 1994.

Social Contract in *The Collected Writings of Rousseau*, ed. Roger D. Masters and Christopher Kelly, trans. Judith R. Bush, Roger D. Masters, and Christopher Kelly. Vol. IV. Hanover, NH, and London: University Press of New England, 1994.

The Discourses *and other early political writings*, ed. and trans. Victor Gourevitch. Cambridge: Cambridge University Press, 1997.

Rudiments of Law and Government Deduced from the Law of Nature in *American Political Writing during the Founding Era: 1760–1805*, ed. Charles S. Hyneman and Donald S. Lutz. Vol 11. Indianapolis: Liberty Press, 1983.

Saint-Evremond, Charles de Marguetel de Saint Denis, Seigneur de. *Reflexions sur les divers genies du peuple romain, dans les divers temps de la Republique* in *Œuvres melées de M. De Saint-Evremond*. Paris, 1693.

St. John, Henry, Viscount Bolingbroke. *Political Writings*, ed. David Armitage. Cambridge: Cambridge University Press, 1997.

Saint-Réal, César Vichard, Abbé de. *Histoire de la conjuration des Gracques* in *Œuvres de M. L'Abbé de Saint-Real*. Vol. 1. Paris, 1724.

Sallust. *Bellum Catilinae*, ed. and trans. J. C. Rolfe. Loeb Classical Library. London and Cambridge, MA: Harvard University Press, 1921.

    Bellum Iugurthinum, ed. and trans. J. C. Rolfe. Loeb Classical Library. London and Cambridge, MA: Harvard University Press, 1921.

Seneca. *De vita beata* in *Moral Essays*, ed. and trans. John W. Basore. Vol. 11. Loeb Classical Library London and Cambridge, MA: Harvard University Press, 1932.

Ps.-Sextus Aurelius Victor. *Liber de Caesaribus*, ed. Fr. Pichlmayr and R. Gruendel. Bibliotheca scriptorum Graecorum et Romanorum Teubneriana. Leipzig: Teubner, 1966.

Shakespeare, William. *Coriolanus*, ed. Philip Brockbank. The Arden Shakespeare. London: Methuen, 1976.

Ps.-Shakespeare. *Sir Thomas More*, ed. Revd. Alexander Dyce. London: The Shakespeare Society, 1844.

Sidney, Algernon. *Discourses Concerning Government*. 2nd edn. London, 1704.

Sigonio, Carlo. *Caroli Sigonii De antiquo iure civium Romanorum: Italicae: provinciarum: Romanae iurisprudentiae iudiciis, tum privati, tum publicis, eorumque ratione libri XI*. Paris, 1576.

    Caroli Sigonii De antiquo iure civium Romanorum . . . quibus adiecti nunc sunt eiusdem de Republica Hebraeorum, libri septem. Frankfurt, 1593.

Smith, Adam. *An Inquiry into the Nature and Causes of the Wealth of Nations*, ed. R. H. Campbell, A. S. Skinner, and W. B. Todd. Vol. 1. Oxford: Clarendon Press, 1976.

Smith, Melancthon. *Speeches Delivered in the Course of Debate by the Convention of the State of New York on the Adoption of the Federal Constitution* in *The Anti-Federalist: Writings by Opponents of the Constitution*, ed. Herbert J. Storing. Chicago: University of Chicago Press, 1981.

Smith, William Moore, "On the Fall of Empires" in *Dunlap's Pennsylvania Packet, or, the General Advertiser* (Philadelphia). Vol. IV, no. 188. May 29, 1775.

Spenser, Edmund. *The Fairie Queene*, ed. A. C. Hamilton. Longman Annotated English Poets. London: Longman, 1977.

Starkey, Thomas. *A Dialogue between Pole and Lupset*, ed. T. F. Mayer. London: Royal Historical Society, 1989.

Tacitus. *The Histories*, ed. and trans. C. H. Moore. Loeb Classical Library. London and Cambridge, MA: Harvard University Press, 1925.

Thacher, Oxenbridge. *The Sentiments of a British North American* in *Pamphlets of the American Revolution: 1750–1776*, ed. Bernard Bailyn. Cambridge, MA: Belknap, 1965.

Tocqueville, Alexis de. *Democracy in America*, ed. J. P. Mayer, trans. George Lawson. New York: Harper & Row, 1966.

De la démocratie en Amérique, ed. André Jardin. 2 vols. Paris: Librairie Gallimard, 1986.

The Old Regime and the Revolution, ed. François Furet and Françoise Mélonio, trans. Alan S. Kahan. Vol. 1. Chicago: University of Chicago Press, 1998.

Democracy in America, ed. and trans. Harvey C. Mansfield and Delba Winthrop. Chicago: University of Chicago Press, 2000.

Trenchard, John and Gordon, Thomas. *Cato's Letters, or Essays on Liberty, Civil, and Religious, and Other Important Subjects*, ed. Ronald Hamowy. 2 vols. Indianapolis: Liberty Fund, 1995.

Valerius Maximus. *Memorable Doings and Sayings*, ed. and trans. D. R. Shackleton Bailey. 2 vols. Loeb Classical Library. London and Cambridge, MA: Harvard University Press, 2000.

Velleius Paterculus. *Res gestae divi Augusti*, ed. and trans. Frederick W. Shipley. Loeb Classical Library. New York: G. P. Putnam's Sons, 1924.

Vertot, René Auber, Abbé de. *Histoire des révolutions de la République romaine*. 3 vols. Paris, 1719.

The History of the Revolutions that happened in the Government of the Roman Republic. Written in French *by the Abbot* de Vertot, *Author of the History of the Revolution in* Sweden *and in* Portugal. *English'd by Mr. Ozell and Others*, trans. John Ozell et al. London: 1720.

Vico, Giambattista. *The New Science*, ed. Thomas Goddard Bergin and Max Harold Fisch. Ithaca, New York: Cornell University Press, 1976.

Voltaire. *Commentaire sur L'Esprit des lois* in *Œuvres complètes de Voltaire*. Vol. xxx. Paris: Garnier Frères, 1880.

Waller, Edmund. *A Speech Made by Master Waller Esquire . . . Concerning Episcopacie*. London, 1641.

Webster, Noah. *Miscellaneous Remarks on Divisions of Property* in *A Collection of Essays and Fugitiv Writings, on Moral, Historical, Political and Literary Subjects*. Boston, 1790.

On the Education of Youth in America in *A Collection of Essays and Fugitiv Writings, on Moral, Historical, Political and Literary Subjects*. Boston, 1790.

Remarks on the Manners, Government, and Debt of the United States in *A Collection of Essays and Fugitiv Writings, on Moral, Historical, Political and Literary Subjects*. Boston, 1790.

"Review" of *Thoughts upon the Political Situation of the United States* in *American Magazine* [New York, 1787–88]. American Periodical Series. Ann Arbor, MI: University Microfilms International, 1942.

An Examination into the leading principles of the Federal Constitution in *Pamphlets on the Constitution of the United States*, ed. Paul L. Ford. New York: Da Capo Press, 1968.

"An Oration on the Anniversary of the Declaration of Independence" in *American Political Writing during the Founding Era: 1760–1805*, ed. Charles S. Hyneman and Donald S. Lutz. Vol. II. Indianapolis: Liberty Press, 1983.

To the Dissenting Members of the late Convention of Pennsylvania in *The Documentary History of the Ratification of the Constitution*, ed. John P. Kaminski and Gaspare J. Saladino. Vol. xv. Madison: State Historical Society of Wisconsin, 1984.

Wittgenstein, Ludwig. *Philosophical Investigations* (*Philosophische Untersuchungen*), ed. G. E. M. Anscombe and R. Rhees, trans. G. E. M. Anscombe. Oxford: Basil Blackwell, 1958.

Xenophon. *Constitution of the Lacedaemonians* in *Scripta minora*, ed. and trans. E. C. Marchant. Loeb Classical Library. London: William Heinemann, 1925.

SECONDARY SOURCES

Adams, Robert P. *The Better Part of Valor: More, Erasmus, Colet, and Vives, on Humanism, War and Peace 1496–1535*. Seattle: University of Washington Press, 1962.

Annas, Julia. "Cicero on Stoic Moral Philosophy and Private Property" in *Philosophia Togata*, vol. I: *Essays on Philosophy and Roman Society*. ed. Miriam Griffith, Jonathan Barnes. Oxford: Oxford University Press, 1989.

Appleby, Joyce. "Commercial Farming and the 'Agrarian Myth' in the Early Republic" in *Journal of American History* 68 (1982): 833–49.

Capitalism and a New Social Order: the Republican Vision of the 1790s. New York: New York University Press, 1984.

"Republicanism in Old and New Contexts" in *The William and Mary Quarterly* 43 (1986): 20–34.

Liberalism and Republicanism in the Historical Imagination. Cambridge, MA: Harvard University Press, 1992.

Aptekar, Jane. *Icons of Justice: Iconography and Thematic Imagery in Book v of* The Fairie Queene. New York and London: Columbia University Press, 1969.

Armitage, David. *The Ideological Origins of the British Empire*. Ideas in Context. Cambridge: Cambridge University Press, 2000.

Badian, Ernst. *Foreign Clientelae*. Oxford: Clarendon Press, 1958.

"From the Gracchi to Sulla: 1940–59" in *Historia* II (1962): 197–245.

Bailyn, Bernard. *The Ideological Origins of the American Revolution*. Cambridge, MA: Belknap Press, 1967.

Faces of the American Revolution: Personalities and Themes in the Struggle for American Independence. New York: Vintage Books, 1992.

To Begin the World Anew: the Genius and Ambiguities of the American Founders. New York: Alfred A. Knopf, 2003.

Bailyn, Bernard, ed. *Pamphlets of the American Revolution: 1750–1776*. Cambridge, MA: Belknap, 1965.

ed. *The Debate on the Constitution: Federalist and Antifederalist Speeches, Articles, and Letters During the Struggle over Ratification*. 2 vols. New York: Library of America, 1993.

Baker, Keith Michael. *Inventing the French Revolution: Essays on French Political Culture in the Eighteenth Century*. Ideas in Context. Cambridge: Cambridge University Press, 1990.

Baker-Smith, Dominic. *More's Utopia*. London: HarperCollins, 1991.

"Uses of Plato by Erasmus and More" in *Platonism and the English Imagination*, ed. Anna Baldwin and Sarah Hutton. Cambridge: Cambridge University Press, 1994.

Banning, Lance. "Republican Ideology and the Triumph of the Constitution" in *The William and Mary Quarterly* 31 (1974): 167–88.

The Jeffersonian Persuasion: Evolution of a Party Ideology. Ithaca: Cornell University Press, 1978.

"Jeffersonian Ideology Revisited: Liberal and Classical Ideas in the New American Republic" in *The William and Mary Quarterly* 42 (1987): 11–19.

Baridon, Michel. "Rome et l'Angleterre dans les Considérations" in *Storia e ragione: le* Considérations sur les causes de la grandeur des Romains et de leur décadence *di Montesquieu nel 250° della pubblicazione. Atti del Convegno internazionale organizato dall'Instituto Universitario Orientale e dalla Società italiana di studi sul secolo XVIII*, ed. Alberto Postigliola. Naples: Liguori Editore, 1987.

Barnouw, Jeffrey. "American Independence: Revolution of the Republican Ideal; a Response to Pocock's Construction of 'the Atlantic Republican Tradition'" in *The American Revolution and Eighteenth-Century Culture: Essays from the 1976 Bicentennial Conference of the American Society for Eighteenth-Century Studies*, ed. Paul J. Korshin. New York: AMS Press, 1986.

Baron, Hans. *The Crisis of the Early Italian Renaissance: Civic Humanism and Republican Liberty in an Age of Classicism and Tyranny*. Princeton, NJ: Princeton University Press, 1955.

Benrekassa, Georges. "Le problème des sources dans les *Considérations*: questions de méthode" in *Storia e ragione: le* Considérations sur les causes de la grandeur des Romains et de leur décadence *di Montesquieu nel 250° della pubblicazione. Atti del Convegno internazionale organizato dall'Instituto Universitario Orientale e dalla Società italiana di studi sul secolo XVIII*, ed. Alberto Postigliola. Naples: Liguori Editore, 1987.

Berlin, Isaiah. *Four Essays on Liberty*. Oxford: Oxford University Press, 1969.

Bernstein, A. H. *Tiberius Gracchus: Tradition and Apostasy*. Ithaca: Cornell University Press, 1978.

Bietenholz, Peter C. and Deutscher, Thomas B., eds. *Contemporaries of Erasmus: a Biographical Register of the Renaissance and Reformation*. 2 vols. Toronto: University of Toronto Press, 1986.

Blitzer, Charles. *An Immortal Commonwealth: the Political Thought of James Harrington*. New Haven, CT: Yale University Press, 1960.

Bock, Gisela. "Civil Discord in Machiavelli's *Istorie Fiorentine*" in *Machiavelli and Republicanism*, ed. Gisela Bock, Quentin Skinner, and Maurizio Viroli. Ideas in Context. Cambridge: Cambridge University Press, 1990.

Boesche, Roger. *The Strange Liberalism of Alexis de Tocqueville*. Ithaca: Cornell University Press, 1987.

Bradshaw, Brendan. "More on Utopia" in *The Historical Journal* 24 (1981): 1– 27.

Brett, Annabel. *Liberty, Right and Nature: Individual Rights in Later Scholastic Thought*. Ideas in Context. Cambridge: Cambridge University Press, 1997.

Brewer, Holly. "Entailing Aristocracy in Colonial Virginia: 'Ancient Feudal Restraints' and Revolutionary Reform" in *The William and Mary Quarterly* 54 (1997): 307–46.

Breyer, Stephen. "Our Democratic Constitution." The Fall 2001 James Madison Lecture. New York University Law School. October 22, 2001.

Bucher, Gregory S. "The Origins, Program, and Composition of Appian's *Roman History*" in *Transactions of the American Philological Association* 130 (2000): 411–58.

Burckhardt, Jacob. *The Civilization of the Renaissance in Italy (Die Kultur der Renaissance in Italien)*, ed. Peter Murray. trans. S. G. C. Middlemore, with an introduction by Peter Burke. London: Penguin Books, 1990.

Burke, Peter. "A Survey of the Popularity of Ancient Historians, 1450–1700" in *History and Theory* 5 (1966): 135–52.

Cambiano, Giuseppe. "Montesquieu e le antiche repubbliche greche" in *Rivista di Filosofia* 65 (1974): 93–144.

Carcopino, Jérome. *Autour des Gracques: études critiques*. Paris: Belles Lettres, 1967.

Cardinali, Giuseppe. *Studi Graccani*. Roma: "L'Erma" di Bretschneider, 1965.

Carrithers, David W. "Montesquieu, Jefferson and the Fundamentals of Eighteenth-Century Republican Theory" in *The French-American Review* 6 (1982): 160–88.

"Not So Virtuous Republics: Montesquieu, Venice, and the Theory of Aristocratic Republicanism" in *Journal of the History of Ideas* 52 (1991): 245–68.

"Democratic and Aristocratic Republics: Ancient and Modern" in *Montesquieu's Science of Politics: Essays on The Spirit of the Laws*, ed. David W. Carrithers, Michael A. Mosher, and Paul A. Rahe. Lanham, MD: Rowman & Littlefield, 2001.

Cassirer, Ernst. *The Platonic Renaissance in England*, trans. James. P. Pettegrove. Austin: University of Texas Press, 1953.

Christi, F. R. "Hegel and Roman Liberalism" in *History of Political Thought* 5 (1984): 281–94.

Condren, Conal. "*Natura naturans*: Natural Law and the Sovereign in the Writings of Thomas Hobbes" in *Natural Law and Civil Sovereignty: Moral Rights and State Authority in Early Modern Political Thought*, ed. Ian Hunter and David Saunders. Houndmills: Palgrave Macmillan, 2002.

Connell, William J. "The Republican Idea" in *Renaissance Civic Humanism: Reappraisals and Reflections*, ed. James Hankins. Ideas in Context. Cambridge: Cambridge University Press, 2000.

Cotton, James. *James Harrington's Political Thought and Its Context*. New York and London: Garland Publishing, 1991.

Courtney, C. P. "Montesquieu and Natural Law" in *Montesquieu's Science of Politics: Essays on The Spirit of the Laws*, ed. David W. Carrithers, Michael A. Mosher, and Paul A. Rahe. Lanham, MD: Rowman & Littlefield, 2001.

Craiutu, Aurelian. "Tocqueville and the Political Thought of the French Doctrinaires (Guizot, Royer-Collard, Rémusat)" in *History of Political Thought* 20 (1999): 456–93.

Crisafulli, A. S. "Parallels to Ideas in the *Lettres persanes*" in *Modern Language Association of America* (1937): 773–77.

Cromartie, Alan. "Harringtonian Virtue: Harrington, Machiavelli, and the Method of the Moment" in *The Historical Journal* 41 (1998): 987–1009.

Curling, Jonathan. *Edward Wortley Montagu 1713–1776: the Man in the Iron Wig*. London: Andrew Melrose, 1954.

Curtis, Catherine M. "Richard Pace on Pedagogy, Counsel, and Satire." Ph.D. dissertation. University of Cambridge, 1996.

Cytowska, Maria. "Erasme de Rotterdam et Marsile Ficin son maître" in *Eos* 63 (1975): 165–79.

Davis, J. C. *Utopia and the Ideal Society: a Study of English Utopian Writing: 1516–1700*. Cambridge: Cambridge University Press, 1981.

Dawson, Doyne. *Cities of the Gods: Communist Utopias in Greek Thought*. New York and Oxford: Oxford University Press, 1992.

Dedieu, Joseph. *Montesquieu et la tradition politique anglaise en France: les sources anglaises de l'"Esprit des lois."* Paris: Librairie Victor Lecoffre, 1909.

Derathé, Robert. "La Place et l'importance de la notion d'égalité dans la doctrine politique de Jean-Jacques Rousseau" in *Rousseau after Two Hundred Years: Proceedings of the Cambridge Bicentennial Colloquium*, ed. R. A. Leigh. Cambridge: Cambridge University Press, 1982.

Desserud, Donald A. "Virtue, Commerce and Moderation in the 'Tale of the Troglodytes': Montesquieu's *Persian Letters*" in *History of Political Thought* 12 (1991): 605–26.

Diamond, Wm. Craig. "Natural Philosophy in Harrington's Political Thought" in *Journal of the History of Philosophy* 16 (1978): 387–98.

Diggins, John Patrick. *The Lost Soul of American Politics: Virtue, Self-Interest, and the Foundations of Liberalism*. Chicago: University of Chicago Press, 1986.

Ditz, Toby L. *Property and Kinship: Inheritance in Early Connecticut, 1750–1820*. Princeton, NJ: Princeton University Press, 1986.

Eden, Kathy. *Friends Hold All Things in Common: Tradition, Intellectual Property, and the* Adages *of Erasmus*. New Haven, CT: Yale University Press, 2001.

Ellison, Charles E. "The Moral Economy of the Modern City: Reading Rousseau's *Discourse on Wealth*" in *History of Political Thought* 12 (1991): 254–61.

Fenlon, D. B. "England and Europe: *Utopia* and Its Aftermath" in *Transactions of the Royal Historical Society* 25 (1975): 115–135.

Fink, Zera S. *The Classical Republicans: an Essay in the Recovery of a Pattern of Thought in Seventeenth-Century England*. Evanston: Northwestern University Press, 1945.

Fitzmaurice, Andrew K. "Classical Rhetoric and the Literature of Discovery, 1570–1630." Ph.D. dissertation. University of Cambridge, 1995.

Humanism and America: an Intellectual History of English Colonisation, 1500–1625. Ideas in Context. Cambridge: Cambridge University Press, 2003.

Fontana, Benedetto. "Sallust and the Politics of Machiavelli" in *History of Political Thought* 24 (2003): 86–108.

Fox, Alistair. "Facts and Fallacies: Interpreting English Humanism" in *Reassessing the Henrican Age: Humanism, Politics, and Reform 1500–1550*, ed. Alistair Fox and John Guy. Oxford: Oxford University Press, 1986.

Fukuda, Arihiro. *Sovereignty and the Sword: Harrington, Hobbes, and Mixed Government in the English Civil Wars*. Oxford: Oxford University Press, 1997.

Gabba, Emilio. *Appiano e la storia delle guerre civili*. Florence: La Nuova Italia, 1956.

Garin, Eugenio. *Italian Humanism [Der italienische Humanismus]: Philosophy and Civic Life in the Renaissance*, trans. Peter Munz. Oxford: Basil Blackwell, 1965.

Garnsey, Peter. *Ideas of Slavery from Aristotle to Augustine*. The W. B. Stanford Memorial Lectures. Cambridge: Cambridge University Press, 1996.

Gibson, Alan. "Ancients, Moderns and Americans: the Republicanism–Liberalism Debate Revisited" in *History of Political Thought* 21 (2000): 261–307.

Gilbert, Felix. *Machiavelli and Guicciardini: Politics and History in Sixteenth-Century Florence*. Princeton, NJ: Princeton University Press, 1965.

Glover, Samuel Dennis. "The Classical Plebeians: Radical Republicanism and the Origins of Leveller Thought." Ph.D. dissertation. University of Cambridge, 1994.

"The Putney Debates: Popular Versus Elitist Republicanism" in *Past and Present* 164 (1999): 47–80.

Goldhill, Simon. *Who Needs Greek?: Contests in the Cultural History of Hellenism*. Cambridge: Cambridge University Press, 2002.

Goldie, Mark. "The Civil Religion of James Harrington" in *The Languages of Political Theory in Early-Modern Europe*, ed. Anthony Pagden. Ideas in Context. Cambridge: Cambridge University Press, 1987.

Goodey, Brian R. "Mapping 'Utopia': a Comment on the Geography of Sir Thomas More" in *The Geographical Review* 60 (1970): 13–30.

Goulemot, Jean Marie. *Le Règne de l'histoire: discours historiques et révolutions (XVIIeme–XVIIIeme siècle)*. Paris: Albin Michel, 1996.

Greenidge, A. H. J. *A History of Rome*. 2 vols. London: Methuen, 1904.

Greenidge, A. H. J. and Clay, A. M., eds. *Sources for Roman History: 133–70 BC*. Oxford: Clarendon Press, 1960.

Griffin, Miriam T. *Seneca: a Philosopher in Politics*. Oxford: Oxford University Press, 1976.

Guerci, Luciano. "La *République romaine* di Louis de Beaufort e la discussione con Montesquieu" in *Storia e ragione: le* Considérations sur les causes de la grandeur des Romains et de leur décadence *di Montesquieu nel 250° della pubblicazione. Atti del Convegno internazionale organizzato dall'Instituto Universitario Orientale e dalla Società italiana di studi sul secolo XVIII*, ed. Alberto Postigliola. Naples: Liguori Editore, 1987.

Gunn, J. A. W. *Beyond Liberty and Property: the Process of Self-Recognition in Eighteenth-Century Political Thought*. Kingston and Montreal: McGill-Queen's University Press, 1983.

Hamowy, Ronald. "*Cato's Letters*, John Locke, and the Republican Paradigm" in *History of Political Thought* 11 (1990): 273–94.

Hampsher-Monk, Iain. "The Political Theory of the Levellers: Putney, Property and Professor Macpherson" in *Political Studies* 24 (1976): 397–422.

"From Virtue to Politeness" in *Republicanism: a Shared European Heritage*, vol. 11, ed. Quentin Skinner and Martin van Gelderen. Cambridge: Cambridge University Press, 2002.

Hankins, James. *Plato in the Italian Renaissance*. New York: E. J. Brill, 1994.

"Humanism and Modern Political Thought" in *The Cambridge Companion to Renaissance Humanism*, ed. Jill Kraye. Cambridge: Cambridge University Press, 1996.

"Pierleone da Spoleto on Plato's Psychogony (Glosses on the *Timaeus* in Barb. lat. 21)" in *Roma, magistra mundi. Itineraria culturae medievalis. Mélanges offerts au Père L. E. Boyle à l'occasion de son 75e anniversaire*, ed. Jaqueline Hamesse. Vol. 1. Louvain-la-Neuve: F.I.D.E.M., 1998.

"Galileo, Ficino, and Renaissance Platonism" in *Humanism and Early Modern Philosophy*, ed. Jill Kraye and M. W. F Stone. New York and London: Routledge, 2000.

"The Study of the *Timaeus* in Early Renaissance Italy" in *Natural Particulars: Nature and the Disciplines in Renaissance Europe*, ed. Anthony Grafton and Nancy Siraisi. Cambridge, MA: MIT Press, 2000.

"Two Twentieth-Century Interpreters of Renaissance Humanism: Eugenio Garin and Paul Oskar Kristeller" in *Comparative Criticism* 23 (2001): 3–19.

Hankins, James, ed. *Renaissance Civic Humanism: Reappraisals and Reflections*. Ideas in Context. Cambridge: Cambridge University Press, 2000.

Hartz, Louis. *The Liberal Tradition in America: an Interpretation of American Political Thought since the Revolution*. New York: Harcourt Brace, 1955.

Heichelheim, Fritz M. *An Ancient Economic History*, trans. Joyce Stevens. 2 vols. Leyden: A. W. Sythoff, 1964.

Heuss, Alfred. *Barthold Georg Niebuhrs wissenschaftliche Anfänge: Untersuchungen und Mitteilungen über die Kopenhagener Manuscripte und zur europäische Tradition der lex agraria (loi agraire)*. Göttingen: Vandenhoeck & Ruprecht, 1981.

Isaac, Jeffrey C. "Republicanism vs. Liberalism? A Reconsideration" in *History of Political Thought* 9 (1988): 349–77.

Jones, J. W. *The Law and Legal Theory of the Greeks: an Introduction*. Oxford: Clarendon Press, 1956.

Jurdjevic, Mark. "Virtue, Commerce, and the Enduring Florentine Moment: Reintegrating Italy into the Atlantic Republican Debate" in *Journal of the History of Ideas* 62 (2001): 721–43.

Kassem, Badreddine. *Décadence et absolutisme dans l'œuvre de Montesquieu*. Geneva: Librairie E. Droz, 1960.

Katz, Stanley N. "Republicanism and the Law of Inheritance in the American Revolutionary Era" in *Michigan Law Review* 76 (1977): 1–29.

Keohane, Nannerl O. "Virtuous Republics and Glorious Monarchies: Two Models in Montesquieu's Political Thought" in *Political Studies* 20 (1972): 383–96.

Philosophy and the State in France: The Renaissance to the Enlightenment. Princeton, NJ: Princeton University Press, 1980.

Ketcham, Ralph. "Publius: Sustaining the Republican Principle" in *The William and Mary Quarterly* 44 (1987): 576–82.

Klein, Lawrence E. *Shaftesbury and the Culture of Politeness: Moral Discourse and Cultural Politics in Early Eighteenth-Century England.* Cambridge: Cambridge University Press, 1994.

Kloppenberg, James T. "The Virtues of Liberalism: Christianity, Republicanism, and Ethics in Early American Political Discourse" in *Journal of American History* 74 (1987): 9–33.

Kontchalkovsky, D. "Recherches sur l'histoire du mouvement agraire des Gracques" in *Revue Historique* 153 (1926): 161–86.

Kramnick, Isaac. "Republican Revisionism Revisited" in *American Historical Review* 87 (1982): 629–64.

Republicanism and Bourgeois Radicalism: Political Ideology in Late 18th Century England and America. Ithaca: Cornell University Press, 1990.

Kristeller, Paul Oskar. "Introduction" to Pico's *Oration on the Dignity of Man* in *The Renaissance Philosophy of Man*, ed. Ernst Cassirer, Paul Oskar Kristeller, and John Herman Randall, Jr. Chicago: University of Chicago Press, 1948.

Eight Philosophers of the Italian Renaissance. Stanford, CA: Stanford University Press, 1964.

Lamberti, Jean-Claude. *Tocqueville and the Two Democracies*, trans. Arthur Goldhammer. Harvard University Press, 1989.

"Montesquieu in America" in *Archives Européenes de Sociologie* 32 (1991): 197–210.

Landi, Lando. *L'Inghilterra e il Pensiero Politico di Montesquieu.* Padua: CEDAM, 1981.

Leigh, R. A., ed. *Rousseau after Two Hundred Years: Proceedings of the Cambridge Bicentennial Colloquium.* Cambridge: Cambridge University Press, 1982.

Levine, Joseph M. *Between the Ancients and the Moderns: Baroque Culture in Restoration England.* New Haven and London: Yale University Press, 1999.

Lewalski, Barbara K. *The Life of John Milton: a Critical Biography.* Blackwell Critical Biographies. Oxford: Blackwell, 2000.

Logan, George M. *The Meaning of More's Utopia.* Princeton, NJ: Princeton University Press, 1983.

Long A. A. "Cicero's Politics in *De Officiis*" in *Justice and Generosity: Studies in Social and Political Philosophy: Proceedings of the Sixth Symposium Hellenisticum*, ed. André Laks and Malcolm Schofield. Cambridge: Cambridge University Press, 1995.

Lowenthal, David. "Montesquieu and the Classics: Republican Government in *The Spirit of the Laws*" in *Ancients and Moderns: Essays on the Tradition of Political Philosophy in Honor of Leo Strauss*, ed. Joseph Cropsey. New York: Basic Books, 1964.

MacDonald, Sara. "Problems with Principles: Montesquieu's Theory of Natural Justice" in *History of Political Thought* 24 (2003): 109–30.

Macpherson, C. B. *The Political Theory of Possessive Individualism: Hobbes to Locke.* Oxford: Oxford University Press, 1962.

Malcolm, Noel. *Aspects of Hobbes.* Oxford: Clarendon Press, 2002.

Malone, Dumas. *Jefferson and His Time: Jefferson the Virginian.* London: Eyre and Spottiswoode, 1948.

Marius, Richard. *Thomas More.* London: Phoenix, 1999.

Mason, Sheila M. *Montesquieu's Idea of Justice.* The Hague: Martinus Nijhoff, 1975.

Masugi, Ken, ed. *Interpreting Tocqueville's* Democracy in America. Savage, MD: Rowman and Littlefield, 1991.

Matthews, Richard K. *The Radical Politics of Thomas Jefferson: a Revisionist View.* Lawrence, KA: University Press of Kansas, 1984.

McConica, James. *English Humanists and Reformation Politics under Henry VIII and Edward VI.* Oxford: Oxford University Press, 1965.

McCoy, Drew R. *The Elusive Republic: Political Economy in Jeffersonian America.* Chapel Hill: University of North Carolina Press, 1980.

Mercer, Christia. *Leibniz's Metaphysics: Its Origins and Development.* Cambridge: Cambridge University Press, 2001.

Meyers, Richard. "Montesquieu on the Causes of Roman Greatness" in *History of Political Thought* 16 (1995): 37–47.

Millar, Fergus. *The Roman Republic in Political Thought.* Hanover and London: University Press of New England, 2002.

Miller, Fred Jr. *Nature, Justice, and Rights in Aristotle's Politics.* Oxford: Clarendon Press, 1995.

Momigliano, Arnaldo. *Essays in Ancient and Modern Historiography.* Oxford: Basil Blackwell, 1977.

Moulakis, Athanasios. "Pride and the Meaning of *Utopia*" in *History of Political Thought* 11 (1990): 241–56.

"Civic Humanism, Realist Constitutionalism, and Francesco Guicciardini's *Discorso di Logrogno*" in *Renaissance Civic Humanism: Reappraisals and Reflections*, ed. James Hankins. Ideas in Context. Cambridge: Cambridge University Press, 2000.

Mulgan, Richard. "Liberty in Ancient Greece" in *Conceptions of Liberty in Political Philosophy*, ed. Zbigniev Pelczynski and John Gray. London: The Athlone Press, 1984.

Nedelsky, Jennifer. *Private Property and the Limits of American Constitutionalism: the Madisonian Framework and Its Legacy.* Chicago: University of Chicago Press, 1990.

Nelson, Eric. "Greek Nonsense in More's *Utopia*" in *The Historical Journal* 44 (2001): 889–917.

"'True Liberty': Isocrates and Milton's *Areopagitica*" in *Milton Studies* 40 (2001): 201–21.

"The Greek Tradition in Early-Modern Republican Thought." Ph.D. dissertation. University of Cambridge, 2002.

Nippel, Wilfried. "Ancient and Modern Republicanism: 'Mixed Constitution' and 'Ephors'" in *The Invention of the Modern Republic*, ed. Biancamaria Fontana. Cambridge: Cambridge University Press, 1994.

Norbrook, David. *Writing the English Republic: Poetry, Rhetoric and Politics, 1627–1660*. Cambridge: Cambridge University Press, 1999.

Oake, Roger. "Montesquieu's Analysis of Roman History" in *Journal of the History of Ideas* 16 (1955): 44–59.

Ober, Josiah. *Political Dissent in Democratic Athens: Intellectual Critics of Popular Rule*. Princeton, NJ: Princeton University Press, 1998.

Ogilvie, R. M. *A Commentary on Livy Books 1–5*. Oxford: Clarendon Press, 1965.

Olin, John C. "Erasmus's *Adagia* and More's *Utopia*" in *Miscellanea Moreana: Essays for Germain Marc'hadour*, ed. Clare M. Murphy, Henri Gibaud, and Mario A. Di Cesare. Binghamton, New York: Medieval & Renaissance Texts & Studies, 1989.

O'Neal, John C. "Rousseau's Theory of Wealth" in *History of European Ideas* 7 (1986): 453–67.

Pagden, Anthony, ed. *The Languages of Political Theory in Early-Modern Europe*. Ideas in Context. Cambridge: Cambridge University Press, 1987.

Pangle, Thomas. *Montesquieu's Philosophy of Liberalism*. Chicago: University of Chicago Press, 1973.

Parrish, John Michael. "A New Source for More's 'Utopia'" in *The Historical Journal* 40 (1997): 493–98.

Peltonen, Markku. *Classical Humanism and Republicanism in English Political Thought: 1570–1640*. Ideas in Context. Cambridge: Cambridge University Press, 1995.

Phillipson, Nicholas and Skinner, Quentin, ed. *Political Discourse in Early Modern Britain*. Ideas in Context. Cambridge: Cambridge University Press, 1993.

Pincus, Steven. "Neither Machiavellian Moment nor Possessive Individualism: Commercial Society and the Defenders of the English Commonwealth" in *American Historical Review* 103 (1998): 705–36.

Pocock, J. G. A. *The Ancient Constitution and the Feudal Law: a Study of English Historical Thought in the Seventeenth Century*. Cambridge: Cambridge University Press, 1957.

The Machiavellian Moment: Florentine Political Thought and the Atlantic Republican Tradition. Princeton, NJ: Princeton University Press, 1975.

Virtue, Commerce, and History: Essays on Political Thought and History, Chiefly in the Eighteenth Century. Cambridge: Cambridge University Press, 1985.

"Communications" in *The William and Mary Quarterly* 45 (1988): 817.

Barbarism and Religion, vol. III: *The First Decline and Fall*. Cambridge: Cambridge University Press, 2003.

Pole, J. R. *Political Representation in England and the Origins of the American Republic*. New York: Macmillan, 1966.

Postigliola, Alberto, ed. *Storia e ragione: le* Considérations sur les causes de la grandeur des Romains et de leur décadence *di Montesquieu nel 250° della pubblicazione. Atti del Convegno internazionale organizato dall'Instituto Universitario Orientale e dalla Società italiana di studi sul secolo XVIII.* Naples: Liguori Editore, 1987.

Putterman, Ethan. "Realism and Reform in Rousseau's Constitutional Projects for Poland and Corsica" in *Political Studies* 49 (2001): 481–94.

Raab, Felix. *The English Face of Machiavelli: a Changing Interpretation 1500–1700.* London: Routledge, 1964.

Rahe, Paul. A. "Forms of Government: Structure, Principle, Object, and Aim" in *Montesquieu's Science of Politics: Essays on The Spirit of the Laws,* ed. David W. Carrithers, Michael A. Mosher, and Paul A. Rahe. Lanham, MD: Rowman & Littlefield, 2001.

Republics Ancient and Modern: Classical Republicanism and the American Revolution. 3 vols. Chapel Hill: University of North Carolina Press, 1992.

"Situating Machiavelli" in *Renaissance Civic Humanism: Reappraisals and Reflections,* ed. James Hankins. Ideas in Context. Cambridge: Cambridge University Press, 2000.

Raskolnikoff, Mouza. "Caius Gracchus ou la révolution introuvable: historiographie d'une 'révolution'" in *Demokratia et Aristokratia à propos de Caius Gracchus: mots grecs et réalités romaines,* ed. Claude Nicolet. Paris: Publication de la Sorbonne, 1983.

Des anciens et des modernes, ed. Ségolène Demougin, avant-propos de Claude Nicolet. Paris: Publications de la Sorbonne, 1990.

Histoire romaine et critique historique dans l'Europe des Lumières: la naissance de l'hypercritique dans l'historiographie de la Rome antique. Strasbourg: AECR, 1992.

Rawson, Elizabeth. *The Spartan Tradition in European Thought.* Oxford: Clarendon Press, 1991.

Reeve, Andrew. "Harrington's Elusive Balance" in *History of European Ideas* 4 (1984): 401–25.

Remer, Gary. "James Harrington's New Deliberative Rhetoric: Reflection of an Anticlassical Republicanism" in *History of Political Thought* 16 (1995): 532–57.

Richard, Carl J. *The Founders and the Classics: Greece, Rome, and the American Enlightenment.* Cambridge, MA, and London: Harvard University Press, 1994.

Robbins, Caroline. *The Eighteenth-Century Commonwealthman: Studies in the Transmission, Development and Circumstance of English Liberal Thought from the Restoration of Charles II until the War with the Thirteen Colonies.* Cambridge, MA: Harvard University Press, 1959.

Robbins, Caroline, ed. *Two English Republican Tracts.* Cambridge: Cambridge University Press, 1969.

Roberts, Jennifer Tolbert. *Athens on Trial: the Antidemocratic Tradition in Western Thought.* Princeton, NJ: Princeton University Press, 1994.

Rodgers, Daniel T. "Republicanism: the Career of a Concept" in *Journal of American History* 79 (1992): 11–38.

Romm, James. "More's Strategy of Naming in the *Utopia*" in *The Sixteenth Century Journal* 22 (1991): 173–83.

Rose, R. B. "The 'Red Scare' of the 1790s: the French Revolution and the 'Agrarian Law'" in *Past and Present* 103 (1984): 113–30.

Russell Smith, H. F. *Harrington and His Oceana: a Study of a 17th Century Utopia and Its Influence in America*. Cambridge: Cambridge University Press, 1914.

Sandys, John Edwin. *A History of Classical Scholarship*. 3 vols. Cambridge: Cambridge University Press, 1903–8.

Saladin, Jean-Christophe. *La bataille du grec à la Renaissance*. Paris: Belles lettres, 2000.

Schleifer, James T. "Jefferson and Tocqueville" in *Interpreting Tocqueville's Democracy in America*, ed. Ken Masugi. Savage, MD: Rowman and Littlefield, 1991.

Schlesinger, Arthur Jr. "Individualism and Apathy in Tocqueville's *Democracy*" in *Reconsidering Tocqueville's Democracy in America*, ed. Abraham S. Eisenstadt. New Brunswick, NJ: Rutgers University Press, 1988.

Schofield, Malcolm. *Saving the City: Philosopher-Kings and Other Classical Paradigms*. London and New York: Routledge, 1999.

Scott, Jonathan. *Algernon Sidney and the English Republic, 1623–1677*. Cambridge: Cambridge University Press, 1988.

"The Rapture of Motion: James Harrington's Republicanism" in *Political Discourse in Early Modern Britain*, ed. Nicholas Phillipson and Quentin Skinner. Ideas in Context. Cambridge: Cambridge University Press, 1993.

England's Troubles: Seventeenth-Century English Political Instability in European Context. Cambridge: Cambridge University Press, 2000.

Review of Ahiro Fukuda, *Sovereignty and the Sword* in *English Historical Review* 115 (2000): 660–62.

Shackleton, Robert. "Montesquieu, Bolingbroke, and the Separation of Powers" in *Essays on Montesquieu and the Enlightenment*, ed. David Gilson and Martin Smith. Oxford: The Voltaire Foundation, 1988.

"Montesquieu and Machiavelli: a Reappraisal" in *Essays on Montesquieu and the Enlightenment*, ed. David Gilson and Martin Smith. Oxford: The Voltaire Foundation, 1988.

Shalhope, Robert E. "Toward a Republican Synthesis: the Emergence of an Understanding of Republicanism in American Historiography" in *The William and Mary Quarterly* 29 (1972): 49–80.

Shammas, Carole, Salmon, Marylynn, and Dahlin, Michel. *Inheritance in America from Colonial Times to the Present*. New Brunswick, NJ, and London: Rutgers University Press, 1987.

Sher, Richard B. "From Troglodytes to Americans: Montesquieu and the Scottish Enlightenment on Liberty, Virtue, and Commerce" in *Republicanism, Liberty, and Commercial Society, 1649–1776*, ed. David Wootton. Stanford, CA: Stanford University Press, 1994.

Shklar, Judith. "Ideology Hunting: The Case of James Harrington" in *American Political Science Review* 53 (1959): 662–92.

Skinner, Quentin. *The Foundations of Modern Political Thought*. 2 vols. Cambridge: Cambridge University Press, 1978.

"Sir Thomas More's *Utopia* and the Language of Renaissance Humanism" in *The Languages of Political Theory in Early-Modern Europe*, ed. Anthony Pagden. Ideas in Context. Cambridge: Cambridge University Press, 1987.

"Political Philosophy" in *The Cambridge History of Renaissance Philosophy*, ed. Charles B. Schmitt, Quentin Skinner, Eckhard Kessler, and Jill Kraye. Cambridge: Cambridge University Press, 1988.

"Machiavelli's *Discorsi* and the Pre-Humanist Origins of Republican Ideas" in *Machiavelli and Republicanism*, ed. Gisela Bock, Quentin Skinner, and Maurizio Viroli. Ideas in Context. Cambridge: Cambridge University Press, 1990.

"The Republican Ideal of Political Liberty" in *Machiavelli and Republicanism*, ed. Gisela Bock, Quentin Skinner, and Maurizio Viroli. Ideas in Context. Cambridge: Cambridge University Press, 1990.

Reason and Rhetoric in the Philosophy of Hobbes. Cambridge: Cambridge University Press, 1996.

Liberty before Liberalism. Cambridge: Cambridge University Press, 1998.

Visions of Politics. 3 vols. Cambridge: Cambridge University Press, 2002.

"Classical Liberty and the Coming of the English Civil War" in *Republicanism: a Shared European Heritage*, vol. 11, ed. Quentin Skinner and Martin van Gelderen. Cambridge: Cambridge University Press, 2002.

Sonenscher, Michael. "Republicanism, State Finances and the Emergence of Commercial Society in Eighteenth-Century France – or from Royal to Ancient Republicanism and Back" in *Republicanism: a Shared European Heritage*, vol. 11, ed. Quentin Skinner and Martin van Gelderen. Cambridge: Cambridge University Press, 2002.

Stockton, David. *The Gracchi*. Oxford: Clarendon Press, 1979.

Strauss, Leo. *Natural Right and History*. Chicago: University of Chicago Press, 1953.

Sullivan, Vickie. "The Civic Humanist Portrait of Machiavelli's English Successors" in *History of Political Thought* 15 (1994): 73–96.

Sutcliffe, Adam. *Judaism and Enlightenment*. Ideas in Context. Cambridge: Cambridge University Press, 2003.

Szatmary, David P. *Shays' Rebellion: the Making of an Agrarian Insurrection*. Amherst, MA: University of Massachusetts Press, 1980.

Tawney, R. H. "Harrington's Interpretation of His Age" in *Proceedings of the British Academy* (1941): 199–223.

"The Rise of the Gentry, 1558–1640" in *Economic History Review* 11 (1941): 1–37.

Tuck, Richard. *Natural Rights Theories: Their Origin and Development*. Cambridge: Cambridge University Press, 1979.

Philosophy and Government: 1572–1651. Ideas in Context. Cambridge: Cambridge University Press, 1993.

Varouxakis, Georgios. "Guizot's Historical Works and J. S. Mill's Reception of Tocqueville" in *History of Political Thought* 20 (1999): 292–312.

Venturi, Franco. *Utopia and Reform in the Enlightenment*. Cambridge: Cambridge University Press, 1971.

White, Thomas. "Aristotle and *Utopia*" in *Renaissance Quarterly* 29 (1976): 635–75.
"Pride and the Public Good: Thomas More's Use of Plato in *Utopia*" in *Journal of the History of Philosophy* 20 (1982): 329–54.
Wilentz, Sean. "America's Lost Egalitarian Tradition" in *Daedalus* (2002): 66–80.
Wilson, Nigel. "The Name Hythlodaeus" in *Moreana* 29 (1992): 33–34.
Winch, Donald. "Commercial Realities, Republican Principles" in *Republicanism: a Shared European Heritage*, vol. 11, ed. Quentin Skinner and Martin van Gelderen. Cambridge: Cambridge University Press, 2002.
Wood, Gordon S. *The Creation of the American Republic: 1776–1787*. Chapel Hill: University of North Carolina Press, 1969.
The Radicalism of the American Revolution. New York: Vintage Books, 1991.
"Afterword" in *The Republican Synthesis Revisited: Essays in Honor of George Athan Billias*, ed. Milton M. Klein, Richard D. Brown, and John B. Hench. Worcester, MA: American Antiquarian Society, 1992.
Wood, Neal. *Foundations of Political Economy: Some Early Tudor Views on State and Society*. Berkeley, CA: University of California Press, 1994.
Wootton, David. "Friendship Portrayed: a New Account of *Utopia*" in *History Workshop Journal* 45 (1998): 25–47.
"Introduction" to *Thomas More, Utopia, with Erasmus's The Sileni of Alcibiades*, ed. and trans. David Wootton. Indianapolis: Hackett Publishing, 2000.
Wootton, David, ed. *Republicanism, Liberty, and Commercial Society, 1649–1776*. Stanford, CA: Stanford University Press, 1994.
Worden, Blair. "Marchamont Nedham and English Republicanism" in *Republicanism, Liberty, and Commercial Society, 1649–1776*, ed. David Wootton. Stanford, CA: Stanford University Press, 1994.
"'Wit in a Roundhead': the Dilemma of Marchamont Nedham" in *Political Culture and Cultural Politics in Early Modern England*, ed. Susan Amussen and Mark Kishlansky. Manchester: Manchester University Press, 1995.
Wright, Johnson Kent. *A Classical Republican in Eighteenth-Century France: the Political Thought of Mably*. Stanford, CA: Stanford University Press, 1997.
Zaggia, Massimo. "La traduzione latina da Appiano di Pier Candido Decembrio: per la storia della tradizione" in *Studi Medievali* 34 (1993): 193–243.
Zuckert, Catherine H. "Political Sociology Versus Speculative Philosophy" in *Interpreting Tocqueville's Democracy in America*, ed. Ken Masugi. Savage, MD: Rowman and Littlefield, 1991.
Zuckert, Michael. *The Natural Rights Republic: Studies in the Foundations of the American Political Tradition*. Notre Dame, IN: University of Notre Dame Press, 1996.

Index

IDEAS IN CONTEXT

Edited by QUENTIN SKINNER (*General Editor*),
LORRAINE DASTON, DOROTHY ROSS and JAMES TULLY